D0577563

the best of

ROSE REISMAN

the best of ROSE REISMAN

20 years of
healthy recipes

whitecap

Copyright © 2013 by Rose Reisman
Whitecap Books

All rights reserved. No part of this publication may be reproduced, stored in a retrieval system or transmitted in any form or by any means, electronic, mechanical, photocopying, recording or otherwise, without the prior written permission of the publisher. For more information contact Whitecap Books, at Suite 210, 314 West Cordova Street, Vancouver, BC V6B 1E8 Canada.

The information in this book is true and complete to the best of the author's knowledge. All recommendations are made without guarantee on the part of the author or Whitecap Books Ltd. The author and publisher disclaim any liability in connection with the use of this information.

Whitecap Books is known for its expertise in the cookbook market, and has produced some of the most innovative and familiar titles found in kitchens across North America. Visit our website at www.whitecap.ca.

EDITED BY Theresa Best and Eva van Emden
DESIGNED BY Setareh Ashrafologhalai
FOOD PHOTOGRAPHY AND STYLING Mike McColl and Mia McColl

Printed in Canada

Library and Archives Canada Cataloguing in Publication

Reisman, Rose, 1953-, author
    The best of Rose Reisman : 20 years of healthy recipes /
Rose Reisman.

Includes index.
ISBN 978-1-77050-199-7 (pbk.)

    1. Cooking. 2. Health. 3. Low-fat diet—Recipes. 4. Cookbooks.
I. Title.

TX714.R446 2013   641.5'63   c2013-904145-1

The publisher acknowledges the financial support of the Government of Canada through the Canada Book Fund (CBF) and the Province of British Columbia through the Book Publishing Tax Credit.

13 14 15 16 17   5 4 3 2 1

The only aspect of my life that never changes is the love and respect
I have for my four children and husband. They are the reason I get up
each day with a zest for life.

NATALIE My eldest daughter, who has a quirky and
delightful personality and such an inquisitive mind.

RICKY My son-in-law, who has the sweetest disposition
and makes my daughter so happy.

DAVID My eldest son, who has a bright aura around him
and with whom you fall in love in an instant.

LAURA Laura's genuine nature inspires her to take care
of everyone around her; "Mother Teresa" could be her
middle name.

ADAM Still the baby, who has found his inner strength
as he matures.

SAM The love of my life and my partner for thirty-seven
years. You are my mentor in all aspects of my being.

My "animal" farm at home keeps me relaxed and
balanced. Rocky, A.J., Misty and Ozzie: the only ones
who don't talk back!

My two best buddies, Kathy Kacer and Susan Gordin,
with whom I share my life.

❧ CONTENTS

⚘ ACKNOWLEDGEMENTS

Whitecap Books: Nick Rundall, publisher—thank you for your continuous support of my work and for bringing *The Best of Rose Reisman* to our country. Michelle Furbacher, art director—your details and the look of the book make it easy to read and use. Eva van Emden and Theresa Best, editors—for your excellent and essential work. Setareh Ashrafologhalai, designer—the book looks incredible with your touch. Jeffrey Bryan and Debby de Groot, publicists—thank you for your work with respect to my many books with Whitecap.

Mike McColl and his wife, Mia, for their excellence in food photography and food styling. The days spent working together and listening to sixties music were so enjoyable.

Barbara Cuden, for the nutritional analysis—to your good health.

Lutfiyya Dhalla, my new assistant—thank you for your energy and spunk.

Dr. Harvey Skinner, dean of health at York University—for bringing me on as an adjunct professor and continually supporting my work.

Rose Reisman Catering: a special thanks to Reagan Macklin (president), Chris Chitty (executive chef), Jennifer Droznika (vice president of corporate sales), Catherine Chalmers (vice president of operations)—for your outstanding commitment to excellence on a daily basis.

Peter Higley, chief executive officer of the Pickle Barrel and Glow Fresh Grill, who has been a mentor for years—for giving me the opportunity to continually develop healthy recipes for the restaurants.

Stokely Wilson, executive chef of the Pickle Barrel Restaurants—for recreating my healthy recipes for the consumer.

My wonderful household assistants: Lily Lim, Dang Idala and Mila Doloricon—for assisting me with my everyday work.

FOREWORD BY
DR. DAVID MACKLIN

To eat well in 2013 is difficult. Food is being reinvented every day, manufactured with higher and higher levels of sugar, fat and salt to overstimulate the areas of our brain where we feel pleasure. These foods are now available on every street corner, and they are aggressively marketed to us and our children. A science of "health washing" has created advertisements and labelling that fool some people into thinking junk food is healthy. Portion sizes have exploded, and the social custom of eating only at meals has dissolved and been replaced with eating any time; while walking down a street, sitting in a meeting, watching television or drinking a coffee.

This is the bad news. The good news is that help is on its way. *The Best of Rose Reisman* stands out as a delicious and comprehensive antidote to our current toxic nutritional environment.

I am a family physician who has committed his career full time to counselling people to manage their weight and health through improved eating practices. My clinical practice uses healthy eating to improve quality of life and to prevent conditions like diabetes, high cholesterol and high blood pressure. I tell all my patients to buy Rose Reisman's cookbooks. This book is a perfect compilation of the recipes I recommend. Make these recipes. Cook them in batches and freeze some. You will be eating some of the world's most nutritious foods, and you will improve your health. The recipes in this book have the right amount of protein and fibre to help you eat the right amounts and be satisfied. Rose's recipes are delicious. To eat well in 2013 is difficult. This book will make it much easier.

DAVID A. MACKLIN, MD, CCFP
DIRECTOR, MEDCAN WEIGHT MANAGEMENT PROGRAM

✤ PREFACE

I've been involved in the food world, and writing food books, since 1988. My first book was a high-fat dessert cookbook that I now regret having written. I didn't know then what I understand today about what we eat and our health. I believed that food only tasted good if it was rich, creamy and decadent.

My personal philosophy changed dramatically in 1993, when I was diagnosed with high cholesterol—I was startled to discover that my health was being compromised by how I ate. I also had a genetic predisposition to heart disease, which was not a comforting thing to know. My family has a history of heart disease, high cholesterol, high blood pressure, type 2 diabetes and obesity. My father and his sister died in their fifties, immediately following heart attacks, and my grandmother died in her early fifties from complications related to type 2 diabetes.

Our diets have a profound impact on our health profile. This may strike those who are battling weight gain and food addictions as bad news, but I believe it is actually an empowering fact—all of us have the capacity to influence our long-term health outlook. It's hard to believe how quickly our lives pass and how the habits we develop now follow us all the days of our lives. I was slim and exercised daily, but my diet contained high quantities of saturated fat, sugar and salt. I was, after all, writing high-fat cookbooks at the time, and testing them turned out to be a not-so-delightful benefit of the business, although a delicious one! I thought that working out daily and keeping my weight down was sufficient evidence of good health and that I had nothing to fear, but my diagnosis told me I was dead wrong. The saying "don't judge a book by its cover" has never been more true. No matter how good you look on the outside, it's more important what you look like on the inside.

I profoundly changed my approach to diet over the ensuing years. I decided to aim for health to make sure I was around for my great husband and our four children. I have now studied nutrition for twenty-five years and have concluded that "healthy" eating is not difficult or in any way a compromise on taste or flavour. In fact it's vastly superior to eating processed foods. Processed foods are not flavourful or satisfying on their own—that's why manufacturers add so much junk to them: to bump up the flavour and keep us buying them. Add fat, sugar or salt to any food and it will taste great.

Living a healthy life, eating well, exercising regularly and spending time with family and friends are what keep me happy. And spreading the word to fellow Canadians about how to improve their health is my passion.

I believe that our diets and lifestyles in many cases significantly undercut our quality of life and, in some cases, kill us. Doctors' offices and hospitals are filled with chronically sick adults and children, with illnesses that could have been prevented by a change in lifestyle. Our medical system is reactive, almost exclusively treating symptoms rather than preventing disease. This situation is as undesirable as it is financially unsustainable.

The connection between diet and disease has never been more clear, and the argument for improving our diet never more compelling. Improving our diet should be as urgent a matter as treating an epidemic. After all, what we are seeing now *is* an epidemic—an epidemic of poor health related to diet and lifestyle.

I used to think that improving one's diet was a matter of personal responsibility only; I have now concluded that it is also a matter of national importance. And as such, a coordinated national effort is needed by everyone at all levels—in government, industry and agriculture, in the medical and education systems, and in our grocery stores and restaurants—to improve our health.

It starts with educating ourselves. Understanding how our bodies process food and convert food to energy is a critical first step. Subsequent steps can be small (such as reducing the cream and sugar taken in a coffee, eating one more piece of fresh fruit a day, preparing a meal without processed foods). Slowly but surely a change in lifestyle, to one that is healthier, will occur. Addictions—to processed food, with its fat, sugar and salt—will be broken. Predispositions to chronic diseases will be enormously reduced. Energy levels will be enormously increased. A switch will flip and the journey to a healthy diet will be complete.

Eating fresh fruits and vegetables, lean proteins and complex carbohydrates can keep our bodies fueled and healthier for years, and can reduce the risk of and in some cases even prevent chronic disease. This book is filled with recipes that call for these foods. I'm delighted to present it to you as a useful step in the direction of a healthy diet.

Enjoy!

ROSE

❧ INTRODUCTION

Over the past few years, I've yearned to write a "best of" cookbook. But the time had to be right. Now, as a restaurant consultant, with a prosperous catering company, having written nineteen books and numerous newspaper articles, and having appeared on television to talk about healthy eating many times, I feel that there won't be a better time to update my favourite recipes and present them in a new form and to include with them new recipes that I hope will become your favourites.

I began writing cookbooks focusing on healthy meals in 1993. It was an uphill battle, since the population believed that healthy recipes were synonymous with low fat and little taste. I learned this was not the case. As the years went on, I saw how creative you could become with healthier cuisine. It is not about deprivation, but about allowing yourself to eat all foods in moderation. You must know how to use Canada's Food Guide and encompass the four food groups in your meals, as well as always include healthy snacks. Fad diets will work in the short term but do not help create a lifetime strategy of eating properly. To maximize your health and energy, you have to change the way you use food to fuel your body.

Food manufacturers and restaurants have led us into an addiction to fat, salt and sugar, and addictions are never easy to break. One way is to reduce the amount of processed, packaged and restaurant food in our diet. Breakfast cereals labelled as healthy are loaded with sugar and high-fructose corn syrup. Low-fat products can still be high in sugar and calories and have few health benefits. Supersizing portions at a low cost is another way food manufacturers "hook" us—or they make mini snacks whose lower calorie counts convince us we're eating healthier, while the sugar, fat and salt add up.

We can't depend on the government, schools or food producers to provide this necessary living skill. Instead, parents must be the role models. Eating together again as a family is one way to teach your children the basics of healthy eating. We must start cooking more at home with fresh and seasonal ingredients. Home-cooked food is not as convenient as ready-to-go food, but it's a better guarantee of a healthier life. Menu planning is one way to succeed at eating better. Know what everyone in your family likes to eat and create a weekly menu around these foods. Shop, plan and prep on the weekend. Make double batches for later meals and freezing purposes.

What should you be eating? All the foods in Canada's food guide. Never ban any one food group. You can never eat enough fruits and vegetables! Include them at every meal and in your snacks. Complex carbohydrates must be included. It's fine to cut back on the simple carbohydrates such as white flour products and sugars, but be sure to include whole grains and beans and lentils in your diet. Lean protein, including beef, poultry, pork, fish and vegetarian proteins are ideal. When selecting dairy products such as milk and cheeses, stay with those with a lower milk fat content. The superfood today in that department is Greek non-fat plain yogurt. Just three-quarters of a cup (185 mL) has eighteen grams of protein!

I have updated my recipe creations in this book to reflect the effect of our ethnic diversity on our food tastes. Supermarkets today carry a large variety of ethnic foods that were never easily available before. I looked back at my previous recipes and added more interesting ingredients and improved on the cooking techniques to bring out the best flavours. With the various ethnic influences I created another batch of new recipes to make this without doubt my most creative and delicious book ever!

Some recipes to whet your appetite? The breakfast section includes a light Huevos Rancheros (page 25) and Pistachio-Crusted French Toast (page 31). Appetizers include Thai Pizza with Shrimp, Asian Vegetables and Peanut Dressing (page 54) and Mediterranean Couscous Cakes (page 46). The salad section has Baby Kale and Apricot Dressing (page 65) as well as Watermelon, Tomato, Pistachio and Feta Salad (page 78). Soups include Soba Noodle Soup with Seared Beef and Enoki Mushrooms (page 100) and Roasted Cauliflower Soup with Crisp Prosciutto Crumbs (page 118). The sandwich section gives you Lobster Grilled Cheese (page 142) and the Hoisin Meatball Sub Sandwich (page 148). How about an easy recipe for *bibimbap*, a Korean stir-fry (Korean Stir-Fried Beef and Crunchy Rice, page 158)? And this is only a sampling of what's in *The Best of Rose Reisman*. I get excited just reading the recipe titles!

I have been blessed to feel like I never work a day in my life. I love what I do seven days a week, and want to share my passion for healthy living with you. With this book I hope you'll join me on my journey towards a better, richer and healthier life.

Facts about Canadian Health

How healthy or unhealthy are we? There are no guarantees in life, as we all know. But I firmly believe that we can reduce and perhaps even prevent chronic diseases by living in a healthier way.

Cancer, heart disease, type 2 diabetes and obesity are serious concerns in Canada today. In 2008, cancer and heart disease were the two leading causes of death, and diabetes was the fifth-leading cause of death. (Source: Statistics Canada)

Lifestyle changes can reduce the risk of these serious diseases, or even prevent them. According to one study, four healthy behaviours, combined, can add up to fourteen years of life. The four behaviours are not smoking, drinking alcohol moderately, keeping active, and eating at least five portions of fruit and vegetables a day. (Source: European Prospective Investigation of Cancer)

CANCER

About one-third of all cancers can be prevented by eating well, being active and maintaining a healthy body weight. People who are overweight or obese are at greater risk for cancer of the breast, colon and rectum, esophagus, kidney, pancreas and uterus. On the other hand, regular physical activity over a lifetime protects against colon, breast and uterine cancer.

A diet high in red meat and processed meat can increase the risk of colorectal cancer. Meats such as ham, bacon, salami, hot dogs and sausages contain preservatives and excess sodium, and can contain cancer-causing substances. Conversely, a diet high in fibre protects against colorectal cancer. Furthermore, eating plenty of fibre (by eating a variety of vegetables and fruit) and staying away from high-calorie foods (such as sugar) and high-fat foods can help you maintain a healthy body weight, which reduces your risk of cancer. Eating too much salty food may increase your risk of stomach cancer.

HEART DISEASE

Heart disease and stroke are leading causes of premature death in Canada. Many Canadians have one or more of the major risk factors for heart disease: high cholesterol or triglycerides, high blood pressure, a smoking habit, type 2 diabetes, poor nutritional habits, a lack of regular exercise, obesity, stress, a family history of the disease and being over sixty-five years of age.

A healthier lifestyle, good eating habits and exercise can have a positive effect on most of these factors.

TYPE 2 DIABETES

Type 2 diabetes is closely linked to obesity and has become increasingly common in recent decades as more people become obese.

Although type 2 diabetes can affect life expectancy, changes in lifestyle can help to prevent it or delay its onset. Regular physical activity, along with healthy eating and weight control, can reduce the incidence of type 2 diabetes.

OBESITY

Obesity no longer affects just the Western world. In fact, it's often referred to as "globesity" to reflect the fact that it's now a global issue. There are many reasons for an increase in obesity:

inactivity, not controlling food portions at meals and the world-wide proliferation of fast-food restaurants. A high percentage of Canadians are overweight or obese, including a high percentage of children.

Many diseases and health problems are the result of obesity, including heart disease and stroke; type 2 diabetes; endometrial, breast, and colon cancer; high blood pressure, cholesterol and triglycerides; liver and gallbladder disease; sleep apnea and respiratory problems; osteoarthritis; and gynecological problems (such as abnormal menses and infertility).

Healthy Eating

THE IMMUNE SYSTEM

The stronger your immune system, the less sick you get and the less prone you are to diseases in general. A healthy diet, vitamin C and regular exercise will keep your immune system strong. Factors that depress your immune system include a diet low in beta carotene (which is found in dark-green or red fruits and vegetables) sleep deprivation, extreme stress and smoking.

ALZHEIMER'S DISEASE AND DIET

Long-term healthy dietary choices may help maintain brain function, slow memory decline and reduce the risk of Alzheimer's disease. Obesity, high blood pressure and high cholesterol may increase the risk. (Source: Alzheimer's Disease Education and Referral Centre)

Dark-skinned fruits and vegetables contain antioxidants that may combat Alzheimer's disease. Fattier cold-water fish, such as halibut, mackerel, salmon, trout and tuna, which contain beneficial omega-3 fatty acids, and nuts, such as almonds, pecans and walnuts, which contain vitamin E, may also be beneficial.

Moderate physical activity promotes brain health. People who exercise regularly are less likely to develop heart disease, stroke or diabetes, all conditions that are associated with an increased risk of Alzheimer's disease. (Source: Alzheimer Society)

Wouldn't it be easy to attribute chronic disease entirely to our genes? They do play a role in our health, but we have more control than we think. Lifestyle trumps genes. Even in older people, exercise and a healthy diet can lower the risk of heart disease and osteoporosis, heart attack and cancer.

FOOD GUIDES

What's the best food guide to follow? Ultimately, it's one that you can stick to for life. You shouldn't feel deprived or hungry, and you should enjoy the food you're eating. For health benefits, you should consume enough fruits and vegetables, lean protein, low-fat dairy products and whole grains. You should also make room for small daily indulgences. A food guide with these features allows you to eat out and travel, while never making you feel that you are on a "diet."

Canada's Food Guide

Canada's Food Guide, revised in 2011 (see Health Canada; www.hc-sc.gc.ca), is an excellent and comprehensive plan to healthy eating. It describes four food groups—vegetables and fruits, grain products, milk and alternatives, and meat and alternatives—and gives suggested daily portions for children, teens and adults. Followed wisely, Canada's Food Guide can help you maintain a healthy body weight and lessen the risk of chronic diseases.

The Mediterranean Food Guide

Unlike Canada's Food Guide, in which food groups are set out in a chart, the Mediterranean food guide is set out as a pyramid, with food groups being the levels in the pyramid; specific amounts are not given. Whole grains are the base (largest) level; fruits and vegetables, and beans (and nuts and legumes) are the two next largest, the primary sources of nutrition. The top (smallest) levels are meat, poultry and eggs.

The Mediterranean food guide has many benefits. It may help heart health and lower cholesterol and blood pressure. It may also reduce the risk of type 2 diabetes and certain cancers (specifically breast and colon), help with weight control and help prevent Alzheimer's disease.

The Health of the Nation

Our nation is facing a chronic health situation, and the main reason for it is the amount of fat, salt and sugar in the processed, packaged and restaurant food we consume. Because of the time it takes to cook from scratch, we eat out on a regular basis and homemade meals are on the decline (Source: Alberta Agriculture and Rural Development). Restaurants, fast-food manufacturers and food manufacturers are killing us with food.

If that statement sounds extremely harsh, it is! Food manufacturers and restaurants do not have our health as their priority. They're in business and need to increase revenues. If that means selling addictive foods and catering to our weaknesses, then that's what they do.

From an early age we become addicted to sugar, fat and salt. We crave these ingredients, but we pay a dear price, with our health.

Getting food corporations to focus on our health is a very complex issue. Consumers are concerned about what corporations use in their foods and how it negatively affects our health. The government has asked corporations and restaurants to reduce the salt in their menus on a voluntary basis. This has not been successful. We are asking restaurants for more disclosure on calories, fat, sugar and sodium. Also with no consistent response; although some restaurants post nutritional information online, this information needs to be accessible in the restaurant itself. When we learned that cigarettes were killing us, we tried to warn people. Also with little success. The government finally came in with various smoking and cigarette bans and the decline in smoking has clearly been seen. We need mandatory regulations to be put into place with respect to our food consumption. The government must set limits on acceptable amounts of sodium, limit the addition of harmful preservatives, and crack down on misleading marketing. Our health care system cannot afford what is happening with respect to chronic disease.

FOOD ADDICTIONS

Packaged and processed foods are filled with fat, salt and sugar, all highly addictive ingredients. The more you eat of them, the more you crave them and become addicted to them.

I believe that food manufacturers are to blame. They spend millions of dollars researching how to get people to eat more of their products. *Salt Sugar Fat: How the Food Giants Hooked Us* (written by *New York Times* reporter Michael Moss) is about food industry executives, who, as far back as 1999, knew and wilfully ignored the role their foods played in the obesity epidemic that we now see escalating. Dr. David Kessler (a former commissioner of the U.S. Food and Drug Administration) says in his book *The End of Overeating* that food companies prey on our biological addictions to salt, fat and sugar in the same way that tobacco companies exploit the addictive properties of nicotine.

The biggest offenders aren't always those companies who produce poor-quality food. Many companies try to pass off food that contains excess fat, sugar or salt as healthy. Examples of these foods are dips that sound healthy because they are called vegetable dips, but contain excess mayonnaise, sour cream or salt; breakfast cereals that promote the vitamins and minerals they contain but still contain excess sugar; yogurt that contains little protein and excess sugar. The list goes on.

THE MANUFACTURERS' TRAP

Labelling can be misleading, and addictions to food that contains excess fat, sugar or salt are tough to break. Manufacturers will not change their formulas for their foods if those foods sell. And remember that they have spent millions of dollars researching how to get us addicted. We need the government to intervene, and we need to demand healthier fare.

What is more, we have to understand our own triggers for eating these foods and become aware of how the food companies lure us into their traps. But we also need to take responsibility for what we eat and put into our shopping carts. We have to read labels more carefully and understand the guidelines for a healthy diet, so we won't get fooled by misleading labelling.

Salt

Nearly eighty percent of the salt in the average North American diet is added by food companies. Ten percent is present in food naturally. These figures mean that only ten percent is controlled by the consumer, with the salt shaker—a good reason to reduce your intake of processed and packaged foods.

Food companies love salt. It encourages consumers to eat more. Salt brings out the flavour of natural foods, yet disguises the artificial taste of processed foods. It is cheap and extends shelf life. It makes you want to drink more. It also makes foods weigh more because it binds with water; the added weight of the item means a higher price tag.

Health Canada now suggests that everyone should consume no more than 1,500 milligrams (mg) of sodium a day. This is equivalent to three-quarters of a teaspoon (4 mL) of salt. Finding low-sodium products among the vast array of frozen dinners, cereals, cheeses, soups, sauces and condiments on the main supermarket shelves, let alone in the snacks, pretzels and chips aisles is difficult. If you are trying to cut down on salt, you must avoid such items or eat them in small amounts.

Salt is put into food to make it taste better, and salted foods do taste better. But salt also makes soups thicker, reduces the dryness in crackers and pretzels, and increases the sweetness of cakes and cookies. Salt also helps disguise the metallic or chemical aftertaste of products such as soft drinks.

To become aware of how much salt you are eating, read the "Nutrition Facts" label of food products carefully. In each hundred-gram serving of food, there should be no more than 150 mg of sodium. This label also lists the sodium in each serving as a percentage of the total recommended daily amount (shown as "% Daily Intake"). Sodium should not be more than five percent—many products are over twenty percent. Also note that salt goes by several other names in the ingredients list of food-product labels. Look for these words: sodium, monosodium glutamate (MSG), baking soda, baking powder and sodium nitrate.

Most processed and packaged foods—crackers, potato chips, frozen dinners, home replacement meals, canned foods, pizzas, sauces, soups, condiments, cured meats—contain excess sodium unless marked "low sodium" or "reduced sodium." Eat less of "pickled," "cured" and "smoked" foods. Some of the worst high-salt offenders are soy sauce, condiments, canned soup and bouillon cubes. Some bouillon cubes contain more than 1,500 mg per cube. Keep in mind that the recommended daily limit is only 1,500 mg per day!

To avoid excess salt, choose foods that are labelled "low sodium" or "reduced sodium" and increase the amount of natural or unprocessed food you eat while decreasing the amount of packaged or processed food you eat. This will dramatically reduce the sodium in your diet. Go for foods such as fresh fruits and vegetables, lean meats, poultry, fish and unprocessed grains. Select roasted rather than smoked or deli meats. And remember, restaurant food, fast food and packaged meals can contain more than two to three times as much sodium as a similar meal cooked at home using fresh ingredients.

Sugar

We are always hearing about how much sugar we consume each day. The problem is not only the sugar we add to our coffee or use in our baking, but the sugars that are hidden in so many food products, not dissimilar to the way salt is hidden.

Manufacturers are continually being attacked for the amount of sugar in their products. Sugar has virtually no nutritional qualities. It does not contain vitamins or minerals and it often displaces nutritious foods in a daily diet. When we eat sugar-filled products, we get full and feel satisfied, which often prevents us from eating nutritious foods. Sugar promotes obesity, which can lead to serious and chronic diseases such as type 2 diabetes.

The most commonly consumed sugar products are canned soft drinks, sweetened fruit drinks, sweets and candies, cakes and cookies, dairy desserts such as ice cream or frozen yogurt, and breakfast cereals. The biggest controversy around sugar right now is the high amount of sugar in food products intended for children.

The newest culprit on the sugar scene is high-fructose corn syrup. A common sweetener and preservative, this syrup is made by changing the sugar (glucose) in cornstarch to fructose—another form of sugar. The end product is a fructose-and-glucose combination. Today high-fructose corn syrup is seen in packaged foods everywhere—canned pop, cookies, energy bars, salad dressings, breakfast cereals—in any foods that traditionally had cane sugar added to them. High-fructose corn syrup also has a longer shelf life than cane sugar, which makes it even more attractive to food manufacturers.

Sugar is used not only to sweeten foods but to give them texture, and is often used just for appearance and colour. It also helps to preserve food, as it prevents bacterial growth.

Other names for sugar include brown sugar, cane sugar, corn syrup, dextrose, fructose, glucose, sucrose, high-fructose corn syrup, lactose—to name just a few. Many foods contain sugar, including pastries, salad dressings, packaged cereals and breakfast bars, ketchup, barbecue sauce, preserves, dried fruit, sports drinks, juices, colas, yogurts and pasta sauces.

Fat

It's a toss-up: which is more addictive, sugar or fat? I think more people are addicted to fat because of its "mouth feel." Fat comes in many forms and isn't easily recognized on food labels. It preserves food so it can sit on grocery shelves for days or weeks. It also gives more bulk and texture to food. But not all fat is bad; certain fats are necessary for good health.

Unsaturated (mono- and poly-) fats are "good" fats. Examples of these fats are canola, olive, peanut and grape-seed oils, and some margarines. These fats play an important role in hormone production, red blood cell formation, joint lubrication and proper insulin function. Eating the right fats in moderation will not cause you to gain excess fat.

Too many people are obsessed with taking all the fat out of their diet. It is actually unhealthy to have no fat in your diet— a healthy diet should consist of twenty-five to thirty percent fat. However, the typical North American diet, which consists of forty percent or more fat, exceeds that considerably.

Fat has nine calories per gram—more than protein or carbohydrates, which have only four calories per gram. And fat doesn't fill you up the same way that protein and carbohydrates do, which means you're hungry soon after you've eaten fatty foods.

Aim to keep your fat intake to less than thirty percent of your total daily calories and your saturated fat intake to less than ten percent.

Saturated fats are "bad" fats. These are mostly found in animal products, such as meat and dairy products. Butter, lard, coconut and palm oils are saturated fats. In excess, these fats can clog your arteries and lead to heart disease and stroke.

Trans fats are also "bad" fats. Stay away from them; they are actually more harmful than saturated fats. They are produced when unsaturated fat is hydrogenated (hydrogenation is a process that changes a liquid oil into a solid fat). Trans fats have traditionally been used to benefit the manufacturer by improving the shelf life, flavour and stability of foods. You'll find trans fats in vegetable shortenings as well as some margarines, crackers and cookies. Since January 2006, food manufacturers have been required to list the amount of trans fat in all their products. Trans fat is listed directly under saturated fat in the Nutrition Facts information label on a food product package. Many cities in North America and Europe have begun the process of banning trans fat from restaurant food as well as from packaged goods. I believe that in time many more cities will join their ranks.

Saturated fat doesn't appear just as "saturated fat" on a food label; it will appear under different names as well: lard, milk solids, palm or coconut oil, shortening, coconut milk, chocolate, cocoa butter, or cream.

PROCESSED FOODS

Processed foods provide convenience and taste, but they often contain excess fat, sugar, salt and calories. They can also contain harmful preservatives, hydrogenated vegetable oil, artificial flavourings, food dyes and artificial sweeteners. Check carefully for these harmful ingredients on the Nutrition Facts label when you are selecting canned, frozen or processed foods.

Generally speaking, you should aim to consume processed food that has, per serving, less than fifteen grams of fat, fewer than 400 calories and less than 800 mg of sodium.

THE BENEFITS OF EXERCISE

The other half of the healthy-lifestyle equation is exercise. You should do some form of exercise every day for at least twenty minutes. If you don't enjoy the gym, just walking briskly is excellent. The benefits of exercise are enormous:

- burns calories
- increases metabolism
- lessens the risk of heart disease, stroke, type 2 diabetes, obesity and cancer
- regulates blood pressure
- boosts the immune system
- increases bone density

This is a lot to digest, no pun intended. But this material is important to help you understand why we have no choice but to try to live a healthier lifestyle. I have devoted the past fifteen years to changing my own eating habits and my family's, and now my mission is to change Canadians' eating habits. Our families depend on us to be as healthy as we can. Our employers need us to do the best work possible, which can only happen when we are feeling healthy and at the top of our game. I am getting my message out to Canadians every day through my catering, books, media appearances, speaking engagements and several health-oriented boards I sit on. I love what I do every day, and I hope I can bring you along on the journey to a longer and healthier life.

About the Nutrition Information

This book uses many reduced-fat or low-sodium ingredients. The table below describes the exact amount of fat or sodium in these ingredients, and the nutrition information that appears in each recipe is based on them. You can use any reduced-fat or low-sodium ingredient you like to make the recipes, just be aware that the calories, fat and sodium of the recipe might then be different from the amount given in the nutrition information of the recipe if you don't use the ingredient listed here.

Where a recipe gives a second option for an ingredient, the nutritional analysis for that recipe is based on the first ingredient. For example, the nutrition information for a recipe that uses "1½ cups (375 mL) liquid egg substitute (or 6 large eggs)" is based on using the liquid egg substitute.

INGREDIENT USED IN THE RECIPE	DESCRIPTION
vegetable oil	canola oil
reduced-fat mayonnaise	35% fat
low-sodium stock	contains 400 mg of sodium per cup (250 mL)
part-skim mozzarella cheese	18% milk fat
reduced-fat feta cheese	14% milk fat
reduced-fat cream cheese	21% milk fat
reduced-fat ricotta cheese	5% milk fat
reduced-fat sour cream	3% milk fat
reduced-fat yogurt	2% milk fat
low-fat condensed milk	4% milk fat
light coconut milk	5%–7% fat

BREAKFAST & BRUNCH

SUNNY-SIDE UP EGGS WITH SPINACH AND MUSHROOMS ON ENGLISH MUFFINS

Adding some vegetables, cheese and whole grains to your eggs gives you a complete and healthy breakfast meal. Cook your eggs until still runny for the best flavour.

1. In a large skillet, add the oil, onions and garlic. Sauté for 5 minutes until tender. Add the mushrooms and sauté for 5 minutes or until the liquid is evaporated. Add the spinach and sauté until wilted. Add the feta cheese. Set aside.

2. In another large skillet, sprayed with vegetable oil, heat and carefully crack the eggs (use two pans if necessary). On medium heat, cook for about 3 to 5 minutes until done to your preference. Meanwhile toast the English muffins.

3. Place the mushroom mixture on the English muffin halves. Carefully slip the eggs overtop.

PREPARATION TIME 10 minutes · **COOKING TIME** 15 minutes ·
MAKE AHEAD Prepare the vegetables up to a day in advance and finish the dish just before serving. · **MAKES** 6 servings.

2 tsp (10 mL) vegetable oil

1½ cups (375 mL) chopped onion

1 tsp (5 mL) minced garlic

4 cups (1 L) diced button mushrooms

4 cups (1 L) fresh baby spinach leaves

¼ cup (60 mL) crumbled reduced-fat feta cheese (1 oz/30 g)

6 eggs

3 whole wheat English muffins

 ROSE'S TIP

Be sure not to overcook your eggs. A soft- to medium-cooked egg has the best flavour for this dish.

 HEALTH TIP

English muffins are much healthier in terms of calories and fat than a bagel. A bagel has 340 calories, and an English muffin has only 100 calories!

NUTRITION INFORMATION PER SERVING (½ ENGLISH MUFFIN)

Calories 173	Protein 10.6 g	Cholesterol 160 mg
Carbohydrates 19.1 g	Total fat 6.2 g	Sodium 214 mg
Fibre 2.9 g	Saturated fat 2 g	

SCRAMBLED EGGS WITH BRIE AND SMOKED SALMON

Scrambled eggs made with velvety brie and savoury smoked salmon are a real treat for a weekend breakfast item. I have used egg substitutes because a healthy portion has three eggs per person, which has too much fat and cholesterol. The egg substitutes available today are excellent and even come in different flavours.

1. In a large skillet sprayed with vegetable oil, add the eggs and milk. On medium heat continue to scramble just until the eggs are almost set. Do not overcook.

2. Serve with smoked salmon and brie overtop. Sprinkle with pepper and garnish with dill sprig.

PREPARATION TIME 5 minutes · **COOKING TIME** 5 minutes ·
MAKES 2 servings.

1½ cups (375 mL) liquid egg substitute (or 6 large eggs)

¼ cup (60 mL) 2% milk

¼ cup (60 mL) diced smoked salmon

2 slices brie (1½ oz/45 g)

pinch of pepper

sprig of dill

 ROSE'S TIP
Be sure not to mix the salmon with the eggs before serving, or you will cook the salmon.

 HEALTH TIP
Eat small amounts of smoked fish due to the sodium content.

NUTRITION INFORMATION PER SERVING

Calories 187	Protein 26.6 g	Cholesterol 25 mg
Carbohydrates 5.2 g	Total fat 6.3 g	Sodium 685 mg
Fibre 0 g	Saturated fat 3.9 g	

CALIFORNIA BURRITO WITH BLACK BEANS AND CHARRED CORN

This Tex-Mex wrap is loaded with flavour from the sautéed vegetables, salsa and aged cheddar cheese. I love the flavour of whole eggs and four split between six servings is acceptable. By using the egg substitute you cut back on extra calories, fat and cholesterol.

1. Heat the oil in a nonstick skillet over medium heat. Add the onion and sauté for 3 minutes or until soft. Add the corn and sauté for 5 to 8 minutes or until the corn begins to char. Add the bell pepper, beans and garlic, and sauté for 2 more minutes. Set aside.

2. Lightly coat a nonstick skillet with cooking spray. Add the eggs and scramble over medium heat for 2 minutes or almost set. Fold in the beans and corn mixture and cook for 1 more minute or until the eggs are set. Keep warm.

3. To assemble the burritos, spread the salsa evenly over the tortillas. Place a third of the eggs along the bottom of each tortilla. Sprinkle with cheese and season with the salt and pepper. Fold in both sides and roll. Cut in half.

4. If desired, toast the burritos in the oven or toaster oven at 400°F (200°C) for 5 minutes before serving.

PREPARATION TIME 15 minutes • **COOKING TIME** 15 minutes •
MAKE AHEAD Prepare early in the day and reheat the burritos wrapped in foil in a 350°F (175°C) oven for 10 minutes. • **MAKES** 6 servings.

2 tsp (10 mL) vegetable oil

⅓ cup (80 mL) finely diced onion

⅓ cup (80 mL) canned corn

¼ cup (60 mL) finely diced red bell pepper

¼ cup (60 mL) canned black beans, drained and rinsed

1 tsp (5 mL) finely chopped garlic

1 cup (250 mL) liquid egg substitute (or 4 eggs)

½ cup (125 mL) medium salsa

3 large whole wheat flour tortillas

½ cup (125 mL) shredded aged cheddar cheese (1.5 oz/45 g)

pinch of salt and pepper

 ROSE'S TIP
Try adding some homemade guacamole to this burrito (see Guacamole on page 362).

 HEALTH TIP
A 10-inch (25 cm) whole wheat flour tortilla has 3.3 grams of fibre versus the white tortilla which has only 1 gram of fibre.

NUTRITION INFORMATION PER SERVING (½ TORTILLA)

Calories 104	Protein 8 g	Cholesterol 7 mg
Carbohydrates 6 g	Total fat 5.3 g	Sodium 248 mg
Fibre 1.1 g	Saturated fat 1.8 g	

EGG MUFFINS WITH SUN-DRIED TOMATOES AND GOAT CHEESE

This is the greatest creation since the McDonald's McMuffin, but much healthier. The egg mixture is baked in a muffin tin and can then be served over an English muffin, toast or bagel. You can use one egg per person, but if you're watching your cholesterol, you may want to use an egg substitute or a combination.

1. Preheat the oven to 350°F (175°C). Lightly coat a 6-cup muffin tin with cooking spray.

2. Combine the eggs with half the sun-dried tomatoes (about 2 Tbsp/30 mL). Divide evenly into the 6 muffin cups. Bake for 15 to 18 minutes or until the eggs are just set.

3. Combine the remaining sun-dried tomatoes with the goat cheese in a small bowl. Top each egg muffin with a little of the tomato and cheese mixture. Carefully remove the eggs with a knife.

PREPARATION TIME 10 minutes • **BAKING TIME** 15 minutes •
MAKE AHEAD Prepare just before serving. • **MAKES** 6 servings.

6 eggs (or 1½ cups/375 mL liquid egg substitute)

¼ cup (60 mL) diced rehydrated sun-dried tomatoes

¼ cup (60 mL) crumbled goat cheese (1 oz/30 g)

 ROSE'S TIP
Always use dry sun-dried tomatoes that you have to hydrate to cut out the fat from the oil used in preserving. Just pour boiling water overtop and let sit for 10 minutes. Drain and dice.

 HEALTH TIP
Combine 3 whole eggs and ¾ of the egg substitute for the best flavour and texture in order to lessen the calories and fat.

NUTRITION INFORMATION PER SERVING (1 EGG MUFFIN)

Calories 74	Protein 9 g	Cholesterol 3 mg
Carbohydrates 2 g	Total fat 3.4 g	Sodium 176 mg
Fibre 0.3 g	Saturated fat 1.1 g	

CHEESE BLINTZ SOUFFLÉ WITH BLUEBERRY SAUCE

I love blintzes, but making individual ones takes time and effort. This baked version is an easy way to prepare this classic dish.

1. Preheat the oven to 350°F (175°C). Lightly coat an 8-inch (20 cm) square baking dish with cooking spray.

2. TO MAKE THE BATTER Purée the batter ingredients in the bowl of a food processor until smooth. Pour a little less than half the mixture in the bottom of the dish. Bake for 10 minutes.

3. TO MAKE THE FILLING Beat the filling ingredients in the bowl of a food processor or with electric beaters until smooth. Pour over the baked blintz mixture. Carefully pour the remaining batter over the filling. Bake for 25 to 30 minutes or until mixture is no longer loose and top is puffy.

4. TO MAKE THE SAUCE Combine the orange juice, sugar, cornstarch and lemon juice in a small bowl and whisk until the cornstarch is dissolved. Add to a small skillet along with berries, bring to a boil, then simmer on low heat for 3 minutes or until thickened. Serve over the blintz soufflé.

PREPARATION TIME 20 minutes • **BAKING TIME** 35 minutes •
MAKE AHEAD Prepare up to a day early. Best baked right before serving. •
MAKES 9 servings.

 ROSE'S TIP
You can always serve this soufflé with maple syrup or sour cream.

 HEALTH TIP
Light (5%) ricotta cheese has 80 calories and 4 grams of fat per ⅓ cup (80 mL), whereas light cream cheese has 180 calories and 13 grams fat.

NUTRITION INFORMATION PER SERVING (1 SQUARE)

Calories 312	Protein 11 g	Cholesterol 104 mg
Carbohydrates 36 g	Total fat 12 g	Sodium 230 mg
Fibre 0.9 g	Saturated fat 4.4 g	

Batter

2 eggs

¾ cup (185 mL) 2% milk

1½ Tbsp (22.5 mL) reduced-fat sour cream

2½ Tbsp (38 mL) vegetable oil

1 tsp (5 mL) vanilla extract

¾ cup (185 mL) all-purpose flour

2 Tbsp (30 mL) granulated sugar

1 tsp (5 mL) baking powder

Filling

2 cups (500 mL) reduced-fat ricotta cheese (1 lb/500 g)

¾ cup (185 mL) softened reduced-fat cream cheese (6 oz/175 g)

1 egg

⅓ cup (80 mL) granulated sugar

2 tsp (10 mL) lemon zest

2 Tbsp (30 mL) lemon juice

Sauce

⅓ cup (80 mL) orange juice

⅓ cup (80 mL) granulated sugar

2 tsp (10 mL) cornstarch

1 Tbsp (15 mL) lemon juice

1 cup (250 mL) fresh or 2 cups (500 mL) frozen blueberries (thawed and drained)

OPEN-FACED OMELETTE WITH BELL PEPPERS, MUSHROOMS AND SWISS CHEESE

To enhance the flavour, use oyster, shiitake or portobello mushrooms. Button mushrooms work as well, but be sure to sauté on higher heat so the excess liquid evaporates.

1. Lightly coat a small nonstick skillet with cooking spray. Add the oil and set over medium heat. Add the onion and garlic and sauté for 3 minutes or until the onion is soft and lightly browned. Add the mushrooms and red pepper and cook for 5 minutes or until the mushrooms are slightly dried. Set aside.

2. Wipe out the skillet and respray. Combine the egg substitute, egg whites and milk. Cook for 4 minutes over medium heat or until the egg begins to set. Add the onion and mushroom mixture, spinach and cheese. Cook for another 2 minutes or until the cheese melts.

3. Slip the omelette onto a serving platter with a spatula. Cut in half, garnish with parsley and serve immediately.

PREPARATION TIME 10 minutes · **COOKING TIME** 14 minutes ·
MAKE AHEAD Sauté the vegetables up to a day before. Cook the omelette just before serving. · **MAKES** 2 servings.

1 tsp (5 mL) vegetable oil

⅓ cup (80 mL) finely chopped onion

½ tsp (2.5 mL) chopped garlic

¾ cup (185 mL) sliced mushrooms

¼ cup (60 mL) diced red bell pepper

½ cup (125 mL) liquid egg substitute (or 2 large eggs)

3 egg whites

⅓ cup (80 mL) 2% milk

1 cup (250 mL) fresh baby spinach

⅓ cup (80 mL) shredded Swiss cheese (1 oz/30 g)

2 Tbsp (30 mL) chopped parsley

ROSE'S TIP
You can make 2 small omelettes instead of 1 large one.

HEALTH TIP
This omelette is a great breakfast consisting of 3 of the 4 food groups. Add some wholegrain bread and you have all the nutrients to start your day.

NUTRITION INFORMATION PER SERVING

Calories 170	Protein 17 g	Cholesterol 12 mg
Carbohydrates 7 g	Total fat 7 g	Sodium 290 mg
Fibre 1.3 g	Saturated fat 3.2 g	

HUEVOS RANCHEROS

My children love to brunch at Glow Fresh Grill, the restaurant that features my healthy menu. Customers kept telling me I was missing Huevos Rancheros, a Mexican egg dish. I created a healthier delicious version. The key is not to overcook your eggs.

1. Preheat the oven to 425°F (220°C).

2. In a skillet sprayed with vegetable spray, add the oil and sauté the onions for 3 minutes. Add the green peppers, garlic, jalapeños and cumin. Sauté for 2 minutes. Add the black beans.

3. Place the tortillas on a baking sheet lined with foil. Divide the vegetable mixture overtop along with the cheese and tomato salsa. Bake for 5 minutes.

4. Meanwhile, crack the eggs gently into a large skillet sprayed with vegetable spray. On medium-low heat, cook the eggs sunny-side up for about 5 minutes, just until yolks are still slightly loose. Place the eggs on the tortillas and garnish with cilantro and salsa. Serve immediately.

PREPARATION TIME 10 minutes · **COOKING TIME** 10 minutes ·
MAKE AHEAD Cook the vegetables up to a day in advance. Cook the remaining dish just before serving. · **MAKES** 4 servings.

 ROSE'S TIP
For the best flavour, cook your eggs until they're still slightly runny.

 HEALTH TIP
One egg contains a high level of choline, which is beneficial for pregnant women since choline can increase brain and memory function of the fetus.

1 tsp (5 mL) vegetable oil

¾ cup (185 mL) diced onion

⅓ cup (80 mL) diced green bell pepper

1 tsp (5 mL) crushed garlic

1 tsp (5 mL) minced jalapeño peppers with seeds

¼ tsp (1 mL) cumin powder

¼ cup (60 mL) canned black beans, drained and rinsed

4 small flour tortillas

½ cup (125 mL) grated Monterey Jack or aged cheddar cheese (1½ oz/45 g)

⅓ cup (80 mL) medium-hot tomato salsa

4 eggs

2 Tbsp (30 mL) chopped cilantro

2 Tbsp (30 mL) medium salsa

NUTRITION INFORMATION PER SERVING

Calories 248	Protein 14 g	Cholesterol 151 mg
Carbohydrates 28 g	Total fat 8.8 g	Sodium 265 mg
Fibre 3 g	Saturated fat 3.8 g	

ITALIAN OMELETTE WITH TOMATOES AND FETA

This omelette fits in perfectly with the Mediterranean food pyramid. This way of eating has been credited with lowering the incidence of heart attacks and strokes, reducing the risk of certain cancers and maintaining weight control. We have it all here in one omelette.

1. Lightly coat a 9-inch (23 cm) nonstick skillet with cooking spray. Add the egg substitute and cook over medium-low heat for 4 minutes. Add the tomatoes, olives, feta and dried basil and cook for another 2 minutes or until the eggs are almost set.

2. Fold the omelette in half and cook for another minute. Garnish with fresh basil.

PREPARATION TIME 10 minutes · **COOKING TIME** 7 minutes ·

MAKES 2 servings.

1 cup (250 mL) liquid egg substitute (or 4 large eggs)

⅓ cup (80 mL) seeded and diced plum tomatoes

3 Tbsp (45 mL) diced black olives

¼ cup (60 mL) crumbled reduced-fat feta cheese (1 oz/30 g)

½ tsp (2.5 mL) dried basil

2 Tbsp (30 mL) chopped fresh basil

 ROSE'S TIP

Egg substitutes today come in various flavours such as Southwestern, three cheese and Florentine.

 HEALTH TIP

Reduced-fat feta cheese has about a third of the calories and fat as regular full fat. The taste is still rich and delicious.

NUTRITION INFORMATION PER SERVING

Calories 157	Protein 18 g	Cholesterol 6.3 mg
Carbohydrates 3.5 g	Total fat 7.8 g	Sodium 509 mg
Fibre 1 g	Saturated fat 2.5 g	

BRAN, BANANA AND DRIED CRANBERRY MUFFINS

You can't claim to have a complete repertoire of muffin recipes without including the traditional bran variety. But my recipe uses both banana and molasses to increase the flavour and moisture. The dried cranberries give a delicious tartness.

1. Preheat the oven to 375°F (190°C). Spray 12 muffin cups with vegetable oil.

2. Combine the oil, molasses, egg, sugar, banana, vanilla, yogurt and milk in a large bowl and mix until well blended.

3. Combine the bran, both flours, baking powder, baking soda, cinnamon, salt and dried cranberries in another bowl and mix well. Add to the wet mixture and stir just until combined. Spoon into the prepared muffin cups and bake in the centre of the oven for about 15 minutes or until the tops are firm to the touch. Turn out and serve immediately or serve at room temperature.

PREPARATION TIME 10 minutes · **BAKING TIME** 15 minutes ·
MAKE AHEAD Bake muffins and store them at room temperature for up to 2 days or freeze them for up to 2 weeks. · **MAKES** 12 servings.

ROSE'S TIP
Adding molasses and ripe banana gives this bran muffin its distinctive flavour. Be sure to use only the ripest bananas.

HEALTH TIP
Regular muffins in coffee shops can have over 600 calories due to their massive size and excess fat and sugar.

¼ cup (60 mL) vegetable oil

3 Tbsp (45 mL) molasses

1 large egg

1 cup (250 mL) sugar

1 medium ripe banana, mashed (about ½ cup/125 mL)

1 tsp (5 mL) pure vanilla extract

½ cup (125 mL) reduced-fat plain yogurt

⅓ cup (80 mL) 2% milk

½ cup (125 mL) wheat bran

¾ cup (185 mL) all-purpose flour

⅓ cup (80 mL) whole wheat flour

1½ tsp (7.5 mL) baking powder

½ tsp (2.5 mL) baking soda

1 tsp (5 mL) ground cinnamon

pinch of salt

½ cup (125 mL) dried cranberries

NUTRITION INFORMATION PER SERVING (1 MUFFIN)

Calories 188	Protein 2.4 g	Cholesterol 18 mg
Carbohydrates 28 g	Total fat 5.4 g	Sodium 129 mg
Fibre 1.8 g	Saturated fat 0.6 g	

CHOCOLATE CHIP BANANA MUFFINS

Coffee-shop muffins are definitely high in calories and fat—often with close to one-third of your daily calories and fat. In this muffin recipe, using mashed bananas and the yogurt eliminates the need for a lot of oil. It's perfect for a snack or a lighter dessert. A favourite for kids.

1. Preheat the oven to 375°F (190°C). Spray 12 muffin cups with vegetable oil.

2. Using an electric mixer, beat together the bananas, sugar, oil, egg and vanilla in a large bowl until well mixed.

3. In another bowl, combine the flour, baking powder and baking soda. Stir the banana and flour mixture together. Stir in the yogurt. Fold in the chocolate chips.

4. Divide the batter among the prepared muffin cups and bake in the centre of the oven for 15 minutes until a tester inserted in the middle of the muffin comes out clean. Turn out and serve immediately.

PREPARATION TIME 5 minutes · **BAKING TIME** 15 minutes ·

MAKE AHEAD Bake muffins and store at room temperature for up to 2 days or freeze for up to 2 weeks. · **MAKES** 12 muffins.

¾ cup (185 mL) ripe bananas, mashed (about 1½ medium bananas)

½ cup (125 mL) granulated sugar

¼ cup (60 mL) vegetable oil

1 egg

1 tsp (5 mL) vanilla

1 cup (250 mL) all-purpose flour

1 tsp (5 mL) baking powder

1 tsp (5 mL) baking soda

½ cup (125 mL) reduced-fat plain yogurt (or reduced-fat sour cream)

⅓ cup (80 mL) semisweet chocolate chips

 ROSE'S TIP

Freeze overripe bananas in their skin. Defrost and use in your baking. The banana flavour will be intense—perfect for low-fat cooking.

 HEALTH TIP

When using reduced-fat yogurt, 1%–2% is fine to use. You don't need 0% fat unless you're eating larger amounts.

NUTRITION INFORMATION PER SERVING (1 MUFFIN)

Calories 150	Protein 2 g	Cholesterol 18 mg
Carbohydrates 21 g	Total fat 6 g	Sodium 158 mg
Fibre 1 g	Saturated fat 1.2 g	

PEANUT BUTTER
AND JAM MUFFINS

You can't find a better combination than peanut butter and jam. Always use natural peanut butter (the kind that contains peanuts only). The other types often contain hydrogenated vegetable oil and icing sugar. If you're baking for someone with a peanut allergy, try using other nut butters or soy butter.

1. Preheat the oven to 350°F (175°C). Lightly coat a 12-cup muffin tin with cooking spray.

2. Using a whisk or electric beaters, combine the oil, sugar, banana, peanut butter, egg, sour cream and vanilla in a large bowl. Beat until smooth.

3. In another bowl, combine both flours, baking powder, baking soda, cinnamon and salt with a wooden spoon. Gradually add the dry ingredients to the wet ingredients and stir until the dry ingredients are just moistened.

4. Divide the mixture among the prepared muffin cups. Bake for 15 to 18 minutes or until a tester inserted in the middle of a muffin comes out clean. Press gently in the centre of each muffin to make an indentation and place a small amount of the jam inside.

PREPARATION TIME 15 minutes · **BAKING TIME** 15 minutes ·
MAKE AHEAD Bake up to a day in advance or freeze for up to 2 weeks. ·
MAKES 12 servings.

3 Tbsp (45 mL) vegetable oil

¼ cup (60 mL) granulated sugar

1 large ripe banana (about ½ cup/125 mL)

3 Tbsp (45 mL) smooth natural peanut butter

1 large egg

⅔ cup (160 mL) reduced-fat sour cream

1 tsp (5 mL) vanilla extract

1 cup (250 mL) all-purpose flour

¼ cup (60 mL) whole wheat flour

1½ tsp (7.5 mL) baking powder

½ tsp (2.5 mL) baking soda

1 tsp (5 mL) cinnamon

pinch of salt

3 Tbsp (45 mL) raspberry jam

ROSE'S TIP
Get your kids to help you make these great muffins. They're perfect for snacks or dessert.

HEALTH TIP
Peanut butter is high in calories and fat but the fat is monoun-saturated, which reduces the risk of heart disease and type 2 diabetes.

NUTRITION INFORMATION PER SERVING (1 MUFFIN)

Calories 251	Protein 3.8 g	Cholesterol 22 mg
Carbohydrates 43 g	Total fat 7.5 g	Sodium 160 mg
Fibre 1.2 g	Saturated fat 1.3 g	

PISTACHIO-CRUSTED FRENCH TOAST

French toast is a classic breakfast item either at home or in restaurants. In our catering kitchen, we developed a great version of French toast, coating it with ground pistachios.

1. Mix the eggs, milk, sugar and vanilla just until combined and pour onto a plate.

2. Combine the pistachios and cinnamon and put on another plate.

3. Dip the bread in the egg mixture, soaking until just before the bread breaks. Dip in the pistachio mixture.

4. Spray a skillet with vegetable oil and brown the bread for 4 minutes on each side or until browned.

5. Garnish with maple syrup and fresh fruit, if using.

PREPARATION TIME 5 minutes · **COOKING TIME** 8 minutes · **MAKES** 4 servings.

½ cup (125 mL) liquid egg substitute (or 2 large eggs)

1 cup (250 mL) 2% milk

1½ tsp (7.5 mL) granulated sugar

1 tsp (5 mL) vanilla extract

1 cup (250 mL) finely ground pistachios

¼ tsp (1 mL) ground cinnamon

4 slices whole wheat bread

2 Tbsp (30 mL) pure maple syrup

fresh fruit (optional)

ROSE'S TIP
Use any variety of nuts you like, such as almonds, pecans, cashews or macademia nuts.

HEALTH TIP
If you want to cut back on the calories and fat, just dip one side of the milk-soaked bread in the ground nuts.

NUTRITION INFORMATION PER SERVING (1 SLICE OF BREAD)

Calories 288	Protein 15.1 g	Cholesterol 1 mg
Carbohydrates 28.2 g	Total fat 14.2 g	Sodium 225 mg
Fibre 5.2 g	Saturated fat 2 g	

UPSIDE-DOWN FRENCH TOAST WITH ORANGE-MAPLE GLAZE

I came across this recipe in a breakfast magazine, but it was made with excess butter, eggs and heavy cream. I played around with it and came out with a delicious healthier version. This is best served hot right from the oven.

1. Lightly coat a 9-inch (23 cm) square ovenproof casserole dish with cooking spray.

2. TO MAKE THE BOTTOM LAYER Combine the brown sugar, oil, maple syrup and apricots in a bowl and spread the mixture across the bottom of the dish. Place the baguette slices over the bottom layer.

3. TO MAKE THE TOP LAYER Whisk together the orange zest, orange juice, milk, brown sugar, cinnamon, vanilla and egg substitute in a large bowl. Pour the mixture over the baguette slices. Cover and refrigerate for at least 4 hours or overnight.

4. Preheat the oven to 350°F (175°C). Take the casserole dish out of the fridge and turn the baguette slices over in the dish. Let sit at room temperature for 15 minutes. Bake for 25 minutes. Serve immediately with sliced strawberries and the sauce from the bottom of the pan served on top of the casserole.

PREPARATION TIME 15 minutes · BAKING TIME 25 minutes ·

MAKE AHEAD Prepare up to a day in advance and bake just before serving. ·

MAKES 9 servings.

Bottom Layer

⅓ cup (80 mL) packed brown sugar

2 Tbsp (30 mL) vegetable oil

2 Tbsp (30 mL) maple syrup

½ cup (125 mL) chopped dried apricots

9 slices whole wheat French baguette (about 1 inch/2.5 cm thick and 2 inches/5 cm in diameter)

Top Layer

2 tsp (10 mL) finely grated orange zest

½ cup (125 mL) orange juice

½ cup (125 mL) 2% milk

¼ cup (60 mL) packed brown sugar

½ tsp (2.5 mL) cinnamon

1 tsp (5 mL) vanilla extract

½ cup (125 mL) liquid egg substitute (or 2 large eggs)

1 cup (250 mL) sliced strawberries for topping

 ROSE'S TIP

If you're in a hurry, just
let the casserole sit for
30 minutes, turn the bread
after 15 minutes and then
bake. The bread won't soak
up the moisture as well as
it will if you leave it for
4 hours, but it will still
be delicious.

 HEALTH TIP

Be sure to buy only pure
maple syrup and never
the artificial kind, which
contains high-fructose
corn syrup.

NUTRITION INFORMATION PER SERVING (1 SLICE)

Calories 160	Protein 3.7 g	Cholesterol 0 mg
Carbohydrates 29.7 g	Total fat 3.2 g	Sodium 109 mg
Fibre 1.1 g	Saturated fat 0.5 g	

ROSE'S NO-BAKE GRANOLA SQUARES

It took me forever to come up with a great and healthy granola square that didn't need baking. This one is so delicious and addictive, I want to produce them in our catering kitchen and distribute them!

1. Line an 8-inch (20 cm) square baking dish with parchment paper or spray with vegetable oil.

2. In a large skillet, add the oats, rice crisp cereal, nuts, flax seeds and cinnamon. On medium heat, lightly brown the mixture for about 3 minutes, stirring constantly. Remove from heat and add the dried fruit.

3. In a small skillet, add the sugar, vanilla, peanut butter and honey. Heat gently just until you can easily blend the mixture. Add to the oat mixture and press into the pan. Refrigerate for about 30 minutes, then cut into 12 squares. Best kept refrigerated to stay crisp.

PREPARATION TIME 10 minutes • **COOKING TIME** 3 minutes •
MAKE AHEAD Can be made 3 days in advance. Cover tightly. •
MAKES 12 servings.

½ cup (125 mL) old-fashioned rolled oats

½ cup (125 mL) brown rice crisp cereal

½ cup (125 mL) finely chopped nuts (any variety)

2 Tbsp (30 mL) whole flax seeds

½ tsp (2.5 mL) cinnamon

½ cup (125 mL) chopped dried fruit (combination)

¼ cup (60 mL) granulated sugar

1 tsp (5 mL) vanilla extract

¼ cup (60 mL) natural smooth peanut butter

¼ cup (60 mL) honey

 ROSE'S TIP
Most granola squares are filled with excess sugar and fat, making them worse than a candy bar, nutrition-wise. These granola squares have more protein and fibre due to the natural peanut butter, dried fruit and nuts.

 HEALTH TIP
The 2 Tbsp (30 mL) of flax seeds contain 4 grams of protein. Sprinkle them into your cereal, yogurt and smoothies.

NUTRITION INFORMATION PER SERVING (1 SQUARE)

Calories 133	Protein 3 g	Cholesterol 0 mg
Carbohydrates 21.1 g	Total fat 3.8 g	Sodium 24 mg
Fibre 2.1 g	Saturated fat 0.6 g	

ROSE'S NUT AND DRIED-FRUIT GRANOLA

You'll never want to eat packaged granola again after you try this. This is the number-one breakfast food in my catering company and a favourite on the brunch menu at Glow Fresh Grill, where I have developed the menu. It also has fewer calories and less fat than other granolas because I have replaced some of the oil with orange juice and maple syrup. Serve with yogurt or milk.

1. Preheat the oven to 300°F (150°C). Line a baking sheet with foil and lightly coat with cooking spray.

2. Combine the oats, flour, brown sugar, cinnamon, ginger, oil, orange juice, maple syrup and nuts in a large mixing bowl and stir to combine. Spread the mixture out on the prepared baking sheet and bake for 35 to 45 minutes, tossing once to prevent burning, just until crisp.

3. Remove the granola from the oven and let it cool to room temperature. Add the dried fruit and stir. Store in an airtight container.

PREPARATION TIME 15 minutes · **BAKING TIME** 35 minutes ·
MAKE AHEAD This can be made and kept in a tight container for up to a week. Freeze for up to a month. · **MAKES** about 4 cups (1 L).

2 cups (500 mL) large rolled oats

½ cup (125 mL) whole wheat flour

½ cup (125 mL) packed brown sugar

1 tsp (5 mL) cinnamon

½ tsp (2.5 mL) ground ginger

3 Tbsp (45 mL) vegetable oil

¼ cup (60 mL) orange juice

3 Tbsp (45 mL) maple syrup

½ cup (125 mL) chopped nuts of your choice

¼ cup (60 mL) chopped dried dates

¼ cup (60 mL) chopped dried cranberries

ROSE'S TIP
Have fun with this granola and add different flours, nuts and dried fruits. For crisper granola, bake an extra 10 minutes.

HEALTH TIP
Add 2 Tbsp (30 mL) of flax seeds or chia seeds for extra omega-3 fatty acids.

NUTRITION INFORMATION PER SERVING (⅓ CUP/80 ML)

Calories 194	Protein 4 g	Cholesterol 0 mg
Carbohydrates 31 g	Total fat 6.2 g	Sodium 5 mg
Fibre 3 g	Saturated fat 0.4 g	

BANANA CHOCOLATE CHIP LOAF

Banana loaf is an all-time favourite. These loaves are traditionally made with an excess of oil and chocolate chips. By using more banana and reduced-fat sour cream, I enhance the flavour so I can use fewer chips. This is great as a dessert, breakfast or snack.

1. Preheat the oven to 350°F (175°C). Lightly coat an 8- × 4-inch (1.5 L) loaf pan with cooking spray.

2. Using a whisk or an electric mixer, combine the banana, oil, sugar, egg, vanilla and sour cream in a large bowl until smooth.

3. In another bowl, combine both flours, baking powder and baking soda. With a wooden spoon, stir the dry mixture into the banana mixture until the dry ingredients are just moistened. Fold in the chocolate chips.

4. Pour into the prepared pan and bake for about 30 to 35 minutes or until a tester inserted in the middle of the loaf comes out clean. Let the loaf cool in the pan on a wire rack before removing and slicing into 8 slices.

5. CHOCOLATE DRIZZLE Melt the chocolate in a microwave oven for 2 minutes on Defrost. Stir until smooth and drizzle over the loaf.

PREPARATION TIME 10 minutes • **BAKING TIME** 30 minutes •
MAKE AHEAD Bake up to 2 days before or freeze for up to 1 month. •
MAKES 8 servings.

---

1 large ripe banana, mashed (about ½ cup/125 mL)

¼ cup (60 mL) vegetable oil

¾ cup (185 mL) granulated sugar

1 large egg

1 tsp (5 mL) vanilla extract

¼ cup (60 mL) reduced-fat sour cream

¾ cup (185 mL) all-purpose flour

2 Tbsp (30 mL) whole wheat flour

1 tsp (5 mL) baking powder

½ tsp (2.5 mL) baking soda

⅓ cup (80 mL) semisweet chocolate chips

Chocolate drizzle (optional)
3 Tbsp (45 mL) semisweet chocolate chips (1 oz/30 g)

 ROSE'S TIP
You can increase the whole wheat flour to half the amount of white flour for extra fibre. You may have to cut down your baking time by 5 minutes.

 HEALTH TIP
Bananas are one of the best sources of potassium, which helps maintain normal blood pressure and heart function.

NUTRITION INFORMATION PER SERVING (1 SLICE)

Calories 254	Protein 3.2 g	Cholesterol 30 mg
Carbohydrates 38 g	Total fat 10.6 g	Sodium 162 mg
Fibre 1.6 g	Saturated fat 2.4 g	

CRUSTLESS QUICHE WITH SPINACH, MUSHROOMS AND CHEESE

The calories and fat of quiche come from the buttery crust and amount of cheese, cream and eggs traditionally used. This crustless version is delicious due to the sautéed vegetables and aged cheddar cheese.

1. Preheat the oven to 350°F (175°C). Lightly coat an 8-inch (20 cm) square baking dish with vegetable oil spray.

2. Heat the oil in a large nonstick skillet over medium heat. Add the garlic, onion and mushrooms and cook until softened, about 5 minutes. Add the spinach and cook for 2 minutes.

3. Remove from heat and add the cheddar and Parmesan cheeses, eggs, egg whites, flour, dill, and salt and pepper. Mix well and pour into the prepared pan.

4. Bake in the centre of the oven for 35 to 40 minutes or until a knife inserted in the centre comes out clean. Serve warm.

PREPARATION TIME 15 minutes · **COOKING TIME** 42 minutes ·

MAKE AHEAD Prepare a day in advance and bake as directed. ·

MAKES 6 servings.

2 tsp (10 mL) vegetable oil

1 tsp (5 mL) minced fresh garlic

1½ cups (375 mL) chopped onion

2½ cups (625 mL) chopped mushrooms

half a 10 oz (300 g) package of frozen chopped spinach, defrosted and squeezed dry or 5 cups (1.25 L) chopped fresh baby spinach

1 cup (250 mL) grated aged cheddar cheese (3 oz/90 g)

3 Tbsp (45 mL) grated Parmesan cheese (¾ oz/23 g)

3 eggs

2 egg whites

2 Tbsp (30 mL) all-purpose flour

3 Tbsp (45 mL) chopped fresh dill (or 1 tsp/5 mL dried)

pinch of salt and pepper

ROSE'S TIP

You can buy a large block of cheddar cheese, grate it and freeze it in containers, using when needed.

HEALTH TIP

Quiche crusts are usually made with butter, shortening or lard. By removing the crust, you're cutting the calories and fat in half.

NUTRITION INFORMATION PER SERVING

Calories 171	Protein 17.5 g	Cholesterol 95 mg
Carbohydrates 8.8 g	Total fat 7.6 g	Sodium 250 mg
Fibre 2.2 g	Saturated fat 3.6 g	

RASPBERRY, BANANA AND GREEK YOGURT SMOOTHIE

If you're in a rush in the morning and need a quick breakfast, try a smoothie. The combination of protein and fruit keeps you satisfied longer. This is also a healthy snack to stave off hunger between meals. Experiment with different fruits, using whatever is in season.

1. Place the yogurt, banana, raspberries, orange juice, honey and ice in a blender and purée. Serve immediately.

PREPARATION TIME 5 minutes · **MAKE AHEAD** Best prepared just before drinking. · **MAKES** 4 servings.

1 cup (250 mL) reduced-fat plain Greek yogurt

1 small ripe banana, sliced

1 cup (250 mL) frozen or fresh sliced raspberries

¾ cup (185 mL) orange juice

2 Tbsp (30 mL) honey

5 ice cubes

ROSE'S TIP
If you are making a smoothie in advance, leave out the ice cubes to prevent excess water.

HEALTH TIP
Plain Greek yogurt has 18 grams of protein per ¾ cup (185 mL) compared to fruit-flavoured regular varieties, which have only 5 grams of protein.

NUTRITION INFORMATION PER SERVING

Calories 104	Protein 3 g	Cholesterol 3.7 mg
Carbohydrates 18 g	Total fat 1 g	Sodium 34 mg
Fibre 1.6 g	Saturated fat 0.4 g	

CHOCOLATE, CAPPUCCINO AND BANANA SMOOTHIE

I'm a chocoholic and I have discovered that 1% chocolate milk (made with cocoa) is the best treat I can have either for breakfast or a snack. Adding chocolate milk to this smoothie satisfies your chocolate cravings and makes it taste like a chocolate milkshake, but without the calories and fat.

1. Combine the milk, yogurt, banana, honey and cocoa powder in a blender and purée. Serve immediately.

PREPARATION TIME 5 minutes · **MAKE AHEAD** Best prepared just before drinking. · **MAKES** 4 servings.

1 cup (250 mL) cold 1% chocolate milk (or soy milk)

1 cup (250 mL) reduced-fat coffee-flavoured yogurt

1 medium-sized ripe banana, sliced

2 Tbsp (30 mL) honey

1 Tbsp (15 mL) cocoa powder

ROSE'S TIP
You can use chocolate soy milk to accommodate a dairy allergy.

HEALTH TIP
Cocoa is chocolate without the cocoa butter, which saves you excess calories and fat.

NUTRITION INFORMATION PER SERVING

Calories 156	Protein 6 g	Cholesterol 6 mg
Carbohydrates 33 g	Total fat 1.5 g	Sodium 81 mg
Fibre 1.6 g	Saturated fat 0.9 g	

APPETIZERS

ROASTED ASPARAGUS AND PROSCIUTTO TORTILLA SLICES

The taste, texture and appearance of this appetizer are wonderful. When you slice these tortillas into rolls, you see the vibrant colours of the green asparagus against the rosy prosciutto and white cheese spread. Replace the prosciutto with smoked salmon or thinly sliced turkey or roast beef. Using a coloured tortilla adds even more visual appeal. For an extra boost of fibre, try whole wheat tortillas.

1. Preheat the oven to 425°F (220°C). Place the asparagus on a baking sheet sprayed with vegetable oil. Bake for 8 minutes or just until bright green.

2. In a food processor, or in a bowl using an electric mixer, beat the ricotta, cream cheese, mayonnaise, green onions, lemon juice, garlic, and salt and pepper until smooth.

3. Spread the cheese mixture evenly over the tortillas. Scatter the spinach leaves overtop. Place the prosciutto on top of the spinach. Place 2 spears of the asparagus near the bottom of each tortilla. Roll up tightly, wrap in plastic wrap, and chill (to get the best flavour).

4. Cut each tortilla on the diagonal into 6 pieces.

PREPARATION TIME 10 minutes · **BAKING TIME** 8 minutes ·
MAKE AHEAD Can be prepared up to 1 day ahead if wrapped well in plastic wrap and chilled. · **MAKES** 18 servings.

NUTRITION INFORMATION PER SERVING (1 PIECE)

Calories 66	Protein 3.4 g	Cholesterol 7 mg
Carbohydrates 7.1 g	Total fat 2.7 g	Sodium 130 mg
Fibre 0.5 g	Saturated fat 1.1 g	

6 medium-thick spears of asparagus

½ cup (125 mL) reduced-fat ricotta cheese (4 oz/125 g)

¼ cup (60 mL) softened reduced-fat cream cheese (2 oz/60 g)

1 Tbsp (15 mL) reduced-fat mayonnaise

2 Tbsp (30 mL) chopped green onions

2 Tbsp (30 mL) fresh lemon juice

½ tsp (2.5 mL) minced garlic

pinch of salt and pepper

3 large flour tortillas

1 cup (250 mL) baby spinach leaves

2 oz (60 g) sliced prosciutto

ROSE'S TIP

You can roast asparagus ahead of time, but put it into the refrigerator immediately to chill so the bright green colour doesn't change. Serve at room temperature.

HEALTH TIP

According to EatingWell.com, asparagus is one of the 15 foods that does not have to be bought organic since it's least likely to be contaminated with pesticide.

CRAB CAKES WITH TAHINI SAUCE

Crab cakes have to be one of the most delicious appetizers you can order in a restaurant if they are made properly. But virtually all crab cakes are fried, adding unnecessarily to calories and fat, not to mention the high-fat tartar sauce or aioli. These cakes are lightly sautéed and served with a light tahini sauce.

1. TO MAKE THE CRAB CAKES Combine the crabmeat, mayonnaise, lemon juice and zest, bell peppers, green onions, cilantro, breadcrumbs, egg, garlic, ginger, jalapeños, and salt and pepper in a bowl until well mixed.

2. Form into 18 small cakes 3 Tbsp (45 mL) each (best chilled for 30 minutes).

3. In a large skillet sprayed with vegetable oil, sauté cakes for 4 minutes on each side until browned and hot.

4. TO MAKE THE TAHINI SAUCE Combine the mayonnaise, sour cream, sesame oil and soy sauce. Serve the crab cakes with the tahini sauce.

PREPARATION TIME 20 minutes · **COOKING TIME** 8 minutes ·
MAKE AHEAD Prepare up to 1 day before and sauté just before serving. ·
MAKES 6 servings.

Crab cakes

12 oz (375 g) finely diced crabmeat chopped (moisture squeezed out and shells removed)

3 Tbsp (45 mL) reduced-fat mayonnaise

2 Tbsp (30 mL) freshly squeezed lemon juice

1 Tbsp (15 mL) lemon zest

⅓ cup (80 mL) finely diced red bell peppers

¼ cup (60 mL) finely chopped green onion

¼ cup (60 mL) finely chopped cilantro

⅓ cup (80 mL) unseasoned dry breadcrumbs

1 large egg

1 tsp (5 mL) crushed fresh garlic

½ tsp (2.5 mL) crushed fresh ginger

2 tsp (10 mL) minced jalapeño peppers

pinch of salt and pepper

 ROSE'S TIP

You can use "surimi" imitation crabmeat, but it won't have the same flavor of crab. You need the real deal! Crabmeat is found frozen in your fish department. Slightly defrost just the amount you need and return the rest to the freezer.

 HEALTH TIP

Crabmeat contains omega-3 fatty acids and is rich in protein. It can lower blood pressure, raise the good cholesterol and lower bad cholesterol, which reduces the risk of heart disease and stroke.

Tahini Sauce

2 Tbsp (30 mL) reduced-fat mayonnaise

2 Tbsp (30 mL) reduced-fat sour cream

2 tsp (10 mL) sesame oil

2 tsp (10 mL) low-sodium soy sauce

NUTRITION INFORMATION PER SERVING (3 CAKES WITH SAUCE)

Calories 176	Protein 11.1 g	Cholesterol 53 mg
Carbohydrates 11.3 g	Total fat 8.6 g	Sodium 397 mg
Fibre 0.7 g	Saturated fat 1.6 g	

MEDITERRANEAN COUSCOUS CAKES

These delicious couscous cakes not only make a delicious appetizer but are also great as a vegetarian meal or side grain dish. You could also serve them in a piece of pita bread with sliced tomatoes, lettuce and cucumbers, similar to a falafel.

1. TO MAKE THE COUSCOUS CAKES In a saucepan over high heat, bring the stock to a boil. Add the couscous and remove from heat. Let stand, covered, for 5 minutes or until the liquid is absorbed and the grain is tender. Fluff with a fork and set aside to cool.

2. In a bowl, combine the cooled couscous, red peppers, green onions, red onions, black olives, garlic, basil, feta cheese, eggs, flour, lemon juice, and salt and pepper. Form each ⅓ cup (80 mL) of the mixture into a flat patty, squeezing it together in your hands. In a large skillet sprayed with vegetable spray, add 2 tsp (10 mL) of oil and sauté patties for about 3 minutes on each side just until hot.

3. TO MAKE THE SAUCE In a bowl, combine the mayonnaise, sour cream, sesame oil and soy sauce. Serve the warm patties with the sauce.

PREPARATION TIME 15 minutes • **COOKING TIME** 15 minutes •
MAKE AHEAD Prepare up to a day before and refrigerate. Sauté right before serving or reheat in a 300°F (150°C) oven for 10 minutes. •
MAKES 10 servings.

Couscous cakes

1 cup (250 mL) low-sodium chicken or vegetable stock

1 cup (250 mL) couscous

½ cup (125 mL) minced red bell peppers

⅓ cup (80 mL) minced green onions

⅓ cup (80 mL) minced red onions

¼ cup (60 mL) minced black olives

1 tsp (5 mL) minced garlic

½ tsp (2.5 mL) dried basil

¾ cup (185 mL) crumbled reduced-fat feta cheese (2½ oz/75 g)

2 large eggs

2 Tbsp (30 mL) all-purpose flour

2 Tbsp (30 mL) fresh lemon juice

pinch of salt and pepper

2 tsp (10 mL) vegetable oil

ROSE'S TIP

To make perfect couscous that's not too wet or too clumpy, you must have a ratio of 1 cup (250 mL) of liquid to 1 cup (250 mL) of couscous. Never cook couscous; just bring the liquid to a boil, add couscous and immediately take off heat and leave covered for 5 minutes.

 HEALTH TIP

Try to purchase whole-grain couscous for an extra boost of fibre. One cup (250 mL) cooked regular couscous has 2 grams of fibre versus 3 grams of fibre for whole-grain couscous.

Sauce

2 Tbsp (30 mL) reduced-fat mayonnaise

¼ cup (60 mL) reduced-fat sour cream

2 tsp (10 mL) sesame oil

2 tsp (10 mL) low-sodium soy sauce

NUTRITION INFORMATION PER SERVING (1 CAKE)

Calories 216	Protein 9 g	Cholesterol 49 mg
Carbohydrates 31 g	Total fat 6 g	Sodium 150 mg
Fibre 2 g	Saturated fat 2.8 g	

ITALIAN PIZZA ROLLS

The number one treat for kids and adults of all ages. All the fat and calories in traditional egg rolls come from the deep-frying. Since these are baked, you can enjoy them without the guilt! Leftovers are great for kids' lunches. Substitute ground chicken or soy-based ground beef substitute.

1. Preheat the oven to 425°F (220°C). Spray a baking sheet with cooking spray.

2. In a nonstick frying pan sprayed with cooking spray, heat the oil over medium heat; cook the carrots, onions and garlic, stirring occasionally, for 8 minutes or until softened and browned. Stir in the peppers; cook 2 minutes longer. Stir in the beef; cook, stirring to break it up, for 2 minutes or until no longer pink. Stir in the tomato sauce and simmer for 2 minutes. Add the mozzarella and Parmesan cheeses.

3. Put one wrapper on the work surface with a corner pointing toward you, keeping the rest of the wrappers covered with a cloth to prevent them drying out. Put 3 Tbsp (45 mL) of the filling in the centre. Fold the lower corner up over the filling, fold in the two side corners and roll the bundle away from you. Put on the prepared pan. Repeat until all the wrappers are filled.

4. Bake in the centre of the oven for 15 minutes or until golden, turning the pizza rolls halfway through the baking time.

PREPARATION TIME 15 minutes · **COOKING TIME** 29 minutes ·
MAKE AHEAD Make these up to 1 day in advance and bake just before serving or reheat for 10 minutes in a 300°F (150°C) oven. · **MAKES** 12 servings.

NUTRITION INFORMATION PER SERVING (1 PIZZA ROLL)

Calories 126	Protein 6.7 g	Cholesterol 10 mg
Carbohydrates 18 g	Total fat 3 g	Sodium 243 mg
Fibre 1.1 g	Saturated fat 1.2 g	

1 tsp (5 mL) vegetable oil

½ cup (125 mL) finely chopped carrots

½ cup (125 mL) finely chopped onions

1 tsp (5 mL) minced garlic

½ cup (125 mL) finely chopped green bell peppers

6 oz (175 g) lean ground beef

¾ cup (185 mL) homemade or store-bought tomato sauce (see Quick Basic Tomato Sauce on page 369)

¾ cup (185 mL) shredded part-skim mozzarella cheese (2 oz/60 g)

3 Tbsp (45 mL) grated Parmesan cheese (¾ oz/23 g)

12 large egg roll wrappers (5½ inches/14 cm square)

 ROSE'S TIP
If you want an appetizer size, purchase the small egg roll or wonton wrappers. You will be able to make about 36 egg rolls.

HEALTH TIP
Egg roll or wonton wrappers have only 75 calories and 0 grams of fat for a 5½-inch (14 cm) square.

SHRIMP POT STICKERS WITH PEANUT SAUCE

Pot stickers are a food you may only enjoy in Asian restaurants. But these are so easy to make and honestly more delicious. You'll never be able to stop at one! Enjoy them as either an appetizer or a main dish. Substitute ground chicken or beef if desired.

1. Measure out about 2 Tbsp (30 mL) of the Peanut Sauce and set aside.

2. TO MAKE THE FILLING In a clean food processor, combine shrimp, garlic, green onion, cilantro and 2 Tbsp (30 mL) of the reserved peanut sauce; pulse on and off until the filling is well mixed and the shrimp is finely chopped.

3. Place 2 tsp (10 mL) of filling in the centre of each wrapper. Pull the edges up, pleating and bunching. Press the edges together to seal.

4. In a large nonstick frying pan sprayed with cooking spray, cook the pot stickers, flat side down, over medium-high heat for 3 minutes or until golden-brown on bottom.

5. Add the stock and reduce heat to low. Cover and cook for 2 minutes or until cooked through. Remove from the pan; discard any remaining stock. Garnish with cilantro and serve with the remaining peanut sauce.

PREPARATION TIME 15 minutes · **COOKING TIME** 5 minutes ·
MAKE AHEAD Make up to a day before and keep covered and refrigerated until ready to cook. · **MAKES** 26 servings.

Peanut sauce

½ cup (125 mL) Peanut Sauce (see page 375), divided

Filling

8 oz (250 g) shrimp, peeled, deveined and diced

1 clove minced garlic

1 chopped green onion

2 Tbsp (30 mL) chopped fresh cilantro

26 small wonton or egg roll wrappers (3 inches/8 cm square)

¾ cup (185 mL) low-sodium seafood or chicken stock

2 Tbsp (30 mL) chopped fresh cilantro

 ROSE'S TIP
If honey crystallizes, just heat gently in a microwave oven for about 20 seconds.

 HEALTH TIP
Only buy pure peanut butter, which has nothing but peanuts. Regular brands are hydrogenated to make them smooth and have added icing sugar.

NUTRITION INFORMATION PER SERVING (1 POT STICKER)

Calories 46	Protein 2.6 g	Cholesterol 11 mg
Carbohydrates 6.2 g	Total fat 1.4 g	Sodium 94 mg
Fibre 0.3 g	Saturated fat 0.3 g	

CHICKEN POT STICKERS WITH HOISIN SAUCE

When I go for dim sum, I enjoy pot stickers. But, as with egg rolls, I often find the fillings boring, and tasty only with the dipping sauce. My version of pot stickers has a delicious filling, and they're easy to prepare. If wontons aren't available, use small egg roll wrappers

1. Measure out about 2 Tbsp (30 mL) of the Hoisin Sauce and set aside.

2. TO MAKE THE FILLING Combine the chicken, garlic, green onion, and cilantro in the bowl of a food processor. Add the 2 Tbsp (30 mL) of reserved sauce, and pulse on and off until the filling is finely and evenly chopped and everything is well combined.

3. Place 2 tsp (10 mL) of the filling in the centre of each wrapper. Pull the edges up to make a small bundle, pleating and bunching. Press the edges together to seal.

4. In a large nonstick skillet lightly coated with cooking spray, cook the pot stickers, flat side down, over medium-high heat for 3 minutes or until they are golden brown on the bottom.

5. Add the stock and reduce the heat to low. Cover and cook for 2 minutes or until cooked through. Remove from the pan and discard any remaining stock. Serve with the remaining sauce. Garnish with cilantro.

PREPARATION TIME 20 minutes • **COOKING TIME** 5 minutes • **MAKE AHEAD** Prepare early in the day and keep refrigerated. Cook just before serving. • **MAKES** 28 servings.

NUTRITION INFORMATION PER SERVING (1 POT STICKER)

Calories 81	Protein 4 g	Cholesterol 12 mg
Carbohydrates 15 g	Total fat 0.6 g	Sodium 230 mg
Fibre 0.6 g	Saturated fat 0.1 g	

Sauce
½ cup (125 mL) Hoisin Sauce (see page 372), divided

Filling
8 oz (250 g) lean ground chicken

1 clove finely chopped garlic

1 chopped green onion

2 Tbsp (30 mL) chopped cilantro

28 small wonton wrappers

½ cup (125 mL) low-sodium beef or chicken stock

3 Tbsp (45 mL) chopped cilantro

 ROSE'S TIP
Feel free to substitute ground beef, pork or veal instead of the chicken. Even ground soy would work.

 HEALTH TIP
In many Asian restaurants, the pot stickers are deep-fried, which doubles their calories and fat.

HOISIN–GINGER MEATBALLS

These are perfect appetizers for a dinner party. Meatballs are usually made from regular ground meat, which has three times the fat and calories of extra-lean. For a lighter version, try ground chicken, turkey, pork or veal. The red currant jelly adds a tart-sweet flavour and gives the sauce the thickness it requires.

1. Preheat the oven to 425°F (220°C). Line a baking sheet with foil and spray with vegetable oil.

2. TO MAKE THE MEATBALLS Combine the beef, breadcrumbs, hoisin sauce, garlic, egg, onion, and salt and pepper. Form into 24 small meatballs about 1 inch (2.5 cm) in diameter. Place on the baking sheet and bake for 10 minutes or just until no longer pink.

3. TO MAKE THE SAUCE Combine the hoisin sauce, jelly, garlic, ginger and water in a small bowl. In a saucepan, combine the sauce with the cooked meatballs and stir well. Cover and simmer on low heat for 10 minutes.

4. Garnish with sesame seeds and cilantro.

PREPARATION TIME 15 minutes · COOKING TIME 20 minutes ·
MAKE AHEAD Prepare and freeze the uncooked meatballs up to 2 weeks in advance. Thaw just before cooking. Can be cooked and refrigerated for up to 2 days. Reheat in a saucepan over low heat until warmed through. · MAKES 6 servings.

Meatballs

8 oz (250 g) extra-lean ground beef

3 Tbsp (45 mL) unseasoned dry breadcrumbs

2 Tbsp (30 mL) hoisin sauce

1 tsp (5 mL) crushed garlic

1 egg

2 Tbsp (30 mL) minced green onion

pinch of salt and pepper

Sauce

⅓ cup (80 mL) hoisin sauce

⅓ cup (80 mL) red currant jelly

1 tsp (5 mL) crushed garlic

½ tsp (2.5 mL) minced fresh ginger

2 Tbsp (30 mL) water

1 tsp (5 mL) toasted sesame seeds

2 Tbsp (30 mL) chopped fresh cilantro or parsley

 ROSE'S TIP
You can turn this into a complete meal by making larger meatballs and serving over rice or rice noodles.

 HEALTH TIP
Hoisin sauce is a delicious and healthier sauce used in Asian cooking. It consists of sweet potatoes, wheat or rice, soybeans and garlic.

NUTRITION INFORMATION PER SERVING (4 MEATBALLS)

Calories 150	Protein 8.1 g	Cholesterol 52 mg
Carbohydrates 19.2 g	Total fat 4.2 g	Sodium 321 mg
Fibre 0.6 g	Saturated fat 1.5 g	

THAI BALLS WITH PEANUT SAUCE

Traditional meatballs have become passé; now you will see these small appetizers served with a variety of ingredients. I've used ground pork and shrimp with Thai flavourings and a light peanut sauce for dipping. Substitute beef or chicken for the pork or you can use all shrimp.

Thai balls

½ lb (250 g) ground pork

½ lb (250 g) chopped shrimp

1 egg

½ cup (125 mL) chopped basil

⅓ cup (80 mL) cilantro

1 tsp (5 mL) chopped chili peppers

¼ cup (60 mL) unseasoned dry breadcrumbs

2 tsp (10 mL) Thai seasoning

1 Tbsp (15 mL) low-sodium soy sauce

1 Tbsp (15 mL) sesame seeds

1½ tsp (7.5 mL) fish sauce

Peanut Sauce

½ cup (125 mL) Peanut Sauce (see page 375)

1. TO MAKE THE THAI BALLS   Combine the pork, shrimp, egg, basil, cilantro, chili peppers, breadcrumbs, Thai seasoning, soy sauce, sesame seeds and fish sauce. Form into 36 meatballs. Roast at 425°F (220°C) for 15 minutes, turning after 10 minutes.

2. Serve the meatballs with the Peanut Sauce.

PREPARATION TIME 20 minutes · **BAKING TIME** 15 minutes ·
MAKE AHEAD Prepare up to 2 days in advance and bake just before serving. ·
MAKES 9 servings.

 ROSE'S TIP
Thai seasoning can be found in your supermarket in the spice section. It's made with a blend of chili peppers, ginger, cilantro, red pepper, cumin, cinnamon and star anise.

 HEALTH TIP
Shrimp contain selenium, which may reduce the risk of cancer of the lung, colon and prostate. Death rates from these cancers are lower in parts of the world where there is an abundance of selenium.

NUTRITION INFORMATION PER SERVING (4 THAI BALLS)

Calories 147	Protein 10 g	Cholesterol 66 mg
Carbohydrates 5.6 g	Total fat 8.7 g	Sodium 421 mg
Fibre 0.7 g	Saturated fat 3.1 g	

THAI PIZZA WITH SHRIMP, ASIAN VEGETABLES AND PEANUT DRESSING

Thai cuisine seems to have taken over North American cuisine. Part of the reason is the influence of immigration from Asia. So move over, Italy: here comes an Eastern version of pizza. The light peanut hoisin sauce makes the entire difference.

1. TO MAKE THE DRESSING In a small food processor, purée the coconut milk, peanut butter, hoisin and soy sauces, vinegar, sesame oil, honey, garlic, ginger and jalapeños.

2. TO ASSEMBLE THE PIZZA Drizzle three-quarters of the dressing over the pizza crust. Save the rest for garnish.

3. Add the mozzarella, snap peas, red peppers, shrimp or chicken, and cashews overtop. Bake at 400°F (200°C) for 12 minutes or until the crust is crisp.

4. Pour the remaining dressing overtop. Garnish with green onions and cilantro.

PREPARATION TIME 20 minutes • **BAKING TIME** 12 minutes •
MAKE AHEAD Prepare the pizza up to a day before. Bake just before serving. •
MAKES 8 servings.

 ROSE'S TIP
Try different nut butters, such as almond or cashew. Soy butter is great for those with nut allergies.

 HEALTH TIP
A small thin pizza crust alone has half the calories of a small deep dish or thick pizza crust.

NUTRITION INFORMATION PER SERVING

Calories 156	Protein 9.4 g	Cholesterol 37 mg
Carbohydrates 9.2 g	Total fat 8.9 g	Sodium 325 mg
Fibre 2 g	Saturated fat 3.3 g	

Dressing

3 Tbsp (45 mL) light coconut milk

3 Tbsp (45 mL) peanut butter

4 tsp (20 mL) hoisin sauce

2 tsp (10 mL) low-sodium soy sauce

2 tsp (10 mL) rice vinegar

2 tsp (10 mL) sesame oil

1 tsp (5 mL) honey

1 tsp (5 mL) crushed garlic

1 tsp (5 mL) crushed ginger

1½ tsp (7.5 mL) minced jalapeño peppers

Pizza

one 12-inch (30 cm) pre-baked thin pizza crust (preferably whole wheat)

1 cup (250 mL) grated part-skim mozzarella cheese (3 oz/90 g)

1 cup (250 mL) sliced sugar snap peas

1 cup (250 mL) sliced red peppers

¾ cup (185 mL) diced raw shrimp or cooked chicken

3 Tbsp (45 mL) chopped cashews

⅓ cup (80 mL) diced green onions

¼ cup (60 mL) cilantro

HOT CRAB, ARTICHOKE AND CHEESE DIP

These hot morsels of artichoke heart, crabmeat, Swiss cheese and dill are outstanding with tasty crackers or flatbread. If you don't have any dill on hand, substitute fresh parsley. This type of dip served in restaurants has close to three times the fat and calories.

1. Preheat the oven to 425°F (220°C). Spray a small decorative baking dish with cooking oil.

2. Combine the artichoke hearts, crabmeat, mozzarella and Swiss cheeses, dill, sour cream, mayonnaise, lemon juice, garlic and chili sauce in a food processor. Pulse until just combined but still chunky. Place in the prepared baking dish. Sprinkle with the Parmesan.

3. Bake in the centre of the oven for 10 minutes. Move to the top rack and broil for 3 to 5 minutes, until the top is slightly browned. Serve warm with crackers.

PREPARATION TIME 10 minutes · **BAKING TIME** 15 minutes · **MAKE AHEAD** Up to 2 days in advance, prepare to the baking stage, cover and refrigerate. Bake just before serving, adding an extra 5 minutes until hot. · **MAKES** 3 cups (750 mL).

one 14 oz (398 mL) can artichoke hearts, drained and halved

4 oz (125 g) chopped crabmeat or surimi (imitation crabmeat)

½ cup (125 mL) shredded part-skim mozzarella (1½ oz/45 g)

⅓ cup (80 mL) shredded Swiss cheese (1 oz/30 g)

⅓ cup (80 mL) minced fresh dill (or 1 tsp/5 mL dried dill) or parsley

⅓ cup (80 mL) reduced-fat sour cream

3 Tbsp (45 mL) reduced-fat mayonnaise

2 Tbsp (30 mL) freshly squeezed lemon juice

1 tsp (5 mL) minced garlic

1 tsp (5 mL) hot chili sauce (Sriracha)

1 Tbsp (15 mL) grated Parmesan cheese (¼ oz/8 g)

ROSE'S TIP

Be sure to squeeze out the excess moisture if using crab to prevent wateriness. Do the same to the canned artichokes.

HEALTH TIP

Artichokes are filled with fibre, vitamin C and folate and are also an excellent source of antioxidants.

NUTRITION INFORMATION PER SERVING (⅓ CUP/80 ML)

Calories 69	Protein 8 g	Cholesterol 25 mg
Carbohydrates 3 g	Total fat 1.8 g	Sodium 94 mg
Fibre 1.8 g	Saturated fat 1 g	

SALMON SATAY WITH PEANUT COCONUT SAUCE

Satays have been the trend for years, as an appetizer or main course. You can substitute fresh, firm fish, such as tuna, halibut or haddock, or chicken, beef or pork cubes. The light Peanut Coconut Sauce is so creamy you'll never believe it's low in calories and fat. Light coconut milk has 3 grams of fat per ¼ cup (60 mL), compared to the 10 grams of regular coconut milk.

1. Preheat the barbecue or oven to 425°F (220°C). If using wooden skewers, soak them in water for 20 minutes.

2. Thread the salmon cubes on the skewers.

3. Divide the Peanut Coconut Sauce in half.

4. Brush the skewers with half the sauce. Spray the grill or a baking sheet with cooking oil and cook the skewers, turning once, for 10 minutes or until the salmon is almost cooked. Do not overcook.

5. Serve with the remaining sauce on the side. Garnish with peanuts and cilantro.

PREPARATION TIME 10 minutes · **COOKING TIME** 10 minutes ·
MAKE AHEAD Prepare the sauce up to 3 days in advance, cover and refrigerate. · **MAKES** 4 servings.

1 lb (500 g) fresh salmon cut into sixteen 1-inch (2.5 cm) cubes

4 medium skewers

Peanut Coconut Sauce
½ cup (125 mL) Peanut Coconut Sauce (see page 376)

3 Tbsp (45 mL) chopped toasted peanuts

3 Tbsp (45 mL) chopped fresh cilantro or parsley

 ROSE'S TIP
Sriracha is a type of hot sauce from Thailand. It's a paste of chili peppers, vinegar, garlic, sugar and salt.

 HEALTH TIP
Salmon contains omega-3 fatty acids, which raise your good cholesterol. Atlantic salmon can have contaminants that are dangerous to your health, so it's wise to buy organic.

NUTRITION INFORMATION PER SERVING (1 SKEWER)

Calories 233	Protein 22.7 g	Cholesterol 161 mg
Carbohydrates 6.1 g	Total fat 13.6 g	Sodium 298 mg
Fibre 1.7 g	Saturated fat 2.6 g	

SMOKED-SALMON SUSHI SQUARES WITH WASABI MAYO

My corporate clients vote this their favourite appetizer. It's the perfect solution for those who shy away from sushi because of concern about eating raw fish. The key is cooking the sushi rice properly. I always use a water-to-rice ratio of one-to-one, never stir the rice and keep it covered even when it's cooling—using a rice cooker is easy, since it can never go wrong. Nori is available in good quality supermarkets and Asian food shops.

2 cups (500 mL) sushi rice

2 cups (500 mL) water

¼ cup (60 mL) rice vinegar

1 Tbsp (15 mL) granulated sugar

16 thin slices English cucumber (unpeeled)

4 oz (125 g) smoked salmon

2 Tbsp (30 mL) reduced-fat mayonnaise

1 tsp (5 mL) wasabi (Japanese horseradish)

1 sheet nori (dried seaweed)

1 tsp (5 mL) toasted sesame seeds

low-sodium soy sauce, wasabi and pickled ginger on the side (optional)

1. Combine the rice and water in a saucepan. Bring to a boil and boil for 1 minute. Reduce the heat to low, cover and cook for 12 minutes. Remove from the heat and let stand, covered, for 10 minutes.

2. While the rice cooks, combine the vinegar and sugar in a small saucepan. Bring to a boil, stirring to dissolve the sugar. Remove from the heat.

3. Turn the rice out into a large bowl. Stir in the vinegar and sugar mixture. Cool just until the rice no longer feels hot. Don't let the rice get cold, or it will dry out.

4. Line an 8-inch (20 cm) square baking dish with plastic wrap. Cover the bottom with the cucumber slices. Lay the smoked salmon overtop. Mix the mayonnaise and wasabi together and spread over the salmon.

5. Place half the rice over the mayonnaise. Pat it firmly to an even thickness, dipping your fingers in water to prevent the rice from sticking to your hands. Top with the nori. Add the remaining rice, patting it firmly to an even thickness.

6. Invert onto a serving platter and cut into 16 pieces. Sprinkle with the sesame seeds. Serve immediately, or cover with plastic wrap and refrigerate for up to 8 hours. Serve at room temperature, garnished with soy sauce, wasabi and pickled ginger (if using).

PREPARATION TIME 15 minutes · **COOKING TIME** 12 minutes ·

MAKE AHEAD Prepare early in the day, cover and refrigerate. If you just want to cook and season the rice earlier in the day, cool before placing in a large plastic bag so it doesn't dry out. · **MAKES** 16 squares.

 ROSE'S TIP

You can now find sushi rice vinegar, which already is sweetened, instead of using the plain version to which you have to add sugar.

 HEALTH TIP

You can add an extra boost of fibre by cooking brown rice instead of white. You would use 4 cups (1 L) of water and simmer for about 25 minutes, or just until tender.

NUTRITION INFORMATION PER SERVING (1 SQUARE)

Calories 97	Protein 3.1 g	Cholesterol 2 mg
Carbohydrates 19 g	Total fat 0.9 g	Sodium 154 mg
Fibre 0.9 g	Saturated fat 0.2 g	

QUESADILLAS WITH GRILLED CHICKEN, PESTO AND CHEESE

These make a great appetizer or main meal. I always like to use my own recipe for pesto, since it has a lot fewer calories and less fat than the store-bought type. In late summer, when basil is abundant, I make pesto in large batches and freeze it in small containers.

1. Spray a nonstick skillet or grill pan with cooking oil and place over medium-high heat. Sauté the chicken just until cooked, about 6 minutes per side. Set aside. Wipe out the skillet and respray.

2. Heat the oil in a skillet over medium-high heat. Sauté the onion and garlic for 5 minutes or until the onions are tender and browned. Stir in the pesto and cheeses. Dice the chicken and add to the skillet.

3. Divide the mixture among the tortillas, placing it on half of each tortilla. Fold the other half overtop. Heat on a grill pan or in a large skillet for 2 minutes on each side. Cut each tortilla into 3 wedges, making 12 wedges in total.

PREPARATION TIME 10 minutes · **COOKING TIME** 20 minutes ·

MAKE AHEAD Make the filling up to 2 days in advance, cover and refrigerate. Heat gently in a small skillet until warm. · **MAKES** 6 servings.

8 oz (250 g) skinless, boneless chicken breast (about 2 breasts)

2 tsp (10 mL) vegetable oil

1 cup (250 mL) chopped onion

2 tsp (10 mL) crushed fresh garlic

¼ cup (60 mL) store-bought or homemade pesto sauce (see Basil Pesto on page 371)

½ cup (125 mL) grated part-skim mozzarella cheese (1½ oz/45 g)

2 Tbsp (30 mL) grated Parmesan cheese (½ oz/15 g)

4 large whole wheat flour tortillas (or any flavour you prefer)

 ROSE'S TIP

I purchase large blocks of mozzarella or cheddar cheese and freeze them for up to 6 months. They are perfect for cooking purposes.

 HEALTH TIP

You can now purchase low-carbohydrate tortillas by La Tortilla Factory recommended by Weight Watchers, if you're concerned about your daily carbohydrate intake.

NUTRITION INFORMATION PER SERVING (2 WEDGES)

Calories 203	Protein 15 g	Cholesterol 31 mg
Carbohydrates 16 g	Total fat 8.7 g	Sodium 400 mg
Fibre 2.1 g	Saturated fat 2.5 g	

TUNA TARTARE
LAYERED WITH AVOCADO

I have been served this exquisite appetizer in the top restaurants I have frequented, and I so badly wanted to create my own simple version. This is quick to prepare, elegant to serve, incredibly healthy and oh so delicious!

1. Place the tuna in a bowl along with the soy sauce, mirin, sesame oil, 1½ tsp (7.5 mL) lemon juice, ginger, garlic, wasabi and sesame seeds. Let marinate in the refrigerator for a minimum of 15 minutes and up to 2 hours.

2. Toss the avocado with the lemon juice.

3. Fill a quarter-cup (60 mL) measuring cup sprayed with vegetable oil halfway with one-sixth of the avocado, then one-sixth of the tuna. Press down firmly, then carefully invert onto a serving plate. Repeat with the remaining tuna and avocado until you've made 6 individual appetizers. Granish with sesame seeds.

PREPARATION TIME 10 minutes · **MAKE AHEAD** You can marinate the tuna early in the day and assemble no earlier than 4 hours before serving. · **MAKES** 6 appetizers.

8 oz (250 g) finely diced raw sushi-grade tuna

1 Tbsp (15 mL) low-sodium soy sauce

1 Tbsp (15 mL) mirin sauce (sweet Japanese wine)

2 tsp (10 mL) sesame oil

1½ tsp (7.5 mL) lemon juice

½ tsp (2.5 mL) minced ginger

½ tsp (2.5 mL) minced garlic

¼ tsp (1 mL) wasabi mustard

1 tsp (5 mL) toasted sesame seeds

1 small avocado, finely diced (¾ cup/185 mL)

½ tsp (2.5 mL) lemon juice

toasted sesame seeds

 ROSE'S TIP
If you don't have mirin, you can substitute sake and a little sugar, or rice wine vinegar and sugar. The ratio is 1 part sugar to 3 parts sake or rice wine vinegar. Heat gently to dissolve the sugar.

 HEALTH TIP
Sushi-grade tuna means the fish is fresh and has been properly stored on ice. It has nothing to do with the grade of tuna.

NUTRITION INFORMATION PER SERVING

Calories 70	Protein 10 g	Cholesterol 15 mg
Carbohydrates 1 g	Total fat 3 g	Sodium 110 mg
Fibre 1 g	Saturated fat 0.5 g	

✕ SALADS

BABY KALE AND APRICOT DRESSING

Baby kale is the new green on the block. I prefer these small leaves because they are sweeter and more tender than the large fibrous leaves, which have to be massaged when eaten raw.

Add some protein such as grilled chicken, shrimp or tofu if you want a main meal salad.

1. Place the kale, onion, cranberries and almonds on a serving platter.

2. TO MAKE THE DRESSING Mix the oil, jam, vinegar, lemon juice and salt and pepper together and pour overtop of the salad.

PREPARATION TIME 15 minutes • **MAKE AHEAD** Prepare early in the day and dress just before serving. • **MAKES** 8 servings.

Salad

8 cups (2 L) baby kale leaves

1 cup (250 mL) sliced red onion

½ cup (125 mL) dried cranberries

½ cup (125 mL) sliced and toasted almonds

Dressing

2 Tbsp (30 mL) olive oil

2½ Tbsp (38 mL) apricot jam

1 Tbsp (15 mL) cider vinegar

1 Tbsp (15 mL) lemon juice

pinch of salt and pepper

 ROSE'S TIP
If you have to use larger kale leaves, you must literally massage the leaves with your fingers, once mixed with the dressing. These originally bitter and tough leaves turn silky and sweet, darken and shrink in size, making them delicious.

 HEALTH TIP
Kale is beyond a powerhouse of nutrients. One cup (250 mL) of cooked kale contains only 36 calories, but provides you with 350% of your daily vitamin A, 90% of your vitamin C and over 1,000% of your vitamin K.

NUTRITION INFORMATION PER SERVING

Calories 161	Protein 4.3 g	Cholesterol 0 mg
Carbohydrates 20.8 g	Total fat 8 g	Sodium 68 mg
Fibre 3.1 g	Saturated fat 0.9 g	

NOUVEAU GREEK SALAD WITH FETA DRESSING

This salad is beautiful with all the ingredients scattered overtop rather than mixed in. The feta dressing is much more interesting than the basic oil and vinegar dressing.

1. Place the lettuce on a large serving platter.

2. Scatter the tomatoes, sun-dried tomatoes, cucumber, olives, onion and feta cheese decoratively overtop.

3. TO MAKE THE DRESSING In a small food processor, add the feta and cream cheeses, sour cream, garlic, lemon juice, water and basil. Purée until smooth, adding more water if too thick. Pour overtop of the salad.

PREPARATION TIME 20 minutes · **MAKE AHEAD** Prepare the salad and dressing early in the day. Dress just before serving. · **MAKES** 4 servings.

ROSE'S TIP
Another trend today is to grill whole romaine lettuces for a minute on both sides. You could do this for this salad and serve the other ingredients scattered over the entire grilled romaine lettuce. Use two leaves per serving.

HEALTH TIP
A head of romaine has more nutrients than iceberg lettuce. One head of romaine has 8 grams of protein, 13 grams of fibre and 200 mg of calcium whereas iceberg has only 5 grams of protein, 7 grams of fibre and 97 mg of calcium.

1 medium head romaine lettuce, cut into bite-sized pieces

1 cup (250 mL) coloured cherry tomatoes, sliced in half

⅓ cup (80 mL) diced sun-dried tomatoes

1 cup (250 mL) sliced baby cucumber, cut in half

⅓ cup (80 mL) halved black olives

⅓ cup (80 mL) diced red onion

½ cup (125 mL) diced reduced-fat feta cheese (2 oz/60 g)

Feta cheese dressing

⅓ cup (80 mL) crumbled reduced-fat feta cheese (1½ oz/45 g)

½ cup (125 mL) softened reduced-fat cream cheese (2 oz/60 g)

3 Tbsp (45 mL) reduced-fat sour cream

½ tsp (2.5 mL) finely chopped garlic

1 Tbsp (15 mL) lemon juice

3 Tbsp (45 mL) water

½ tsp (2.5 mL) dried basil

NUTRITION INFORMATION PER SERVING

Calories 135	Protein 6.9 g	Cholesterol 14 mg
Carbohydrates 10 g	Total fat 7 g	Sodium 420 mg
Fibre 2.5 g	Saturated fat 4 g	

SPINACH SALAD WITH CANDIED PECANS, RASPBERRIES AND GOAT CHEESE

This salad is perfect for entertaining, with all its vibrant colours, flavours and textures. The combination of spinach, spiced nuts, berries and goat cheese gives it loads of character. Add a grilled fish or chicken and you have a complete meal.

1. Preheat the oven to 350°F (175°C). Line a baking sheet with foil and lightly coat with cooking spray.

2. TO MAKE THE PECANS Rinse the pecans with cold water. Drain but do not let them dry. Place them in a bowl and add the brown sugar, cinnamon, nutmeg and ground ginger. Toss to coat. Spread out on the prepared baking sheet and bake for 15 minutes, tossing once. Let cool, then remove from the baking sheet and chop coarsely.

3. TO MAKE THE SALAD Place the spinach, red pepper, raspberries and goat cheese in a large serving bowl.

4. TO MAKE THE DRESSING Whisk together the cider vinegar, olive oil, apple juice concentrate, brown sugar, garlic and mustard in a small bowl. Pour the dressing over the salad and toss. Top with the chopped nuts.

PREPARATION TIME 15 minutes · **BAKING TIME** 15 minutes ·
MAKE AHEAD Prepare the salad early in the day. Dress just before serving. · **MAKES** 6 servings.

Pecans
¼ cup (60 mL) whole pecans

3 Tbsp (45 mL) brown sugar

½ tsp (2.5 mL) cinnamon

¼ tsp (1 mL) nutmeg

¼ tsp (1 mL) ground ginger

Salad
8 cups (2 L) baby spinach

1 cup (250 mL) thinly sliced red bell pepper

1 cup (250 mL) fresh raspberries

½ cup (125 mL) crumbled goat cheese (2 oz/60 g)

Dressing
1½ Tbsp (22.5 mL) cider vinegar

1 Tbsp (15 mL) olive oil

1 Tbsp (15 mL) apple or orange juice concentrate

1 tsp (5 mL) brown sugar

½ tsp (2.5 mL) chopped garlic

½ tsp (2.5 mL) Dijon mustard

ROSE'S TIP

Prepare the nuts in larger quantities and keep them in an airtight container for up to 2 weeks. Substitute any nut, fruit and cheese of your choice.

 HEALTH TIP

Pecans contain more than 19 vitamins and minerals, including vitamin A, vitamin E, folic acid, calcium, magnesium and potassium. One ounce (30 g) of pecans (19 halves) provides 10% of your daily recommended fibre and is an excellent source of protein.

NUTRITION INFORMATION PER SERVING

Calories 138	Protein 4.2 g	Cholesterol 4 mg
Carbohydrates 14 g	Total fat 7 g	Sodium 160 mg
Fibre 3 g	Saturated fat 1.7 g	

SOUTHWESTERN SALAD WITH RANCH SALSA DRESSING

I love these Tex-Mex salads. You can find light ranch dressings easily today if you don't want to make your own. Also add some grilled chicken or beef overtop. If you have time, prepare your own individual baked tortilla shells for a special treat (see Rose's tip).

1. In a skillet sprayed with vegetable oil, sauté the corn just until seared (about 5 minutes).

2. Meanwhile, arrange on a serving plate the lettuce, onion, tomatoes, avocado, beans, jalapeños and cheese. Add the corn.

3. TO MAKE THE RANCH SALSA DRESSING Combine the ranch dressing and salsa. Pour overtop the salad and garnish with cilantro and tortilla chips.

PREPARATION TIME 15 minutes · COOKING TIME 5 minutes ·
MAKE AHEAD Prepare the salad early in the day and dress just before serving. ·
MAKES 6 servings.

ROSE'S TIP
Preheat the oven to 400°F (200°C). Brush 2 large flour tortillas with a mixture of 1 Tbsp (15 mL) of olive oil and water. Place the tortillas over the 2 empty cans from the corn and beans and bake for 5 minutes just until browned. Fill with salad.

HEALTH TIP
A baked tortilla shell contains 210 calories with 5 grams of fat. The fried shells in restaurants have 260 calories and 13 g of fat.

1 cup (250 mL) corn

8 cups (2 L) chopped romaine lettuce

½ cup (125 mL) diced sweet onion

1 cup (250 mL) halved cherry tomatoes

½ cup (125 mL) sliced avocado

½ cup (125 mL) canned black beans, drained and rinsed

2 tsp (10 mL) minced jalapeño peppers

¾ cup (185 mL) grated Monterey Jack cheese or aged cheddar (2¼ oz/65 g)

Ranch Salsa Dressing
⅔ cup (160 mL) Ranch Dressing on page 357

⅓ cup (80 mL) medium salsa

¼ cup (60 mL) chopped cilantro

1 cup (250 mL) broken baked tortilla chips (1 oz/30 g)

NUTRITION INFORMATION PER SERVING (NOT INCLUDING TORTILLA SHELLS)

Calories 255	Protein 9 g	Cholesterol 22 mg
Carbohydrates 22 g	Total fat 10.3 g	Sodium 530 mg
Fibre 5 g	Saturated fat 4.5 g	

WARM ARUGULA AND SPINACH SALAD WITH PARMESAN AND MUSHROOMS

This salad has to be served warm so the cheese softens over the warmed mushrooms. Use any variety of mushroom you like. The key is to cook the mushrooms on medium-high heat until all the moisture evaporates so the mushrooms aren't wet.

1. TO MAKE THE SALAD Lightly coat a nonstick skillet with cooking spray and sauté the mushrooms over medium heat for about 8 minutes, or just until they are no longer wet and are slightly browned. Respray pan or add 2 Tbsp (30 mL) water if mushrooms begin to burn. Keep warm.

2. TO MAKE THE DRESSING Whisk together the olive oil, balsamic vinegar, mayonnaise, honey, garlic, mustard, and salt and pepper.

3. Place the spinach, arugula, sautéed mushrooms and Parmesan in a large serving bowl. Pour the dressing over the salad and toss. Serve immediately.

PREPARATION TIME 10 minutes · COOKING TIME 8 minutes ·
MAKE AHEAD Sauté the mushrooms and mix the dressing up to a day in advance. Dress just before serving. · MAKES 4 servings.

Salad

3 cups (750 mL) oyster mushrooms, sliced in half (or any variety)

4 cups (1 L) baby spinach

4 cups (1 L) arugula

½ cup (125 mL) grated Parmesan cheese (2 oz/60 g)

Dressing

2 Tbsp (30 mL) olive oil

1 Tbsp (15 mL) balsamic vinegar

1 Tbsp (15 mL) reduced-fat mayonnaise

2 tsp (10 mL) honey

½ tsp (2.5 mL) finely chopped garlic

½ tsp (2.5 mL) Dijon mustard

pinch of salt and pepper

 ROSE'S TIP
Arugula has a distinctive peppery flavour that goes well with the mildness of spinach. Buy baby arugula, which has a milder flavour than the larger leaves.

 HEALTH TIP
Arugula is a nutritional powerhouse; it contains significant folic acid and calcium. Arugula has nine times as much calcium as iceberg lettuce, contains cancer-fighting antioxidants and has more vitamin C than any other leaf.

NUTRITION INFORMATION PER SERVING

Calories 178	Protein 6 g	Cholesterol 14 mg
Carbohydrates 11 g	Total fat 13 g	Sodium 328 mg
Fibre 3.1 g	Saturated fat 3.5 g	

CHICKEN BLT SALAD

No, not a sandwich but a delicious salad with all the ingredients except for the bread. I don't often use iceberg lettuce, but it goes so well in this salad.

1. Preheat the oven to 400°F (200°C).

2. Combine the milk and egg in one bowl. Combine the panko, Parmesan and salt and pepper in another bowl.

3. Dip the chicken breast in the egg mixture, then the panko mixture.

4. Heat a small skillet until hot. Add the oil and sauté the chicken breast just until browned on both sides, about 2 minutes per side. Place in a 400°F (200°C) oven and bake for 10 minutes, until the temperature reaches 165°F (74°C) or until it's no longer pink. Let cool, then slice thinly.

5. Meanwhile, in a small skillet, cook the prosciutto until crisp (about 5 minutes). Dice and sprinkle over the lettuce wedges and sprinkle with the crumbled feta and tomatoes. Add chicken.

6. Pour the dressing overtop.

PREPARATION TIME 20 minutes · **COOKING TIME** 10 minutes ·
MAKE AHEAD Prepare the salad early in the day and dress just before serving. ·
MAKES 6 servings.

½ cup (125 mL) 2% milk

1 egg

½ cup (125 mL) panko crumbs or unseasoned dry breadcrumbs

2 Tbsp (30 mL) grated Parmesan cheese (½ oz/15 g)

pinch of salt and pepper

8 oz (250 g) boneless chicken breast

2 tsp (10 mL) vegetable oil

2 oz (60 g) prosciutto

1 large iceberg lettuce cut into 6 wedges

½ cup (125 mL) reduced-fat feta cheese (2 oz/60 g)

½ cup (125 mL) diced tomatoes

⅔ cup (160 mL) Ranch Dressing (page 357)

 ROSE'S TIP

Panko crumbs are lighter and crunchier than regular breadcrumbs, making them perfect for baking or binding meat and as a topping for casseroles.

 HEALTH TIP

For coating your chicken or fish, use panko crumbs rather than bread because the panko doesn't need or absorb as much oil, reducing the calories and fat.

NUTRITION INFORMATION PER SERVING

Calories 220	Protein 17.3 g	Cholesterol 78 mg
Carbohydrates 11.5 g	Total fat 10 g	Sodium 560 mg
Fibre 0.7 g	Saturated fat 3.5 g	

GRILLED CHICKEN CAESAR

Consider this: a not-so-innocent traditional caesar salad can have over 500 calories and 30 grams of fat per plate! Try this delicious version; you don't need your salad to be swimming in dressing—there is just enough here.

1. Preheat the oven to 425°F (220°C).

2. Spray a grill or nonstick grill pan with cooking oil and heat to medium-high. Cook the chicken for 6 minutes per side or until cooked through and no longer pink in the centre. Dice.

3. Place the bread cubes on a baking sheet. Spray with cooking oil. Bake for 8 to 10 minutes or until golden.

4. Combine the egg, 3 Tbsp (45 mL) of the Parmesan cheese, the anchovies, lemon juice, mustard, garlic and pepper in a small food processor and process until smooth (or use a whisk). Slowly add the olive oil, mixing until thickened.

5. Toss the chicken, croutons and romaine in a large serving bowl. Pour the dressing over the top and toss to coat. Sprinkle with the remaining 2 Tbsp (30 mL) of Parmesan cheese.

PREPARATION TIME 15 minutes · **COOKING TIME** 15 minutes ·
MAKE AHEAD Prepare early in the day and dress just before serving. ·
MAKES 6 servings.

8 oz (250 g) boneless skinless chicken breast

2 cups (500 mL) 1-inch (2.5 cm) Italian bread cubes

1 egg

5 Tbsp (75 mL) grated Parmesan cheese (1¼ oz/40 g)

3 minced anchovy fillets

1 Tbsp (15 mL) fresh lemon juice

1 tsp (5 mL) Dijon mustard

1½ tsp (7.5 mL) minced fresh garlic

pinch of ground black pepper

2 Tbsp (30 mL) olive oil

6 cups (1.5 L) torn romaine lettuce

 ROSE'S TIP
Substitute the grilled chicken for lean beef, fish, seafood or grilled tofu.

HEALTH TIP
Having just a caesar salad in a restaurant gives you virtually no nutrition, just loads of calories and fat. By adding some protein such as chicken and keeping the dressing to a smaller amount, you're getting a nutritious meal.

NUTRITION INFORMATION PER SERVING

Calories 164	Protein 14 g	Cholesterol 61 mg
Carbohydrates 9.8 g	Total fat 7.9 g	Sodium 239 mg
Fibre 1.4 g	Saturated fat 1.9 g	

THAI BEEF SALAD WITH NAPA CABBAGE AND HOISIN DRESSING

I created this salad for Glow Fresh Grill, and it's our number-one-selling salad. You can serve the beef warm or cold and even switch to grilled chicken, shrimp, fish or tofu. This is a main course salad—delicious for lunch or dinner

1. Grill the steak just until cooked to your preference. Cool for 10 minutes, then slice thinly.

2. On a large serving platter, add the cabbage, lettuce, bell peppers, peas, orange segments, onion, cilantro, cashews and steak slices.

3. TO MAKE THE DRESSING Combine the hoisin, lemon juice, soy sauce, garlic, ginger, honey and hot sauce and pour overtop.

PREPARATION TIME 20 minutes · **COOKING TIME** 10 minutes ·
MAKE AHEAD Prepare the salad early in the day and dress just before serving. · **MAKES** 4 servings.

ROSE'S TIP
You can serve the steak either warm, cold or at room temperature. You can use any lean cut of beef such as flank, tenderloin or top sirloin.

HEALTH TIP
New York strip is a lean cut. Four ounces (125 g) has only 190 calories and 6 grams of fat, which means each individual serving of meat in this salad adds only an extra 47 calories and 1.5 grams of fat.

4 oz (125 g) New York strip steak

3 cups (750 mL) chopped napa cabbage

3 cups (750 mL) chopped romaine lettuce

1 cup (250 mL) sliced red bell peppers

1 cup (250 mL) sugar snap peas, cut in half

¾ cup (185 mL) diced orange segments

⅓ cup (80 mL) sliced red onion

3 Tbsp (45 mL) chopped cilantro

3 Tbsp (45 mL) chopped toasted cashews

Dressing

2 Tbsp (30 mL) hoisin sauce

1 Tbsp (15 mL) fresh lemon juice

2 Tbsp (30 mL) low-sodium soy sauce

1½ tsp (7.5 mL) minced garlic

1 tsp (5 mL) chopped ginger

1½ tsp (7.5 mL) honey

½ tsp (2.5 mL) hot sauce

NUTRITION INFORMATION PER SERVING

Calories 210	Protein 11.6 g	Cholesterol 21 mg
Carbohydrates 27.1 g	Total fat 6.6 g	Sodium 433 mg
Fibre 6.5 g	Saturated fat 2.2 g	

TOMATO SALAD WITH PARMESAN CRISPS, SPINACH AND ORANGES

This is an elegant salad to serve to company. Add a grilled protein such as chicken, beef, pork, fish or tofu and make it an entire meal. These Parmesan crisps are so addictive you'll have to lock them away before serving.

1. TO MAKE THE PARMESAN CRISPS Preheat the oven to 375°F (190°C). Line a baking sheet with parchment paper. With a 1 Tbsp (15 mL) measuring spoon, place the cheese on a baking sheet, making 12 rounds. Bake for 8 minutes.

2. TO MAKE THE SALAD In a hot skillet, sear the whole tomatoes just until slightly charred. Set aside to cool.

3. On a large platter add the spinach, orange wedges, onion, tomatoes and crisps.

4. TO MAKE THE DRESSING Combine the garlic, mustard, vinegar, maple syrup, olive oil, lemon juice, and salt and pepper and pour overtop of the salad.

PREPARATION TIME 15 minutes · **COOKING TIME** 8 minutes ·
MAKE AHEAD Prepare crisps up to a week in advance and the remainder of the salad early in the day. Dress just before serving. · **MAKES** 6 servings.

 ROSE'S TIP
Be sure to use only freshly grated cheese, not the prepared ground Parmesan. You can make these crisps in advance and store them at room temperature in an airtight container.

 HEALTH TIP
Oranges are a superfruit; they have over 100% of your daily vitamin C requirement and are rich in vitamin A, calcium, magnesium, potassium, fibre and antioxidants that can reduce the risk of cancer.

NUTRITION INFORMATION PER SERVING

Calories 171	Protein 7.2 g	Cholesterol 10 mg
Carbohydrates 12.9 g	Total fat 10.4 g	Sodium 340 mg
Fibre 1.8 g	Saturated fat 3.4 g	

Parmesan crisps
1 cup (250 mL) freshly grated Parmesan cheese (4 oz/125 g)

Salad
2 cups (500 mL) small grape tomatoes

6 cups (1.5 L) baby spinach leaves

1 small orange, peeled and cut into small wedges

⅓ cup (80 mL) thinly sliced red onion

Maple dressing
1 tsp (5 mL) minced garlic

½ tsp (2.5 mL) Dijon mustard

1 Tbsp (15 mL) cider vinegar

2½ Tbsp (38 mL) maple syrup

3 Tbsp (45 mL) olive oil

2 tsp (10 mL) lemon juice

pinch of salt and pepper

WATERMELON, TOMATO, PISTACHIO AND FETA SALAD

Nothing beats a spring or summer salad that combines watermelon, tomatoes and feta. The balsamic dressing is sensational, and you avoid the calories and fat of oil-based dressings.

1. TO MAKE THE SALAD Place arugula, tomatoes, watermelon, feta, pistachios and mint in a large serving bowl.

2. TO MAKE THE DRESSING In a small skillet, add the vinegar and maple syrup, bring to a boil and cook at a rapid boil for 8 to 10 minutes or just until the mixture bubbles on the entire surface and is slightly syrupy. Do not overcook, or the syrup will get too thick.

PREPARATION TIME 10 minutes · COOKING TIME 8 minutes ·
MAKE AHEAD Prepare the salad and dressing early in the day. ·
MAKES 4 servings.

 ROSE'S TIP
The balsamic dressing can harden very quickly if you overcook it. Quickly remove it from the heat and let it cool. If it is still too loose, put it back on the heat for a minute. If it is too thick, add a little more maple syrup.

 HEALTH TIP
The balsamic dressing has only about 35 calories with 0 grams of fat per serving compared to regular dressings, which have about 100 calories and 10 grams of fat per serving.

Salad

4 cups (1 L) baby arugula or baby spinach

1 cup (250 mL) small red or yellow grape tomatoes

4 cups (1 L) cubed watermelon

⅓ cup (80 mL) diced reduced-fat feta cheese (2½ oz/75 g)

⅓ cup (80 mL) toasted chopped pistachios

¼ cup (60 mL) chopped mint or parsley

Dressing

1 cup (250 mL) balsamic vinegar

¼ cup (60 mL) maple syrup

NUTRITION INFORMATION PER SERVING

Calories 191

Carbohydrates 28 g

Fibre 2.7 g

Protein 7.3 g

Total fat 8.4 g

Saturated fat 2.4 g

Cholesterol 5 mg

Sodium 280 mg

CALIFORNIA SUSHI SALAD WITH SMOKED SALMON

If you like sushi but can't be bothered making it at home, try this fabulous sushi salad using smoked salmon. The combination of the sushi rice, crisp nori sheets, avocado and smoked salmon is perfect.

1. **TO PREPARE THE SALAD** Bring the rice and water to a boil. Reduce the heat to low, cover the rice and cook for 12 minutes. Remove the pan from the heat and let the rice stand, covered, for 10 minutes.

2. While the rice is hot, add the rice vinegar and sugar and stir well. Place the rice mixture in a serving bowl to cool until the rice is still warm, but not hot.

3. Stir in the smoked salmon, cucumber, red pepper, carrots, green onions, avocado and nori. Let it cool.

4. **TO MAKE THE DRESSING** Whisk together the mayonnaise, sour cream, wasabi, soy sauce and sesame oil in a small bowl. Pour the dressing over the cooled rice mixture and toss to coat. Top with the sesame seeds and serve.

PREPARATION TIME 15 minutes · **COOKING TIME** 12 minutes ·

MAKE AHEAD Prepare the salad and dressing early in the day. Dress just before serving to maintain moisture. · **MAKES** 6 servings.

Salad

1 cup (250 mL) sushi rice

1 cup (250 mL) water

2 Tbsp (30 mL) rice vinegar

1½ tsp (7.5 mL) granulated sugar

4 oz (125 g) diced smoked salmon

¾ cup (185 mL) finely chopped cucumbers

¾ cup (185 mL) finely chopped red bell pepper

⅓ cup (80 mL) finely chopped carrots

¼ cup (60 mL) finely chopped green onions

½ cup (125 mL) chopped avocado

½ sheet nori, cut into very thin strips

Dressing

¼ cup (60 mL) reduced-fat mayonnaise

¼ cup (60 mL) reduced-fat sour cream

½ tsp (2.5 mL) wasabi paste

4 tsp (20 mL) low-sodium soy sauce

2 tsp (10 mL) toasted sesame oil

1 tsp (5 mL) toasted sesame seeds for garnish

ROSE'S TIP

You can prepare the sushi rice a few hours earlier if you place it on a baking sheet and cover it with a wet towel or keep it airtight in a large Ziploc bag.

 HEALTH TIP

Wasabi has similar anti-cancer chemicals found in broccoli and cabbage known as isothiocyanates. These chemicals also help to reduce inflammation causing arthritis, asthma and allergic reactions. Double up the wasabi when eating sushi since it's also known to stop the growth of certain strains of bacteria that cause food poisoning.

NUTRITION INFORMATION PER SERVING

Calories 183	Protein 9.1 g	Cholesterol 26.9 mg
Carbohydrates 22.3 g	Total fat 6.2 g	Sodium 444 mg
Fibre 2.3 g	Saturated fat 1.6 g	

GREEK BARLEY SALAD

This is my variation on the traditional Mediterranean salad. I like to have it as a main meal with some protein or as a side dish instead of rice or pasta. If you want more fibre, use pot barley, which takes about 50 minutes to cook.

1. Bring the stock to a boil in a medium saucepan and add the barley. Cover, reduce the heat and simmer for 25 to 30 minutes, or just until tender. Do not overcook. Drain well.

2. Place the barley in a large serving bowl. Add the cucumber, tomato, onion, green pepper, olives and feta. Toss well.

3. TO MAKE THE DRESSING Whisk the oil, lemon juice, garlic, dried basil, oregano and fresh basil in a small bowl. Pour the dressing over the salad and toss well. Refrigerate until chilled.

PREPARATION TIME 15 minutes · **COOKING TIME** 25 minutes · **MAKE AHEAD** Make the salad early in the day. · **MAKES** 6 servings.

 ROSE'S TIP
This salad is delicious served warm, cold or at room temperature. You could also substitute the barley for other ancient grains such as wheat berry, farro or buckwheat. Check for cooking times for different grains.

 HEALTH TIP
Pearl barley is much more nutritious than rice. One cup (250 mL) cooked has 190 calories and 44 grams of carbohydrates compared to rice, which has 250 calories and 53 grams of carbohydrates per cup (250 mL). Pot barley is more nutritious than pearl barley.

NUTRITION INFORMATION PER SERVING

Calories 197	Protein 5 g	Cholesterol 9 mg
Carbohydrates 29 g	Total fat 8 g	Sodium 290 mg
Fibre 6 g	Saturated fat 2 g	

3 cups (750 mL) low-sodium chicken stock or water

¾ cup (185 mL) pearl barley

1½ cups (375 mL) diced cucumber

1½ cups (375 mL) diced plum tomatoes

¾ cup (185 mL) chopped red onion

¾ cup (185 mL) chopped green bell pepper

⅓ cup (80 mL) sliced black olives

⅓ cup (80 mL) crumbled reduced-fat feta cheese (1½ oz/45 g)

Dressing
2 Tbsp (30 mL) olive oil

2 Tbsp (30 mL) freshly squeezed lemon juice

1½ tsp (7.5 mL) minced fresh garlic

1 tsp (5 mL) dried basil

½ tsp (2.5 mL) dried oregano

⅓ cup (80 mL) chopped fresh basil or parsley

BROWN RICE, ARUGULA AND BLACK BEAN SALAD

I won rave reviews with my family when I developed this salad. It's delicious, colourful and so nutritious. Feel free to replace the arugula with spinach or baby kale leaves.

1. Add the rice to the water with the oregano and cumin. Bring to a boil, cover and simmer for 25 to 30 minutes or until the rice is cooked. Drain any excess liquid. Set aside.

2. Meanwhile in a large skillet, add the oil and onion and sauté for 5 minutes until tender. Add the garlic and corn and sauté until the corn begins to brown. Add the tomatoes and cook until slightly charred (about 3 minutes).

3. Add the beans, arugula, feta, olive oil, lemon juice, salt and pepper, cilantro and rice. Heat just until warm.

PREPARATION TIME 15 minutes · **COOKING TIME** 30 minutes ·
MAKE AHEAD Prepare the salad early in the day and dress just before serving. ·
MAKES 8 servings.

 ROSE'S TIP
Brown basmati rice gets longer, not fatter, when cooked and develops a firm, dry consistency perfect for this salad. It's considered a non-glutinous rice.

 HEALTH TIP
Brown basmati rice is the most nutritious of all the varieties of brown rice. It is an excellent source of manganese, containing 88% of your daily require-ment in one cup (250 mL) of cooked rice. Manga-nese is essential for the metabolism of protein and carbohydrates.

1 cup (250 mL) brown rice

3 cups (750 mL) water or low-sodium chicken stock

½ tsp (2.5 mL) dried oregano

½ tsp (2.5 mL) ground cumin

2 tsp (10 mL) vegetable oil

1 cup (250 mL) chopped onion

2 tsp (10 mL) crushed garlic

1 cup (250 mL) corn

2 cups (500 mL) grape tomatoes

2 cups (500 mL) canned black beans, drained and rinsed (one 19 oz/540 mL can)

2 cups (500 mL) arugula

¾ cup (185 mL) crumbled reduced-fat feta cheese (2½ oz/75 g)

2 Tbsp (30 mL) olive oil

3 Tbsp (45 mL) lemon juice

pinch of salt and pepper

⅓ cup (80 mL) chopped cilantro or parsley

NUTRITION INFORMATION PER SERVING

Calories 239	Protein 8.9 g	Cholesterol 2 mg
Carbohydrates 37.5 g	Total fat 6.5 g	Sodium 159 mg
Fibre 6.2 g	Saturated fat 1.6 g	

ASIAN SOBA NOODLE SALAD WITH COCONUT GINGER DRESSING

Soba noodles are Japanese noodles made of buckwheat and wheat flour. They are perfect to use in either hot or cold pasta dishes and don't soak up the sauce as quickly as regular pasta. Combine them with a coconut-peanut dressing and a variety of vegetables to make this great appetizer or main course.

1. Bring a large saucepan of water to a boil and cook the noodles for 3 to 5 minutes or until tender. Drain. Rinse under cold running water and drain again.

2. Combine the noodles, snow peas, red pepper, green onion, cilantro and peanuts in a large serving bowl.

3. TO MAKE THE DRESSING Combine the coconut milk, peanut butter, soy sauce, vinegar, sesame oil, sesame seeds, garlic, brown sugar, ginger and chili sauce in a bowl or a small food processor. Whisk or process the mixture until smooth.

4. Pour the dressing over the vegetable-noodle mixture and toss to coat.

PREPARATION TIME 20 minutes • COOKING TIME 3 to 5 minutes •
MAKE AHEAD Prepare the salad early in the day and dress just before serving. •
MAKES 8 servings.

8 oz (250 g) thin soba noodles

1½ cups (375 mL) finely chopped snow peas

1½ cups (375 mL) finely chopped red bell pepper

½ cup (125 mL) finely chopped green onion

⅓ cup (80 mL) chopped cilantro or parsley

¼ cup (60 mL) chopped peanuts

Dressing

½ cup (125 mL) light coconut milk

3 Tbsp (45 mL) natural peanut butter

2 Tbsp (30 mL) low-sodium soy sauce

2 Tbsp (30 mL) rice vinegar

1 Tbsp (15 mL) sesame oil

1 Tbsp (15 mL) toasted sesame seeds

2 tsp (10 mL) minced fresh garlic

2 Tbsp (30 mL) brown sugar

1 tsp (5 mL) minced fresh ginger

1 tsp (5 mL) hot chili sauce, or to taste

 ROSE'S TIP

Light coconut milk makes
this dish much lower in
calories and fat. Add
4 ounces (125 g) of protein
if desired such as grilled
chicken, shrimp or tofu to
make this a complete meal.

 HEALTH TIP

Soba noodles are lower
in calories and carbo-
hydrates than regular
pasta. One cup (250 mL)
(4 ounces/125 grams) of
cooked soba noodles has
112 calories and 24 grams
of carbohydrates, whereas
white pasta has 182 calories
and 35 grams of carbohy-
drates per 4-ounce
(125-gram) serving.

NUTRITION INFORMATION PER SERVING

Calories 214	Protein 6.8 g	Cholesterol 0 mg
Carbohydrates 28 g	Total fat 7.9 g	Sodium 116 mg
Fibre 2.2 g	Saturated fat 1.3 g	

GRILLED CALAMARI SALAD WITH LEMON CAPER DRESSING

Grilled is the best way to serve calamari. Keep away from the deep fried version due to excess calories and fat.

1. Lightly coat a nonstick grill pan with cooking spray and set over medium-high heat. Or preheat your barbecue to medium-high heat. Cut the calamari on one side to open and lay flat. Score the calamari by making slits on both sides with a sharp knife. Do not cut all the way through. Grill the calamari for 5 minutes, turning halfway, just until charred and no longer translucent. Let cool for 5 minutes. Slice thinly.

2. In a bowl, add the tomatoes, red onion, bell pepper, olives, olive oil, lemon juice, garlic, capers, feta, salt and pepper, and calamari. Place on a serving plate and garnish with parsley.

PREPARATION TIME 15 minutes · **COOKING TIME** 5 minutes ·
MAKE AHEAD If serving at room temperature or cold, prepare early in the day. If serving hot, prepare just before serving. · **MAKES** 4 servings.

 ROSE'S TIP
Scoring the calamari makes it more tender and allows it to cook more quickly and retain moisture. Marinating calamari in milk for a couple of hours before cooking tenderizes it. Dry the calamari completely with a paper towel before grilling.

 HEALTH TIP
A 3-ounce (90 g) serving of grilled calamari has only 78 calories per ounce (30 g) and 1 gram of fat. Three ounces (90 g) of fried calamari has 200 calories and 11 grams of fat.

12 oz (375 g) cleaned calamari

¾ cup (185 mL) grape tomatoes sliced in half

⅓ cup (80 mL) diced red onion

⅓ cup (80 mL) roasted red pepper

⅓ cup (80 mL) diced black olives

2 Tbsp (30 mL) olive oil

1 Tbsp (15 mL) lemon juice

1 tsp (5 mL) finely chopped garlic

1 tsp (5 mL) capers

¼ cup (60 mL) crumbled reduced-fat feta cheese (1 oz/30 g)

pinch of salt and pepper

2 Tbsp (30 mL) chopped parsley

NUTRITION INFORMATION PER SERVING

Calories 192	Protein 15 g	Cholesterol 201 mg
Carbohydrates 8.2 g	Total fat 11 g	Sodium 394 mg
Fibre 1.6 g	Saturated fat 2 g	

MALAYSIAN SALAD WITH MISO DRESSING

Napa cabbage is great in a salad because of its crunchiness and flavour. You can find miso paste in the refrigerator section of a good quality supermarket, your local health food store or Asian food stores. It's a fermented soybean paste. The lighter the colour, the milder the flavour.

1. **TO MAKE THE SALAD** In a large bowl, combine the cabbage, bean sprouts, carrot, red pepper, snow peas, green onion and almonds.

2. **TO MAKE THE DRESSING** In another bowl, whisk the miso, water, vinegar, soy sauce, brown sugar, sesame oil, garlic and mustard until smooth. Pour over the salad and toss to coat. Garnish with sesame seeds and parsley.

PREPARATION TIME 20 minutes · **MAKE AHEAD** Prepare the salad early in the day and dress just before serving. · **MAKES** 6 servings.

 ROSE'S TIP
Store miso in the refrigerator, where it will keep for months! If you see a white mould on top, it's harmless; just scrape it off.

 HEALTH TIP
Miso contains a lot of sodium. One tablespoon (15 mL) has 600 mg sodium! But remember that you use very small quantities in any recipe.

Salad

3 cups (750 mL) thinly sliced napa cabbage

1 cup (250 mL) bean sprouts

1 cup (250 mL) grated carrot

1½ cups (375 mL) thinly sliced red bell pepper

1 cup (250 mL) halved snow peas

⅓ cup (80 mL) diced green onion

¼ cup (60 mL) sliced toasted almonds

Dressing

2 Tbsp (30 mL) mild yellow miso paste

2 Tbsp (30 mL) water

1 Tbsp (15 mL) rice vinegar

1 Tbsp (15 mL) low-sodium soy sauce

4 tsp (20 mL) brown sugar

2 tsp (10 mL) sesame oil

1 tsp (5 mL) minced garlic

½ tsp (2.5 mL) Dijon mustard

2 tsp (10 mL) toasted sesame seeds

¼ cup (60 mL) chopped parsley or cilantro

NUTRITION INFORMATION PER SERVING

Calories 102	Protein 4 g	Cholesterol 0 mg
Carbohydrates 9 g	Total fat 4.6 g	Sodium 375 mg
Fibre 2.9 g	Saturated fat 0.5 g	

GREEN MANGO RED PEPPER SALAD WITH FRESH MINT

Thai menus always feature this sweet and savoury salad. For the traditional version, the key is finding an unripe mango, one that's still firm. But a ripe mango makes for a delicious sweeter salad, equally good. This salad is perfect to serve before a rice-noodle type of dish such as Pad Thai.

1. TO MAKE THE SALAD Place the mango, red pepper, onion, mint and cilantro in a serving bowl.

2. TO MAKE THE DRESSING Whisk together the soy sauce, lime juice, sesame oil, fish sauce and brown sugar in a small bowl. Stir in the jalapeños, garlic and ginger.

3. Pour the dressing over the salad and toss. Garnish with cashews.

PREPARATION TIME 15 minutes · **MAKE AHEAD** Prepare early in the day. · **MAKES** 4 servings.

 ROSE'S TIP
A great mango salad should be crunchy, juicy, tart, sweet and sour all in one bite, which this is. You could also try papaya in this dish. Make it a complete meal by adding some shrimp or grilled chicken.

 HEALTH TIP
The antioxidants found in mango can help reduce the risk of colon, breast and prostate cancers and leukemia. They have high levels of fibre and vitamin C to help lower cholesterol and also have 25% of the recommended vitamin A, which promotes good eyesight.

NUTRITION INFORMATION PER SERVING

Calories 132	Protein 3 g	Cholesterol 0 mg
Carbohydrates 17 g	Total fat 7 g	Sodium 316 mg
Fibre 2.5 g	Saturated fat 1.3 g	

Salad

1 large green (unripe) mango, thinly sliced

¾ cup (185 mL) thinly sliced red bell pepper

⅓ cup (80 mL) thinly sliced red onion

¼ cup (60 mL) chopped fresh mint

¼ cup (60 mL) chopped cilantro

Dressing

1 Tbsp (15 mL) low-sodium soy sauce

1 Tbsp (15 mL) lime or lemon juice

2 tsp (10 mL) sesame oil

1½ tsp (7.5 mL) fish (or oyster) sauce

2 tsp (10 mL) brown sugar

1 tsp (5 mL) finely chopped jalapeño pepper

½ tsp (2.5 mL) finely chopped garlic

½ tsp (2.5 mL) finely chopped ginger

¼ cup (60 mL) chopped toasted cashews

MANGO SLAW WITH NUTTY COCONUT DRESSING

If you want a variation on typical coleslaw, this is outstanding. Cabbage, mango and a light peanut dressing are perfect for any time of year. Be sure to choose a ripe mango, which will be sweeter and more tender.

1. **TO MAKE THE SALAD** Combine the cabbage, mango, carrots, onion, bell peppers, water chestnuts, sesame seeds and cilantro in a large serving bowl.

2. **TO MAKE THE DRESSING** In a small food processor, purée the coconut milk, peanut butter, soy sauce, vinegar, sesame oil, honey, garlic, ginger and jalapeño until smooth. Pour over the salad.

PREPARATION TIME 20 minutes · **MAKE AHEAD** Make early in the day if you'd like it to marinate. · **MAKES** 6 servings.

 ROSE'S TIP
This salad tastes great if prepared and eaten immediately, since it has a crisp, crunchy texture. Allowing it to marinate produces a more intense flavour, but the vegetables become softer.

 HEALTH TIP
Green cabbage is a low-calorie cruciferous vegetable. One cup (250 mL) shredded cabbage contains 66% of your daily vitamin K requirement, which is important for blood clotting, and 42% of your daily vitamin C requirement.

Salad

3½ cups (875 mL) thinly sliced green cabbage

½ large ripe mango, thinly sliced

½ cup (125 mL) grated carrots

¼ cup (60 mL) thinly sliced red onion

1 cup (250 mL) thinly sliced red bell pepper

½ cup (125 mL) thinly sliced water chestnuts

1 tsp (5 mL) sesame seeds

3 Tbsp (45 mL) chopped cilantro

Dressing

¼ cup (60 mL) light coconut milk

2 Tbsp (30 mL) almond or peanut butter

1 Tbsp (15 mL) low-sodium soy sauce

1 Tbsp (15 mL) rice vinegar

2 tsp (10 mL) sesame oil

1 tsp (5 mL) honey

1 tsp (5 mL) crushed garlic

1 tsp (5 mL) crushed ginger

1 tsp (5 mL) minced jalapeño peppers or Sriracha

NUTRITION INFORMATION PER SERVING

Calories 130	Protein 3.4 g	Cholesterol 0 mg
Carbohydrates 16.4 g	Total fat 6.5 g	Sodium 134 mg
Fibre 3.5 g	Saturated fat 2.7 g	

THREE PEA SALAD WITH DATES, ALMONDS AND ORANGE DRESSING

The green peas, edamame (Japanese soybeans) and snap peas make this a unique salad. Green beans and haricots verts also work. The dates and orange dressing complement the peas beautifully.

1. TO MAKE THE SALAD Place 2 cups (500 mL) of water into a large saucepan and bring to a boil. Add the green peas, edamame and snap peas, cover and bring back to a boil and cook for 1 minute. Drain quickly and rinse with cold water until no longer warm. Place in a serving bowl.

2. In small skillet sprayed with vegetable oil, sauté the onion and garlic until soft (about 3 minutes). Add to the peas and beans along with the dates and nuts.

3. TO MAKE THE DRESSING Combine the olive oil, orange juice concentrate, lemon juice, orange rind, honey, sesame oil and salt and pepper. Pour overtop. Garnish with mint.

PREPARATION TIME 15 minutes • **COOKING TIME** 4 minutes •
MAKE AHEAD Make the salad early in the day. • **MAKES** 6 servings.

 ROSE'S TIP
I buy my dried fruits and nuts in bulk and store them in the freezer.

 HEALTH TIP
Green peas are a good source of protein and insoluble fibre. They are also an excellent source of folic acid, which prevents defects in the nervous system of newborns.

Salad

2 cups (500 mL) frozen green peas

2 cups (500 mL) frozen shelled edamame

3 cups (750 mL) halved sugar snap peas or snow peas

1 cup (250 mL) diced onion

1 tsp (5 mL) crushed garlic

½ cup (125 mL) diced dried dates

⅓ cup (80 mL) toasted slivered almonds

Orange dressing

1 tsp (5 mL) olive oil

2 Tbsp (30 mL) frozen orange juice concentrate

2 tsp (10 mL) lemon juice

1 tsp (5 mL) grated orange rind

1½ Tbsp (22.5 mL) honey

2 tsp (10 mL) sesame oil

pinch of salt and pepper

2 Tbsp (30 mL) mint or parsley, chopped

NUTRITION INFORMATION PER SERVING

Calories 299	Protein 15.8 g	Cholesterol 0 mg
Carbohydrates 41.8 g	Total fat 9 g	Sodium 65 mg
Fibre 8.4 g	Saturated fat 1.6 g	

EDAMAME, WATER CHESTNUTS AND RED PEPPER SALAD WITH SESAME DRESSING

Edamame (Japanese soybeans) is here to stay. You can use edamame in a salad, add it to grain dishes, eat it on its own or use it as a garnish. This salad is always featured in my catering company and in the restaurants I consult with.

1. **TO MAKE THE SALAD** Boil the edamame just until bright green, approximately 3 minutes. Drain and rinse with cold water. Place in a serving bowl.

2. In a nonstick skillet sprayed with the vegetable oil, sauté the corn just until browned, approximately 5 minutes. Add to the edamame along with the water chestnuts, bell pepper, green onions and cilantro.

3. **TO MAKE THE DRESSING** Mix the soy sauce, rice vinegar, sesame oil, honey, garlic and ginger and pour over the salad. Garnish with sesame seeds.

PREPARATION TIME 10 minutes · **COOKING TIME** 8 minutes ·
MAKE AHEAD Make the salad early in the day. · **MAKES** 4 servings.

 ROSE'S TIP
For snacking, buy edamame in the shell, but for all other cooking purposes buy shelled. You'll find them in the frozen section of your supermarket.

 HEALTH TIP
Edamame makes for a nutritious snack and can help stabilize your blood sugar. One half cup (125 mL) contains 125 calories, 3 grams of fat and 4 grams of protein.

Salad
3 cups (750 mL) frozen shelled edamame

1 cup (250 mL) corn

½ cup (125 mL) diced water chestnuts

½ cup (125 mL) diced red bell pepper

¼ cup (60 mL) chopped green onions

¼ cup (60 mL) chopped cilantro

Dressing
2 Tbsp (30 mL) low-sodium soy sauce

1½ Tbsp (22.5 mL) rice vinegar

1 Tbsp (15 mL) sesame oil

2 tsp (10 mL) honey

1 tsp (5 mL) crushed garlic

½ tsp (2.5 mL) minced ginger

1 tsp (5 mL) toasted sesame seeds

NUTRITION INFORMATION PER SERVING

Calories 257 · Protein 17 g · Cholesterol 0 mg
Carbohydrates 29 g · Total fat 7.9 g · Sodium 398 mg
Fibre 3.6 g · Saturated fat 0.5 g

SOUPS

THAI SWEET POTATO SOUP

Sweet potatoes and light coconut milk make a creamy and rich-tasting soup without the calories and fat. Add some lemongrass for a more authentic Thai flavour.

1. Lightly coat a large nonstick pot with cooking spray. Add the oil and set over medium heat. Sauté the onion, garlic and ginger for 5 minutes or until the onions are just softened.

2. Add the sweet potatoes, stock, chili sauce, fish sauce and salt. Bring to a boil, then reduce the heat to low. Cover and simmer for about 25 minutes or until the potatoes are tender.

3. Purée the soup in a blender or food processor in batches. Return the soup to the saucepan and add the coconut milk and honey. Heat through. Serve the soup in bowls and garnish with cilantro.

PREPARATION TIME 10 minutes · **COOKING TIME** 30 minutes ·

MAKE AHEAD Make the soup up to 2 days in advance. Add more stock when reheating. · **MAKES** 6 servings.

2 tsp (10 mL) vegetable oil

1 cup (250 mL) diced onion

2 tsp (10 mL) finely chopped garlic

1 tsp (5 mL) finely chopped ginger

6 cups (1.5 L) cubed peeled sweet potatoes

3 cups (750 mL) low-sodium chicken stock

1½ tsp (7.5 mL) hot chili sauce (Sriracha)

½ tsp (2.5 mL) fish sauce (optional)

pinch of salt

1 cup (250 mL) light coconut milk

1 tsp (5 mL) honey

¼ cup (60 mL) chopped fresh cilantro or basil

 ROSE'S TIP
You can substitute butternut squash for the sweet potato.

 HEALTH TIP
Honey is actually higher in calories and sugar than granulated sugar, but is a natural ingredient, so it's better to use.

NUTRITION INFORMATION PER SERVING

Calories 239	Protein 3.6 g	Cholesterol 0 mg
Carbohydrates 47.3 g	Total fat 3.8 g	Sodium 375 mg
Fibre 6.7 g	Saturated fat 2.3 g	

THAI COCONUT CHICKEN SOUP

We all have a standard chicken soup in our repertoire, but now let's add a Southeastern twist. If you don't have lemongrass, add 2 tsp (10 mL) of grated lemon zest. Sriracha is a great hot sauce to use.

1. In a skillet or on a grill, cook the chicken breast just until no longer pink or the temperature reaches 165°F (74°C) (about 12 minutes), depending upon the thickness. Cool and dice.

2. Meanwhile, sauté the onions in oil for 5 minutes. Add the garlic, ginger and corn and sauté until the corn browns. Add the red pepper and curry paste and sauté for 3 minutes. Add the stock, lemongrass and potato and simmer for 15 minutes or until the potato is tender.

3. Add the fish and soy sauces, sesame oil, chili flakes and coconut milk. Simmer for 5 minutes. Remove the lemongrass.

4. Remove 1½ cups (375 mL) soup and place in a food processor. Purée until smooth. Add back to the soup and add the chicken.

5. Garnish with cilantro, cashews and avocado.

PREPARATION TIME 15 minutes • **COOKING TIME** 28 minutes •
MAKE AHEAD Make the soup up to 2 days in advance, adding more stock when reheating. • **MAKES** 4 servings.

---

4 oz (125 g) boneless chicken breast

1½ cups (375 mL) diced onions

2 tsp (10 mL) vegetable oil

2 tsp (10 mL) chopped garlic

2 tsp (10 mL) chopped ginger

1 cup (250 mL) corn

¾ cup (185 mL) diced red pepper

2 tsp (10 mL) red curry paste or hot chili sauce

2½ cups (625 mL) low-sodium chicken stock

1 stick lemongrass, cut in half and smashed

1 cup (250 mL) diced potato

1½ tsp (7.5 mL) fish sauce (optional)

2 tsp (10 mL) low-sodium soy sauce

2 tsp (10 mL) sesame oil

¼ tsp (1 mL) chili flakes

¾ cup (185 mL) light coconut milk

3 Tbsp (45 mL) chopped cilantro

3 Tbsp (45 mL) toasted diced cashews

¼ cup (60 mL) diced avocado

ROSE'S TIP

When a recipe calls for chili peppers or hot sauce you can add virtually anything with heat. Hot sauces, jalapeños, cayenne, chili powder and chili flakes are great substitutes.

HEALTH TIP

Fish sauce is a common flavourful ingredient in Asian cooking but use it sparingly since 1 Tbsp (15 mL) has 1,200 mg of sodium! That's close to an entire day's worth.

NUTRITION INFORMATION PER SERVING

Calories 239	Protein 11.2 g	Cholesterol 14 mg
Carbohydrates 26.1 g	Total fat 10.5 g	Sodium 375 mg
Fibre 3.7 g	Saturated fat 3.6 g	

SOBA NOODLE SOUP WITH SEARED BEEF AND ENOKI MUSHROOMS

This is my simplified version of the Vietnamese soup called pho. It's simple to make and is a complete meal in one bowl. Enoki mushrooms are small, creamy white mushrooms with tall stalks. They are available in the fresh Asian section of your supermarket. If you can't find them, use button mushrooms, but it's best to cook these before adding them to the soup.

1. Spray a grill pan with vegetable oil. Sear the steak for 2 minutes per side, just until still rare in the middle. Let rest, then slice very thinly.

2. In a large saucepan sprayed with cooking oil, add the ginger and garlic and sauté for 2 minutes.

3. Bring the stock and soy sauce to a boil in a large saucepan. Add the noodles and return to a boil. Reduce the heat to medium-high and cook for 4 minutes or until the noodles are tender.

4. Add the bok choy, snow peas and mushrooms and cook for 2 minutes.

5. Add the sliced beef, green onions and sesame oil. Serve immediately.

6. Ladle into individual bowls and garnish each serving with bean sprouts and cilantro.

PREPARATION TIME 10 minutes · **COOKING TIME** 8 minutes ·
MAKE AHEAD Best to prepare just before serving so the noodles don't overcook. · **MAKES** 6 servings.

NUTRITION INFORMATION PER SERVING

Calories 144	Protein 11.6 g	Cholesterol 10 mg
Carbohydrates 19 g	Total fat 2.7 g	Sodium 641 mg
Fibre 0.8 g	Saturated fat 0.7 g	

6 oz (175 g) New York strip sirloin steak (fat trimmed)

2 tsp (10 mL) minced fresh ginger

2 tsp (10 mL) minced fresh garlic

8 cups (2 L) low-sodium chicken or beef stock

2 Tbsp (30 mL) low-sodium soy sauce

3 oz (90 g) soba noodles

1 cup (250 mL) sliced bok choy

½ cup (125 mL) sliced snow peas

1 cup (250 mL) enoki mushrooms

2 large green onions, chopped

2 tsp (10 mL) sesame oil

½ cup (125 mL) bean sprouts

3 Tbsp (45 mL) chopped cilantro or parsley

 ROSE'S TIP
You can use chicken, pork or tofu instead of beef. If using chicken, be sure it cooks until done in the broth before serving.

 HEALTH TIP
One cup (250 mL) of enoki mushrooms has 2 grams of protein and 2 grams of fibre, with only 24 calories and 0 grams of fat.

WILD MUSHROOM SOUP

Everyone loves a delicious mushroom soup, but most are filled with cream and butter. This soup gets its flavour from mixed mushrooms and evaporated milk. Use any variety of mushrooms you enjoy.

1. In a large nonstick pot lightly coated with cooking spray, add 1 tsp (5 mL) of the oil and the mushrooms. Sauté for 15 minutes on medium-high heat or until the mushrooms are no longer wet. Remove and save ½ cup (125 mL) for garnish. Add the remaining oil to the pan.

2. Add the onions and garlic and sauté on medium heat for 5 minutes. Add the carrots and sauté for 3 minutes. Add all of the cooked mushrooms (except the reserved ½ cup/ 125 mL) and the stock, potato, rosemary and salt and pepper. Bring to a boil, cover and simmer for 15 minutes or until the potato is tender.

3. Purée in a food processor until smooth. Pour back into the saucepan and add the milk, Parmesan and the remaining ½ cup (125 mL) cooked mushrooms. Heat gently and serve. Garnish with parsley.

PREPARATION TIME 15 minutes · **COOKING TIME** 30 minutes ·
MAKE AHEAD Cook up to 2 days in advance. Add more stock when reheating. · **MAKES** 8 servings.

2 tsp (10 mL) vegetable oil

8 cups (2 L) chopped mixed wild mushrooms (about 1⅓ lb/600g)

1 cup (250 mL) chopped onion

2 tsp (10 mL) finely chopped garlic

½ cup (125 mL) diced carrots

4 cups (1 L) low-sodium chicken (or vegetable) stock

1 cup (250 mL) peeled and diced potato

½ tsp (2.5 mL) dried rosemary

¼ tsp (1 mL) salt

¼ tsp (1 mL) ground pepper

½ cup (125 mL) canned evaporated 2% milk

3 Tbsp (45 mL) grated Parmesan cheese (¾ oz/23 g)

3 Tbsp (45 mL) chopped parsley

 ROSE'S TIP
Try oyster, button, brown and portobello mushrooms. Portobellos will make the soup darker.

 HEALTH TIP
I like to use 2% evaporated milk versus 0% fat because the flavour and texture are better, and 2% has only 0.5 grams of fat per 2 tablespoons (30 mL).

NUTRITION INFORMATION PER SERVING

Calories 126	Protein 8.9 g	Cholesterol 8 mg
Carbohydrates 15 g	Total fat 3.8 g	Sodium 290 mg
Fibre 2.2 g	Saturated fat 1.4 g	

CARAMELIZED ONION SOUP WITH TOASTED CHEESE BAGUETTE

Everyone loves onion soup with all that thick melted cheese spilling over the bowl—but when it's made like that, it's not a healthy choice. This soup has delicious caramelized onions and a small sliced baguette with a tablespoon of cheese melted on top. You'll find this is the perfect amount of cheese to satisfy your appetite.

1. Lightly coat a large nonstick pot with cooking spray, add the oil and set over medium heat. Add the onions and sauté for 10 minutes, stirring constantly, until softened but not browned. Stir in the garlic and sugar and continue cooking over low heat for 20 minutes, stirring often or until the onions are golden brown.

2. Preheat the oven to 425°F (220°C).

3. Stir in the stock, wine, thyme, salt and pepper and Worcestershire sauce. Bring to a boil, then reduce the heat to low and simmer, covered, for about 12 minutes.

4. Meanwhile, lightly coat the baguette slices on both sides with cooking spray and place them on a baking sheet. Bake for 8 to 10 minutes or until golden on top. Turn the slices over and sprinkle the toasted side with the 2 cheeses. Turn the oven to broil, and broil the toasts for about 30 seconds or until the cheese melts.

5. Serve the soup in bowls with 1 cheese toast placed on top, and garnish with parsley.

PREPARATION TIME 15 minutes · **COOKING TIME** 42 minutes ·

MAKE AHEAD Make the soup 2 days in advance. Add cheese toast just before serving. · **MAKES** 6 servings.

---

2 tsp (10 mL) vegetable oil

6 cups (1.5 L) Spanish onion, cut into ¼-inch (6 mm) rings

2 tsp (10 mL) finely chopped garlic

4 tsp (20 mL) brown sugar

5 cups (1.25 L) low-sodium chicken (or beef) stock

½ cup (125 mL) dry red wine

½ tsp (2.5 mL) dried thyme or 1 Tbsp (15 mL) fresh

pinch of salt and pepper

2 tsp (10 mL) Worcestershire sauce

6 slices whole wheat baguette, cut ½ inch (1 cm) thick

3 Tbsp (45 mL) shredded Swiss cheese (½ oz/15 g)

3 Tbsp (45 mL) shredded part-skim mozzarella cheese (½ oz/15 g)

3 Tbsp (45 mL) chopped parsley

ROSE'S TIP

Remember the old saying regarding wine. "If you wouldn't drink it, don't cook with it." So true. Use a good leftover wine from a night's meal. Good dry wines include cabernet sauvignon, merlot and pinot noir.

HEALTH TIP

The antioxidants in an onion are more concentrated in the outer layers of the flesh. So peel off as few of the outside layers as possible after removing the skin. A red onion can lose about 20% of its quercetin and 75% of its anthocyanins if overpeeled. These are the main antioxidants.

NUTRITION INFORMATION PER SERVING

Calories 210	Protein 8 g	Cholesterol 7 mg
Carbohydrates 31 g	Total fat 2.7 g	Sodium 635 mg
Fibre 2.7 g	Saturated fat 0.8 g	

POTATO, CORN AND RED PEPPER CHOWDER

Traditional corn chowder is usually prepared with excess cream and butter. My version uses evaporated milk, and you'll be surprised at how creamy and rich the soup tastes. Charring the corn gives the soup a fresher flavour.

1. Lightly coat a nonstick skillet with cooking spray and set over medium heat. Sauté the corn, stirring often, for about 8 minutes or just until lightly browned. Purée half the corn in a small food processor. Combine the puréed corn with the whole corn in a small bowl and set aside.

2. Add the oil to a large nonstick pot and set over medium heat. Add the onion and garlic and sauté for about 4 minutes. Add the red pepper and sauté for another 2 minutes. Add the potato, stock, chili sauce and corn mixture. Bring to a boil, then reduce the heat to low and simmer, covered, for about 15 minutes or until the potato is tender.

3. Whisk together the flour and milk in a small bowl and gradually add to the soup. Add the salt and pepper. Simmer, stirring occasionally for 3 minutes or until slightly thickened and heated through. Serve in bowls, and garnish with parsley.

PREPARATION TIME 15 minutes · **COOKING TIME** 30 minutes ·

MAKE AHEAD Make up to 2 days in advance. Add more stock when reheating. ·

MAKES 4 servings.

2 cups (500 mL) corn

1½ tsp (7.5 mL) vegetable oil

1 cup (250 mL) chopped onion

1½ tsp (7.5 mL) finely chopped garlic

½ cup (125 mL) chopped red bell pepper

1 cup (250 mL) peeled and diced potato

2½ cups (625 mL) low-sodium chicken stock

½ tsp (2.5 mL) hot chili sauce (or finely chopped jalapeño pepper)

2 tsp (10 mL) all-purpose flour

1 cup (250 mL) canned evaporated 2% milk

pinch of salt and pepper

3 Tbsp (45 mL) chopped parsley

ROSE'S TIP

In season, fresh corn is fantastic to use. Boil the corn for just 2 minutes, cool, and then with a sharp knife remove the kernels.

 HEALTH TIP

Sweet corn that you eat is not genetically modified, as field corn given to animals may be. Corn has only 100 calories per cup (250 mL) and 3 grams of fibre, the same as an apple.

NUTRITION INFORMATION PER SERVING

Calories 211	Protein 10 g	Cholesterol 5 mg
Carbohydrates 35 g	Total fat 3.7 g	Sodium 565 mg
Fibre 3.9 g	Saturated fat 0.9 g	

OLD-FASHIONED SPLIT PEA AND BARLEY SOUP

Split pea soup can be an entire meal if you like. It's such a hearty and filling soup that all you'll need is a green salad to accompany it. But it's also a great way to start off a meal. Having a soup like this is a great tool for weight management, since it's so nutritious and satisfying.

1. Combine the barley and the 2 cups (500 mL) of water in a large saucepan and bring to a boil. Reduce the heat and simmer, covered, for 25 minutes or until the barley is just tender. Drain any excess liquid. Set aside.

2. Lightly coat a large nonstick pot with cooking spray, add the oil and set over medium heat. Add the onion and sauté for 5 minutes or until just softened. Add the carrots and garlic, and cook for another 5 minutes or until the carrots are slightly softened.

3. Stir in the 4 cups (1 L) of stock and the potato, split peas, and salt and pepper. Bring to a boil, then reduce the heat to low and simmer, covered, for 35 minutes or until the split peas are tender.

4. Purée 2 cups (500 mL) of the soup in a blender or food processor. Return the puréed soup to the saucepan and stir in the barley. Heat through and serve.

PREPARATION TIME 15 minutes · **COOKING TIME** 45 minutes (cook the soup while cooking the barley) · **MAKE AHEAD** Make the soup up to 2 days in advance. Add more stock when reheating. · **MAKES** 6 servings.

¼ cup (60 mL) pearl barley

2 cups (500 mL) water (or low-sodium vegetable or chicken stock)

2 tsp (10 mL) vegetable oil

1 cup (250 mL) chopped onion

⅔ cup (160 mL) chopped carrots

2 tsp (10 mL) finely chopped garlic

4 cups (1 L) low-sodium vegetable (or chicken) stock

1 cup (250 mL) peeled and chopped potato

¾ cup (185 mL) green split peas

¼ tsp (1 mL) salt

¼ tsp (1 mL) pepper

ROSE'S TIP

You can now buy garlic cloves that are peeled and refrigerated for easier use in cooking. Or buy bottled pre-chopped garlic packed in oil. Use double the amount, since once the garlic has been cut it loses some of its flavour.

 HEALTH TIP

Pearl barley is quicker to cook than pot barley but not as nutritious. A 1-cup (250 mL) serving of pot barley has 14 grams of fibre, which is half your daily requirement, whereas pearl barley has only 6 grams per cup (250 mL). It takes pot barley close to double the time to cook.

NUTRITION INFORMATION PER SERVING

Calories 167	Protein 11 g	Cholesterol 0 mg
Carbohydrates 24 g	Total fat 3 g	Sodium 396 mg
Fibre 7.6 g	Saturated fat 0.5 g	

MEATBALL AND SMALL SHELL PASTA SOUP

This is a great soup for children and teens. It's a complete meal in a bowl. Try using ground chicken, turkey or pork instead of beef. (Add an extra 1 Tbsp/15 mL of breadcrumbs if you're using chicken or turkey.)

1. Preheat the oven to 425°F (220°C). Line a baking sheet with foil sprayed with vegetable oil.

2. TO MAKE THE MEATBALLS Combine the ground beef, breadcrumbs, barbecue sauce, egg, garlic, basil and 2 Tbsp (30 mL) of the Parmesan cheese. Form into 1-inch (2.5 cm) meatballs (you should have enough for about 24 meatballs). Place on baking sheet and cook for 10 minutes, turning after 6 minutes.

3. TO MAKE THE SOUP Lightly coat a large nonstick pot with cooking spray. Add the oil and set over medium heat. Add the onion and garlic and sauté for 5 minutes or until just softened and browned. Stir in the green pepper and carrots and cook for 3 minutes. Stir in the stock, tomato sauce, tomato paste, chili powder and meatballs. Bring to a boil, then reduce the heat to low and simmer, covered, for 15 minutes.

4. Stir in the pasta and simmer for 5 minutes or until tender. Serve the soup in bowls, and garnish with Parmesan cheese.

PREPARATION TIME 20 minutes · **COOKING TIME** 38 minutes ·
MAKE AHEAD Make the soup up to 2 days in advance, leaving out the pasta. Add pasta when reheating and more stock if necessary. · **MAKES** 6 servings.

Meatballs

6 oz (175 g) lean ground beef

3 Tbsp (45 mL) seasoned dry breadcrumbs

2 Tbsp (30 mL) barbecue sauce

1 egg

1 tsp (5 mL) finely chopped garlic

½ tsp (2.5 mL) dried basil

2 Tbsp (30 mL) Parmesan cheese (½ oz/15 g)

Soup

2 tsp (10 mL) vegetable oil

1 cup (250 mL) chopped onion

1½ tsp (7.5 mL) finely chopped garlic

½ cup (125 mL) chopped green bell pepper

½ cup (125 mL) chopped carrots

4 cups (1 L) low-sodium beef (or chicken) stock

1¾ cups (435 mL) homemade or store-bought tomato sauce (see Quick Basic Tomato Sauce on page 369)

ROSE'S TIP

You can always make 6 large meatballs and serve one per bowl.

HEALTH TIP

Homemade tomato sauce is much lower in sodium than jarred or canned sauce. A ½-cup (125 mL) serving of jarred tomato sauce has 500 mg of sodium, whereas a ½ cup (125 mL) of home-made sauce (see Quick Basic Tomato Sauce on page 369) has only 360 mg (using canned tomatoes). If you use fresh tomatoes, there is virtu-ally no sodium.

2 Tbsp (30 mL) tomato paste

1 tsp (5 mL) chili powder

⅓ cup (80 mL) small shell pasta

¼ cup (60 mL) grated Parmesan cheese (1 oz/30 g)

NUTRITION INFORMATION PER SERVING

Calories 187	Protein 14 g	Cholesterol 58 mg
Carbohydrates 21 g	Total fat 6.3 g	Sodium 568 mg
Fibre 3 g	Saturated fat 1.7 g	

BEEF BARLEY SOUP WITH ROASTED ROOT VEGETABLES

Everyone loves a hearty beef barley soup, especially in the colder months. But I found that roasting the vegetables gave an incredible flavour. The soup takes some time to prepare, but you can double the batch and freeze the remains for later.

1. Preheat the oven to 425°F (220°C). Place the root vegetables on a baking sheet lined with foil and sprayed with vegetable oil. Spray the vegetables with oil.

2. Roast for 20 minutes, just until tender. Set aside.

3. Meanwhile, dust the beef with flour. In a large skillet sprayed with vegetable oil, sear the beef just until browned on all sides (about 3 minutes). Set aside.

4. In a large saucepan, add the oil and sauté the onions with the garlic over medium heat for 5 minutes. Add the mushrooms and sauté for 5 minutes or until no longer wet. Add the beef and stock and cover and simmer for 30 minutes or until the beef is almost tender. Add the barley and root vegetables and cover and simmer for 20 minutes or just until the barley is cooked. Add the Worcestershire sauce and salt and pepper.

5. Ladle into individual bowls and garnish with parsley.

PREPARATION TIME 15 minutes · **COOKING TIME** 80 minutes ·
MAKE AHEAD Make the soup up to 2 days in advance. Add more stock when reheating. · **MAKES** 6 servings.

¾ cup (185 mL) diced potato

¾ cup (185 mL) diced sweet potato

¾ cup (185 mL) diced parsnip

8 oz (250 g) stewing beef, cut into small cubes

2 Tbsp (30 mL) all-purpose flour

2 tsp (10 mL) vegetable oil

1½ cups (375 mL) diced onions

2 tsp (10 mL) crushed garlic

2 cups (500 mL) sliced button mushrooms

4 cups (1 L) low-sodium beef stock

¼ cup (60 mL) barley

1 Tbsp (15 mL) Worcestershire sauce

pinch of salt and pepper

¼ cup (60 mL) chopped parsley

 ROSE'S TIP

The smaller you cut the beef cubes, the more quickly they will become tender. You can always use large cubes, but you may have to double the cooking time.

 HEALTH TIP

Stewing beef is very lean, which is why it has to be cooked on low heat for a longer time. An 8-ounce (250 g) serving has only 8 grams of fat compared to regular beef, which would have 40 grams of fat!

NUTRITION INFORMATION PER SERVING

Calories 243	Protein 11.9 g	Cholesterol 26 mg
Carbohydrates 27 g	Total fat 9.1 g	Sodium 440 mg
Fibre 4.7 g	Saturated fat 3.8 g	

PASTA AND BEAN SOUP (FAGIOLI)

This classic Italian soup is a medley of vegetables, beans and pasta. Serve it with some Italian bread for a wonderful lunch. Use any variety of beans you prefer, such as chickpeas, white kidney beans or white navy beans. Try adding a teaspoon of pesto as a garnish.

1. Spray a large nonstick saucepan with cooking oil. Add the vegetable oil and place over medium heat. Sauté the onions, carrots, celery and garlic for 5 minutes.

2. Stir in the stock, tomatoes, sugar, dried basil, oregano, salt, pepper and beans. Bring to a boil, reduce the heat to a simmer and cook covered for 15 minutes, stirring occasionally. Remove 2 cups (500 mL) of the soup, purée and add back to the soup.

3. Stir in the pasta. Cook for 5 to 8 minutes, until the pasta is tender but firm. Add half the Parmesan cheese. Ladle into individual bowls and garnish with Parmesan cheese and basil.

PREPARATION TIME 15 minutes · **COOKING TIME** 28 minutes ·
MAKE AHEAD Make the soup up to 2 days in advance, leaving out the pasta. Add the pasta when reheating and add more stock if necessary. · **MAKES** 6 servings.

2 tsp (10 mL) vegetable oil

½ cup (125 mL) chopped onion

⅓ cup (80 mL) chopped carrot

⅓ cup (80 mL) chopped celery

2 tsp (10 mL) minced fresh garlic

3½ cups (875 mL) low-sodium vegetable or chicken stock

one 19 oz can (540 mL) diced tomatoes

2 tsp (10 mL) granulated sugar

1½ tsp (7.5 mL) dried basil

1 tsp (5 mL) dried oregano

pinch of salt and pepper

3 cups (750 mL) canned red kidney beans, drained and rinsed (about 1½ 19 oz/540 mL cans)

⅓ cup (80 mL) elbow macaroni or small shell pasta

⅓ cup (80 mL) grated Parmesan cheese (1¼ oz/40 g)

¼ cup (60 mL) chopped fresh basil or parsley

ROSE'S TIP

If you like the taste of
freshly cooked beans
instead of canned ones, use
the quick-soak-and-cook
method. Bring the beans
and water to a boil, cover
and boil for 2 minutes. Let
sit for 1 hour. Drain the
water and add fresh water,
bring to a boil, cover and
simmer just until beans
are tender.

 HEALTH TIP

The beans and pasta
combine to make this
soup a complete protein.
Perfect for vegetarians.
You don't have to combine
incomplete proteins at
the same meal to get an
entire protein. Just eat the
incomplete proteins within
a few hours of each other
and you'll get the complete
protein benefit.

NUTRITION INFORMATION PER SERVING

Calories 284	Protein 14.6 g	Cholesterol 3.5 mg
Carbohydrates 46.6 g	Total fat 4.2 g	Sodium 593 mg
Fibre 13.1 g	Saturated fat 1 g	

NAVY BEAN PESTO SOUP

These small pearl-like beans go so well with pesto. You can always substitute white kidney beans if necessary. Cooking your own beans will save you the excess sodium that is in canned beans.

1. Sauté the onion in oil until soft. Add the garlic and carrot and cook for 5 minutes. Add the red pepper and sauté for 2 minutes. Add the potato, salt and pepper, stock and beans and bring to a boil. Cover and simmer for 25 minutes just until the carrots and potatoes are soft.

2. Remove 2 cups (500 mL) of the soup mixture; purée until smooth and add back to the soup. Add the pesto and Parmesan cheese.

PREPARATION TIME 10 minutes · **COOKING TIME** 32 minutes ·

MAKE AHEAD Make the soup up to 2 days in advance. Add more stock when reheating. · **MAKES** 4 servings.

2 tsp (10 mL) vegetable oil

1½ cups (375 mL) diced onion

2 tsp (10 mL) crushed garlic

1 cup (250 mL) diced carrot

½ cup (125 mL) diced red bell pepper

1 cup (250 mL) diced potato

pinch of salt and pepper

3 cups (750 mL) low-sodium chicken stock

1 cup (250 mL) canned small white navy beans, drained and rinsed

3 Tbsp (45 mL) pesto (see Basil Pesto on page 371)

¼ cup (60 mL) grated Parmesan cheese (1 oz/30 g)

ROSE'S TIP

The addition of pesto highlights the flavour of the mild navy beans. Try making your own pesto to save on calories, fat and sodium (see Basil Pesto on page 371).

HEALTH TIP

One cup (250 mL) of cooked white navy beans has 76% of your daily fibre requirement, which helps to reduce the bad cholesterol (LDL) and contributes to heart health. It also has significant amounts of folate and magnesium.

NUTRITION INFORMATION PER SERVING

Calories 254	Protein 13.9 g	Cholesterol 9 mg
Carbohydrates 31.8 g	Total fat 7.9 g	Sodium 569 mg
Fibre 6.4 g	Saturated fat 3.1 g	

TUSCAN WHITE BEAN SOUP WITH PROSCIUTTO

You'll feel like you're in Tuscany when enjoying this soup. Have a glass of wine and some wonderful bread, and you've got a meal! You can leave out the prosciutto if you want it vegetarian.

1. Sauté the prosciutto until crisp (about 3 minutes). Drain off the fat and crumble the prosciutto. Set aside.

2. Heat the oil in a large soup pot. Sauté the onions for 5 minutes. Add the carrots and sauté for 3 minutes. Add the garlic, basil, oregano, bay leaves, potato, stock, salt and pepper, and beans.

3. Cover and simmer for 20 minutes. Remove 2 cups (500 mL), purée and add back to the soup. Add the spinach and cook for 2 minutes. Garnish with Parmesan cheese and the sautéed prosciutto.

PREPARATION TIME 15 minutes · **COOKING TIME** 33 minutes ·
MAKE AHEAD Make up to 2 days in advance, but add cheese and spinach just before reheating. Add more stock if necessary. · **MAKES** 6 servings.

 ROSE'S TIP
I purchase whole Parmesan cheese wedges, grate the cheese, place it in containers and keep them in the freezer. Perfect for cooking purposes.

 HEALTH TIP
When bay leaves are cooked, they release powerful antioxidants. The best nutrition will come from fresh bay leaves with the darkest green colour. They have a milder flavour than dried ones, so use more.

4 slices prosciutto (2 oz/60 g)

2 tsp (10 mL) vegetable oil

1½ cups (375 mL) chopped onions

1 cup (250 mL) chopped carrots

2 tsp (10 mL) crushed garlic

1½ tsp (7.5 mL) dried basil

1 tsp (5 mL) dried oregano

2 dried bay leaves

1½ cups (375 mL) chopped potato

3½ cups (875 mL) low-sodium chicken stock

pinch of salt and pepper

7½ oz (213 mL) can white kidney beans, drained and rinsed

2 cups (500 mL) baby spinach leaves

¼ cup (60 mL) grated Parmesan cheese (1 oz/30 g)

NUTRITION INFORMATION PER SERVING

Calories 182	Protein 11.1 g	Cholesterol 9 mg
Carbohydrates 23.7 g	Total fat 4.8 g	Sodium 486 mg
Fibre 5.7 g	Saturated fat 2 g	

BLACK BEAN SOUP WITH AVOCADO

This creamy, rich-tasting soup is very nutritious. I like to serve it garnished with reduced-fat sour cream, diced plum tomatoes or a sprinkle of shredded cheddar cheese. If you cook your own black beans, use the quick-soak-and-cook method (see Rose's tip on page 113). You'll need 1 cup (250 mL) of dried beans, and they'll take about 40 minutes to cook.

1. Spray a nonstick saucepan with cooking oil, add the vegetable oil and place over medium heat. Cook the onion, carrot and garlic, stirring occasionally, for 5 minutes or until softened.

2. Set aside ½ cup (125 mL) of the black beans. Add the remaining beans, stock, sugar and cumin to the vegetable mixture. Bring to a boil, then reduce the heat to medium-low. Cover and cook for 15 minutes or until the carrots are tender.

3. Purée the soup in a blender or food processor, working in batches if necessary. Return the purée to the saucepan. Stir in the reserved beans.

4. Ladle into individual bowls and garnish with cilantro and avocado and sour cream (if using).

PREPARATION TIME 10 minutes · **COOKING TIME** 20 minutes ·
MAKE AHEAD Make the soup up to 2 days in advance. Add more stock when reheating. · **MAKES** 4 servings.

NUTRITION INFORMATION PER SERVING

Calories 140	Protein 8.2 g	Cholesterol 0 mg
Carbohydrates 25 g	Total fat 3.2 g	Sodium 460 mg
Fibre 7.1 g	Saturated fat 0.2 g	

2 tsp (10 mL) vegetable oil

1 cup (250 mL) chopped onion

1 cup (250 mL) chopped carrot

2 tsp (10 mL) minced fresh garlic

one 19 oz (540 mL) can black beans, drained and rinsed

2½ cups (625 mL) low-sodium chicken or vegetable stock

½ tsp (2.5 mL) granulated sugar

¾ tsp (4 mL) cumin

¼ cup (60 mL) chopped cilantro or parsley

¼ cup (60 mL) diced avocado and reduced-fat sour cream (optional)

ROSE'S TIP
This is a great soup to freeze. Place in large Ziploc bags and freeze for up to 2 months. If it's slightly watery when cooking, simmer without a lid and it will thicken.

HEALTH TIP
Cumin has a long history of being used as a treatment for indigestion and diarrhea. It stimulates the liver to secrete more bile, which helps in the breakdown of fats and absorption of nutrients, leading to better digestion.

ROASTED CAULIFLOWER SOUP WITH CRISP PROSCIUTTO CRUMBS

Roasting the cauliflower makes this soup sensational. You can omit the prosciutto if you want it vegetarian and add a couple of tablespoons (30 mL) of grated Parmesan cheese.

1. In 450°F (230°C) oven, place the cauliflower on a baking sheet lined with foil and sprayed with vegetable oil. Drizzle the olive oil overtop and sprinkle with salt and pepper. Bake for 30 minutes, turning halfway.

2. In a soup pan, add the oil and sauté the onion and garlic until soft. Add the stock, potato and cauliflower. Cover and simmer for 20 minutes.

3. Add to a large food processor along with the milk and purée until smooth.

4. In a small skillet, sauté the prosciutto for 5 minutes or until crisp. Crumble.

5. Serve with the sautéed prosciutto.

PREPARATION TIME 15 minutes · **COOKING TIME** 55 minutes ·

MAKE AHEAD Make the soup up to 2 days in advance. Add more stock when reheating. · **MAKES** 6 servings.

8 cups (2 L) of cauliflower florets (1 large head)

2 tsp (10 mL) olive oil

pinch of salt and pepper

2 tsp (10 mL) vegetable oil

1 cup (250 mL) diced onion

2 tsp (10 mL) crushed garlic

4 cups (1 L) low-sodium chicken stock

1 cup (250 mL) diced peeled potato

½ cup (125 mL) canned evaporated 2% milk

3 slices thinly sliced prosciutto (1½ oz/45 g)

 ROSE'S TIP
You can also substitute broccoli for the cauliflower if you wish. I would avoid using frozen vegetables, since the water content is too high for roasting.

 HEALTH TIP
One cup (250 mL) of raw cauliflower contains 86% of your daily vitamin C requirement and half your daily fibre requirement.

NUTRITION INFORMATION PER SERVING

Calories 176	Protein 10.8 g	Cholesterol 15 mg
Carbohydrates 21.6 g	Total fat 5.4 g	Sodium 519 mg
Fibre 3.8 g	Saturated fat 2 g	

THAI SEAFOOD STEW

The Italian version is known as cioppino; I have just added a Thai twist. This stew is wonderful served with salad and a French baguette for dipping. The light coconut milk is the magic ingredient here, making this a healthy version.

1. In a large nonstick skillet sprayed with cooking spray, heat the oil over medium heat; cook the onions and garlic for 5 minutes. Stir in the tomatoes, stock, fish sauce, brown sugar and lemongrass. Bring to a boil. Reduce the heat to a simmer, cover and cook for 5 minutes.

2. Stir in the seafood, cover and cook for 3 minutes or just until the mussels open and the seafood is just cooked. Do not overcook. Stir in the coconut milk and hot sauce and cook for 1 minute. Garnish with cilantro and serve.

PREPARATION TIME About 15 minutes • **COOKING TIME** About 15 minutes • **MAKE AHEAD** Make the soup base up to a day in advance. Add the seafood just before serving. • **MAKES** 6 servings.

ROSE'S TIP
Buy the freshest fish possible for this dish. You can use any variety of fish and seafood. Clam juice is easier to find in your supermarket than fish stock. You should find it in the canned fish aisles.

HEALTH TIP
Lemongrass contains several flavonoids that function as antioxidants and anti-inflammatory agents that can kill cancer cells. You can add 1 tsp (5 mL) minced lemongrass to your tea and get these benefits.

---

2 tsp (10 mL) vegetable oil

1 cup (250 mL) chopped onions

2 tsp (10 mL) minced garlic

2 cups (500 mL) seeded, chopped plum tomatoes

½ cup (125 mL) clam juice or low-sodium fish stock

1 Tbsp (15 mL) fish sauce or oyster sauce

1 Tbsp (15 mL) packed brown sugar

1 stalk lemongrass, finely chopped or 2 tsp (10 mL) grated lemon rind

16 mussels

8 oz (250 g) deveined peeled shrimp

8 oz (250 g) scallops

½ cup (125 mL) light coconut milk

1 tsp (5 mL) Asian hot sauce

¼ cup (60 mL) chopped fresh cilantro or parsley

NUTRITION INFORMATION PER SERVING

Calories 172	Protein 21 g	Cholesterol 82 mg
Carbohydrates 10.8 g	Total fat 5 g	Sodium 290 mg
Fibre 1.4 g	Saturated fat 1.5 g	

SANDWICHES & WRAPS

PANINI CLUBHOUSE WITH CRISP PROSCIUTTO, AVOCADO AND CHEESE

Panini—grilled sandwiches filled with vegetables—have taken the place of regular sandwiches. I like this take on a clubhouse sandwich. I use prosciutto instead of bacon since it has less fat and fewer calories. One ounce (30 g) of prosciutto has 50 calories and 3 grams of fat, whereas bacon has 130 calories and 10 grams of fat per ounce (30 g). Sautéing prosciutto gives it the texture of bacon.

1. Spray a nonstick skillet with cooking oil and place over medium heat. Sauté the prosciutto for 5 minutes or just until dry and beginning to crisp. Remove from the pan, cool slightly and crumble. Wipe the skillet and respray.

2. Working with one at a time, pound the chicken breasts between two sheets of waxed paper to an even ¼-inch (6 mm) thickness. Sauté the chicken for 5 minutes, or just until cooked and no longer pink in the centre, turning halfway. Cool for 5 minutes, then dice.

3. Combine the mayonnaise, lemon juice, mustard, garlic and pepper in a small bowl and mix thoroughly. Spread evenly over the entire surface of the tortillas. Scatter the chicken, prosciutto, cheese, tomato, onion and avocado overtop. Fold in the sides of each tortilla and roll it up tightly.

4. Preheat a nonstick grill pan to hot and spray with cooking oil. Sear the rolls on both sides until browned, approximately 2 minutes per side. Slice in half before serving.

PREPARATION TIME 20 minutes · **COOKING TIME** 14 minutes · **MAKE AHEAD** Make the panini early in the day. Cover and refrigerate and heat just before serving. · **MAKES** 8 servings.

NUTRITION INFORMATION PER SERVING (½ WRAP)

Calories 143	Protein 12 g	Cholesterol 28 mg
Carbohydrates 12 g	Total fat 6.1 g	Sodium 333 mg
Fibre 1.6 g	Saturated fat 2.2 g	

2 oz (60 g) sliced prosciutto

8 oz (250 g) boneless skinless chicken breast

2 Tbsp (30 mL) reduced-fat mayonnaise

2 tsp (10 mL) lemon juice

1 tsp (5 mL) Dijon mustard

½ tsp (2.5 mL) crushed fresh garlic

pinch of ground black pepper

4 large whole wheat tortillas

⅔ cup (160 mL) grated Parmesan or Swiss cheese (2½ oz/75 g)

⅓ cup (80 mL) diced, seeded plum tomatoes

⅓ cup (80 mL) diced sweet onion

½ diced ripe avocado

ROSE'S TIP

If you love making panini and grilled cheese sandwiches, invest in a grill press. The heat is easier to control.

HEALTH TIP

One tablespoon (15 mL) of Dijon mustard contains only 15 calories and 0 grams of fat compared to mayonnaise, which has 90 calories and 10 grams of fat per tablespoon (15 mL).

SPINACH, CHICKEN AND HUMMUS WRAP

This is a wrap I developed for the Pickle Barrel chain of restaurants in Toronto. When the customers want a healthier wrap, this is what they order. The combination of spinach, sautéed chicken and hummus is a winner. Homemade hummus always has considerably fewer calories and less fat than the store-bought type.

1. Working with one at a time, pound the chicken breasts to an even ½-inch (1 cm) thickness between two sheets of waxed paper.

2. Spray a nonstick grill pan with cooking oil and sauté the chicken for approximately 8 minutes or until no longer pink in the centre. Slice into thin strips.

3. Stir the green and red pepper, onion, feta, tomatoes, olives, oil, basil and garlic together in a large bowl.

4. Spread the hummus over the entire surface of the tortillas. Place the vegetable mixture over the hummus. Scatter the spinach leaves overtop and add the chicken. Roll the bottom of each tortilla up and over the filling, fold in both sides, and continue to roll up tightly. Cut each roll in half before serving.

PREPARATION TIME 15 minutes · **COOKING TIME** 8 minutes ·
MAKE AHEAD Prepare early in the day, cover and refrigerate. ·
MAKES 8 servings.

8 oz (250 g) boneless skinless chicken breast

1 cup (250 mL) sliced green bell pepper

1 cup (250 mL) sliced red bell pepper

⅓ cup (80 mL) sliced red or sweet onion

⅓ cup (80 mL) crumbled reduced-fat feta cheese (1½ oz/45 g)

½ cup (125 mL) chopped rehydrated sun-dried tomatoes

⅓ cup (80 mL) diced black olives

1 Tbsp (15 mL) olive oil

1½ tsp (7.5 mL) dried basil

1½ tsp (7.5 mL) minced fresh garlic

⅔ cup (160 mL) hummus (see Hummus on page 363)

4 large whole wheat tortillas (or flavour of your choice)

1 cup (250 mL) baby spinach leaves

 ROSE'S TIP
Try different greens such as arugula or even baby kale instead of the spinach.

 HEALTH TIP
Hummus can be a good source of protein in vegetarian diets.

NUTRITION INFORMATION PER SERVING (½ WRAP)

Calories 256	Protein 13 g	Cholesterol 22 mg
Carbohydrates 11 g	Total fat 10.5 g	Sodium 280 mg
Fibre 4.5 g	Saturated fat 1.5 g	

COBB SALAD WRAPS WITH CHICKEN, AVOCADO AND BLACK BEANS

A cobb salad traditionally has loads of chicken, blue cheese, bacon and heavy dressing. I've lightened up this classic and tossed the main ingredients into a wrap. It's delicious.

1. Lightly coat a nonstick grill pan with vegetable spray and set over medium heat. Grill the chicken for 4 minutes on each side or until no longer pink. Cool slightly, then slice thinly.

2. Combine the tomatoes, red pepper, avocado, black beans, green onions and parsley in a large bowl. Add the lemon juice, sour cream, olive oil, garlic, chili sauce and salt and pepper and mix well.

3. Spread half of each tortilla with some of the tomato mixture. Top with slices of chicken and the shredded cheese. Fold the 2 sides in and roll up. Place the wraps in a clean grill pan and cook for 5 minutes, turning halfway, just enough to warm through. (Or heat in a 400°F/200°C oven for 5 minutes until warm.) Cut in half and serve.

PREPARATION TIME 15 minutes • **COOKING TIME** 12 minutes •
MAKE AHEAD Make wraps up to 2 hours in advance. Cover and refrigerate. •
MAKES 8 servings.

8 oz (250 g) boneless skinless chicken breasts (about 2 breasts)

½ cup (125 mL) diced plum tomatoes

½ cup (125 mL) diced red bell pepper

½ cup (125 mL) diced ripe avocado

⅓ cup (80 mL) canned black beans, drained and rinsed

¼ cup (60 mL) finely chopped green onions

¼ cup (60 mL) chopped parsley

4 tsp (20 mL) lemon juice

1 Tbsp (15 mL) reduced-fat sour cream

1 Tbsp (15 mL) olive oil

1 tsp (5 mL) finely chopped garlic

½ tsp (2.5 mL) hot chili sauce

pinch of salt and pepper

4 large whole wheat flour tortillas

½ cup (125 mL) shredded aged cheddar cheese (1½ oz/45 g)

 ROSE'S TIP
Low-carbohydrate tortillas contain about a third of the carbohydrates of regular tortillas, which have about 40 grams of carbohydrates.

 HEALTH TIP
Most cheeses have a reduced-fat version. For example, ½ cup (125 mL) of regular cheddar has 18 grams of fat, whereas a light cheddar has only 11 grams of fat.

NUTRITION INFORMATION PER SERVING (½ WRAP)

Calories 132	Protein 11 g	Cholesterol 19 mg
Carbohydrates 19 g	Total fat 5.1 g	Sodium 193 mg
Fibre 2.4 g	Saturated fat 1.2 g	

CHICKEN SHAWARMAS (MIDDLE EASTERN PITAS)

Often beef or pork is used instead of chicken in shawarmas. The chicken skin is traditionally not removed, which adds excess fat and calories. My version is much lighter.

1. **TO MAKE THE SAUCE** Combine the hummus, lemon juice, sour cream, garlic and salt and pepper in a small bowl. Set aside.

2. **TO MAKE THE CHICKEN** Place the chicken between 2 pieces of waxed paper, pound it flat and cut into thin strips. Coat the chicken strips with the flour. Lightly coat a nonstick skillet with cooking spray and set over medium-high heat. Add the oil and onion and sauté for 5 minutes or just until browned. Add the chicken and sauté for 10 minutes, stirring constantly, until the chicken is no longer pink. Respray the pan if necessary.

3. **TO MAKE THE PITAS** Slice each pita in half. Divide the chicken and onion mixture among the half-pitas. Sprinkle with tomatoes, cucumber and cilantro and spoon the hummus sauce over the pitas.

PREPARATION TIME 20 minutes · **COOKING TIME** 15 minutes ·
MAKE AHEAD Make the chicken mixture and hummus sauce early in the day. Reheat the chicken gently just to warm and assemble the pitas. ·
MAKES 8 servings.

Sauce
¾ cup (185 mL) hummus (see Hummus, page 363)

1½ Tbsp (22.5 mL) lemon juice

2 Tbsp (30 mL) reduced-fat sour cream

1 tsp (5 mL) finely chopped garlic

pinch of salt and pepper

Chicken
12 oz (375 g) boneless skinless chicken breasts (about 3 breasts)

¼ cup (60 mL) all-purpose flour

2 tsp (10 mL) vegetable oil

1½ cups (375 mL) sliced onion

Pitas
4 large whole wheat pitas

½ cup (125 mL) chopped tomatoes

½ cup (125 mL) chopped cucumber

¼ cup (60 mL) chopped cilantro

 ROSE'S TIP
Dusting the chicken with flour maintains the moisture without having to use excess oil when sautéing.

 HEALTH TIP
One large white flour pita has only 1.5 grams of fibre. The whole wheat pita has close to 5 grams.

NUTRITION INFORMATION PER SERVING (½ PITA)

Calories 212	Protein 14 g	Cholesterol 25 mg
Carbohydrates 25 g	Total fat 6.7 g	Sodium 240 mg
Fibre 3.8 g	Saturated fat 1.3 g	

CALIFORNIA CHICKEN, AVOCADO AND ROASTED RED PEPPER GRILLED CHEESE

The owner of the Pickle Barrel opened Glow Press, a healthy option for grilled cheese sandwiches at Yorkdale Shopping Centre in Toronto. I had the opportunity to create my own recipes, and here is one of my favourites, easy to duplicate at home.

1. TO MAKE THE SANDWICH Preheat the oven to 425°F (220°C). Line a small baking sheet with foil sprayed with vegetable oil. Roast the bell pepper until charred (about 20 minutes). Cool, then remove the skin and slice thinly.

2. Meanwhile, either grill or sauté the chicken breast in a nonstick skillet sprayed with vegetable oil just until no longer pink or temperature reaches 165°F (74°C). Cool, then slice thinly.

3. TO MAKE THE SAUCE Combine the mayo and chipotle. Spread over the bread slices. Over 3 slices of the bread, divide the chicken, cheese, bell pepper, avocado and cilantro. Place the other bread slices overtop.

4. Spray vegetable oil over the outside of the sandwiches and grill for at least 5 minutes, turning halfway just until browned and the cheese begins to melt.

PREPARATION TIME 10 minutes · **COOKING TIME** 25 minutes ·
MAKE AHEAD Prepare sandwich up to 2 hours in advance. Grill just before serving. · **MAKES** 3 servings.

Sandwich

1 small red bell pepper, top and seeds removed and cut into 4 wedges

4 oz (120 g) boneless skinless chicken breast

6 slices of crusty bread (½ inch/1 cm thick)

¾ cup (185 mL) grated Monterey Jack or aged cheddar cheese (2¼ oz/65 g)

⅓ cup (80 mL) sliced avocado

3 Tbsp (45 mL) chopped cilantro

Sauce

3 Tbsp (45 mL) reduced-fat mayonnaise

1½ tsp (7.5 mL) chopped chipotle pepper or jalapeños

ROSE'S TIP

Monterey Jack cheese origi-
nated along the central
California coast. It is a
semi-firm cheese with a
creamy, mild flavour. It is
perfect for grilled cheese
sandwiches, since it
melts well.

 HEALTH TIP

Typical grilled cheese
sandwiches are loaded with
calories and fat because the
bread slices are coated in
butter or oil. By spraying
the bread with vegetable
oil you can save over
200 calories and 28 grams
of fat per sandwich.

NUTRITION INFORMATION PER SERVING (1 SANDWICH)

Calories 287	Protein 18.9 g	Cholesterol 38 mg
Carbohydrates 25.1 g	Total fat 10.3 g	Sodium 380 mg
Fibre 2.6 g	Saturated fat 5.6 g	

PULLED CHICKEN BURRITOS

Pulled meats have become a trendy food item. The key is to cook the meat on lower heat until it's very tender, then with two forks separate the meat into tiny strands. This is the process called "pulling."

1. Preheat the oven to 425°F (220°C). Line a baking sheet with foil.

2. Brush the chicken with the barbecue sauce. In a hot skillet or grill pan, cook the chicken breast on medium-low heat just until no longer pink or until temperature reaches 165°F (74°C), about 8 minutes per side. Let cool, then pull the chicken apart with two forks. Set aside.

3. In a large skillet sprayed with vegetable oil, add the onions and garlic and sauté for 3 minutes. Add the corn and sauté just until browned, about 3 minutes. Add the bell pepper, cumin and salt and pepper and sauté just until tender. Add the chipotle peppers, beans, cilantro, lemon juice, pulled chicken and brown rice.

4. Lay out the tortillas and place the chicken filling in the middle of each tortilla. Place the guacamole, cheese and salsa overtop. Fold in the corners and wrap tightly.

5. Bake for 5 minutes, just until hot. Cut in half.

PREPARATION TIME 20 minutes • **COOKING TIME** 21 minutes •
MAKE AHEAD Make wraps early in the day. Bake just before serving. •
MAKES 6 servings.

4 oz (125 g) boneless skinless chicken breast

2 Tbsp (25 mL) store-bought barbecue sauce

1 cup (250 mL) chopped onion

1 tsp (5 mL) crushed garlic

½ cup (125 mL) corn

½ cup (125 mL) chopped red pepper

¼ tsp (1 mL) cumin

pinch of salt and pepper

1½ tsp (7.5 mL) canned chopped chipotle peppers or jalapeño peppers

½ cup (125 mL) canned black beans, drained and rinsed

¼ cup (60 mL) chopped cilantro

1 Tbsp (15 mL) lemon juice

1½ cups (375 mL) cooked brown rice (½ cup/125 mL raw rice)

3 large flour tortillas

⅓ cup (80 mL) guacamole (see Guacamole on page 362)

¾ cup (185 mL) grated Monterey Jack cheese or aged cheddar (2¼ oz/65 g)

¼ cup (60 mL) medium salsa

ROSE'S TIP

Chipotle peppers are
small peppers that have
been dried by a smoking
process that gives them a
dark colour and distinct
smoky flavour. You can use
what's needed and freeze
any remaining. Defrost
what you need and use over
a period of time.

 HEALTH TIP

Pulled meats of any kind,
such as beef brisket and
pork, can be a lean meal as
long as you remove the fat
and skin after cooking.

NUTRITION INFORMATION PER SERVING (½ WRAP)

Calories 220	Protein 12.9 g	Cholesterol 20 mg
Carbohydrates 29.6 g	Total fat 6.2 g	Sodium 430 mg
Fibre 4.3 g	Saturated fat 2.8 g	

CALIFORNIA AVOCADO AND SURIMI WRAP

This recipe came to me one day when I couldn't decide if I wanted sushi or a wrap for lunch. What about a combination? I took the elements of a California roll and put them into a wrap, and it turned out great!

1. TO MAKE THE RICE In a saucepan, combine the rice and water. Bring to a boil and boil for 1 minute. Reduce the heat to low; cover and cook for 12 minutes. Remove from the heat and let stand covered for 10 minutes. Meanwhile, in a small saucepan, combine the vinegar and sugar. Bring to a boil, stirring to dissolve sugar. Remove from the heat.

2. Turn the rice out into a large bowl. Stir in the vinegar and sugar mixture. Cool.

3. In a bowl, stir together the surimi, cucumber, avocado, green onions, sesame seeds, soy sauce and cooled rice.

4. In a small bowl, combine the mayonnaise, sour cream and wasabi. Remove 2 Tbsp (30 mL) and add the remainder to the crabmeat mixture.

5. Spread 2 Tbsp (30 mL) of the reserved mayonnaise mixture thinly over the tortillas, about 2 tsp (10 mL) per tortilla.

6. Divide the crab mixture evenly among the tortillas, placing on the bottom third of each tortilla. Roll once away from you, fold in both sides and continue to roll. Cut in half to serve.

PREPARATION TIME 20 minutes • **COOKING TIME** 10 minutes •
MAKE AHEAD Prepare wraps early in the day, cover and keep refrigerated. • **MAKES** 12 servings.

Sushi rice

¾ cup (185 mL) sushi rice

¾ cup (185 mL) water

1 Tbsp (15 mL) rice vinegar

1½ tsp (7.5 mL) granulated sugar

Filling

6 oz (175 g) imitation (surimi) or real crabmeat, chopped and squeezed dry

¾ cup (185 mL) diced peeled English cucumber

½ cup (125 mL) diced avocado (half a medium avocado)

⅓ cup (80 mL) chopped green onions

1½ tsp (7.5 mL) toasted sesame seeds

2 Tbsp (30 mL) low-sodium soy sauce

3½ Tbsp (55 mL) reduced-fat mayonnaise

3 Tbsp (45 mL) reduced-fat sour cream

½ tsp (2.5 mL) wasabi (Japanese horseradish)

6 large flour tortillas

ROSE'S TIP

Crabmeat is always a better
choice, since it's a pure
fish, but surimi is easy to
use and very affordable.
This is imitation crabmeat
consisting of a mixture of
various white fish, mostly
Alaskan pollock. The fish
is formed into various
shapes before cooking.

 HEALTH TIP

A 3-ounce (90 g) serv-
ing of surimi contains
only 87 calories with
1 gram of fat but has about
700 mg of sodium. The
same size serving of crab
has 60 calories, 0.5 grams
of fat and 395 mg of
sodium.

NUTRITION INFORMATION PER SERVING (½ WRAP)

Calories 191	Protein 5 g	Cholesterol 5 mg
Carbohydrates 30 g	Total fat 5 g	Sodium 460 mg
Fibre 0.8 g	Saturated fat 1.4 g	

FALAFEL WITH TAHINI LEMON DRESSING

Middle Eastern cuisine is known for its falafels—chickpea-based deep-fried balls served with tahini sauce. My version is baked, with a light lemony and creamy tahini dressing. You can make double the falafels by making them smaller. Serve them in mini pitas as an appetizer. You'll have a few tablespoons of leftover dressing; store it in the refrigerator and use it as a salad dressing or sauce over chicken or fish.

1. TO MAKE THE FALAFELS Preheat the oven to 400°F (200°C). Spray a baking sheet with cooking oil.

2. Combine the chickpeas, green onion, cilantro, breadcrumbs, tahini, lemon juice, garlic, baking powder, cumin, egg and pepper in a food processor. Pulse on and off until well-mixed. Form into 16 balls (about 2 Tbsp/30 mL each). Flatten slightly and place on the prepared baking sheet.

3. Bake in the centre of the oven, turning once, for 15 to 20 minutes or until golden.

4. Wrap the pitas in foil and heat in a 400°F (200°C) oven for 10 minutes. Place two falafels in the pocket of each pita half. Drizzle about 2 Tbsp (30 mL) of dressing over each. Tuck the tomato slices and lettuce inside each pita.

PREPARATION TIME 20 minutes · **COOKING TIME** 25 minutes · **MAKE AHEAD** Make the falafels and sauce a day in advance. Gently reheat the falafels in a 300°F (150°C) oven for 10 minutes, then assemble the pitas. · **MAKES** 8 servings.

Falafels

one 19 oz (540 mL) can chickpeas, drained and rinsed

¼ cup (60 mL) chopped green onion

¼ cup (60 mL) chopped fresh cilantro or parsley

¼ cup (60 mL) unseasoned dry breadcrumbs

2 Tbsp (30 mL) tahini (sesame seed paste)

1 Tbsp (15 mL) fresh lemon juice

1½ tsp (7.5 mL) minced fresh garlic

¼ tsp (1 mL) baking powder

¼ tsp (1 mL) ground cumin

1 egg

pinch of ground black pepper

⅔ cup (160 mL) Tahini Lemon Dressing (page 366)

4 large pitas, sliced in half

8 tomato slices and 4 chopped romaine lettuce leaves

ROSE'S TIP

Tahini is a thick paste made of ground sesame seeds. You can find it in your supermarket in the ethnic foods section. If you can't find it, you can substitute another nut butter like peanut butter.

 HEALTH TIP

One cup (250 mL) of canned chickpeas has 660 mg of sodium! Rinsing them well with water will eliminate 30% of the sodium.

NUTRITION INFORMATION PER SERVING (½ PITA WITH 2 FALAFELS)

Calories 242	Protein 8 g	Cholesterol 29 mg
Carbohydrates 33 g	Total fat 8 g	Sodium 433 mg
Fibre 4.1 g	Saturated fat 1.3 g	

PORTOBELLO PITAS WITH RED BELL PEPPER HUMMUS AND GOAT CHEESE

When you're in the mood for a vegetarian alternative, look no further than this. Portobellos are called the meat of the vegetable family. They have a firm texture and delicious taste and are wonderful with hummus and goat cheese.

1. **TO MAKE THE FILLING** On either a barbecue or a nonstick grill pan sprayed with cooking spray, grill the mushrooms over medium-high heat for 12 minutes, turning halfway or until tender and grill marked. Spray the mushrooms with vegetable spray if they look dry. Slice into thick slices.

2. Spread the inside of the pita halves with the hummus. Place half of the mushroom slices in each pita, sprinkle with cheese, and garnish with lettuce, tomatoes and onions.

PREPARATION TIME 10 minutes · **COOKING TIME** 12 minutes · **MAKE AHEAD** Make the hummus up to a day in advance. Cook the mushrooms early in the day. Assemble the sandwiches just before serving. · **MAKES** 6 servings.

Red Bell Pepper Hummus

¾ cup (185 mL) Red Bell Pepper Hummus (see page 365)

Wraps

3 large portobello mushroom caps, wiped (stems removed)

3 medium-sized pitas, sliced in half

½ cup (125 mL) crumbled goat cheese (2 oz/60 g)

lettuce

sliced tomatoes

sliced onions

 ROSE'S TIP

This is a vegetarian's dream meal, consisting of vegetables, beans and pitas as the grain.

 HEALTH TIP

A whole red pepper has over 300% of your daily vitamin C—more than orange juice or strawberries. Vitamin C is a powerful antioxidant and is also needed for the proper absorption of iron.

NUTRITION INFORMATION PER SERVING (½ PITA)

Calories 222	Protein 5.5 g	Cholesterol 33 mg
Carbohydrates 8.3 g	Total fat 1.6 g	Sodium 310 mg
Fibre 0.7 g	Saturated fat 0.4 g	

ROASTED VEGGIE
SANDWICH WITH BRIE

After tasting this sandwich, you might decide to go vegetarian! The grilled vegetables, pesto and brie are a sensational combination. And, yes, you can enjoy brie when you're eating light—just watch the amounts. Each sandwich contains only ½ ounce (15 grams), which you'll find is enough. For the rolls, I like to use either focaccia or sourdough rolls. If using store-bought pesto, remember it is higher in fat and calories than my homemade version (see Basil Pesto on page 371); use a smaller amount or thin it with a little water.

1. Preheat the oven to 425°F (220°C). Line a rimmed baking sheet with foil.

2. Place the onion, red pepper, mushroom and zucchini on the baking sheet. Spray foil lightly with cooking oil. Roast the vegetables, turning once, for 25 to 30 minutes or until tender. Remove and allow to cool.

3. While the vegetables are roasting, combine the pesto and sour cream in a small bowl.

4. Cut the roasted vegetables into pieces that fit the shape of the bread. Place them in a bowl and toss with the oil, vinegar and garlic.

5. Spread the pesto mixture over the bottom half of each roll. Top with the vegetable mixture and brie. Replace the top half of the roll and cut in half to serve.

PREPARATION TIME 15 minutes · **COOKING TIME** 25 minutes ·
MAKE AHEAD Make the sandwiches up to 4 hours in advance, keep covered and refrigerated. · **MAKES** 8 servings.

NUTRITION INFORMATION PER SERVING (½ SANDWICH)

Calories 187	Protein 6 g	Cholesterol 9 mg
Carbohydrates 29 g	Total fat 6 g	Sodium 298 mg
Fibre 2.5 g	Saturated fat 2.2 g	

½ large red onion, sliced

1 red bell pepper, cut into 8 wedges

1 large portobello mushroom, thickly sliced

1 zucchini, cut in 3 slices lengthwise

2 Tbsp (30 mL) store-bought or homemade pesto sauce (see Basil Pesto on page 371)

2 Tbsp (30 mL) reduced-fat sour cream

1 Tbsp (15 mL) olive oil

2 tsp (10 mL) balsamic vinegar

½ tsp (2.5 mL) minced fresh garlic

4 large rolls (3½ oz/110 g each), split

2 oz (60 g) brie, thinly sliced

ROSE'S TIP

If you want to reduce the calories of the bread roll by half, scoop out some of the inside bread.

HEALTH TIP

Red onions are packed with quercetin, which is an antioxidant that fights free radicals. It prevents and controls the formation of intestinal polyps that lead to cancer.

SMOKED SALMON AND AVOCADO WRAP

My version of a lox and cream cheese sandwich has fewer calories, less fat and more interesting and tasty ingredients! The light ricotta and cream cheese combination is the key substitute for regular cream cheese.

1. Purée the ricotta, cream cheese, goat cheese, mayonnaise, lemon juice, mustard, garlic and pepper in a small food processor, or with a hand beater, until smooth.

2. Divide the cheese mixture among the tortillas, spreading it to ¼ inch (6 mm) from the edges. Place the lettuce overtop.

3. Scatter the salmon, onion, avocado and capers over the lettuce. Roll the bottom of each tortilla up and over the filling, fold in the sides and roll the tortilla up tightly. Cut in half before serving.

PREPARATION TIME 15 minutes · **MAKE AHEAD** Prepare up to 2 hours in advance. · **MAKES** 8 servings.

 ROSE'S TIP
When buying Atlantic smoked salmon, look for salmon produced in Norway or on the east coast of Canada for the best quality.

 HEALTH TIP
If you want to avoid smoked fish, try buying gravlax, which is raw salmon cured with salt, sugar and dill. You can find it at specialty stores.

⅓ cup (80 mL) reduced-fat ricotta cheese (3 oz/90 g)

2 Tbsp (30 mL) reduced-fat cream cheese (1 oz/30 g)

⅓ cup (80 mL) goat cheese (3 oz/90 g)

2 Tbsp (30 mL) reduced-fat mayonnaise

2 tsp (10 mL) freshly squeezed lemon juice

1 tsp (5 mL) Dijon mustard

½ tsp (2.5 mL) crushed fresh garlic

pinch of ground black pepper

4 large tortillas (preferably whole wheat)

4 pieces leafy lettuce

4 oz (125 g) diced smoked salmon

½ cup (125 mL) diced red onion

½ cup (125 mL) diced ripe avocado

1 Tbsp (15 mL) capers

NUTRITION INFORMATION PER SERVING (½ WRAP)

Calories 124	Protein 7 g	Cholesterol 12 mg
Carbohydrates 14 g	Total fat 6.1 g	Sodium 324 mg
Fibre 1.8 g	Saturated fat 2.1 g	

AHI TUNA CLUB

For those who love seared tuna, this is the perfect sandwich for you.
Overcooking fresh tuna results in a dry texture.

1. Dip the tuna in sesame seeds, and in a hot skillet sprayed with vegetable oil, sear the tuna for about 2 minutes per side, depending upon the thickness. The tuna will continue to cook after searing. Remove from the heat, cool, then thinly slice.

2. Toast the bread slices.

3. Combine the guacamole, mayonnaise, wasabi and cilantro. Spread over the bread slices. Place the tomato slices, prosciutto and spinach leaves on 4 slices of the bread. Add the tuna. Place the other bread slices overtop and serve.

PREPARATION TIME 10 minutes · **COOKING TIME** 4 minutes ·

MAKE AHEAD Cook the tuna early in the day, refrigerate and slice before using. Assemble the sandwich just before serving. · **MAKES** 4 servings.

8 oz (250 g) raw ahi tuna

1 Tbsp (15 mL) sesame seeds

8 slices crusty bread (⅓ inch/ 1 cm thick)

⅓ cup (80 mL) guacamole (see Guacamole on page 362)

1 Tbsp (15 mL) reduced-fat mayonnaise

1 tsp (5 mL) wasabi

2 Tbsp (30 mL) chopped cilantro

12 thin slices plum tomato

4 pieces prosciutto (2 oz/60 g)

⅓ cup (80 mL) baby spinach leaves

 ROSE'S TIP

If you want to cook the tuna earlier in the day, just sear and place in the refrigerator for 10 minutes to prevent it from cooking through.

 HEALTH TIP

Traditional chicken club sandwiches are loaded with mayonnaise and three slices of bread, increasing the calories and fat to over double what's in the Ahi Tuna Club.

NUTRITION INFORMATION PER SERVING (1 SANDWICH)

Calories 330	Protein 24.1 g	Cholesterol 37 mg
Carbohydrates 39.2 g	Total fat 8 g	Sodium 600 mg
Fibre 4.7 g	Saturated fat 2 g	

LOBSTER GRILLED CHEESE

Lobster is definitely a luxury food item, but today you can find great frozen products in your grocery. You can always substitute shrimp, crabmeat or surimi (artificial crabmeat). The avocado, corn and jalapeño are a perfect match with seafood.

1. Sauté the corn in a skillet sprayed with vegetable oil for 5 minutes just until lightly charred. Place it in a bowl along with the avocado, jalapeño, onion, salt and pepper, lemon juice and olive oil.

2. Place the salsa over 4 slices of bread along with the lobster meat and cheese. Place the other slices overtop. Brush the mayo over the outside of the bread slices. Grill for 5 minutes or just until the bread is browned and the cheese is melted.

PREPARATION TIME 15 minutes · **COOKING TIME** 10 minutes ·
MAKE AHEAD Prepare the salsa up to 2 hours in advance. Assemble the sandwich just before serving. · **MAKES** 4 servings.

1 cup (250 mL) corn, drained and rinsed

½ cup (125 mL) diced avocado

1 tsp (5 mL) minced jalapeño

3 Tbsp (45 mL) diced red onion

pinch of salt and pepper

1½ Tbsp (22.5 mL) lemon juice

1½ tsp (7.5 mL) olive oil

8 slices crusty bread (½ inch/ 1 cm thick)

6 oz (175 g) lobster meat, chopped (if frozen and defrosted, squeeze out excess moisture)

1 cup (250 mL) grated Havarti cheese (or other mild cheese) (3 oz/90 g)

2 Tbsp (30 mL) reduced-fat mayonnaise

 ROSE'S TIP
A grilled cheese sandwich is best made with a sourdough crusty loaf. Cut the slices thinly (½ inch/1 cm) to save calories. One slice should weigh about 1½ oz (45 g), which contains about 100 calories.

 HEALTH TIP
If you use whole wheat bread, you will double your fibre. One slice of white bread has only 0.8 grams of fibre, whereas 1 slice of whole wheat has 2 grams of fibre.

NUTRITION INFORMATION PER SERVING (1 SANDWICH)

Calories 153	Protein 11 g	Cholesterol 7 mg
Carbohydrates 15.6 g	Total fat 4.8 g	Sodium 484 mg
Fibre 3.4 g	Saturated fat 1.1 g	

SHRIMP PO'BOYS

This is a classic Louisiana sandwich that is traditionally made with fried shrimp and a high-fat remoulade sauce. My version lightens it up by baking the shrimp balls and serving them with a reduced-fat mayonnaise ketchup sauce.

1. Preheat the oven to 400°F (200°C). Line a baking sheet with parchment paper.

2. In a large bowl or food processor, add the diced shrimp, mayonnaise, lemon juice and zest, garlic, egg, panko crumbs, red pepper, green onion, cilantro, salt and pepper, and hot sauce. Process on and off just until coarsely combined. Form into 18 (2 Tbsp/30 mL) balls.

3. Bake for 10 minutes.

4. TO MAKE THE SAUCE Combine the mayonnaise, ketchup, soy sauce and lemon juice.

5. Spread some of the sauce over the bread rolls. Add 3 balls on top, divide the lettuce and tomatoes overtop and serve with the extra sauce.

PREPARATION TIME 20 minutes · **COOKING TIME** 10 minutes ·
MAKE AHEAD Prepare the shrimp mixture and sauce early in the day.
Bake just before serving. · **MAKES** 6 servings.

8 oz (250 g) diced cleaned raw shrimp, cut into large pieces

3 Tbsp (45 mL) reduced-fat mayonnaise

1½ Tbsp (22.5 mL) lemon juice

2 tsp (10 mL) lemon zest

1 large clove garlic

1 egg

¾ cup (185 mL) panko crumbs

¼ cup (60 mL) finely diced red bell peppers

3 Tbsp (45 mL) finely diced green onion

3 Tbsp (45 mL) chopped cilantro

pinch of salt and pepper

1 tsp (5 mL) hot sauce

Sauce
½ cup (125 mL) reduced-fat mayonnaise

1½ Tbsp (22.5 mL) ketchup

1–2 tsp (5-10 mL) low-sodium soy sauce

1 tsp (5 mL) lemon juice

six 3 oz (90 g) whole wheat sandwich rolls

 ROSE'S TIP

When you're using shrimp in a recipe where it will be processed, you can buy small to medium shrimp and not spend a lot on jumbo shrimp.

 HEALTH TIP

Shrimp is a low-calorie and low-fat seafood. Four large shrimp contain only 30 calories with 0.5 grams of fat and 6 grams of protein.

½ cup (125 mL) chopped romaine lettuce

½ cup (125 mL) sliced plum tomatoes

NUTRITION INFORMATION PER SERVING (1 SANDWICH)

Calories 354	Protein 14.4 g	Cholesterol 78 mg
Carbohydrates 53.5 g	Total fat 5.3 g	Sodium 890 mg
Fibre 7.1 g	Saturated fat 1.9 g	

ROSE'S PHILADELPHIA CHEESE STEAK

Philly steaks—grilled thin steak topped with loads of cooked vegetables, cheese and mayo—can be a healthy meat sandwich if prepared well. The original version, naturally, from Philadelphia, contains a lot of calories and fat. Try my lighter version of this classic sandwich.

1. Preheat the oven to 425°F (220°C). Line a baking sheet with foil.

2. Spray a large nonstick skillet with cooking oil, add the vegetable oil and place over medium heat. Add the onions and sauté for 8 minutes. Add the garlic, brown sugar, salt and pepper, and bell pepper. Sauté for another 5 minutes. Set aside and keep warm.

3. Meanwhile, spray a nonstick grill or skillet with cooking oil and place it over high heat. Cook the steak just until done to your preference, approximately 5 to 8 minutes. Cool for 5 minutes before cutting it into thin slices. Add it to the vegetable mixture.

4. Combine the mayonnaise, sour cream and horseradish. Spread thinly over both sides of the rolls. Divide the filling among the 4 rolls, sprinkle with the cheese and replace the top half of the bun. Place on the prepared baking sheet and bake for 5 minutes. Slice in half before serving.

PREPARATION TIME 15 minutes · **COOKING TIME** 18 minutes ·
MAKE AHEAD Cook the beef and vegetables early in the day. Assemble and heat just before serving. · **MAKES** 4 servings.

---

2 tsp (10 mL) vegetable oil

2 cups (500 mL) sliced onions

2 tsp (10 mL) crushed fresh garlic

2 tsp (10 mL) brown sugar

⅛ tsp (0.5 mL) each salt and ground black pepper

1 cup (250 mL) sliced red bell pepper

1 cup (250 mL) sliced green bell pepper

8 oz (250 g) grilling steak

2 Tbsp (30 mL) reduced-fat mayonnaise

3 Tbsp (45 mL) reduced-fat sour cream

2 tsp (10 mL) jarred horseradish

4 small (6-inch/15 cm) whole-grain rolls, split

¾ cup (185 mL) grated provolone or Gruyère cheese (2¼ oz/65 g)

ROSE'S TIP

You can substitute chicken breast, tofu or shrimp for the beef. There's no mandate to make this a beef dish!

 HEALTH TIP

Horseradish is a member of the cruciferous vegetable group. This means it's a powerful antioxidant that can fight cancer of the lungs and colon. It's also high in vitamin C and contains virtually no calories, so use it liberally in sauces, in dips or with your meat.

NUTRITION INFORMATION PER SERVING (1 SANDWICH)

Calories 340	Protein 24 g	Cholesterol 56 mg
Carbohydrates 18 g	Total fat 16 g	Sodium 200 mg
Fibre 4 g	Saturated fat 7 g	

HOISIN MEATBALL SUB SANDWICH

Forget your next trip to the submarine shop. A make-it-yourself sub at home will save you calories, fat and sodium and taste better!

1. Combine the soy sauce and hoisin sauce, garlic, ginger, sesame oil and vinegar. Set aside.

2. Combine the beef, breadcrumbs, onions, cilantro, 2 Tbsp (30 mL) of the sauce, ginger, garlic and egg until well combined. Make into small 1-inch (2.5 cm) balls (about 36). Brush with some of the remaining sauce. Bake at 400°F (200°C) for 12 minutes or just until cooked.

3. Sauté the onions in a nonstick skillet sprayed with vegetable oil until tender. Add the mushrooms and sauté until soft; add the bell peppers and sauté until tender. Add 3 Tbsp (45 mL) of the sauce mixture.

4. Toast the submarine buns. Divide the meatballs overtop the buns and add the sautéed vegetables. Drizzle remaining sauce mixture overtop and garnish with the sesame seeds.

PREPARATION TIME 20 minutes · **COOKING TIME** 15 minutes ·

MAKE AHEAD Make the meatballs and stir-fry early in the day. Gently reheat the meatballs in a 300°F (150°C) oven for 10 minutes, reheat the stir-fry and assemble. · **MAKES** 6 servings.

 ROSE'S TIP
You can reduce the amount of sodium in soy sauce by diluting it to a ratio of half soy sauce, half water.

 HEALTH TIP
If you're looking for a gluten-free soy sauce, buy tamari made by San-J.

NUTRITION INFORMATION PER SERVING (1 SANDWICH)

Calories 348	Protein 26.4 g	Cholesterol 70 mg
Carbohydrates 43.2 g	Total fat 7.7 g	Sodium 562 mg
Fibre 4.6 g	Saturated fat 2.6 g	

¼ cup (60 mL) low-sodium soy sauce

¼ cup (60 mL) hoisin sauce

2 tsp (10 mL) chopped garlic

2 tsp (10 mL) chopped ginger

5 tsp (25 mL) sesame oil

5 tsp (25 mL) rice vinegar

1 lb (500 g) lean ground beef

¼ cup (60 mL) unseasoned dry breadcrumbs

¼ cup (60 mL) chopped green onions

3 Tbsp (45 mL) chopped fresh cilantro or parsley

1 tsp (5 mL) minced ginger

1 tsp (5 mL) minced garlic

1 egg

1½ cups (375 mL) sliced onions

2 cups (500 mL) chopped mushrooms

1½ cups (375 mL) sliced red bell pepper

six 4-inch (10 cm) whole wheat submarine buns sliced in half

1 tsp (5 mL) toasted sesame seeds

STIR-FRIES, BURGERS & CHILIES

PORK, BOK CHOY AND MUSHROOM STIR-FRY

This is a great stir-fry, with its tender cut of pork, crisp bok choy and savoury hoisin sauce. Feel free to substitute boneless chicken breast, beef, tofu or shrimp for the pork.

1. TO MAKE THE SAUCE Combine the stock, hoisin sauce, soy sauce, cornstarch, brown sugar, sesame oil, garlic and ginger in a small bowl. Whisk together until smooth.

2. TO MAKE THE STIR-FRY Dust the pork pieces with flour. Lightly coat a large nonstick skillet with cooking spray, set over medium-high heat and add the oil. Sauté the pork for 3 minutes or just until browned. Do not cook through. Set aside and wipe the pan clean.

3. Respray the pan and sauté the mushrooms for 5 minutes or until they are soft and the liquid has evaporated. Add the bok choy and sauté for 2 minutes or it begins to wilt. Add the sauce, water chestnuts and pork and stir-fry for 2 minutes or until the sauce thickens. Place on a platter and garnish with cashews, green onion and cilantro.

PREPARATION TIME 15 minutes • **COOKING TIME** 12 minutes •
MAKE AHEAD Make the sauce and prepare vegetables early in the day. Cook just before serving. • **MAKES** 4 servings.

 ROSE'S TIP
This sauce can be made up in batches and frozen in containers for use over stir-fries, vegetables and even grains.

 HEALTH TIP
Pork tenderloin is lower in calories and fat than beef tenderloin.

NUTRITION INFORMATION PER SERVING

Calories 275	Protein 22 g	Cholesterol 37 mg
Carbohydrates 25 g	Total fat 11 g	Sodium 600 mg
Fibre 3.3 g	Saturated fat 2.1 g	

Sauce

1 cup (250 mL) low-sodium chicken (or beef) stock

¼ cup (60 mL) hoisin sauce

2 Tbsp (30 mL) low-sodium soy sauce

5 tsp (25 mL) cornstarch

1 Tbsp (15 mL) brown sugar

2 tsp (10 mL) sesame oil

1½ tsp (7.5 mL) finely chopped garlic

1 tsp (5 mL) finely chopped ginger

Stir-fry

12 oz (375 g) pork tenderloin cut into 1-inch (2.5 cm) cubes

2 Tbsp (30 mL) all-purpose flour

2 tsp (10 mL) vegetable oil

2 cups (500 mL) chopped mushrooms (any variety)

2 small baby bok choy, sliced (or 2 cups/500 mL sliced)

½ cup (125 mL) sliced water chestnuts

½ cup (125 mL) coarsely chopped cashews

1 large green onion, chopped

¼ cup (60 mL) chopped cilantro

CHICKEN, SNOW PEA AND BELL PEPPER STIR-FRY

A simple and delicious stir-fry. The flavours blend so well together. Substitute any protein you like, such as steak, shrimp, pork or firm tofu. Serve it over rice, soba or rice noodles.

1. **TO MAKE THE SAUCE** Place the stock, soy sauce, hoisin sauce, cornstarch, brown sugar, sesame oil, garlic and ginger in a small bowl and whisk to combine. Set aside.

2. **TO MAKE THE STIR-FRY** Dust the chicken with the flour. Spray a nonstick wok or frying pan with cooking oil and place over medium heat. Brown the chicken on all sides for 3 minutes, in total, or until browned but not cooked through. Remove from the pan.

3. Respray the pan and heat the oil over medium heat. Add the red pepper and snow peas; stir-fry for 2 minutes or until the vegetables are tender-crisp. Stir the sauce and add it to the pan along with the chicken and water chestnuts. Cook for 2 minutes, until the chicken is cooked through and the sauce has thickened.

4. Serve immediately, garnished with cashews and green onion.

PREPARATION TIME 15 minutes · **COOKING TIME** 10 minutes ·
MAKE AHEAD Make the sauce up to a day in advance. Prepare the stir-fry early in the day and cook just before serving. · **MAKES** 4 servings.

Sauce

1 cup (250 mL) low-sodium chicken stock

2 Tbsp (30 mL) low-sodium soy sauce

3 Tbsp (45 mL) hoisin sauce

4 tsp (20 mL) cornstarch

1 Tbsp (15 mL) brown sugar

1 tsp (5 mL) sesame oil

1½ tsp (7.5 mL) crushed fresh garlic

1 tsp (5 mL) minced fresh ginger

Stir-fry

8 oz (250 g) boneless skinless chicken breast, cut into 1-inch (2.5 cm) cubes

2 Tbsp (30 mL) all-purpose flour

2 tsp (10 mL) vegetable oil

1½ cups (375 mL) thinly sliced red bell pepper

1½ cups (375 mL) halved snow peas

½ cup (125 mL) sliced water chestnuts

¼ cup (60 mL) coarsely chopped cashews

1 large green onion, chopped

ROSE'S TIP

Dusting the chicken with flour keeps it moist before sautéing.

 HEALTH TIP

Cashews have a lower fat content than most other nuts, and the fat is in the form of oleic acid, which is the same heart-healthy fat found in olive oil. This benefits heart health by reducing triglyceride levels.

NUTRITION INFORMATION PER SERVING

Calories 277	Protein 17 g	Cholesterol 37 mg
Carbohydrates 20 g	Total fat 11 g	Sodium 503 mg
Fibre 2.8 g	Saturated fat 1.4 g	

BEEF AND MANGO STIR-FRY WITH HOISIN COCONUT SAUCE

The combination of beef, mangoes and coconut sauce is incredible. If you can't find fish sauce, use either soy sauce or oyster sauce. The steaks I like to use that are tender yet lower in calories and fat are sirloin, flank, filet or New York strip, but chicken (shown in photo), pork, shrimp or tofu make good substitutes for the beef.

1. TO MAKE THE SAUCE Whisk the coconut milk, hoisin sauce, sugar, fish sauce, peanut butter, water, cornstarch, garlic, ginger and hot sauce in a bowl until smooth. Set aside.

2. TO MAKE THE STIR-FRY Spray a barbecue or a nonstick grill pan with cooking oil and heat to high. Grill the beef until medium-rare, about 5 to 8 minutes. Slice the steak thinly and keep covered.

3. Spray a nonstick skillet with cooking oil, add the vegetable oil and place over medium heat. Stir-fry the onions until softened, about 5 minutes. Add the red pepper and stir-fry for 3 minutes.

4. Add the sauce and beef. Stir-fry until the sauce thickens, about 2 minutes, being careful not to overcook the beef.

5. Transfer to a serving platter. Garnish with mango, cilantro and green onion and serve immediately. If desired, serve with rice.

PREPARATION TIME 15 minutes · **COOKING TIME** 15 minutes ·
MAKE AHEAD Prepare the sauce up to a day in advance. It's best to stir-fry the vegetables and cook the meat just before serving. · **MAKES** 4 servings.

Sauce

½ cup (125 mL) light coconut milk

¼ cup (60 mL) hoisin sauce

3 Tbsp (45 mL) brown sugar

2 Tbsp (30 mL) fish sauce

1 Tbsp (15 mL) natural peanut butter

1 Tbsp (15 mL) water

2 tsp (10 mL) cornstarch

1½ tsp (7.5 mL) minced fresh garlic

1 tsp (5 mL) minced fresh ginger

1 tsp (5 mL) hot sauce (Sriracha)

Stir-fry

12 oz (375 g) boneless grilling steak

2 tsp (10 mL) vegetable oil

1½ cups (375 mL) sliced onion

2 cups (500 mL) sliced red bell pepper

¾ cup (185 mL) diced mango

¼ cup (60 mL) chopped cilantro or parsley

3 Tbsp (45 mL) chopped green onion

 ROSE'S TIP

The most delicious mangoes are from Indonesia—they're sweet and tender and smaller than regular mangoes.

 HEALTH TIP

Natural peanut butter and commercial peanut butter have almost identical amounts of calories and fat but commercial peanut butter often contains icing sugar and is hydrogenated.

NUTRITION INFORMATION PER SERVING

Calories 290	Protein 18 g	Cholesterol 48 mg
Carbohydrates 28 g	Total fat 9 g	Sodium 460 mg
Fibre 3 g	Saturated fat 3 g	

KOREAN STIR-FRIED BEEF AND CRUNCHY RICE

My children love Korean food and their favourite dish is bibimbap, consisting of crunchy rice, beef, Asian sauce and a cooked egg overtop. Here's my simplified version.

1. Preheat the oven to 450°F (230°C). Spray a 9-inch (23 cm) square baking dish with vegetable oil.

2. Bring the rice and water or stock to a boil. Cover and simmer on the lowest heat for 10 minutes. Let cool, covered, for 10 minutes.

3. TO MAKE THE SAUCE Combine the stock, hoisin and soy sauce, vinegar, sesame oil, cornstarch, garlic, ginger and hot sauce. Set aside.

4. Heat a large skillet sprayed with vegetable oil until very hot. Spread the rice evenly overtop. On medium-high heat, let the rice sit for 10 minutes or until the rice begins to slightly brown and become crisp. Toss rice for another 5 minutes or just until the rice is crisp. Spread over the bottom of the baking dish.

5. TO MAKE THE STIR-FRY Meanwhile, dust the meat with the flour. Wipe out the skillet, respray and on high heat sear the beef just until cooked to medium. Set aside.

6. Wipe out the skillet, respray and sauté the mushrooms until no longer wet, about 5 minutes. Add the onions and sauté for 3 minutes; add the carrots and sauté another 3 minutes. Add the sauce and cook just until the sauce thickens, about 2 minutes. Place the meat over the rice, then pour the sauce overtop. Add the cilantro and sesame seeds and bake for 5 minutes.

---

1 cup (250 mL) basmati rice

1 cup (250 mL) water or low-sodium stock

Sauce

¾ cup (185 mL) low-sodium beef or chicken stock

¼ cup (60 mL) hoisin sauce

1½ Tbsp (22.5 mL) low-sodium soy sauce

1½ Tbsp (22.5 mL) rice vinegar

1½ tsp (7.5 mL) sesame oil

4 tsp (20 mL) cornstarch

2 tsp (10 mL) finely chopped garlic

1½ tsp (7.5 mL) finely chopped ginger

1 tsp (5 mL) hot sauce (Sriracha)

Stir-fry

1 lb (500 g) sirloin beef, sliced thinly

2 Tbsp (30 mL) all-purpose flour

3 cups (750 mL) thinly sliced mushrooms (any variety)

1½ cups (375 mL) thinly sliced onions

7. **(OPTIONAL) EGGS** Prepare 2 sunny-side up eggs in a skillet sprayed with vegetable oil just until barely cooked. Slip the eggs overtop of the beef dish.

PREPARATION TIME 20 minutes · **COOKING TIME** 35 minutes ·
MAKE AHEAD Prepare the rice and sauce early in the day. Finish the dish just before serving. · **MAKES** 6 servings.

 ROSE'S TIP
Getting the rice crispy is key to the texture of this dish. Be patient while waiting for the rice to get crispy. Do not turn the heat up too high or the rice will burn.

HEALTH TIP
This is a great nutritious meal all in one dish. You have your grains, vegetables and protein. Use brown rice if you want more nutrients, especially fibre.

1½ cups (375 mL) thinly sliced carrots

¼ cup (60 mL) cilantro

2 tsp (10 mL) toasted sesame seeds

2 eggs (optional)

NUTRITION INFORMATION PER SERVING (WITHOUT EGGS)

Calories 306	Protein 20.8 g	Cholesterol 28 mg
Carbohydrates 43.1 g	Total fat 5.8 g	Sodium 366 mg
Fibre 2.6 g	Saturated fat 1.5 g	

SUN-DRIED TOMATO BURGERS WITH BARBECUE MAYO

The sun-dried tomatoes give this burger the best flavour along with the garnishing sauce.

1. **TO MAKE THE BURGERS** In a large bowl, combine the ground beef, breadcrumbs, tomatoes, barbecue sauce, egg, garlic, basil and oregano. Form into 4 patties. On a grill sprayed with cooking spray, cook patties on one side over medium heat for 7 minutes. Turn and cook 3 to 8 minutes longer or until cooked through. (Alternatively, bake in a preheated 450°F/230°C oven for 10 to 15 minutes or until cooked through, turning once.)

2. **TO MAKE THE SAUCE** In a small bowl, mix the barbecue sauce and mayonnaise. Serve over the burgers with the onions, tomatoes and lettuce.

PREPARATION TIME 10 minutes · **COOKING TIME** About 10 minutes ·
MAKE AHEAD Prepare the burgers up to 1 day in advance or freeze for up to
a month. Cook just before serving. · **MAKES** 4 servings.

 ROSE'S TIP
Pre-chop dry sun-dried tomatoes and keep them in your freezer. Rehydrate by pouring hot water overtop and letting stand for 10 minutes. Drain and use.

 HEALTH TIP
Sun-dried tomatoes soaked in water have 140 calories, 8 grams of protein and 7 grams of fibre per cup. They also have 40% of your recommended daily potassium.

Burgers

1 lb (500 g) extra-lean ground beef

¼ cup (60 mL) seasoned dry breadcrumbs

¼ cup (60 mL) finely chopped rehydrated sun-dried tomatoes

3 Tbsp (45 mL) barbecue sauce or ketchup

1 egg

2 tsp (10 mL) minced garlic

1 tsp (5 mL) dried basil

½ tsp (2.5 mL) dried oregano

Sauce

3 Tbsp (45 mL) barbecue sauce

2 tsp (10 mL) reduced-fat mayonnaise

4 slices onion and tomato

4 lettuce leaves

NUTRITION INFORMATION PER SERVING

Calories 192	Protein 19 g	Cholesterol 68 mg
Carbohydrates 8 g	Total fat 9 g	Sodium 398 mg
Fibre 1.3 g	Saturated fat 2.9 g	

MEDITERRANEAN BURGERS WITH MUSHROOMS AND FETA

Add some mushrooms, feta cheese and oregano and you have a whole new burger. Try substituting ground chicken, turkey or veal. Forget the bun—I love to serve these over a bed of couscous.

1. TO MAKE THE BURGERS spray a nonstick frying pan with cooking oil. Add the mushrooms and onions and cook over medium-high heat for 4 minutes or until softened and browned. Remove from the heat.

2. Combine the beef, oregano, barbecue sauce, breadcrumbs, garlic and egg in a bowl. Stir in the onion mixture. Mix thoroughly. Form into 4 patties.

3. Spray a nonstick grill pan or barbecue grill with cooking oil and heat to medium-high. Grill the patties for 3 to 5 minutes per side or until no longer pink in the centre. (Alternatively, place on a baking sheet in the centre of a preheated 450°F/230°C oven for 10 to 15 minutes or until cooked through, turning once.)

4. TO MAKE THE SAUCE Place the feta and cream cheeses, yogurt, garlic, lemon juice, water and basil in a small food processor and purée. Drizzle over the burgers.

PREPARATION TIME 10 minutes · **COOKING TIME** 15 minutes ·

MAKE AHEAD Make burgers up to a day in advance or freeze raw for up to a month. Cook just before serving. · **MAKES** 4 servings.

 ROSE'S TIP
Be sure to finely chop your mushrooms and onion so the burger binds better.

 HEALTH TIP
Lean ground beef can taste great as long as you add lots of flavour to the mixture.

Burgers

1 cup (250 mL) finely chopped mushrooms

½ cup (125 mL) finely chopped onion

1 lb (500 g) extra-lean ground beef or lamb

½ tsp (2.5 mL) dried oregano

2 Tbsp (30 mL) barbecue sauce

3 Tbsp (45 mL) seasoned dry breadcrumbs

2 tsp (10 mL) minced fresh garlic

1 egg

Sauce

¼ cup (60 mL) crumbled reduced-fat feta cheese (1 oz/30 g)

¼ cup (60 mL) softened reduced-fat cream cheese (2 oz/60 g)

3 Tbsp (45 mL) reduced-fat plain yogurt (or reduced-fat sour cream)

½ tsp (2.5 mL) finely chopped garlic

1 Tbsp (15 mL) lemon juice

1 Tbsp (15 mL) water

½ tsp (2.5 mL) dried basil

NUTRITION INFORMATION PER SERVING (1 BURGER)

Calories 258	Protein 22.7 g	Cholesterol 96 mg
Carbohydrates 7.4 g	Total fat 14.9 g	Sodium 318 mg
Fibre 0.8 g	Saturated fat 7.2 g	

CARAMELIZED ONION SIRLOIN STEAK BURGER STUFFED WITH BRIE

My version of a "gourmet" burger is stuffed with brie and topped with caramelized onions. It's sensational!

1. Spray a large nonstick skillet with cooking oil, add the vegetable oil and place over medium heat. Add the onion and sauté for 5 minutes, just until soft. Reduce the heat to low, add the sugar and continue cooking for 10 minutes until browned and caramelized. Set aside.

2. Combine the meat, green onion, breadcrumbs, barbecue sauce, garlic, salt and pepper, egg and basil in a large bowl. Mix thoroughly and shape into 4 burgers. Form a pocket in each burger and stuff evenly with the diced brie. Make sure the beef encloses the cheese completely.

3. Preheat a barbecue or indoor grill and spray with cooking oil. Cook the burgers for about 4 minutes per side or until no longer pink in the centre. Mound the onions on top of each serving and garnish with the parsley.

PREPARATION TIME 10 minutes • **COOKING TIME** 23 minutes •
MAKE AHEAD Make the burgers up to a day in advance or freeze raw up to a month. Cook just before serving. • **MAKES** 4 servings.

1 tsp (5 mL) vegetable oil

3 cups (750 mL) sliced sweet onion

1 Tbsp (15 mL) packed brown sugar

1 lb (500 g) ground lean sirloin steak

3 Tbsp (45 mL) minced green onion

¼ cup (60 mL) seasoned dry breadcrumbs

3 Tbsp (45 mL) barbecue sauce

1½ tsp (7.5 mL) crushed fresh garlic

pinch of salt and ground black pepper

1 large egg

1 tsp (5 mL) dried basil

⅓ cup (80 mL) diced brie (1½ oz/45 g)

2 Tbsp (30 mL) chopped fresh parsley

 ROSE'S TIP

Stuffing a burger with cheese or sautéed finely diced vegetables takes it to another level. Try a combination of sautéed onions, garlic, spinach and feta cheese.

 HEALTH TIP

A 4-ounce (125 g) serving of ground sirloin steak has only 200 calories and 6 grams of fat, which is lower than that in regular ground beef.

NUTRITION INFORMATION PER SERVING (1 BURGER)

Calories 264	Protein 30 g	Cholesterol 120 mg
Carbohydrates 15 g	Total fat 11 g	Sodium 289 mg
Fibre 2.4 g	Saturated fat 5 g	

TURKEY BURGERS WITH DRIED APRICOT AND CRANBERRY SALSA

Glow Fresh Grill's number-one-selling burger is the turkey patty. The flavours of the meat and dried fruit salsa go together so well. Feel free to substitute another meat, such as ground chicken or pork.

1. TO MAKE THE BURGERS   In a skillet, add oil and onions. Sauté until tender, about 5 minutes.

2. Place turkey in a bowl, add garlic, barbecue sauce, egg, breadcrumbs, and salt and pepper and form into 6 burgers. Grill or sauté just until cooked to 160°F (71°C) (about 15 minutes).

3. TO MAKE THE SALSA   Meanwhile, in a bowl, add the apricots, cranberries, bell pepper, green onion, garlic, cilantro, jam, maple syrup, mustard and apple cider. Divide the topping over the burgers.

PREPARATION TIME 20 minutes · **COOKING TIME** 20 minutes · **MAKE AHEAD** Make the burgers and sauce up to a day in advance and cook just before serving. · **MAKES** 6 servings.

 ROSE'S TIP
You could make these burgers into a meat loaf and serve the salsa on top. Place in an 8- × 5-inch (1.5 L) loaf pan and bake for about 30 minutes or until the temperature reaches 165°F (74°C).

 HEALTH TIP
Ground turkey is one of the leanest meats to make a burger with. Four ounces (125 g) of white ground turkey has only 120 calories, 1 gram of fat and 28 grams of lean protein!

Burgers

2 tsp (10 mL) vegetable oil

1 cup (250 mL) diced onions

1½ lb (750 g) ground turkey

2 tsp (10 mL) crushed garlic

3 Tbsp (45 mL) barbecue sauce

1 egg

3 Tbsp (45 mL) seasoned dry breadcrumbs

pinch of salt and pepper

Salsa

3 Tbsp (45 mL) diced dried apricots

3 Tbsp (45 mL) dried cranberries

¾ cup (185 mL) diced red bell pepper

¼ cup (60 mL) diced green onion

½ tsp (2.5 mL) minced garlic

3 Tbsp (45 mL) chopped cilantro

2 Tbsp (30 mL) apricot jam

2 tsp (10 mL) maple syrup

½ tsp (2.5 mL) Dijon mustard

1½ tsp (7.5 mL) apple cider

NUTRITION INFORMATION PER SERVING (1 BURGER)

Calories 320	Protein 21 g	Cholesterol 120 mg
Carbohydrates 22 g	Total fat 15 g	Sodium 280 mg
Fibre 1.6 g	Saturated fat 4 g	

CALIFORNIA GRILLED
CHICKEN PESTO BURGERS

The West Coast is known for its fresh chicken burgers with all the toppings including cheese, avocado and tomatoes. These are simple to make and a real crowd pleaser.

1 lb (500 g) ground white and dark ground turkey or chicken

1 egg

⅓ cup (80 mL) seasoned dry breadcrumbs

2 Tbsp (30 mL) pesto sauce (see Basil Pesto on page 371)

2 tsp (10 mL) crushed garlic

3 Tbsp (45 mL) minced green onions

pinch of salt and pepper

4 thin slices Monterey Jack or aged cheddar cheese (about 1 oz/30 g)

¼ cup (60 mL) diced avocado

4 slices ripe tomatoes

8 basil leaves (optional)

1. Combine the turkey, egg, breadcrumbs, pesto, garlic, green onions, and salt and pepper. Form into 4 burgers. Either grill or bake at 425°F (220°C) until no longer pink, about 8 minutes per side. Add the cheese and cook just until melted.

2. Garnish with avocado, tomatoes and basil leaves.

PREPARATION TIME 15 minutes · **COOKING TIME** 16 minutes ·

MAKE AHEAD Prepare the burgers up to a day in advance. Cook just before serving. · **MAKES** 4 servings.

ROSE'S TIP

I save time by grating a pound (500 g) of cheese, placing it in airtight containers and freezing it for later cooking. No need to defrost.

HEALTH TIP

If you want to keep calories and fat lower, select only white ground chicken, not the dark. A 3-ounce (90 g) serving of white ground chicken has 140 calories and 3 grams of fat, and dark meat has 180 calories and 9 grams of fat.

NUTRITION INFORMATION PER SERVING (1 BURGER)

Calories 304	Protein 23.7 g	Cholesterol 100 mg
Carbohydrates 3.5 g	Total fat 20.8 g	Sodium 361 mg
Fibre 0.6 g	Saturated fat 7.6 g	

FRESH SALMON AND HOISIN BURGERS

For those who don't eat meat, here's a perfectly cooked salmon burger that is sensational. The hoisin mayonnaise sauce is the perfect accompaniment.

1. **TO MAKE THE BURGERS** In a food processor, process burger ingredients until coarsely ground by turning processor on and off. Do not purée. Mixture will be loose. Form into 4 patties.

2. Either barbecue or, on a nonstick grill pan sprayed with cooking spray, grill the burgers until medium done, about 3 minutes per side on medium heat. Do not overcook.

3. **TO MAKE SAUCE** In a small bowl, mix the hoisin and mayonnaise.

4. Place the lettuce leaves on a serving dish. Top with the burgers and spread with the sauce.

PREPARATION TIME 10 minutes · **COOKING TIME** 6 minutes ·
MAKE AHEAD These burgers can be prepared 1 day in advance or frozen raw for 1 month. It's best to cook them just before serving. ·
MAKES 4 servings.

 ROSE'S TIP
You can replace the salmon with any other firm fish of your choice. Tuna, tilapia, halibut or snapper taste great as well.

 HEALTH TIP
Beware of grilling on too high a heat. Flare-ups can cause carcinogens to develop by charring the fish.

Burgers

1 lb (500 g) boneless skinless salmon fillet, cut into 1-inch (2.5 cm) pieces

1 egg

¼ cup (60 mL) chopped fresh cilantro or parsley

2 Tbsp (30 mL) hoisin sauce

1 tsp (5 mL) reduced-fat mayonnaise

¼ cup (60 mL) chopped green onions

1 tsp (5 mL) minced garlic

Sauce

2 Tbsp (30 mL) hoisin sauce

1 Tbsp (15 mL) reduced-fat mayonnaise

Boston lettuce leaves

NUTRITION INFORMATION PER SERVING (1 BURGER)

Calories 186	Protein 18 g	Cholesterol 80 mg
Carbohydrates 6 g	Total fat 9 g	Sodium 304 mg
Fibre 0.8 g	Saturated fat 0.9 g	

CHICKEN FAJITAS WITH SAUTÉED BELL PEPPERS AND ONIONS

Tex-Mex food is an all-time kids' favourite. These fajitas are creamy and rich tasting but without the fat of regular fajitas, which are loaded with a lot of cheese, sour cream, guacamole and fatty cuts of beef. My version has plenty of vegetables, along with some light cheese and sour cream. They're easy to make, and the whole family loves them.

1. Preheat the oven to 425°F (220°C). Line a baking sheet with foil and lightly coat with cooking spray.

2. Lightly coat a nonstick skillet with cooking spray and place over medium-high heat. Cook the chicken for about 8 minutes or until cooked and no longer pink. Let rest for 10 minutes, then slice thinly. Wipe out pan.

3. Meanwhile, add the oil to the pan and brown the onion and garlic, about 4 minutes. Reduce the heat to medium. Stir in the red pepper strips and cook until softened, about 5 minutes. Remove the pan from the heat. Stir in the parsley, green onions and cooked chicken.

4. Divide the mixture among the tortillas. Top with the cheese, salsa and sour cream. Roll up.

5. Place on the prepared baking sheet. Bake in the centre of the oven for 5 minutes or until the fajitas are heated through and the cheese has melted. Cut in half and serve immediately.

PREPARATION TIME 20 minutes · **COOKING TIME** 22 minutes ·
MAKE AHEAD Prepare the ingredients early in the day. Cook just before serving. · **MAKES** 6 servings.

NUTRITION INFORMATION PER SERVING (1 FAJITA)

Calories 220	Protein 14 g	Cholesterol 29 mg
Carbohydrates 23 g	Total fat 7.5 g	Sodium 340 mg
Fibre 2.1 g	Saturated fat 2.5 g	

8 oz (250 g) boneless skinless chicken breasts (about 2 breasts)

2 tsp (10 mL) vegetable oil

1½ cups (375 mL) thinly sliced white onion

1½ tsp (7.5 mL) finely chopped garlic

1½ cups (375 mL) red bell pepper, cut into strips

¼ cup (60 mL) chopped parsley or cilantro

3 Tbsp (45 mL) chopped green onions

6 small (6-inch/15 cm) flour tortillas

½ cup (125 mL) shredded cheddar cheese (1½ oz/45 g)

⅓ cup (80 mL) medium salsa

¼ cup (60 mL) reduced-fat sour cream

ROSE'S TIP

You can serve these fajitas in a buffet style. Place all separate ingredients on a plate and have everyone create their own fajitas.

HEALTH TIP

To reduce the calories and fat of fajitas in restaurants, order either fish or poulty rather than beef and add reduced amounts of guacamole, cheese and sour cream.

FISH FAJITAS WITH CORN AND BLACK BEAN SALSA

You can't easily find fish fajitas that aren't deep-fried or served in a fried taco shell. Try my take for an outstanding, healthier recipe. Be sure to use a firm white fish so it doesn't flake.

1. Preheat the oven to 425°F (220°C). Line a baking sheet with foil sprayed with vegetable oil.

2. Sauté the corn until light brown and add the red pepper and sauté for 2 minutes. Remove from the heat, cool and add the red onion, beans, cilantro, jalapeños, garlic, lemon juice, olive oil and salt and pepper.

3. Mix the egg and milk in a bowl. Mix the panko and chili powder in a bowl. Dip the fish pieces in the milk mixture, then in the crumbs. Place on a baking sheet and bake for 10 minutes or just until fish is cooked.

4. Warm the tortillas in a microwave oven for 20 seconds. Divide the fish, guacamole, corn salsa, lettuce and sour cream among the tortillas. Fold and serve.

PREPARATION TIME 20 minutes · **COOKING TIME** 12 minutes ·

MAKE AHEAD Prepare the salsa and fish early in the day. Cook just before serving. · **MAKES** 6 servings.

ROSE'S TIP
The key to making a delicious fish fajita without deep-frying is not to overcook the fish. Make the tastiest salsa to put overtop, such as this one.

HEALTH TIP
Corn tortillas can be used instead of flour. They are higher in calories but lower in fat and sodium.

NUTRITION INFORMATION PER SERVING (1 FAJITA)

Calories 342	Protein 23 g	Cholesterol 88 mg
Carbohydrates 42.7 g	Total fat 8.3 g	Sodium 490 mg
Fibre 5.7 g	Saturated fat 2.4 g	

Salsa

1 cup (250 mL) corn

¾ cup (185 mL) diced red pepper

¼ cup (60 mL) diced red onion

¾ cup (185 mL) canned black beans, drained and rinsed

¼ cup (60 mL) cilantro

1 tsp (5 mL) minced jalapeño peppers

1 tsp (5 mL) garlic

2 Tbsp (30 mL) lemon juice

2 tsp (10 mL) olive oil

pinch of salt and pepper

1 egg

1 Tbsp (15 mL) 2% milk

1½ cups (375 mL) panko crumbs

¼ tsp (1 mL) chili powder

1 lb (500 g) basa cut into 2-inch (5 cm) cubes

6 small flour tortillas

⅓ cup (80 mL) guacamole (see Guacamole on page 362)

2 cups (500 mL) chopped romaine lettuce

⅓ cup (80 mL) reduced-fat sour cream

WHITE BEAN CHILI

I once had this served to me on a ski trip in Colorado. I immediately created my own version. You may never go back to classic chili again!

1. Dust the turkey with flour. Sauté in 2 tsp (10 mL) oil just until browned on all sides (about 3 minutes). Do not cook through. Set aside.

2. Sauté the onion in 1 tsp (5 mL) oil for 5 minutes. Add the corn and sauté for 5 minutes until lightly browned. Add the red pepper, garlic, cumin, jalapeños and salt and pepper and sauté for 3 minutes.

3. Add 1½ cups (375 mL) of the beans. Purée the remaining ½ cup (125 mL) with ½ cup (125 mL) of chicken stock. Add to the pot along with the remaining stock. Cover and simmer for 15 minutes until thickened. Add the turkey and cheese and cook for 2 minutes.

4. Garnish with avocado, cilantro and cheddar.

PREPARATION TIME 15 minutes · **COOKING TIME** 33 minutes ·
MAKE AHEAD Make the chili up to 2 days in advance. Add more stock when reheating. · **MAKES** 6 servings.

ROSE'S TIP
Dusting your turkey with flour before sautéing saves the moisture. I use this technique for stir-frying turkey as well.

HEALTH TIP
Regular chilies are loaded with calories and fat due to the high-fat ground beef used and toppings such as regular sour cream, cheddar cheese and avocado.

NUTRITION INFORMATION PER SERVING

Calories 255	Protein 25.4 g	Cholesterol 35 mg
Carbohydrates 26.5 g	Total fat 5.8 g	Sodium 400 mg
Fibre 6.4 g	Saturated fat 1.7 g	

12 oz (375 g) diced turkey breast

3 Tbsp (45 mL) all-purpose flour

2 tsp (10 mL) vegetable oil

1½ cups (375 mL) diced onion

1 tsp (5 mL) vegetable oil

1 cup (250 mL) corn

¾ cup (185 mL) diced red pepper

2 tsp (10 mL) chopped garlic

2 tsp (10 mL) cumin powder

½ tsp (2.5 mL) minced jalapeño peppers (add a few seeds for extra heat)

pinch of salt and pepper

2 cups (500 mL) canned white cannellini beans, drained and rinsed (one 19 oz/540 mL can)

2 cups (500 mL) low-sodium chicken stock

½ cup (125 mL) grated white aged cheddar cheese (1½ oz/45 g)

⅓ cup (80 mL) diced avocado

¼ cup (60 mL) chopped cilantro

¼ cup (60 mL) grated aged cheddar (¾ oz/23 g)

SOUTHWESTERN CHICKEN CHILI WITH CORN AND BEANS

This is a great, lighter chili typically served in the Southwest. Using chicken rather than beef reduces the calories and fat. Aged cheddar is the perfect accompaniment. Add diced avocado to the list of garnishes if you like.

1. Place the chicken and flour in a bowl and toss to coat. Lightly coat a nonstick saucepan with cooking spray, add 1 tsp (5 mL) of the vegetable oil and set over medium heat. Sauté the chicken for 5 minutes or until it is lightly browned on all sides, but do not cook through. Set aside.

2. Respray the same saucepan, add the remaining vegetable oil and set over medium heat. Add the onion and cook until soft, stirring frequently, about 5 minutes. Stir in the corn and garlic and continue to cook and stir for 5 minutes or until the corn is browned.

3. Stir in the beans, tomato sauce, stock, chili powder, basil, oregano, jalapeño pepper and salt and pepper. Bring to a boil, reduce the heat and cover. Simmer for 15 minutes. Add the diced chicken and simmer, uncovered, for 5 minutes or until the chicken is just cooked through and the chili thickens. Serve the chili in bowls and garnish with cilantro, cheddar cheese and sour cream.

PREPARATION TIME 15 minutes · **COOKING TIME** 35 minutes ·
MAKE AHEAD Make the chili up to 2 days in advance. Warm just before serving and serve with the garnishes. · **MAKES** 6 servings.

12 oz (375 g) diced boneless skinless chicken breasts (about 3 breasts)

¼ cup (60 mL) all-purpose flour

2 tsp (10 mL) vegetable oil

1½ cups (375 mL) chopped onion

1 cup (250 mL) corn

2 tsp (10 mL) finely chopped garlic

1½ cups (375 mL) canned black beans, drained and rinsed

2½ cups (625 mL) homemade or store-bought tomato sauce (see Quick Basic Tomato Sauce on page 369)

¾ cup (185 mL) low-sodium chicken (or beef) stock

1 Tbsp (15 mL) chili powder

1½ tsp (7.5 mL) dried basil

1 tsp (5 mL) dried oregano

1½ tsp (7.5 mL) seeded and finely chopped jalapeño pepper (or 1½ tsp/7.5 mL hot chili sauce)

pinch of salt and pepper

ROSE'S TIP

This chili is perfect on its own or served over pasta, rice or a baked potato.

 HEALTH TIP

A bowl of chili is a complete meal, with beans, protein, dairy and vegetables. This keeps your blood sugar under control, which is good for diabetics and those with low blood sugar.

¼ cup (60 mL) chopped cilantro or parsley

½ cup (125 mL) shredded aged cheddar cheese (1½ oz/45 g)

¼ cup (60 mL) reduced-fat sour cream

NUTRITION INFORMATION PER SERVING

Calories 333	Protein 27 g	Cholesterol 68 mg
Carbohydrates 33 g	Total fat 11 g	Sodium 550 mg
Fibre 6 g	Saturated fat 3.9 g	

BEEF AND BARLEY CHILI WITH AGED CHEDDAR AND SOUR CREAM

Chili has to be one of the most versatile, healthy and easy foods to prepare. It's the perfect dish to make for your own family, but also works great for entertaining. The key to keeping it nutritious is to use extra-lean or lean ground beef. The addition of barley makes this a complete meal.

1. Lightly coat a large saucepan with cooking spray, add the oil and set over medium heat. Add the onion and garlic and sauté for 3 minutes. Add the beef, chili powder, basil and oregano and sauté for another 4 or 5 minutes or until the beef is no longer pink.

2. Add the barley, tomato sauce, stock and kidney beans. Cover and simmer for 30 minutes or until the barley is tender.

3. Serve in bowls and garnish with the sour cream, cheddar cheese, green onions and basil.

PREPARATION TIME About 10 minutes · **COOKING TIME** 50 minutes · **MAKE AHEAD** Make the chili up to 2 days in advance. Add more stock when reheating · **MAKES** 6 servings.

ROSE'S TIP
Substitute ground chicken, turkey, pork or soy for the beef. Also, any variety of beans work well.

HEALTH TIP
Canned beans versus home-cooked have excess sodium. One cup (250 mL) has 900 mg; home-cooked beans have none. To cook beans, use the quick-soak-and-cook boil method (see page 113).

2 tsp (10 mL) vegetable oil

1 cup (250 mL) chopped onion

2 tsp (10 mL) chopped garlic

1 lb (500 g) extra-lean ground beef

2 tsp (10 mL) chili powder (or to taste)

1½ tsp (7.5 mL) dried basil

1 tsp (5 mL) dried oregano

¼ cup (60 mL) pearl barley

2½ cups (625 mL) homemade or store-bought tomato sauce (see Quick Basic Tomato Sauce on page 369)

1 cup (250 mL) low-sodium beef (or chicken) stock

one 19 oz (540 mL) can red kidney beans, drained and rinsed

¼ cup (60 mL) reduced-fat sour cream

¼ cup (60 mL) shredded aged cheddar cheese (¾ oz/23 g)

¼ cup (60 mL) chopped green onions

¼ cup (60 mL) chopped fresh basil or parsley

NUTRITION INFORMATION PER SERVING

Calories 321	Protein 26 g	Cholesterol 47 mg
Carbohydrates 40 g	Total fat 7.4 g	Sodium 490 mg
Fibre 10 g	Saturated fat 2.2 g	

✧ FISH & SEAFOOD

SALMON WITH SUN-DRIED TOMATO-OLIVE STUFFING

This olive and sun-dried tomato mixture is incredible with salmon, but it also goes well with halibut or sea bass and even chicken or pork. If you don't have both types of olives, either is fine. If you like, add some thinly sliced olives as a garnish.

1. Preheat the oven to 425°F (220°C). Spray a baking sheet with cooking oil.

2. Finely chop the olives, sun-dried tomatoes, breadcrumbs, oil, garlic and mustard, either by hand or using a small food processor.

3. Make a ¼-inch (6 mm) vertical slit through the top of each salmon fillet to within ¼ inch (6 mm) of each end. Divide the filling and stuff the fish. Bake in the centre of the oven for 10 minutes per inch (2.5 cm) of thickness. Garnish with fresh parsley or basil.

PREPARATION TIME 10 minutes · **COOKING TIME** 10 to 15 minutes · **MAKE AHEAD** Prepare the olive stuffing up to a week in advance. Bake the fish just before serving. · **MAKES** 4 servings.

3 Tbsp (45 mL) chopped black olives

3 Tbsp (45 mL) chopped green olives

3 Tbsp (45 mL) chopped rehydrated sun-dried tomatoes

2 Tbsp (30 mL) unseasoned dry breadcrumbs

2 tsp (10 mL) olive oil

1 tsp (5 mL) crushed fresh garlic

1 tsp (5 mL) Dijon mustard

1½ lb (750 g) salmon fillets (4 fillets)

3 Tbsp (45 mL) chopped fresh parsley or basil

ROSE'S TIP

Another way to present this is to spread the olive topping overtop of the entire fish instead of stuffing into the slit.

HEALTH TIP

Seasoned breadcrumbs have 3 times the sodium of unseasoned ones. Read the labels carefully. A hundred grams of seasoned breadcrumbs has 1,759 mg of sodium and the same amount of unseasoned breadcrumbs has 700 mg.

NUTRITION INFORMATION PER SERVING

Calories 386	Protein 37 g	Cholesterol 112 mg
Carbohydrates 7.5 g	Total fat 22 g	Sodium 436 mg
Fibre 2.1 g	Saturated fat 4.9 g	

SALMON WITH MANGO, BLACK BEAN AND CORN SALSA

*The combination of black beans and sweet mango is outstanding.
I serve this salsa over chicken or other fish and even as a salad
dressing. Sautéing the corn adds a barbecued flavour.*

1. **TO MAKE THE SALSA** In a nonstick skillet sprayed with
cooking spray, cook the corn on medium-high heat for
8 minutes or just until the corn is dry and beginning to
brown. Place it in a serving dish. Stir in the remaining
salsa ingredients.

2. Either on a barbecue or in a nonstick grill pan sprayed
with cooking spray, grill the salmon on medium-high
heat for 5 minutes per side or just until medium done
(10 minutes per inch/2.5 cm of fish thickness). Serve
the salsa overtop of the fish.

PREPARATION TIME About 10 minutes · **COOKING TIME** About 20 minutes ·
MAKE AHEAD The salsa can be made early in the day. Cook the fish just before
serving. · **MAKES** 4 servings.

 ROSE'S TIP
In the summer a fresh corn
and fruit salsa is perfect
over fish. This salsa would
also suit any variety of
white fish, such as tilapia,
sole or basa.

 HEALTH TIP
Mangoes help improve
digestion for those who
suffer from acidity. As well,
mangoes are a good source
of soluble fibre and vitamin
C and can lower cholesterol
levels.

Salsa

½ cup (125 mL) corn

½ cup (125 mL) diced mango

½ cup (125 mL) canned black
beans, drained and rinsed

¼ cup (60 mL) diced red
bell peppers

¼ cup (60 mL) diced
sweet onions

¼ cup (60 mL) chopped
fresh cilantro or parsley

1 Tbsp (15 mL) fresh lime
or lemon juice

1 tsp (5 mL) liquid honey

1 tsp (5 mL) minced garlic

½ tsp (2.5 mL) hot pepper sauce

Salmon

1½ skin-on salmon fillets
(about 6 oz/175 g each)

NUTRITION INFORMATION PER SERVING

Calories 309	Protein 36.2 g	Cholesterol 93 mg
Carbohydrates 15.6 g	Total fat 11.3 g	Sodium 267 mg
Fibre 11.3 g	Saturated fat 1.8 g	

SALMON WITH PECAN AND MAPLE SYRUP SAUCE

The pecan and maple syrup sauce gets thick and sticky—almost candy-like—upon cooling. If you like the sauce looser, heat it just before serving or add more maple syrup. Use any nuts of your choice.

1. Heat the oven to 425°F (220°C). Spray a nonstick baking pan or grill pan with cooking oil.

2. Place the pecans in a small nonstick frying pan and toast over medium-high heat for 3 minutes or until golden and fragrant. Stir in the honey, maple syrup and butter. Reduce the heat to low and cook for 3 minutes or until slightly thickened. Whisk in the mustard. Pour half the sauce over the salmon.

3. Grill or bake the salmon, cooking for 10 minutes per inch (2.5 cm) thickness of the fish or until the fish flakes easily when pierced with a fork.

4. Reheat the remaining sauce and serve with the fish. Garnish with cilantro.

PREPARATION TIME 5 minutes · **COOKING TIME** 16 minutes ·
MAKE AHEAD Make the sauce up to 2 days in advance. Reheat gently before using. Bake the fish just before serving. · **MAKES** 4 servings.

3 Tbsp (45 mL) finely chopped pecans

3 Tbsp (45 mL) liquid honey

2 Tbsp (30 mL) maple syrup

2 tsp (10 mL) butter or margarine

½ tsp (2.5 mL) Dijon mustard

four 6 oz (175 g) portions salmon fillet

Garnish
3 Tbsp (45 mL) chopped cilantro or fresh parsley

 ROSE'S TIP
You can always use a food thermometer when cooking fish. Place the prong into the thickest part of the fish, and when the temperature reaches 125°F (52°C) the fish is medium-cooked. The fish continues cooking for at least 5 minutes after this time, so you don't want to overcook the fish or it will be dry.

 HEALTH TIP
Pecans contain vitamin E, which is a natural antioxidant that helps protect against cell damage and fight Alzheimer's, Parkinson's, cancer and heart disease. They are also a naturally good source of protein.

NUTRITION INFORMATION PER SERVING

Calories 397	Protein 34.3 g	Cholesterol 102 mg
Carbohydrates 21 g	Total fat 19.2 g	Sodium 120 mg
Fibre 0.6 g	Saturated fat 3.9 g	

ROASTED TERIYAKI–HOISIN SALMON

This is a twist on my original teriyaki recipe. By adding just one table-spoon of hoisin sauce, the flavour completely changes. Salmon and Asian sauces always go well together. This sauce goes well with other fish, chicken and pork.

1. Preheat the oven to 425°F (220°C). Line a rimmed baking sheet with foil and lightly coat it with cooking spray.

2. TO MAKE THE SAUCE Combine the brown sugar, soy sauce, rice vinegar, hoisin sauce, water, oil, cornstarch, garlic and ginger in a small saucepan. Bring to a boil, reduce the heat and simmer for 2 minutes or just until the mixture thickens.

3. Place the salmon on the prepared baking sheet and pour half the sauce over it. Bake for 10 minutes per inch (2.5 cm) of thickness or until the fish just flakes when tested with a fork.

4. Gently reheat the remaining sauce and serve over the baked salmon. Garnish with the sesame seeds and cilantro before serving.

PREPARATION TIME 5 minutes • **COOKING TIME** 15 minutes •
MAKE AHEAD Prepare the sauce a few days in advance and keep refrigerated. Bake the fish just before serving. • **MAKES** 4 servings.

Sauce

3 Tbsp (45 mL) packed brown sugar

2 Tbsp (30 mL) low-sodium soy sauce

1 Tbsp (15 mL) rice vinegar

1 Tbsp (15 mL) hoisin sauce

1 Tbsp (15 mL) water

2 tsp (10 mL) sesame oil

2 tsp (10 mL) cornstarch

1 tsp (5 mL) finely chopped garlic

1 tsp (5 mL) finely chopped ginger

Salmon

1½ lb (750 g) salmon fillet

Garnish

1 tsp (5 mL) sesame seeds

3 Tbsp (45 mL) chopped cilantro or parsley

ROSE'S TIP
Store your garlic and ginger in a dark, cool pantry. No need to refrigerate until cut.

HEALTH TIP
Garlic contains allicin, which gives garlic its odour and protects us from cancer and heart disease. To activate this compound, chop the garlic and let it sit for 10 minutes before using.

NUTRITION INFORMATION PER SERVING

Calories 350	Protein 39 g	Cholesterol 108 mg
Carbohydrates 10.5 g	Total fat 15 g	Sodium 420 mg
Fibre 0.3 g	Saturated fat 1.8 g	

SALMON STUFFED WITH PESTO CREAM CHEESE

This is an easy and delicious way to serve salmon. I prefer to use homemade pesto, which has fewer calories and less fat than store-bought pesto. To toast the pine nuts or almonds, just place them in a dry skillet over high heat, add the nuts and stir often for about 3 minutes or until they are lightly browned.

1. Preheat the oven to 425°F (220°C). Line a rimmed baking sheet with foil and lightly coat with cooking spray.

2. Combine the cream cheese and pesto in a small bowl until smooth.

3. Make a small vertical slit on the top of each salmon fillet to within ¼ inch (6 mm) of each end and about ½ inch (1 cm) deep. Divide the pesto filling between the fillets and stuff each fillet.

4. Place on the prepared baking sheet and bake for 10 minutes per inch (2.5 cm) of thickness.

5. Garnish with the toasted nuts before serving.

PREPARATION TIME 5 minutes · **COOKING TIME** 10 to 15 minutes ·
MAKE AHEAD Make the stuffing up to 2 days in advance. Bake the fish just before serving. · **MAKES** 4 servings.

¼ cup (60 mL) softened reduced-fat cream cheese (2 oz/60 g)

2 Tbsp (30 mL) store-bought or homemade pesto (see Basil Pesto on page 371)

Salmon
1½ lb (750 g) salmon fillet, cut into 4 fillets (about 6 oz/175 g each)

Garnish
2 Tbsp (30 mL) toasted pine nuts (or chopped toasted almonds)

 ROSE'S TIP
You can toast your nuts and freeze in large Ziploc bags for later use.

 HEALTH TIP
Pine nuts are rich in vitamin E, an antioxidant that protects our cells from free radicals that cause cancer. A 3-ounce (90 gram) serving has over 62% of our daily vitamin E requirements. They also help lower the risk of heart disease.

NUTRITION INFORMATION PER SERVING

Calories 362	Protein 40.5 g	Cholesterol 115.5 mg
Carbohydrates 1.5 g	Total fat 19.5 g	Sodium 162 mg
Fibre 0.3 g	Saturated fat 4.2 g	

ROASTED PROSCIUTTO-WRAPPED WHITE FISH WITH PESTO

I had a version of this in a restaurant while on a ski trip in Colorado, and I had to recreate it. Prosciutto used sparingly is fine in your diet. You can experiment with different herbs and nuts to make the pesto. You can try this recipe with boneless chicken breasts as well.

1. Preheat the oven to 400°F (200°C). Line a rimmed baking pan with foil and lightly coat with cooking spray.

2. TO MAKE THE PESTO Combine the basil, parsley, pine nuts, Parmesan, olive oil, garlic and salt and pepper in the bowl of a food processor and process until all the ingredients are finely chopped and well combined. Do not purée.

3. Place the prosciutto slices horizontally on a flat surface. Spread the pesto down the middle of each slice. Place a fish fillet vertically on each slice and wrap the prosciutto around the fish.

4. Lightly coat a nonstick skillet with cooking spray and set over medium-high heat. Add the fish and sauté on each side for 1 minute or until the prosciutto begins to get crisp.

5. Place the fish on the prepared baking pan and bake for 10 minutes or until the fish just flakes when tested with a fork.

PREPARATION TIME 15 minutes · **COOKING TIME** 12 minutes ·
MAKE AHEAD Prepare the fish early in the day. Refrigerate and bake just before serving. · **MAKES** 6 servings.

NUTRITION INFORMATION PER SERVING

Calories 415	Protein 42 g	Cholesterol 118.5 mg
Carbohydrates 4.5 g	Total fat 25.5 g	Sodium 450 mg
Fibre 2 g	Saturated fat 3.8 g	

Pesto

⅔ cup (160 mL) fresh basil leaves

⅔ cup (160 mL) fresh parsley leaves

¼ cup (60 mL) toasted pine nuts (or almonds)

2 Tbsp (30 mL) grated Parmesan cheese (½ oz/15 g)

2 Tbsp (30 mL) olive oil

½ tsp (2.5 mL) finely chopped garlic

pinch of salt and pepper

6 thin slices prosciutto (about 3 oz/90 g in total)

1½ lb (750 g) firm white fish (such as halibut, sea bass or black cod), cut into six 4 oz (125 g) fillets

 ROSE'S TIP
This pesto contains both basil and parsley. You can create your own versions by using combinations of basil, cilantro, mint, parsley, spinach or arugula.

 HEALTH TIP
Prosciutto is a cured ham that has very few calories when used sparingly in a recipe like this. One slice contains only 50 calories and 1.5 grams of fat. Beware, though, of the high sodium content.

HALIBUT WITH ORANGE–MISO GLAZE

This miso glaze is so easy to make and tastes so authentic. Miso is a fermented soybean paste that comes in a variety of flavours and colours. The most common are red, brown and white or yellow. I like using the lighter varieties because they are sweeter and less pungent.

1. Preheat the oven to 425°F (220°C). Spray a baking sheet with cooking oil.

2. TO MAKE THE GLAZE Combine the miso, orange juice, soy sauce, sesame oil, sugar and orange peel in a small bowl.

3. Remove 2 Tbsp (30 mL) of the glaze and brush lightly over the fish. Sprinkle with the sesame seeds.

4. Place the fish on the prepared baking sheet and bake for about 10 minutes per inch (2.5 cm) of thickness of fish or until the fish flakes easily when pierced with a fork.

5. Serve with the remaining sauce on the side. Garnish each serving with a sprinkling of green onions and cilantro.

PREPARATION TIME 5 minutes · **COOKING TIME** 10 minutes ·
MAKE AHEAD Prepare the sauce up to 2 days in advance and refrigerate. Cook the fish just before serving. · **MAKES** 4 servings.

Glaze

2 Tbsp (30 mL) white miso paste

¼ cup (60 mL) orange juice concentrate

2 tsp (10 mL) low-sodium soy sauce

2 tsp (10 mL) sesame oil

5 tsp (25 mL) brown sugar

½ tsp (2.5 mL) grated orange peel

1½ lb (750 g) halibut fillets

2 tsp (10 mL) sesame seeds

Garnish

3 Tbsp (45 mL) diced green onions

2 Tbsp (30 mL) chopped cilantro

 ROSE'S TIP
Miso paste is found in the refrigerator section of your supermarket, specialty or health food store.

 HEALTH TIP
Miso has a high sodium content, yet recent studies show that diets containing miso lower the risk of heart disease. This may be due to the unique soy protein of miso.

NUTRITION INFORMATION PER SERVING

Calories 302	Protein 38 g	Cholesterol 77 mg
Carbohydrates 12 g	Total fat 11 g	Sodium 551 mg
Fibre 0.6 g	Saturated fat 2.1 g	

PISTACHIO-CRUSTED BASA

Basa is a white fish that is delicate tasting, quick to cook and incredibly affordable. You can always substitute another white fish. Pistachios give this fish a bright green colour and sweet nutty flavour.

1. Preheat the oven to 400°F (200°C) and spray a 9-inch (23 cm) baking dish with vegetable oil.

2. TO MAKE THE TOPPING Place the topping ingredients in a small food processor and pulse just until combined.

3. Divide the topping overtop of the fish. Bake for 10 minutes per inch (2.5 cm) of thickness or just until cooked.

PREPARATION TIME 10 minutes · **COOKING TIME** 10 minutes ·
MAKE AHEAD Prepare the nut crust up to a day in advance, cover and refrigerate. Bake the fish just before serving. · **MAKES** 4 servings.

Topping

⅔ cup (160 mL) toasted pistachios

¼ cup (60 mL) Parmesan cheese (1 oz/30 g)

2 Tbsp (30 mL) olive oil

2 Tbsp (30 mL) lemon juice

1 tsp (5 mL) lemon zest

1 tsp (5 mL) garlic

Basa

1½ lb (750 g) basa fillets (or any white fish)

 ROSE'S TIP

Basa is the newest trendiest fish on the market. But basa is not a new fish, it just has a new name. Better known as a type of catfish, they are native to Vietnam and Thailand.

 HEALTH TIP

Basa is one of the lowest-calorie fish available. A 4-ounce (125 g) serving has only 70 calories, 2 grams of fat and 15 grams of protein.

NUTRITION INFORMATION PER SERVING

Calories 358	Protein 35.6 g	Cholesterol 141 mg
Carbohydrates 6.6 g	Total fat 17 g	Sodium 212 mg
Fibre 2.2 g	Saturated fat 2.9 g	

TILAPIA WITH TOMATO AND GREEN-OLIVE SALSA

Olives have such a distinctive flavour, they go best with a milder-tasting fish. This is a very Mediterranean-tasting dish. Chicken would also be a great substitute.

1. Dust the fish with the flour and salt and pepper. In a large skillet sprayed with vegetable spray, add oil and fish. Sauté for about 5 to 8 minutes, turning halfway just until cooked.

2. TO MAKE THE SALSA Combine the tomatoes, garlic, olives, capers, olive oil, jalapeños and cilantro and spoon overtop of the fish.

PREPARATION TIME 15 minutes · **COOKING TIME** 8 minutes ·
MAKE AHEAD Prepare the salsa early in the day. Bake the fish just before serving. · **MAKES** 4 servings.

ROSE'S TIP
Capers are not a type of fish! Capers are the unripened flower buds of the *Capparis spinosa* plant native to the Mediterranean. The buds are harvested and dried, then pickled in vinegar, brine or salt.

HEALTH TIP
There are no nutritional differences between green and black olives. They have the same benefits of extra virgin olive oil. This is a monounsaturated fat that lessens the risk of heart disease, cancer and obesity.

1½ lb (750 g) white fish fillets (basa or tilapia)

3 Tbsp (45 mL) all-purpose flour

pinch of salt and pepper

2 tsp (10 mL) vegetable oil

Salsa

2 cups (500 mL) quartered cherry tomatoes (different colours)

1 tsp (5 mL) crushed garlic

¼ cup (60 mL) diced green olives with pimentos

2 tsp (10 mL) chopped capers

1 Tbsp (15 mL) olive oil

1 tsp (5 mL) minced jalapeño peppers

¼ cup (60 mL) chopped cilantro

NUTRITION INFORMATION PER SERVING

Calories 248	Protein 31.7 g	Cholesterol 136 mg
Carbohydrates 7.1 g	Total fat 9 g	Sodium 195 mg
Fibre 0.9 g	Saturated fat 1.7 g	

FISH CRUSTED WITH BLACK AND GREEN OLIVES

The topping for this dish, which combines two types of olives, breadcrumbs, garlic and lemon juice, is delicious. Olives contain monounsaturated fat, which means they're heart-healthy, but you still have to watch the amount you consume since they are high in calories and fat. I use them to highlight this dish.

1. Preheat the oven to 425°F (220°C). Spray a rimmed baking sheet with cooking spray.

2. TO MAKE THE TOPPING In a food processor, combine bread-crumbs, black and green olives, oregano, garlic, oil, and lemon juice. Process until finely chopped.

3. Place the fish on the prepared baking sheet. Sprinkle with the topping. Bake 10 minutes per inch (2.5 cm) thickness of fish and topping or until the fish flakes easily when prodded with a fork.

4. Serve garnished with lemon wedges and parsley sprigs.

PREPARATION TIME 10 minutes • **COOKING TIME** 10 minutes •
MAKE AHEAD Prepare the topping up to a day in advance. Bake just
before serving. • **MAKES** 4 servings.

NUTRITION INFORMATION PER SERVING

Calories 253	Protein 36.4 g	Cholesterol 64 mg
Carbohydrates 8.1 g	Total fat 7.9 g	Sodium 464 mg
Fibre 0.5 g	Saturated fat 1.1 g	

Topping

½ cup (125 mL) seasoned dry breadcrumbs

3 Tbsp (45 mL) sliced black olives

3 Tbsp (45 mL) sliced green olives

½ tsp (2.5 mL) dried oregano

½ tsp (2.5 mL) minced garlic

2 tsp (10 mL) olive oil

1 Tbsp (15 mL) fresh lemon juice

Fish

four 6 oz (175 g) skinless white fish fillet portions such as halibut, tilapia, haddock or cod

lemon wedges and sprigs of fresh parsley

 ROSE'S TIP
Olives packed in oil have more calories but are tastier than those canned in water. Since you're using such a small amount, I wouldn't be concerned.

 HEALTH TIP
White fish has fewer calories and less fat than salmon or tuna. A 4-ounce (125 g) serving of tilapia has 100 calories and 2 grams of fat. A 4-ounce (125 g) serving of salmon has over 200 calories and 12 grams of fat. But salmon contains a heart-healthy fat that consists of omega-3 fatty acids.

HOISIN-SESAME STEAMED SEA BASS

Steaming is a wonderful cooking technique in Asian cuisine. It keeps calories and fat to a minimum. If sea bass or halibut isn't within your budget, try salmon, which also goes well with this hoisin sauce.

1. Use a steamer over 2 inches (5 cm) of water or create a makeshift steamer by filling a large pot with 2 inches (5 cm) of water and setting a metal rack inside to fit in the pan.

2. **TO MAKE THE SAUCE** Combine the stock, soy sauce, hoisin sauce, sesame oil, ginger and garlic. Place the sauce in a heatproof bowl small enough to fit on the steamer.

3. Add the fish. Cover, bring the water to a boil, then simmer, covered, on medium heat for about 10 minutes per inch (2.5 cm) of thickness of the fish.

4. Garnish with green onions and cilantro.

PREPARATION TIME 10 minutes · **COOKING TIME** 10 minutes ·
MAKE AHEAD Make the sauce early in the day. Steam just before serving. · **MAKES** 4 servings.

 ROSE'S TIP
To bake the fish place it in foil and pour the sauce overtop. Wrap tightly and bake at 425°F (220°C) for 12 to 15 minutes.

 HEALTH TIP
Steaming allows food to cook in its own juices, which minimizes the loss of nutrients and retains its texture and flavour.

Sauce

¼ cup (60 mL) low-sodium fish or chicken stock

2 Tbsp (30 mL) low-sodium soy sauce

2 Tbsp (30 mL) hoisin sauce

2 tsp (10 mL) sesame oil

1 Tbsp (15 mL) chopped fresh ginger

2 tsp (10 mL) chopped garlic

Fish

1½ lb (750 g) sea bass or halibut fillets

Garnish

3 Tbsp (45 mL) chopped green onions

2 Tbsp (30 mL) chopped cilantro or parsley

NUTRITION INFORMATION PER SERVING

Calories 201	Protein 32 g	Cholesterol 70 mg
Carbohydrates 3.7 g	Total fat 6 g	Sodium 490 mg
Fibre 0.8 g	Saturated fat 1.3 g	

SOLE STUFFED WITH CRAB

Sole is one of the few fish that is difficult to overbake. This is a plus for those intimidated by cooking fish. The tasty stuffing adds flavour to this delicate fish. Sole can be gently reheated the next day and still stay moist. Crabmeat is always the preferred choice, but surimi is a good substitute.

1. Preheat the oven to 425°F (220°C). Spray a baking dish with cooking oil.

2. TO MAKE THE STUFFING Combine the crabmeat, mayonnaise, lemon juice, green onion and dill in the bowl of a food processor. Pulse just until still chunky. Alternatively, chop finely by hand.

3. TO MAKE THE TOPPING Combine the breadcrumbs, oil and garlic.

4. Divide the filling over the sole fillets. Roll them up and fasten with a toothpick. Sprinkle the crumb mixture overtop. Place them in the prepared baking dish and bake in the centre of the oven for 10 minutes or until the fish flakes and is no longer translucent. Remove toothpicks.

5. Garnish with dill and serve immediately.

PREPARATION TIME 10 minutes · **COOKING TIME** 10 minutes ·
MAKE AHEAD Prepare the stuffing up to a day in advance and refrigerate.
Bake just before serving. · **MAKES** 4 servings.

Stuffing

4 oz (125 g) crabmeat (or surimi)

2 Tbsp (30 mL) reduced-fat mayonnaise

1 Tbsp (15 mL) freshly squeezed lemon juice

¼ cup (60 mL) chopped green onion

2 Tbsp (30 mL) chopped fresh dill

Topping

2 Tbsp (30 mL) seasoned dry breadcrumbs

1 tsp (5 mL) olive oil

½ tsp (2.5 mL) crushed fresh garlic

Sole

1½ lb (750 g) sole (4 fillets)

Garnish

2 Tbsp (30 mL) chopped fresh parsley

ROSE'S TIP

Purchase frozen crabmeat. Defrost just the amount you need and keep the rest frozen. Be sure to squeeze out all excess moisture from the crab before using. Surimi is an inexpensive version of crabmeat made up of a variety of white fishes.

 HEALTH TIP

Sole is one of the leanest fish. A 3-ounce (90 g) serving contains only 100 calories, 1 gram of fat and 21 grams of protein, a third of your daily protein requirement.

NUTRITION INFORMATION PER SERVING

Calories 215	Protein 39 g	Cholesterol 109 mg
Carbohydrates 3.4 g	Total fat 4.6 g	Sodium 354 mg
Fibre 0.6 g	Saturated fat 1.2 g	

SEARED TUNA WITH MEDITERRANEAN SALSA

This Mediterranean-flavoured dish tastes like a Greek salad. Tuna goes well with the salsa. Serving the tuna slightly undercooked is the key to excellent tuna. Searing the tuna is exceptionally great tasting. Feel free to substitute another firm fish, such as sea bass. If you use another fish, cook it right through.

1. TO MAKE THE SALSA In a bowl, combine the tomatoes, peppers, onions, olives, lemon juice, feta, olive oil, garlic and oregano together.

2. Either on a barbecue or in a nonstick grill pan sprayed with cooking spray, sear the tuna on both sides just until cooked to your preference. Place on a serving dish. Sprinkle with the basil and serve the salsa overtop.

PREPARATION TIME 15 minutes · **COOKING TIME** 8 to 10 minutes · **MAKE AHEAD** The salsa can be made early in the day, but remove the seeds of the tomatoes. · **MAKES** 6 servings.

ROSE'S TIP

When I buy fresh tuna for cooking I like to use bluefin tuna, which has the most flavour. The flesh is dark red with the appearance of raw beef. The best flavour is when the tuna is just seared and still pink inside.

HEALTH TIP

Tuna is rich in high-quality protein and an excellent source of nutrients such as selenium, potassium, magnesium and of course omega-3 essential fatty acids, which are known to reduce the risk of heart disease and cancer.

Salsa

1 cup (250 mL) diced plum tomatoes

⅓ cup (80 mL) diced sweet green peppers

¼ cup (60 mL) diced green onions

3 Tbsp (45 mL) chopped black olives

2 Tbsp (45 mL) fresh lemon juice

⅓ cup (80 mL) crumbled reduced-fat feta cheese (1½ oz/45 g)

2 tsp (10 mL) olive oil

1½ tsp (7.5 mL) finely chopped garlic

½ tsp (2.5 mL) dried oregano

Tuna

6 tuna fillets (about 6 oz/ 175 g each)

Garnish

¼ cup (60 mL) chopped fresh basil or parsley

NUTRITION INFORMATION PER SERVING

Calories 241	Protein 36.8 g	Cholesterol 74 mg
Carbohydrates 4.2 g	Total fat 7.8 g	Sodium 258 mg
Fibre 1 g	Saturated fat 2.1 g	

SHRIMP WITH WHITE BEANS, LEMON AND PESTO

This is similar to a classic Northern Italian dish. The beans and pesto blend so well with the olives and grilled shrimp.

1. Either grill or sauté shrimp in a skillet sprayed with vegetable oil just until cooked (about 5 minutes). Set aside.

2. In a large skillet sprayed with vegetable spray, add the oil and sauté the onion and garlic for 5 minutes on medium heat until soft and lightly browned. Add the beans, pesto, stock, lemon juice, and olives and cook for 2 minutes until the dish is warm.

3. Place on serving plate and top with shrimp, feta and tomatoes.

PREPARATION TIME 15 minutes · **COOKING TIME** 12 minutes ·
MAKE AHEAD Cook the onion and bean dish early in the day, but cook the shrimp just before serving. · **MAKES** 4 servings.

 ROSE'S TIP
Be sure to weigh your shrimp after it's been defrosted and shelled.

 HEALTH TIP
Six ounces (175 g) of shrimp gives 34 grams of protein, which is over half your daily protein requirement. This amount also contains over 100% of your daily tryptophan requirement, which is responsible for your sleep, mood and appetite.

12 oz (375 g) large shelled shrimp (tail left on)

2 tsp (10 mL) vegetable oil

1 cup (250 mL) chopped onion

1 tsp (5 mL) minced garlic

1½ cups (375 mL) canned white navy beans or kidney beans, drained and rinsed

¼ cup (60 mL) store-bought or homemade pesto (see Basil Pesto on page 371)

⅓ cup (80 mL) low-sodium chicken stock

1½ Tbsp (22.5 mL) lemon juice

¼ cup (60 mL) chopped black olives

Garnish
⅓ cup (80 mL) crumbled reduced-fat feta cheese (1½ oz/45 g)

½ cup (125 mL) diced tomatoes

NUTRITION INFORMATION PER SERVING

Calories 197	Protein 20.5 g	Cholesterol 110 mg
Carbohydrates 19 g	Total fat 5.3 g	Sodium 350 mg
Fibre 1.3 g	Saturated fat 1.6 g	

SCALLOPS WITH AVOCADO, CORN AND BELL PEPPER SALSA

Scallops have a sweet and mild taste with a delicious fleshy texture. They are perfect either grilled or sautéed to sear the surface. This fresh salsa rather than a butter sauce is superb overtop.

1. Preheat grill to 425°F (220°C) or spray a grill pan with vegetable oil.

2. TO MAKE THE SALSA In a small skillet sprayed with vegetable oil, sauté the corn for about 5 minutes just until lightly browned. Place it in a small serving bowl along with the avocado, red pepper, jalapeños, onions, salt and pepper, lemon juice, olive oil and cilantro.

3. In a grill pan sprayed with vegetable oil, grill the scallops, about 2 minutes per side or just until done to your liking.

4. Serve with the salsa.

PREPARATION TIME 15 minutes · **COOKING TIME** 9 minutes ·
MAKE AHEAD Prepare the salsa early in the day, leaving out the avocado.
Add the avocado just before grilling the scallops. · **MAKES** 4 servings.

Salsa

1 cup (250 mL) corn

½ cup (125 mL) finely diced avocado

⅓ cup (80 mL) finely diced red bell pepper

1½ tsp (7.5 mL) minced jalapeño

3 Tbsp (45 mL) finely diced red onion

pinch of salt and pepper

1½ Tbsp (22.5 mL) lemon juice

1½ tsp (7.5 mL) olive oil

3 Tbsp (45 mL) finely chopped cilantro

Scallops

1½ lb (750 g) large scallops

 ROSE'S TIP
When using fresh herbs like cilantro, cut off the bottoms of the stems and do not wash until ready to use. Fill a glass jar with water and place the stems in the water. Cover loosely with a plastic bag and refrigerate for up to one week.

 HEALTH TIP
Canned and frozen corn retain the same nutritional benefits as fresh corn, provided they are processed immediately after being harvested. Canned will contain added sodium.

NUTRITION INFORMATION PER SERVING

Calories 314	Protein 39 g	Cholesterol 108 mg
Carbohydrates 7.5 g	Total fat 13 g	Sodium 120 mg
Fibre 2.1 g	Saturated fat 2.2 g	

CASHEW- AND LEMON-CRUSTED TILAPIA

I created this recipe for the Pickle Barrel restaurant chain in Toronto. It's a real winner for fish lovers. The mild taste of tilapia goes well with nuts, and this lemon-nut combination is outstanding. If you want to substitute another fish, try sole.

1. Preheat the oven to 425°F (220°C). Line a baking sheet with foil and spray with cooking oil.

2. TO MAKE THE NUT CRUST Place the cashews, cheese, oil, lemon juice and garlic in the bowl of a food processor and process just until coarsely ground. Do not purée. Alternatively, finely chop by hand.

3. Place the fish on the prepared baking sheet and divide the nut mixture overtop, pressing it onto the fillets to help it adhere. Bake for 10 minutes per inch (2.5 cm) of thickness or until the fish flakes when pierced with a fork.

4. Garnish with the dill and lemon wedges.

PREPARATION TIME 5 minutes · **COOKING TIME** 10 minutes ·
MAKE AHEAD Prepare the nut crust early in the day. Cover tightly.
Bake the fish just before serving. · **MAKES** 4 servings.

Nut crust
⅓ cup (80 mL) finely chopped toasted cashews

¼ cup (60 mL) grated Parmesan cheese (1 oz/30 g)

1 Tbsp (15 mL) olive oil

1 Tbsp (15 mL) freshly squeezed lemon juice

½ tsp (2.5 mL) crushed fresh garlic

Tilapia
1½ lb (750 g) tilapia

Garnish
3 Tbsp (45 mL) chopped fresh dill or basil

lemon wedges

 ROSE'S TIP
Tilapia is a very mild fish, perfect for those who are not fish lovers, especially children.

HEALTH TIP
Tilapia is very lean fish. One 3-ounce (90 g) serving has 128 calories and 3 grams of fat and contains over 50% of your daily protein requirement.

NUTRITION INFORMATION PER SERVING

Calories 294	Protein 37 g	Cholesterol 85 mg
Carbohydrates 5.1 g	Total fat 14 g	Sodium 143 mg
Fibre 0.6 g	Saturated fat 3 g	

CHICKEN

LETTUCE CUPS WITH HOISIN CHICKEN

I created this recipe originally with peanut sauce and beef, but then redeveloped it for Glow Fresh Grill using tender chicken breasts or thighs with a hoisin sauce. It's great as a main meal or starter.

1. Dust the chicken with the flour and sauté in a skillet sprayed with vegetable oil just until cooked. Set aside.

2. In a large nonstick skillet sprayed with vegetable spray, heat the oil then sauté the onions for 5 minutes or just until browned. Add the carrots and mushrooms and sauté for another 8 minutes until tender and no moisture is left from the mushrooms. Add the red pepper and sauté for 3 minutes. Add the chicken, water chestnuts, green onions and cilantro.

3. Add half of the Hoisin Sauce to the chicken mixture.

4. Serve the chicken mixture with the lettuce and the remaining sauce on the side. Garnish with sesame seeds.

PREPARATION TIME 20 minutes · **COOKING TIME** 16 minutes ·
MAKE AHEAD Prepare the entire dish early in the day. Reheat gently in a skillet just before serving. · **MAKES** 4 servings.

ROSE'S TIP
You can substitute pork, tender beef cubes or tofu for the chicken and use the vegetables of your choice.

HEALTH TIP
Hoisin sauce has around 35 calories per tablespoon (15 mL), but it is high in sodium with about 250 mg per tablespoon (15 mL). Use it in a sauce rather than as a condiment.

12 oz (375 g) diced boneless skinless chicken breasts or thighs

3 Tbsp (45 mL) all-purpose flour

2 tsp (10 mL) vegetable oil

1⅓ cups (335 mL) chopped onion

⅔ cup (160 mL) diced carrots

2 cups (500 mL) diced mushrooms

¾ cup (185 mL) diced red bell pepper

⅔ cup (160 mL) diced water chestnuts

½ cup (125 mL) diced green onions

⅓ cup (80 mL) chopped cilantro

Hoisin Sauce
½ cup (125 mL) Hoisin Sauce (see page 372), divided

8 large Boston lettuce leaves

2 tsp (10 mL) sesame seeds

NUTRITION INFORMATION PER SERVING

Calories 262	Protein 21.3 g	Cholesterol 45 mg
Carbohydrates 31.4 g	Total fat 6.7 g	Sodium 525 mg
Fibre 4.1 g	Saturated fat 0.9 g	

CHICKEN WITH AVOCADO, TOMATO AND LEMON SALSA

I love to serve this chicken in the summer outdoors or at a Sunday brunch. The salsa is fresh tasting, and the contrasting colours are beautiful.

1. Between 2 sheets of waxed paper, pound the chicken breasts to an even ½-inch (1 cm) thickness. Dust the chicken with flour. In a nonstick skillet sprayed with cooking spray, heat the oil over medium-high heat. Cook the chicken for 5 to 8 minutes, turning once, or until cooked through. Place on a serving dish.

2. TO MAKE THE SALSA In a bowl, stir together the tomatoes, avocado, cilantro, oil, lemon juice, garlic, honey, hot sauce and salt and pepper.

3. Spoon the salsa over the chicken before serving.

PREPARATION TIME 15 minutes • **COOKING TIME** 5 to 8 minutes •
MAKE AHEAD Prepare the salsa a few hours in advance. Cook the chicken right before serving. • **MAKES** 4 servings.

4 boneless skinless chicken breasts (about 1½ lb/750 g total)

3 Tbsp (10 mL) all-purpose flour

2 tsp (10 mL) vegetable oil

Salsa

1 cup (250 mL) chopped plum tomatoes

½ cup (125 mL) diced avocado

3 Tbsp (45 mL) chopped fresh cilantro

1 Tbsp (15 mL) olive oil

2 tsp (10 mL) fresh lemon juice

1 tsp (5 mL) minced garlic

½ tsp (2.5 mL) liquid honey

½ tsp (2.5 mL) hot sauce

pinch of salt and pepper

 ROSE'S TIP
Avocados are a perfect match with tomatoes and lemon. It's best to cut it just before using to avoid the avocado turning brown. You can always cut it early in the day and keep it in a bowl of water and lemon juice.

 HEALTH TIP
Avocados are a great source of monounsaturated fat, which can prevent heart disease. But watch the amount you eat, since one avocado has over 300 calories and 30 grams of fat. But on the positive side, one avocado has 13 grams of fibre—half your daily intake.

NUTRITION INFORMATION PER SERVING

Calories 317	Protein 40.4 g	Cholesterol 98.8 mg
Carbohydrates 12.5 g	Total fat 11.3 g	Sodium 133 mg
Fibre 2.7 g	Saturated fat 1.9 g	

BRUSCHETTA-STYLE CHICKEN

I've always loved bruschetta in Italian restaurants, so I adapted the topping for chicken. It's outstanding and dramatic looking. The trick is not to overcook the tomato topping. Plum tomatoes are best, but if you have to use field tomatoes, seed them first to reduce the amount of liquid. You can replace the basil with fresh parsley or even cilantro.

1. Preheat the oven to 425°F (220°C). Line a baking sheet with foil and coat lightly with cooking oil.

2. Working with one at a time, place the chicken breasts between two sheets of waxed paper and pound to an even ½-inch (1 cm) thickness.

3. Place the flour on a plate. Beat the egg and milk together in a shallow bowl. Place the breadcrumbs and 2 Tbsp (30 mL) of the Parmesan on a separate plate.

4. Spray a large nonstick frying pan with cooking oil, add the vegetable oil and place over medium-high heat.

5. Coat each flattened chicken breast in flour, dip in the egg mixture, then coat in the breadcrumbs and Parmesan. Cook for 3 minutes per side or until browned and almost cooked through. Transfer to the prepared baking sheet.

6. Stir the tomatoes, onions, oil, garlic and salt and pepper together in a bowl. Spoon over the chicken breasts. Sprinkle with the 3 Tbsp (45 mL) of Parmesan. Bake in the centre of the oven for 5 minutes or until the chicken is cooked through and the tomato topping is hot. Sprinkle the basil overtop and serve immediately.

PREPARATION TIME 15 minutes • **COOKING TIME** 11 minutes •

MAKE AHEAD Make the entire chicken dish early in the day and refrigerate. Bake just before serving. • **MAKES** 4 servings.

4 boneless skinless chicken breasts (approximately 1½ lb/750 g)

¼ cup (60 mL) all-purpose flour

1 egg

2 Tbsp (30 mL) 2% milk

⅔ cup (160 mL) seasoned dry breadcrumbs

2 Tbsp (30 mL) grated Parmesan cheese (½ oz/15 g)

2 tsp (10 mL) vegetable oil

1½ cups (375 mL) diced plum tomatoes

¼ cup (60 mL) chopped green onion

1 Tbsp (15 mL) olive oil

1 tsp (5 mL) minced fresh garlic

pinch of salt and ground black pepper

3 Tbsp (45 mL) grated Parmesan cheese (¾ oz/23 g)

¼ cup (60 mL) chopped fresh basil

ROSE'S TIP

If preparing the tomato
topping early in the day,
seed the tomatoes to avoid
excess liquid.

 HEALTH TIP

Tomatoes contain lycopene,
which gives the tomato its
red colour and reduces the
risk of colorectal, prostate,
breast, lung and pancreatic
cancer.

NUTRITION INFORMATION PER SERVING

Calories 402	Protein 49.1 g	Cholesterol 156 mg
Carbohydrates 27 g	Total fat 11.7 g	Sodium 437 mg
Fibre 2.4 g	Saturated fat 2.8 g	

CHICKEN AND EGGPLANT PARMESAN

Eggplant, a healthy vegetable, is often loaded with fat and calories from the amount of oil used in frying or sautéing it. This baked version omits the oil, and it turns out great! Purchase fresh young eggplant; when overripe, it becomes bitter. If the skin doesn't spring back when pressed, then it's too old.

1. Preheat the oven to 425°F (220°C). Spray a baking sheet with cooking oil.

2. Whisk the egg with the water in a small bowl. Combine the breadcrumbs, parsley, Parmesan and garlic on a plate, mixing well. Dip the eggplant in the egg mixture, then coat with the breadcrumb mixture. Place on the prepared pan. Bake, turning once, for 20 minutes or until tender.

3. While the eggplant is baking, prepare the chicken. Working with one at a time, place the chicken breasts between two sheets of waxed paper and pound to an even ¼-inch (6 mm) thickness. Spray a large nonstick frying pan with cooking oil, add the vegetable oil and place over medium-high heat. Dip the chicken in the egg mixture, then coat with the remaining breadcrumb mixture. Cook the chicken, turning once, for 4 minutes or until golden brown and almost cooked through.

4. Spread 1 Tbsp (15 mL) of the tomato sauce on each baked eggplant slice. Place a chicken breast on top of each eggplant slice. Spread another 1 Tbsp (15 mL) tomato sauce on each chicken piece. Sprinkle with the mozzarella and Parmesan cheeses. Bake for 5 minutes or until the cheese is golden and the chicken fully cooked.

PREPARATION TIME 10 minutes · **COOKING TIME** 25 minutes (cook the chicken while eggplant bakes) · **MAKE AHEAD** Prepare the entire chicken dish early in the day and refrigerate. Bake just before serving. · **MAKES** 4 servings.

---

1 whole egg

2 Tbsp (30 mL) water or 2% milk

¾ cup (185 mL) seasoned dry breadcrumbs

3 Tbsp (45 mL) chopped fresh parsley

3 Tbsp (45 mL) grated Parmesan cheese (¾ oz/23 g)

1 tsp (5 mL) minced fresh garlic

4 crosswise slices of eggplant, skin on, approximately ½-inch (1 cm) thick

4 boneless skinless chicken breasts (approximately 1½ lb/750 g)

2 tsp (10 mL) vegetable oil

½ cup (125 mL) homemade or store-bought tomato sauce (see Quick Basic Tomato Sauce on page 369)

½ cup (125 mL) shredded part-skim mozzarella cheese (1½ oz/45 g)

2 Tbsp (30 mL) grated Parmesan cheese (½ oz/15 g)

ROSE'S TIP

Eggplant can be bitter. By salting the slices and leaving them in a colander to drain for about 15 minutes, you will remove the juices that produce the bitterness. Then rinse in cold water and press dry with paper towels.

 HEALTH TIP

Eggplant is a low-calorie and low-fat vegetable if cooked properly. Deep-frying in oil makes it a high-fat vegetable. Two slices baked have only 40 calories and 0 grams of fat. Deep-fried, you're looking at 200 calories and 6 grams of fat!

NUTRITION INFORMATION PER SERVING

Calories 374	Protein 50.1 g	Cholesterol 162 mg
Carbohydrates 22 g	Total fat 9.1 g	Sodium 487 mg
Fibre 2.7 g	Saturated fat 3 g	

CHICKEN WITH THREE CHEESES, TOMATOES AND BASIL

I initially created this recipe for white fish; I then tried the delicious topping over a grain. Now I've found it works well with chicken. Use a variety of cheeses of your choice, but be sure to include a couple of stronger-tasting ones.

1. Preheat the oven to 425°F (220°C). Lightly coat a 9- × 13-inch (3.5 L) casserole dish with cooking spray.

2. Working with one at a time, place a chicken breast between 2 sheets of waxed paper and pound to an even ½-inch (1 cm) thickness.

3. Beat the egg and milk together in a shallow bowl. Place the breadcrumbs on a separate plate or shallow dish.

4. Lightly coat a large nonstick skillet with cooking spray, add the oil and place over medium-high heat. Dip each flattened chicken breast into the egg mixture, then coat in the breadcrumbs. Cook for 3 minutes per side or until browned and almost cooked through. Transfer to the prepared casserole dish.

5. Combine the tomatoes, Havarti, goat and Parmesan cheeses, olives, garlic and dried basil in a bowl. Spoon over the chicken breasts. Cover and bake for 10 minutes or until the cheese melts and the chicken is done (has reached an internal temperature of 165°F/74°C). Garnish with fresh basil and serve.

PREPARATION TIME 15 minutes · **COOKING TIME** 16 minutes ·
MAKE AHEAD Prepare the entire dish early in the day and bake just before serving. · **MAKES** 4 servings.

1½ lb (750 g) boneless skinless chicken breasts (about 4 breasts)

1 egg

2 Tbsp (30 mL) 2% milk

¾ cup (185 mL) seasoned dry breadcrumbs

2 tsp (10 mL) vegetable oil

1⅓ cups (335 mL) diced plum tomatoes

½ cup (125 mL) shredded Havarti cheese (1½ oz/45 g)

¼ cup (60 mL) crumbled goat cheese (1 oz/30 g)

2 Tbsp (30 mL) grated Parmesan cheese (½ oz/15 g)

¼ cup (60 mL) finely chopped black olives

1 tsp (5 mL) finely chopped garlic

1 tsp (5 mL) dried basil

3 Tbsp (45 mL) chopped fresh basil or parsley

ROSE'S TIP

You can use other varieties of cheeses if you like. Try stronger cheeses, such as a combination of blue, Swiss and provolone, for a more intense flavour.

 HEALTH TIP

I love the taste of olives that have been packed in oil versus those canned in water. But the calories and fat are higher. If you rinse the olives with water, you'll eliminate half the calories and fat and still retain the flavour.

NUTRITION INFORMATION PER SERVING

Calories 473   Protein 48 g   Cholesterol 174 mg

Carbohydrates 19.5 g   Total fat 19.5 g   Sodium 568.5 mg

Fibre 2.3 g   Saturated fat 8.6 g

SOY-MAPLE SESAME-CRUSTED CHICKEN OVER SOBA NOODLES

I literally created this recipe after my book was sent to the publisher. Fortunately I squeezed it in. This is a simple and delicious trendy Asian chicken dish that goes well over soba noodles. The sesame seed coating gives a crunchy texture to this meal.

1. Preheat the oven to 375°F (190°C). Line a baking sheet with foil sprayed with vegetable spray.

2. In a bowl, beat the egg. Add the milk and mix. Dip the chicken breast in the egg mixture, then in the sesame seeds and salt and pepper. Place on the baking sheet and bake for 15 minutes or until the temperature reaches 160°F (71°C). Let cool for 5 minutes. Slice thinly.

3. Boil the soba noodles until just tender (about 5 minutes). Drain well and place on a serving dish. Place chicken overtop.

4. TO MAKE THE GLAZE Place soy sauce, maple syrup and cornstarch in a small saucepan and whisk until the cornstarch is dissolved. Bring to a boil and simmer for 2 minutes just until thickened.

5. Drizzle the glaze over the chicken and garnish with cilantro.

PREPARATION TIME 10 minutes · **COOKING TIME** 22 minutes ·
MAKE AHEAD Prepare chicken in advance and refrigerate until ready to bake. Make glaze early in the day. · **MAKES** 4 servings.

NUTRITION INFORMATION PER SERVING

Calories 285	Protein 32 g	Cholesterol 35 mg
Carbohydrates 31 g	Total fat 11 g	Sodium 700 mg
Fibre 2 g	Saturated fat 2 g	

1 egg

2 Tbsp (30 mL) 2% milk

1 lb (500 g) boneless chicken breast

½ cup (125 mL) toasted sesame seeds

pinch of salt and pepper

4 oz (125 g) soba noodles

Glaze
¼ cup (60 mL) low-sodium soy sauce

¼ cup (60 mL) maple syrup

2 tsp (10 mL) cornstarch

2 Tbsp (30 mL) chopped cilantro

 ROSE'S TIP
If you have the time, sauté some veggies such as broccoli, red bell peppers or snow peas with some sesame oil and soy sauce and serve this vegetable stir-fry alongside.

 HEALTH TIP
Sesame seeds are a very good source of manganese, copper, calcium, magnesium, iron and fibre. Sesame seeds are known to lower cholesterol and prevent high blood pressure.

TORTILLA-CRUSTED CHICKEN WITH GUACAMOLE AND SALSA

The tortilla chip crust is crunchier than a regular breadcrumb crust and gives the chicken a different texture. This is my version of a Southwestern chicken dish; it has much less fat and fewer calories than the traditional Mexican version. If you can't find baked tortilla chips, use regular ones. The number of calories and amount of fat will be only slightly higher.

1. Preheat the oven to 400°F (200°C). Lightly coat a baking sheet lined with foil with cooking spray.

2. Make the guacamole. Cover and set aside.

3. Working with one at a time, place a chicken breast between 2 sheets of waxed paper and pound to an even ½-inch (1 cm) thickness. Set aside. Whisk together the egg and milk and pour into a shallow dish. Set aside. In the bowl of a food processor, combine the tortilla chips, breadcrumbs and chili powder. Process until crumbly. Dip the pounded chicken breasts in the egg and milk mixture, then into the tortilla crumb mixture.

4. Lightly coat a large nonstick skillet with cooking spray, add the oil and sauté the chicken breasts for about 3 minutes per side or until browned. Place the chicken on the prepared baking sheet.

5. Divide the salsa over the chicken. Top with the beans and cheese. Bake for 10 minutes or until the chicken is just cooked. Serve with the guacamole.

PREPARATION TIME 25 minutes • **COOKING TIME** 16 minutes •
MAKE AHEAD Prepare the dish early in the day, refrigerate and bake just before serving. • **MAKES** 4 servings.

NUTRITION INFORMATION PER SERVING

Calories 638	Protein 49.5 g	Cholesterol 171 mg
Carbohydrates 55.5 g	Total fat 24 g	Sodium 450 mg
Fibre 6.8 g	Saturated fat 7.1 g	

⅔ cup (160 mL) Guacamole (see page 362)

1½ lb (750 g) boneless skinless chicken breasts (about 4 breasts)

1 egg

2 Tbsp (30 mL) 2% milk

2½ cups (625 mL) baked tortilla chips

⅓ cup (80 mL) seasoned dry breadcrumbs

¼ tsp (1 mL) chili powder

2 tsp (10 mL) vegetable oil

⅓ cup (80 mL) medium salsa

¼ cup (60 mL) canned black beans, drained and rinsed

½ cup (125 mL) shredded aged white cheddar cheese (1½ oz/45 g)

ROSE'S TIP

You can purchase excellent ready-made guacamole, but be sure to read the label to ensure you're getting mostly avocado, not mayonnaise or sour cream.

HEALTH TIP

Store-bought salsa contains excess sodium. If you prepare your own (See Fresh Tomato Salsa on page 370), you'll only be getting 30 mg of sodium!

PARMESAN-CRUSTED CHICKEN WITH SUN-DRIED TOMATO SAUCE

A great twist on traditional chicken Parmesan. The combination of sun-dried tomatoes with sweet peppers and tomato sauce is delicious over boneless chicken breasts. I buy sun-dried tomatoes in bulk and use as needed. Just pour boiling water over them and let sit for 15 minutes. Drain, then chop.

1. Preheat the oven to 400°F (200°C).

2. In a nonstick saucepan sprayed with cooking spray, heat 2 tsp (10 mL) of the oil over medium heat; cook the onions and garlic for 5 minutes or until softened. Stir in the peppers and sun-dried tomatoes; cook for 3 minutes. Stir in the tomato sauce, chicken stock, basil and oregano. Bring to a boil. Reduce the heat to a simmer; cook, uncovered, for 10 minutes or until thickened.

3. Meanwhile, between 2 sheets of waxed paper, pound the chicken breasts to an even ½-inch (1 cm) thickness. In a shallow bowl, whisk the egg with water. On a separate plate, stir together the breadcrumbs and Parmesan cheese.

4. In a large nonstick skillet sprayed with cooking spray, heat the remaining oil over medium-high heat. Dip each chicken breast in the egg mixture; coat each with the breadcrumb mixture. Cook for 5 minutes, turning once or until golden on both sides.

5. Place half the sauce in a 9-inch (23 cm) casserole dish; place the chicken on top. Spoon the remaining sauce overtop. Sprinkle with the mozzarella and Parmesan. Bake, uncovered, for 10 minutes or until the chicken is cooked through and the cheese is melted. Garnish with parsley.

PREPARATION TIME 15 minutes · **COOKING TIME** 30 minutes · **MAKE AHEAD** Cook the sauce and bread the chicken up to 1 day in advance. Bake just before serving. · **MAKES** 4 servings.

4 tsp (20 mL) vegetable oil

1 cup (250 mL) chopped onions

1 tsp (5 mL) minced garlic

1 cup (250 mL) chopped sweet red or green peppers

⅓ cup (80 mL) chopped rehydrated sun-dried tomatoes

1 cup (250 mL) tomato pasta sauce (see Quick Basic Tomato Sauce on page 369)

½ cup (125 mL) low-sodium chicken stock

1 tsp (5 mL) dried basil

½ tsp (2.5 mL) dried oregano

4 boneless skinless chicken breasts (about 1½ lb/750 g total)

1 egg

2 Tbsp (30 mL) water

¾ cup (185 mL) seasoned dry breadcrumbs

3 Tbsp (45 mL) grated Parmesan cheese (¾ oz/23 g)

½ cup (125 mL) shredded part-skim mozzarella cheese (1½ oz/45 g)

2 Tbsp (30 mL) grated Parmesan cheese (½ oz/15 g)

3 Tbsp (45 mL) chopped fresh parsley

ROSE'S TIP

When using sun-dried tomatoes, only purchase dried versus those already soaked in oil. You can toss these in the freezer and use when needed. Just pour boiling water overtop, let stand for 10 minutes, drain and chop.

 HEALTH TIP

One cup (250 mL) of plain sun-dried tomatoes contains around 140 calories and 1.5 grams of fat. One cup (250 mL) that has been sitting in oil contains 235 calories and 15 grams of fat. Big difference!

NUTRITION INFORMATION PER SERVING

Calories 443

Carbohydrates 35 g

Fibre 4.8 g

Protein 51.1 g

Total fat 11.7 g

Saturated fat 3.1 g

Cholesterol 160 mg

Sodium 477 mg

CHICKEN BREAST STUFFED WITH THAI PESTO

I developed this chicken dish for our catering company and Glow Fresh Grill. The cilantro and cashew pesto is incredible. If you have the time, make the peanut sauce to serve overtop, but it stands on its own as is.

1. Preheat the oven to 400°F (200°C). Spray a baking dish with vegetable oil.

2. TO MAKE THE PESTO Purée all the Thai pesto ingredients into a thick paste.

3. Make a horizontal pocket in each chicken breast. Divide the filling into the pockets and close the breasts with toothpicks.

4. Mix the egg and water. Dip the breasts into the egg mixture, then the breadcrumbs.

5. In a large hot skillet sprayed with vegetable spray, add the oil and sauté the chicken just until browned on both sides, about 5 minutes.

6. Place the chicken in a baking dish. Bake in the oven just until the temperature reaches 160°F (71°C), about 12 minutes.

7. Serve with peanut sauce if desired.

PREPARATION TIME 20 minutes · **COOKING TIME** 17 minutes ·
MAKE AHEAD Prepare and sear the chicken early in the day and refrigerate.
Bake just before serving. · **MAKES** 4 servings.

Thai pesto

1⅓ cups (335 mL) cilantro leaves

1½ tsp (7.5 mL) chopped garlic

1 tsp (5 mL) chopped ginger

2 Tbsp (30 mL) olive oil

1 Tbsp (15 mL) sesame oil

⅓ cup (80 mL) chopped cashews

1 Tbsp (15 mL) lemon juice

pinch of salt and pepper

½ tsp (2.5 mL) jalapeño peppers

1 Tbsp (15 mL) low-sodium soy sauce

Chicken

1½ lb (750 g) boneless and skinless chicken breasts (about 4 breasts)

1 egg

2 Tbsp (30 mL) water or 2% milk

¾ cup (185 mL) seasoned dry breadcrumbs

1 tsp (5 mL) oil

Peanut Sauce (see page 375)

ROSE'S TIP

Pesto doesn't have to be
made the Italian way with
Parmesan cheese, olive oil
and pine nuts. This Asian
version is a wonderful twist
on this classic.

HEALTH TIP

Cilantro, also known as
Chinese parsley, is packed
with nutrients. It contains
the antioxidant quercetin,
which helps eliminate free
radicals that cause cancer
and has powerful antihis-
tamine and anti-inflam-
matory properties.

NUTRITION INFORMATION PER SERVING

Calories 351	Protein 38.8 g	Cholesterol 125 mg
Carbohydrates 10.1 g	Total fat 19 g	Sodium 617 mg
Fibre 0.9 g	Saturated fat 2.9 g	

CHICKEN BREAST STUFFED WITH ASPARAGUS, RED PEPPER AND BRIE

This is a simple and elegant recipe for a boneless chicken breast. I like to serve this sliced to show the attractive interior. If you want a stronger flavour, use a sharp cheese such as Swiss or Asiago instead of the brie. You could even try blue cheese.

1. Preheat the oven to 400°F (200°C). Lightly coat a 9- × 13-inch (3.5 L) casserole dish with cooking spray.

2. Working with one at a time, place a chicken breast between 2 sheets of waxed paper and pound to an even 2-inch (5 cm) thickness. Set aside.

3. TO MAKE THE STUFFING Boil or steam the asparagus until just tender, about 2 minutes. Drain and rinse with cold water. Dice and place it in a bowl. Add the brie, Parmesan, red pepper and dried basil.

4. Lay the chicken breasts flat and divide the stuffing equally among them. Roll up and secure with a toothpick. Whisk together the egg and milk and place them in a shallow bowl. Combine the breadcrumbs and Parmesan in another shallow bowl or plate.

5. Lightly coat a large nonstick skillet with cooking spray, add the oil and set over medium–high heat. Dip the rolled chicken into the egg mixture and then into the bread-crumbs. Sauté the rolled chicken just until browned on all sides, about 5 minutes.

6. Place in the prepared casserole dish and bake another 10 to 15 minutes or until the chicken is no longer pink (or reaches an internal temperature of 165°F/74°C). Slice in half or into medallions to serve. Garnish with basil.

PREPARATION TIME 15 minutes · **COOKING TIME** 17 minutes ·
MAKE AHEAD Prepare the entire dish and sauté. Refrigerate and bake just before serving. · **MAKES** 4 servings.

1½ lb (750 g) boneless skinless chicken breasts (about 4 breasts)

1 egg

2 Tbsp (30 mL) 2% milk (or water)

⅔ cup (160 mL) seasoned dry breadcrumbs

2 Tbsp (30 mL) grated Parmesan cheese (½ oz/15 g)

2 tsp (10 mL) vegetable oil

Stuffing

12 small (or 4 large) asparagus spears (about ¼ lb/125 g), trimmed

¼ cup (60 mL) diced brie (1 oz/30 g)

2 Tbsp (30 mL) grated Parmesan cheese (½ oz/15 g)

¼ cup (60 mL) chopped roasted red pepper (about 2 small roasted red peppers)

½ tsp (2.5 mL) dried basil

3 Tbsp (45 mL) chopped fresh basil

ROSE'S TIP

Who says you can't enjoy brie when eating healthy? It's all about portions! You could also use pounded turkey, veal or pork cutlets instead of the chicken.

 HEALTH TIP

When buying brie, avoid the double-cream variety, which means higher calories and fat. There is now a light brie available with about 20% less fat.

NUTRITION INFORMATION PER SERVING

Calories 333	Protein 40.5 g	Cholesterol 156 mg
Carbohydrates 16 g	Total fat 10.8 g	Sodium 331.5 mg
Fibre 2 g	Saturated fat 3.2 g	

PEANUT-CRUSTED CHICKEN WITH PEANUT COCONUT SAUCE

Nuts and chicken go hand in hand. The peanut and panko crust is outstanding and the double flavour of added Peanut Coconut Sauce finishes this dish perfectly.

1. Preheat the oven to 375°F (190°C). Line a baking sheet with foil sprayed with vegetable oil.

2. Between 2 sheets of waxed paper, pound the chicken breasts to an even ½-inch (1 cm) thickness. Combine the egg and milk in a bowl.

3. Place the panko, peanuts and salt and pepper into a small food processor and grind until very fine. Dip the chicken breasts in the egg mixture, then the crumbs. Place on a baking sheet and bake for 10 minutes or until the chicken is no longer pink.

4. Serve the chicken with the Peanut Coconut Sauce and garnish with cilantro and peanuts.

PREPARATION TIME 15 minutes · **COOKING TIME** 10 minutes ·
MAKE AHEAD Prepare the chicken and sauce up to a day in advance. Bake just before serving. · **MAKES** 4 servings.

1½ lb (750 g) boneless chicken breast

1 egg

½ cup (125 mL) 2% milk

1 cup (250 mL) panko crumbs

⅓ cup (80 mL) toasted peanuts

pinch of salt and pepper

Sauce

½ cup (125 mL) Peanut Coconut Sauce (see page 376)

2 Tbsp (30 mL) chopped cilantro

3 Tbsp (45 mL) chopped toasted peanuts

ROSE'S TIP

Feel free to substitute
other nuts of your choice
as well as the nut butter.
Try pecan, almond or
cashew nuts and nut
butters. These nut butters
are available in specialty
grocery or health food
shops.

 HEALTH TIP

Coconut milk is a satu-
rated fat despite the fact
there is no animal fat.
The light version is excep-
tional tasting, and used
in moderation is perfect
for Thai and curry dishes.
One-third cup (80 mL) of
regular coconut milk has
120 calories and 11 grams
of fat versus the light,
which has only 50 calories
and 4 grams of fat!

NUTRITION INFORMATION PER SERVING

Calories 469	Protein 47.8 g	Cholesterol 125 mg
Carbohydrates 28.3 g	Total fat 20.8 g	Sodium 776 mg
Fibre 3.6 g	Saturated fat 4.3 g	

HOISIN ORANGE CHICKEN WITH COUSCOUS

This chicken seems to be a hit with adults and the younger folk. This hoisin orange sauce tastes wonderful, especially with the fluffy bed of couscous.

1. Preheat the oven to 400°F (200°C). Spray a 9- × 13-inch (3.5 L) casserole dish with cooking spray.

2. Dust the chicken with flour. In a large skillet sprayed with vegetable spray, add the oil and sauté the chicken just until lightly browned on both sides, about 5 minutes. Place it in the prepared casserole dish.

3. TO MAKE THE SAUCE Mix the hoisin, ketchup, orange juice concentrate, honey, soy sauce, cornstarch, garlic, ginger and chili sauce. Pour over the chicken. Sprinkle with the sesame seeds. Cover and bake in the centre of the oven for 10 minutes or until cooked through (when the temperature reaches 165°F/74°C).

4. TO MAKE THE COUSCOUS Meanwhile, bring the stock to a boil. Add the couscous. Cover, turn off heat and let sit for 5 minutes. Uncover and fluff with a fork. Serve the chicken over the couscous. Garnish with cilantro.

PREPARATION TIME 10 minutes · **COOKING TIME** 15 minutes ·
MAKE AHEAD Prepare the entire dish early in the day and refrigerate.
Bake just before serving. · **MAKES** 4 servings.

4 boneless skinless chicken breasts (about 1½ lb/750 g total)

3 Tbsp (45 mL) all-purpose flour

2 tsp (10 mL) oil

Sauce

¼ cup (60 mL) hoisin sauce

2 Tbsp (30 mL) ketchup

2 Tbsp (30 mL) thawed orange juice concentrate

2 Tbsp (30 mL) liquid honey

1 Tbsp (15 mL) low-sodium soy sauce

1½ tsp (7.5 mL) cornstarch

1 tsp (5 mL) minced garlic

1 tsp (5 mL) minced ginger

½ tsp (2.5 mL) hot Asian chili sauce

1 tsp (5 mL) toasted sesame seeds

Couscous

1 cup (250 mL) low-sodium chicken stock

1 cup (250 mL) couscous

3 Tbsp (45 mL) chopped fresh cilantro or parsley

ROSE'S TIP

This sauce works well over fish and tofu and can be used as a marinade

HEALTH TIP

Couscous is merely semolina pasta, that is, crushed durum wheat. One cup (250 mL) provides 60% of your daily selenium requirements, which protects your heart vessels from plaque buildup, as well as 40% of your daily potassium requirements.

NUTRITION INFORMATION PER SERVING

Calories 452	Protein 47.1 g	Cholesterol 99.2 mg
Carbohydrates 57.6 g	Total fat 3.6 g	Sodium 742.5 mg
Fibre 3.2 g	Saturated fat 0.8 g	

CHICKEN MEATLOAF LAYERED WITH MONTEREY JACK CHEESE AND ROASTED RED PEPPER

This is a healthier alternative to a regular meatloaf. The layered effect, using roasted red peppers, sun-dried tomatoes and Monterey Jack cheese, not only adds flavour but is beautiful when sliced.

1. Preheat the oven to 375°F (190°C). Line the bottom and sides of a 9- × 5-inch (2 L) loaf pan with foil or parchment paper.

2. In a bowl, combine the ground chicken, breadcrumbs, garlic, egg, onion, ketchup, dried basil and salt and pepper until well mixed. Pat half the chicken mixture into the prepared loaf pan. Sprinkle with the green onions, red pepper and sun-dried tomatoes. Mix the Monterey Jack and Parmesan cheeses and add all but 2 Tbsp (30 mL) of the cheese mixture to the loaf. Pat the remaining chicken mixture over the filling. Bake for 40 minutes or until the interior temperature reaches 165°F (74°C). Sprinkle with the remaining cheese and bake for 2 minutes or until the cheese melts. Let stand for 10 minutes, then slice and serve.

PREPARATION TIME 15 minutes · **COOKING TIME** 40 minutes ·
MAKE AHEAD Bake the meatloaf up to a day in advance. Reheat in a 300°F (150°C) oven for 15 minutes. · **MAKES** 6 servings.

ROSE'S TIP
Try making mini meatloaves by using either a muffin cup mould or mini loaf pan mould. Divide mixture into 12 servings.

HEALTH TIP
Four ounces (125 g) of ground chicken has only 108 calories and 1 gram of fat compared to regular ground beef, with 310 calories and 20 grams of fat!

1½ lb (750 g) ground chicken

½ cup (125 mL) seasoned dry breadcrumbs

1½ tsp (7.5 mL) finely chopped garlic

1 large egg

¼ cup (60 mL) finely chopped yellow onion

¼ cup (60 mL) ketchup

½ tsp (2.5 mL) dried basil

pinch of salt and pepper

⅓ cup (80 mL) finely diced green onions

2 oz (60 g) roasted red pepper, chopped (about ½ red bell pepper, roasted)

¼ cup (60 mL) diced rehydrated sun-dried tomatoes

½ cup (125 mL) shredded Monterey Jack cheese or white aged cheddar (2¼ oz/65 g)

2 Tbsp (30 mL) grated Parmesan cheese (½ oz/15 g)

NUTRITION INFORMATION PER SERVING

Calories 280	Protein 22 g	Cholesterol 130 mg
Carbohydrates 13 g	Total fat 14.3 g	Sodium 420 mg
Fibre 1.8 g	Saturated fat 4.9 g	

CURRIED CHICKEN WITH BELL PEPPERS

Indian cuisine is the latest trend in Canadian homes, but the ingredients often make it difficult to make at home. This variation gives you the flavours without all the work and expertise.

1. Coat the chicken in the flour. In a large skillet sprayed with vegetable oil, add 2 tsp (10 mL) oil and sauté the chicken on medium heat until almost cooked through, about 5 minutes. Remove from the skillet, wipe the skillet and respray with vegetable oil.

2. Add the onions and sauté on medium heat for 5 minutes. Add the bell peppers, garlic, ginger, curry paste, hot sauce and salt and pepper and sauté for 3 minutes.

3. Combine the coconut milk and cornstarch until dissolved and add to the vegetables along with the salsa, lemon juice and sugar. Add the chicken, cover and simmer for 3 minutes or until the sauce thickens slightly.

4. Garnish with the cilantro and cashews. Serve over jasmine rice if using.

PREPARATION TIME 20 minutes • **COOKING TIME** 16 minutes •
MAKE AHEAD Cook chicken and prepare the sauce early in the day.
Complete the dish just before serving. • **MAKES** 4 servings.

 ROSE'S TIP
You can substitute pork, tender beef or tofu cubes for the chicken. Also, large shrimp are delicious sautéed, then added.

 HEALTH TIP
Curries in restaurants are high in fat and calories due to regular coconut milk. If you can't find light coconut milk, add half 2% milk to regular coconut milk.

NUTRITION INFORMATION PER SERVING

Calories 284	Protein 24.9 g	Cholesterol 59 mg
Carbohydrates 22.2 g	Total fat 10.9 g	Sodium 343 mg
Fibre 3.3 g	Saturated fat 4.4 g	

1 lb (500 g) boneless chicken breast cut into 1-inch (2.5 cm) cubes

3 Tbsp (45 mL) all-purpose flour

2 tsp (10 mL) vegetable oil

2 cups (500 mL) sliced onions

2 cups (500 mL) sliced red bell pepper

1 cup (250 mL) sliced green bell pepper

1½ tsp (7.5 mL) minced garlic

2 tsp (10 mL) minced ginger

1 Tbsp (15 mL) red curry paste

1 tsp (5 mL) hot sauce (Sriracha)

pinch of salt and pepper

1 cup (250 mL) light coconut milk

1 tsp (5 mL) cornstarch

½ cup (125 mL) medium salsa

1½ Tbsp (22.5 mL) lemon or lime juice

2 tsp (10 mL) brown sugar

Garnish
3 Tbsp (45 mL) chopped cilantro

¼ cup (60 mL) chopped toasted cashews

jasmine rice (optional)

PAELLA WITH CHICKEN, SHRIMP AND MUSSELS

This is my version of paella—a rice, sausage and seafood dish originating in Spain. Using skinless chicken breasts and draining the sausage after it's been cooked keeps the calories and fat to a minimum. The key to this dish is the arborio rice, which gives it a wonderful creamy texture.

1. Dust the chicken with flour. Lightly coat a large nonstick skillet with cooking oil, add the vegetable oil and place over medium-high heat. Brown the chicken on all sides (about 3 minutes). Remove from the pan and set aside.

2. Respray the pan with cooking oil. Add the sausage and cook over medium-high heat for 5 minutes or until cooked through. Remove from the pan with a slotted spoon, draining as much fat as possible. Set aside.

3. Wipe out the pan and respray. Cook the onions and garlic over medium-high heat for 4 minutes or until softened. Stir in the red and green peppers; cook for 3 minutes. Stir in the rice and cook for 1 minute. Add the sausage, chicken stock, tomatoes, basil, oregano, bay leaf, saffron (if using) and salt and pepper. Bring to a boil. Cover, lower the heat to a simmer and cook for 20 minutes, stirring occasionally, until the rice is almost tender.

4. If the shrimp are large or jumbo, cut them in half length-wise. Add the shrimp, mussels and reserved chicken to the sausage mixture. Increase the heat to medium-high and cook for 5 minutes, covered, or until the rice is soft and the mussels have opened. (If the rice begins to stick to the bottom, add another ½ cup/125 mL stock.) Discard the bay leaf and any mussels that do not open. Distribute evenly among large individual bowls, garnish with parsley and serve immediately.

PREPARATION TIME 20 minutes · **COOKING TIME** About 45 minutes · **MAKE AHEAD** Sauté the vegetables early in the day. Complete just before serving. · **MAKES** 6 servings.

12 oz (375 g) cubed boneless skinless chicken breast (about 3 breasts)

3 Tbsp (45 mL) all-purpose flour

2 tsp (10 mL) vegetable oil

6 oz (175 g) medium Italian sausage, cut into ½-inch (1 cm) pieces

1 cup (250 mL) chopped onion

2 tsp (10 mL) minced fresh garlic

1 cup (250 mL) chopped red bell pepper

1 cup (250 mL) chopped green bell pepper

1 cup (250 mL) short-grain arborio rice

2½ cups (625 mL) low-sodium chicken stock

2 cups (500 mL) chopped plum tomatoes

1½ tsp (7.5 mL) dried basil

½ tsp (2.5 mL) dried oregano

1 bay leaf

½ tsp (2.5 mL) crumbled saffron threads (optional)

pinch of salt and ground black pepper

continued . . .

Paella with Chicken, Shrimp and Mussels (continued)

 ROSE'S TIP

You can use basmati rice instead of arborio. The texture will be firmer and drier than with the creamy arborio.

 HEALTH TIP

Paella is a healthy one-dish meal with protein, complex carbohydrates and vegetables.

6 oz (175 g) peeled and deveined shrimp

12 mussels, scrubbed and beards removed

¼ cup (60 mL) chopped fresh parsley

NUTRITION INFORMATION PER SERVING

Calories 407	Protein 49 g	Cholesterol 139 mg
Carbohydrates 36 g	Total fat 7.3 g	Sodium 624 mg
Fibre 3 g	Saturated fat 2.2 g	

MEAT

SOUTHWESTERN STEAK
WITH CORN SALSA

*With the sauce and corn salsa accompaniment, this is a great
Southwestern dish. Sautéing the corn gives it a barbecued flavour.
Be sure to allow time for marinating the steak. Leftovers taste just as
good the next day, either reheat gently or serve at room temperature.*

1. Whisk the barbecue sauce, vinegar, molasses and hot
   pepper sauce in a bowl. Place the flank steak in a shallow,
   nonreactive baking dish and pour the sauce over the steak.
   Cover with plastic wrap and refrigerate for 2 hours or
   overnight.

2. TO MAKE THE SALSA Spray a nonstick skillet with cooking
   oil. Place over medium heat and sauté the corn and red
   pepper until the corn begins to brown, about 5 minutes.
   Stir in the beans, onion and cilantro. Set aside.

3. Remove the steak from the marinade and set the marinade aside in a small saucepan.

4. Preheat the barbecue or a nonstick grill pan to medium-
   high and spray with cooking oil. Cook the beef over
   medium-high heat for 5 to 8 minutes per side or until
   it's done to your liking.

5. While the steak is cooking, bring the reserved marinade
   to a boil and boil for 5 minutes. Serve the steak with the
   sauce and salsa on the side.

PREPARATION TIME 10 minutes • **COOKING TIME** 25 minutes •
MAKE AHEAD Prepare the sauce and salsa up to a day in advance. The longer
the meat marinates, the better. • **MAKES** 4 servings.

NUTRITION INFORMATION PER SERVING

Calories 429	Protein 39 g	Cholesterol 90 mg
Carbohydrates 24 g	Total fat 13 g	Sodium 690 mg
Fibre 2.5 g	Saturated fat 5.8 g	

1 cup (250 mL) barbecue sauce

⅓ cup (80 mL) cider vinegar

2 Tbsp (30 mL) molasses

½ tsp (2.5 mL) hot pepper sauce

1½ lb (750 g) flank steak

Salsa

1 cup (250 mL) corn

1 cup (250 mL) diced red
bell pepper

1 cup (250 mL) canned black
beans, drained and rinsed

⅓ cup (80 mL) chopped
green onion

¼ cup (60 mL) chopped cilantro

 ROSE'S TIP
Dishes in Mexican restau-
rants are often high in calories because of the oil and the
fattier cuts of meat. This dish
contains no oil and uses a lean
flank steak.

 HEALTH TIP
Black beans are very high in
fibre, folate, protein and antioxidants. The fibre helps regulate blood sugar and reduces
the risk of type 2 diabetes as
well as heart disease.

STEAK WITH OLIVE PARSLEY PESTO

This delicious olive pesto goes so well with a perfectly cooked cut of beef. The key with flank steak is to marinate it if you have the time for the best flavour and texture. Remember to cut across the grain.

1. TO MAKE THE OLIVE PARSLEY PESTO In a food processor, add the parsley, oil, garlic, nuts, cheese, olives and lemon juice. Purée until smooth. If too thick, add the water. Set aside.

2. Grill or sauté the steak on medium heat for about 5 to 8 minutes per side or until done to your preference. Let rest for 10 minutes, then slice thinly across the grain. Serve with the pesto.

PREPARATION TIME 10 minutes • **COOKING TIME** 10 to 16 minutes •
MAKE AHEAD Marinate the steak for up to 2 days in advance if desired. Make the pesto early in the day. Cook the steak just before eating. • **MAKES** 4 servings.

Olive Parsley Pesto

1 cup (250 mL) well-packed parsley leaves

3 Tbsp (45 mL) olive oil

1 clove garlic

¼ cup (60 mL) toasted pine nuts or almonds

¼ cup (60 mL) grated Parmesan cheese (1 oz/30 g)

¼ cup (60 mL) pitted green olives

2 Tbsp (30 mL) lemon juice

2 Tbsp (30 mL) water

Steak

1½ lb (750 g) flank steak

 ROSE'S TIP

Use green olives packed in oil rather than water since the flavour is much better. It adds only a little extra in calories and fat.

 HEALTH TIP

Flank steak is one of the leanest cuts you can buy. There's virtu- ally no marbled fat throughout. A 3-ounce (90 g) serving has only 165 calories and 7 grams of fat compared to a rib-eye, which has 275 calories and 18 grams of fat.

NUTRITION INFORMATION PER SERVING

Calories 481	Protein 42.5 g	Cholesterol 120 mg
Carbohydrates 2.9 g	Total fat 28.1 g	Sodium 380 mg
Fibre 0.6 g	Saturated fat 9.4 g	

FLANK STEAK WITH SHIITAKE MUSHROOMS AND MIRIN HOISIN SAUCE

Flank steak is one of the leanest cuts. The key is to marinate it to make it more tender. You can find mirin (sweet rice wine) in a good grocery store or in a Chinese market; Chinese five-spice powder is in the dried herb section. Feel free to use another mushroom of your choice, being sure to cook it until all the moisture evaporates.

1. Combine the mirin, five-spice powder, hoisin, sesame seeds, vinegar, soy sauce and sesame oil. Remove ¼ cup (60 mL) and pour over the flank steak. Let marinate for at least 1 hour, preferably overnight.

2. In a large skillet sprayed with the vegetable oil, sauté the mushrooms for 12 minutes or until tender. Add another ¼ cup (60 mL) sauce and cook one minute.

3. In a grill pan or barbecue sprayed with vegetable oil, grill the steak on medium-high heat for about 8 minutes per side or until done to your preference. Let sit 10 minutes.

4. Slice the steak against the grain into thin slices, scatter the whole mushrooms overtop, garnish with the green onions and serve with extra sauce.

PREPARATION TIME 10 minutes · **COOKING TIME** 20 minutes ·
MAKE AHEAD Marinate the beef up to a day in advance and cook the mushrooms early in the day. Cook the steak just before serving. This dish is delicious at room temperature. · **MAKES** 4 servings.

⅓ cup (80 mL) mirin

1½ tsp (7.5 mL) Chinese five-spice powder

⅓ cup (80 mL) hoisin sauce

2 Tbsp (30 mL) toasted sesame seeds

3 Tbsp (45 mL) rice vinegar

2 Tbsp (30 mL) low-sodium soy sauce

2 Tbsp (30 mL) sesame oil

1 lb (500 g) whole shiitake mushrooms, cleaned with stem removed

2 green onions, sliced for garnish

1½ lb (750 g) flank steak

 ROSE'S TIP
Chinese five-spice powder is a combination of star anise, fennel seeds, ground cloves, cinnamon and salt and pepper.

 HEALTH TIP
The Chinese have used the shiitake mushroom for medicinal purposes for over 6,000 years. It's a rich source of selenium, iron, fibre, protein and vitamin C.

NUTRITION INFORMATION PER SERVING

Calories 429	Protein 41 g	Cholesterol 111 mg
Carbohydrates 21.4 g	Total fat 18 g	Sodium 680 mg
Fibre 4.7 g	Saturated fat 6.6 g	

CHERRY TOMATO AND OLIVE TOPPING OVER SLICED STEAK

A grilled steak by itself needs an interesting topping. The combo of tomatoes and olives goes so well with this tender beef.

1. Combine the tomatoes, olives, cilantro, oil, capers, lemon juice and jalapeños.

2. Grill or sauté the steak on medium temperature just until done to your preference. Let cool for 10 minutes, then slice. Spoon the tomato-olive topping overtop. Garnish with cilantro.

PREPARATION TIME 15 minutes · **COOKING TIME** 10 minutes ·

MAKES 4 servings.

2 cups (500 mL) red and yellow cherry tomatoes, sliced in half

⅓ cup (80 mL) coarsely chopped pimiento-stuffed olives

⅓ cup (80 mL) coarsely chopped black olives

¼ cup (60 mL) chopped fresh cilantro

1 Tbsp (15 mL) extra-virgin olive oil

1 Tbsp (15 mL) drained chopped capers

1 Tbsp (15 mL) fresh lemon juice

2 tsp (10 mL) finely chopped jalapeño peppers

1½ lb (750 g) New York strip steak, trimmed of fat

2 Tbsp (30 mL) chopped cilantro

 ROSE'S TIP

Capers are packed in a strongly acidic brine, which, as long as they're refrigerated, protects them against spoilage. In other words, they last for a very long time.

 HEALTH TIP

A New York strip steak trimmed of fat is a leaner cut of beef than a rib-eye, porterhouse or prime rib. A 3-ounce (90 g) serving only has 160 calories and 10 grams of fat, whereas a porterhouse has 250 calories and 18 grams of fat.

NUTRITION INFORMATION PER SERVING

Calories 398	Protein 35.6 g	Cholesterol 127 mg
Carbohydrates 3.6 g	Total fat 23.3 g	Sodium 267 mg
Fibre 1.2 g	Saturated fat 9.4 g	

PULLED PORK WITH APPLE CIDER BARBECUE SAUCE

A delicious tender pork shoulder takes time to cook, but you will never taste a more delicate meat. The idea is to cook a large pork shoulder and package the extra meat in the freezer for leftovers.

1. Preheat the oven to 300°F (150°C).

2. Rub the roast with Cajun seasoning. In a large skillet or grill pan, sear the pork on all sides just until browned.

3. TO MAKE THE BASTING SAUCE   Combine the cider vinegar and brown sugar and pour 1 cup (250 mL) in the bottom of a large roasting pan. Add the pork and roast, covered tightly, until 190°F (88°C) temperature is reached (approximately 3 to 4 hours). Baste with the mixture of cider vinegar and brown sugar every hour.

4. TO MAKE THE BARBECUE SAUCE   Combine the ketchup, brown and white sugar, salt and pepper, onion powder, mustard, lemon juice, Worcestershire, cider vinegar, corn syrup and molasses until smooth.

5. TO MAKE THE CARAMELIZED ONIONS   In a large skillet, add the oil and sauté the sliced onions with brown sugar on low heat for 15 minutes or until tender.

6. When the pork is cooked, pull pork apart with two forks, removing all visible fat and the skin. Add just enough of the barbecue sauce to wet all the meat. Save any remaining sauce for extra. Serve with the caramelized onions (if using).

PREPARATION TIME 15 minutes • **COOKING TIME** 3 to 4 hours •
MAKE AHEAD Beef can be cooked up to 2 days in advance and gently reheated in a 300°F (150°C) oven. • **MAKES** 6 servings.

3 lb (1.5 kg) pork shoulder—Boston butt

1 Tbsp (15 mL) Cajun or Southwestern seasoning

Basting sauce

2 cups (500 mL) cider vinegar

½ cup (125 mL) brown sugar

Barbecue sauce

1 cup (250 mL) ketchup or Heinz chili sauce

2 Tbsp (30 mL) packed light brown sugar

2 Tbsp (30 mL) granulated sugar

pinch of salt and pepper

¾ tsp (4 mL) onion powder

¾ tsp (4 mL) dry mustard

1 Tbsp (15 mL) fresh lemon juice

1 Tbsp (15 mL) Worcestershire sauce

¼ cup (60 mL) cider vinegar

1 Tbsp (15 mL) light corn syrup

1 Tbsp (15 mL) molasses

Caramelized onions (optional)

2 tsp (10 mL) vegetable oil

1 large sweet onion sliced thinly

2 tsp (10 mL) brown sugar

ROSE'S TIP

You can find Cajun seasoning in your grocery spice section. It's a combination of paprika, oregano, garlic and onion powder, cayenne, salt and pepper.

 HEALTH TIP

Pulled pork in restaurants has excessive calories and fat due to the fat and skin of the meat being added to the mixture after it's been cooked. In my recipe, all the visible fat and skin have been removed.

NUTRITION INFORMATION PER SERVING

Calories 452	Protein 51.8 g	Cholesterol 136 mg
Carbohydrates 38.8 g	Total fat 7 g	Sodium 529 mg
Fibre 0.5 g	Saturated fat 2.5 g	

SESAME PORK TENDERLOIN WITH HOISIN SWEET CHILI SAUCE

Pork tenderloin goes beautifully with this sweet Asian hoisin sauce. Serve alongside rice noodles or rice.

1. Preheat the oven to 425°F (220°C). Line a baking sheet with parchment paper.

2. Spray a nonstick pan with cooking oil and heat to medium-high. Sear the tenderloin for approximately 2 minutes per side, or just until browned. Place on the prepared baking sheet.

3. Combine the hoisin, chili sauce, sugar, oil, garlic, ginger and soy sauce in a small bowl.

4. Brush approximately 2 Tbsp (30 mL) of the mixture over the tenderloin and sprinkle with sesame seeds. Bake for approximately 15 minutes or until a meat thermometer reads 145°F (63°C) for medium. Let rest for 10 minutes before slicing.

5. Slice and serve with the remaining sauce on the side. Garnish with cilantro.

PREPARATION TIME 10 minutes · **COOKING TIME** 19 minutes ·
MAKE AHEAD The sauce can be made up to 2 days in advance. ·
MAKES 4 servings.

1½ lb (750 g) pork tenderloin

¼ cup (60 mL) hoisin sauce

2 Tbsp (30 mL) sweet chili sauce or barbecue sauce

2 Tbsp (30 mL) brown sugar

2 tsp (10 mL) sesame oil

1½ tsp (7.5 mL) crushed fresh garlic

1½ tsp (7.5 mL) crushed fresh ginger

1 tsp (5 mL) low-sodium soy sauce

1 tsp (5 mL) toasted sesame seeds

¼ cup (60 mL) chopped fresh cilantro or parsley

 ROSE'S TIP
Pork can now be cooked to medium and medium-rare if desired. In the past, the parasitic disease called trichinosis was caused by eating rare pork. Today, due to improved sanitary conditions, this illness is rare.

 HEALTH TIP
Pork tenderloin is one of the leanest cuts of pork. A 3-ounce (90 g) serving has only 100 calories and 3 grams of fat.

NUTRITION INFORMATION PER SERVING

Calories 344	Protein 38 g	Cholesterol 117 mg
Carbohydrates 15 g	Total fat 14 g	Sodium 326 mg
Fibre 0.6 g	Saturated fat 4.1 g	

ROSE'S TIP

These mashed potatoes are light due to the addition of a little olive oil and light sour cream. No butter or cream is necessary.

 HEALTH TIP

Potatoes are a great vegetable as long as they're not deep-fried! One potato has only 128 calories, 0 grams of fat, 3 grams of fibre and 800 mg of potassium, which is a quarter of your daily requirement of potassium.

½ tsp (2.5 mL) dried basil leaves

pinch of salt and pepper

2 Tbsp (30 mL) shredded cheddar cheese (½ oz/15 g)

1 Tbsp (15 mL) grated Parmesan cheese (¼ oz/8 g)

NUTRITION INFORMATION PER SERVING

Calories 222	Protein 14 g	Cholesterol 50 mg
Carbohydrates 19 g	Total fat 9 g	Sodium 200 mg
Fibre 2.3 g	Saturated fat 3 g	

CHINESE MEATLOAF WITH MUSHROOMS, BELL PEPPERS AND HOISIN SAUCE

The Sunday meatloaf may be a meal of the past, but this trendy rolled version will revive the tradition. It's even elegant enough for a special dinner. Serve it with mashed white or sweet potatoes. Be sure to let it cool slightly before slicing to reveal the beautiful spiral design of the filling. If you don't feel like rolling the meatloaf, just spoon the vegetable filling over the glaze, cover with foil and bake.

1. Preheat the oven to 375°F (190°C). Spray an 8½- × 4½-inch (1.5 L) loaf pan with cooking oil.

2. TO MAKE THE FILLING Lightly spray a nonstick skillet with cooking oil, add the vegetable oil and place over medium heat. Sauté the onion for 3 minutes. Add the mushrooms and sauté until no liquid is left, about 5 minutes. Add the bell pepper and sauté for 2 minutes. Add the soy sauce, hoisin sauce, water, garlic, ginger, sesame oil and rice vinegar, and cook for 1 minute. Set aside.

3. TO MAKE THE MEAT MIXTURE Combine the ground beef, breadcrumbs, green onion, cilantro, hoisin sauce, ginger, garlic and egg. Mix well. Turn the mixture out onto waxed paper and pat into an approximate 10-inch (25 cm) square.

4. Spread the vegetable filling over the meatloaf and roll it up jellyroll-fashion with the help of the waxed paper. Place it in the prepared loaf pan, seam side down.

5. TO MAKE THE GLAZE Whisk the water, hoisin sauce and sesame oil in a small bowl. Pour over the meatloaf and bake in the centre of the oven for 35 minutes or until a meat thermometer inserted in the centre of the loaf registers 160°F (71°C). Let cool for at least 10 minutes before inverting the pan and slicing into 6 pieces.

PREPARATION TIME 15 minutes · **COOKING TIME** 45 minutes ·

MAKE AHEAD The entire loaf and vegetable filling can be made up to a day in advance. Bake just before serving. · **MAKES** 6 servings.

Vegetable filling

2 tsp (10 mL) vegetable oil

½ cup (125 mL) chopped onion

1 cup (250 mL) chopped mushrooms (any variety)

½ cup (125 mL) chopped red bell pepper

1 Tbsp (15 mL) low-sodium soy sauce

1 Tbsp (15 mL) hoisin sauce

1 Tbsp (15 mL) water

2 tsp (10 mL) finely chopped garlic

2 tsp (10 mL) minced fresh ginger

2 tsp (10 mL) sesame oil

2 tsp (10 mL) rice vinegar

Meat mixture

1 lb (500 g) extra-lean ground beef

¼ cup (60 mL) seasoned dry breadcrumbs

¼ cup (60 mL) chopped green onion

3 Tbsp (45 mL) chopped cilantro or parsley

ROSE'S TIP

An Asian flair to a meat-loaf gives a whole different meaning to this classic dish. Select any variety of mushrooms, just make sure to sauté them until all the liquid evaporates.

 HEALTH TIP

Extra-lean beef has 110 calories and 4 grams of fat per 3 ounces (90 g), whereas regular ground beef has 150 calories and 9 grams of fat per 3 ounces (90 g).

2 Tbsp (30 mL) hoisin sauce

1 tsp (5 mL) minced fresh ginger

1 tsp (5 mL) minced fresh garlic

1 large egg

Glaze

2 Tbsp (30 mL) water

2 Tbsp (30 mL) hoisin sauce

1 tsp (5 mL) sesame oil

NUTRITION INFORMATION PER SERVING (1 SLICE)

Calories 330	Protein 26 g	Cholesterol 80 mg
Carbohydrates 16 g	Total fat 16 g	Sodium 398 mg
Fibre 3 g	Saturated fat 4.6 g	

SHEPHERD'S PIE TOPPED WITH AGED CHEDDAR AND OLIVE OIL MASHED POTATOES

This is a real classic that families still love to eat. It's a great one-dish meal and leftovers taste wonderful. You can freeze as well for up to 2 months.

1. Preheat the oven to 350°F (175°C). Lightly coat an 8-inch (20 cm) square baking dish with cooking spray.

2. Place a large nonstick skillet lightly coated with cooking spray over medium-high heat. Add the oil and onion and sauté for 3 minutes. Add the garlic and carrots and sauté for 3 minutes. Add the ground beef and sauté for 5 minutes or until no longer pink, breaking up the meat as it cooks.

3. Add the flour and cook for 1 minute. Add the tomato paste, stock, tomato sauce, basil and salt and pepper. Cover and cook on low heat for 3 minutes or until thickened. Add the frozen peas. Place in a baking dish.

4. Meanwhile, cover the potatoes with water in a pot, and boil for 10 minutes or just until tender. Drain and add the olive oil, milk, Parmesan cheese and salt and pepper. Mash until smooth.

5. Spread the mashed potatoes over the beef mixture in the baking dish. Sprinkle with cheddar cheese and bake for 20 minutes or until hot.

PREPARATION TIME 20 minutes · **COOKING TIME** 35 minutes ·
MAKE AHEAD The entire dish can be made up to a day in advance. Bake just before serving. · **MAKES** 8 servings.

2 tsp (10 mL) vegetable oil

1½ cups (375 mL) finely diced onion

2 tsp (10 mL) crushed garlic

¾ cup (185 mL) finely diced carrots

1 lb (500 g) extra-lean ground beef

1½ Tbsp (22.5 mL) all-purpose flour

1½ Tbsp (22.5 mL) tomato paste

⅓ cup (80 mL) low-sodium beef (or chicken) stock

¾ cup (185 mL) homemade or store-bought tomato sauce (see Quick Basic Tomato Sauce on page 369)

½ tsp (2.5 mL) dried basil

pinch of salt and pepper

¾ cup (185 mL) frozen green peas

1½ lb (750 g) Yukon Gold potatoes, peeled and cubed

2 Tbsp (30 mL) olive oil

3 Tbsp (45 mL) canned evaporated 2% milk (or 2% milk)

3 Tbsp (45 mL) grated Parmesan cheese (¾ oz/23 g)

pinch of salt and pepper

¾ cup (185 mL) shredded aged cheddar cheese (2¼ oz/65 g)

ROSE'S TIP
Substitute edamame
(Japanese soybeans) for
the green peas and add
some sautéed corn to
increase the vegetable
content.

 HEALTH TIP
You can leave the skin on
the potatoes to boost the
fibre. A medium potato
with the skin has 4 grams
of fibre versus only
1.5 grams of fibre with-
out the skin.

NUTRITION INFORMATION PER SERVING

Calories 260	Protein 25.6 g	Cholesterol 40 mg
Carbohydrates 15 g	Total fat 11 g	Sodium 223 mg
Fibre 2.3 g	Saturated fat 3.4 g	

BEEF ENCHILADAS FILLED WITH BEEF SALSA AND AGED CHEDDAR SAUCE

Traditional enchiladas in Mexican restaurants are loaded with fat, calories and cholesterol. The excess cheese and fatty cuts of beef that are usually used are to blame, as well as the deep-fried corn tortilla shells. You'll enjoy my light version. Feel free to try ground chicken or pork.

1. Preheat the oven to 425°F (220°C). Lightly coat a 9- × 13-inch (3.5 L) casserole dish with cooking oil.

2. TO MAKE THE SALSA Lightly coat a large nonstick skillet with cooking spray. Add the oil and set over medium heat. Add the onion and garlic and sauté for 5 minutes or until the onion begins to brown. Add the ground beef and sauté for 5 minutes or until the beef is no longer pink. Add the green pepper and sauté for 3 more minutes. Add the salsa and jalapeño, cover and simmer for 5 minutes. Add the cilantro and set aside.

3. TO MAKE THE SAUCE Place the evaporated milk, stock, flour, mustard and salt and pepper in a medium saucepan over medium-high heat. Bring to a boil while whisking together. Reduce the heat to medium and simmer until slightly thickened, about 3 minutes. Add the cheese and simmer, while whisking continuously, for another 2 minutes.

4. Add half the sauce to the beef filling and stir to combine.

5. TO ASSEMBLE THE ENCHILADAS Lay the tortillas on your work surface. Divide the filling-and-sauce mixture among the tortillas, spreading it along the centre of each. Roll the tortillas up, leaving the ends open. Place them in the casserole dish, seam side down, and pour the remaining sauce over the tortillas. Sprinkle with the ¼ cup (60 mL) cheese and bake uncovered for 12 to 15 minutes or until heated all the way through. Serve immediately, garnished with cilantro.

PREPARATION TIME 20 minutes • **COOKING TIME** 35 minutes •
MAKE AHEAD The filling and sauce can be made up to a day in advance. •
MAKES 6 servings.

Beef Salsa

2 tsp (10 mL) vegetable oil

1½ cups (375 mL) diced onion

2 tsp (10 mL) finely chopped garlic

12 oz (375 g) lean ground beef

1 cup (250 mL) diced green bell pepper

1 cup (250 mL) medium salsa

1 tsp (5 mL) finely chopped jalapeño pepper

⅓ cup (80 mL) chopped cilantro

Sauce

1½ cups (375 mL) canned evaporated 2% milk

1 cup (250 mL) low-sodium chicken stock

3½ Tbsp (55 mL) all-purpose flour

1 tsp (5 mL) Dijon mustard

pinch of salt and pepper

1 cup (250 mL) shredded aged cheddar cheese (3 oz/90 g)

Enchiladas

6 large flour tortillas

¼ cup (60 mL) shredded aged cheddar cheese (¾ oz/23 g)

2 Tbsp (30 mL) chopped cilantro

ROSE'S TIP

If you can find well-made corn tortillas, this would make the dish more authentic. A specialty grocer would carry them.

 HEALTH TIP

Evaporated milk takes the place of heavy cream in many of my recipes. A quarter-cup (60 mL) 2% evaporated milk has 50 calories and 1 gram of fat, whereas heavy cream has 207 calories and 22 grams of fat!

NUTRITION INFORMATION PER SERVING

Calories 315	Protein 26 g	Cholesterol 47 mg
Carbohydrates 38 g	Total fat 9.7 g	Sodium 724 mg
Fibre 3.4 g	Saturated fat 4.3 g	

THAI GINGER MEATBALLS IN COCONUT SAUCE

You've never tried meatballs like these before! Forget spaghetti and meatballs. Thai flavours have taken over. These are beautiful to serve as an appetizer or main dish over rice noodles, rice or couscous.

1. Preheat the oven to 425°F (220°C). Line a baking sheet with foil and spray with vegetable oil.

2. TO MAKE THE SAUCE In a bowl, stir together the coconut milk, stock, lemon juice, hoisin sauce, sugar, cornstarch, ginger, garlic and hot sauce until the cornstarch is dissolved.

3. TO MAKE THE MEATBALLS In a bowl, stir together the beef, egg, hoisin, onions, breadcrumbs, cilantro, garlic, ginger and salt and pepper. Form into 1-inch (2.5 cm) meatballs, making about 30. Place on a baking sheet and bake for 10 minutes or just until no longer pink.

4. Add the sauce and meatballs to the saucepan, cover and simmer for 5 minutes just until sauce thickens slightly.

5. Boil the noodles (if using) just until cooked. Place on a serving plate and top with the meatballs and sauce. Garnish with cilantro.

PREPARATION TIME 20 minutes • COOKING TIME 15 minutes • MAKE AHEAD This dish can be made 1 day in advance and gently heated before serving. • MAKES 4 servings.

Sauce

¾ cup (185 mL) light coconut milk

⅓ cup (80 mL) low-sodium beef or chicken stock

2 tsp (10 mL) fresh lemon juice

2 Tbsp (30 mL) hoisin sauce

2 tsp (10 mL) packed brown sugar

1 tsp (5 mL) cornstarch

1 tsp (5 mL) minced ginger

1 tsp (5 mL) minced garlic

1 tsp (5 mL) hot sauce (Sriracha)

Meatballs

1 lb (500 g) extra-lean ground beef

1 egg

¼ cup (60 mL) hoisin sauce

¼ cup (60 mL) finely diced green onions

¼ cup (60 mL) unseasoned dry breadcrumbs

2 Tbsp (30 mL) finely chopped fresh cilantro

2 tsp (10 mL) minced garlic

1½ tsp (7.5 mL) crushed ginger

pinch each salt and ground black pepper

ROSE'S TIP

You can substitute the
ground beef for ground
chicken, veal or pork.

HEALTH TIP

Ginger root can relieve
gastrointestinal prob-
lems, motion sickness,
and nausea and vomiting
during pregnancy.

4 oz (125 g) wide rice noodles
(optional)

2 Tbsp (30 mL) chopped
fresh cilantro

NUTRITION INFORMATION PER SERVING

Calories 295	Protein 27.1 g	Cholesterol 95 mg
Carbohydrates 17 g	Total fat 12 g	Sodium 420 mg
Fibre 1.3 g	Saturated fat 6 g	

TEX-MEX LASAGNA WITH AGED CHEDDAR AND MONTE-REY JACK CHEESES

If you want a change from regular beef lasagna, this take on a Southwestern combo is perfect. The tomato sauce is combined with salsa to give you that kick!

1. Preheat the oven to 375°F (190°C). Lightly spray a 9-inch (23 cm) baking dish with vegetable oil.

2. Cook the lasagna sheets in a large pot of boiling water just until tender (about 12 minutes). Drain and rinse with cold water.

3. TO MAKE THE MEAT SAUCE Spray a large skillet with vegetable oil and sauté beef just until cooked, about 3 minutes. Remove the beef and set aside.

4. Add the onion to the pan and sauté on medium heat for 3 minutes until soft. Add the garlic, corn and bell pepper and sauté for 5 minutes until the corn begins to brown. Add the black beans, tomato sauce, salsa, jalapeño and cooked beef and cover and simmer for 10 minutes. Add the cilantro and salt and pepper

5. TO MAKE THE CHEESE MIXTURE Combine the ricotta with 1 cup (250 mL) of cheddar, ½ cup (125 mL) mozzarella cheese and the milk. Reserve the remaining cheese for topping.

6. Place one quarter of the sauce over the bottom of the dish just to cover. Cut lasagna sheets to fit 3 on the bottom of the baking dish. Place half the cheese mixture overtop. Add another quarter of the sauce overtop and add 3 more lasagna sheets cut to fit. Add the remaining cheese mixture, another quarter of the sauce, the remaining noodles and the remaining sauce. Sprinkle with the remaining cheese.

7. Bake for 30 minutes uncovered or until hot. Let cool 10 minutes before cutting.

6 lasagna sheets (any flavour)

Meat sauce
8 oz (250 g) lean ground beef

2 tsp (10 mL) vegetable oil

1 cup (250 mL) diced onion

2 tsp (10 mL) crushed garlic

¾ cup (185 mL) corn

¾ cup (185 mL) diced red bell pepper

¾ cup (185 mL) canned black beans, drained and rinsed

1¼ cups (310 mL) basic tomato sauce (see Quick Basic Tomato Sauce on page 369)

1¼ cups (310 mL) medium salsa

2 tsp (10 mL) chopped jalapeño with seeds

⅓ cup (80 mL) chopped cilantro

pinch of salt and pepper

Cheese mixture
1 cup (250 mL) reduced-fat ricotta cheese (8 oz/250 g)

1¼ cups (310 mL) grated aged cheddar or Monterey Jack cheese (3¼ oz/95 g)

¾ cup (185 mL) grated part-skim mozzarella cheese (2 oz/60 g)

⅓ cup (80 mL) 2% milk

PREPARATION TIME 25 minutes · **COOKING TIME** 1 hour ·

MAKE AHEAD Make the entire lasagna up to a day in advance. Best baked just before serving. Reheat leftovers on low heat. · **MAKES** 8 servings.

 ROSE'S TIP

To increase your fibre, use whole wheat lasagna sheets. You can also use the precooked lasagna sheets, but be sure to keep the dish covered tightly when baking.

 HEALTH TIP

Ricotta cheese allows you to reduce the calories of the mixture by not using more of the harder cheeses, which are higher in calories and fat. There are only 80 calories and 4 grams of fat in ⅓ cup (80 mL) of ricotta versus 130 calories and 12 grams of fat in aged cheddar.

NUTRITION INFORMATION PER SERVING

Calories 415	Protein 24.8 g	Cholesterol 81 mg
Carbohydrates 35.2 g	Total fat 18.2 g	Sodium 543 mg
Fibre 4.9 g	Saturated fat 10.5 g	

PRIME VEAL CHOP COATED WITH FETA AND PESTO

I created this recipe for the Pickle Barrel chain of restaurants in Toronto. The veal chop is beautifully lean and tender. The combination of pesto and feta complements it beautifully and gives the dish a Mediterranean twist.

1. Preheat the oven to 425°F (220°C). Line a baking sheet with foil and spray with cooking oil.

2. Spray a nonstick skillet with cooking oil and place over medium-high heat. Cook the veal on both sides just until seared and browned, approximately 2 minutes per side. Place on the prepared baking sheet.

3. Spread both sides of the veal with pesto sauce and sprinkle with the feta on one side, patting the cheese down firmly.

4. Bake for approximately 15 minutes, until the internal temperature registers about 135°F (57°C) for medium-rare, or to desired doneness. Let rest 5 minutes before serving.

PREPARATION TIME 10 minutes · **COOKING TIME** 19 minutes ·
MAKES 4 servings.

four 6 oz (175 g) prime veal chops with bone in (also known as the French cut)

2 Tbsp (30 mL) homemade or store-bought pesto (see Basil Pesto on page 371)

⅓ cup (80 mL) reduced-fat feta cheese (1 oz/30 g)

ROSE'S TIP
This is the same meat as in a veal chop, but it is trimmed. It's referred to as a French cut and is considered the "crème de la crème" of veal. The key is to cook it to 135°F (57°C) for medium. Do not overcook or it will be dry.

HEALTH TIP
A 4-ounce (125 g) portion of the edible meat (not including the bone) contains only 184 calories and 10 grams of fat.

NUTRITION INFORMATION PER SERVING

Calories 250	Protein 26 g	Cholesterol 115 mg
Carbohydrates 0.8 g	Total fat 14 g	Sodium 235 mg
Fibre 0.2 g	Saturated fat 4 g	

PASTA & GRAINS

ISRAELI COUSCOUS WITH TOMATOES, THREE CHEESES AND BASIL

Israeli couscous is a small, round semolina pasta, different from the tiny, yellow North African couscous. It's often referred to as pearl pasta because of its shape and texture. Although it is becoming more readily available, you may have to go to a specialty store to purchase it. You can substitute another very small pasta.

1. Bring a large pot of salted water to a boil and add the Israeli couscous. Boil for about 8 minutes or just until couscous is tender. Drain well and add to a serving bowl.

2. Add the tomatoes, goat cheese, Havarti, green onions, basil, Parmesan, olive oil, garlic and salt and pepper. Toss well and serve warm.

PREPARATION TIME 15 minutes • **COOKING TIME** 8 minutes •
MAKE AHEAD Can be prepared early in the day and served at room temperature. • **MAKES** 4 servings.

1 cup (250 mL) Israeli couscous

1 cup (250 mL) diced Roma tomatoes

¼ cup (60 mL) crumbled goat cheese (1 oz/30 g)

½ cup (125 mL) shredded Havarti cheese (1½ oz/45 g)

⅓ cup (80 mL) chopped green onions

⅓ cup (80 mL) chopped fresh basil or parsley

2 Tbsp (30 mL) grated Parmesan (or Asiago) cheese (½ oz/15 g)

1 Tbsp (15 mL) olive oil

1 tsp (5 mL) finely chopped garlic

pinch of salt and pepper

 ROSE'S TIP
You can now find Israeli couscous, also known as Jerusalem couscous, in most supermarkets and specialty groceries. Bulk stores are also carrying this versatile grain.

 HEALTH TIP
A 1-cup (250 mL) serving (cooked) Israeli couscous contains 9 grams of your daily fibre and 42% of your daily vitamin C requirement.

NUTRITION INFORMATION PER SERVING

Calories 265	Protein 12 g	Cholesterol 19 mg
Carbohydrates 34 g	Total fat 11 g	Sodium 300 mg
Fibre 4.5 g	Saturated fat 5.4 g	

COUSCOUS WITH DRIED FRUIT AND HONEY LEMON DRESSING

This simple dish is delicious served at room temperature, which makes it perfect for a potluck or buffet. The key to perfect couscous is the one-to-one ratio of the stock and couscous. Try spraying a little vegetable oil into the stock to prevent the couscous from clumping. Add some protein, such as fish or chicken, and you have a complete meal.

1. Bring the stock to a boil in a small saucepan. Stir in the couscous and remove from the heat. Cover and let stand until the liquid is absorbed, approximately 5 minutes. Place in a large serving bowl and fluff with a fork.

2. Spray a nonstick saucepan with cooking oil, add the vegetable oil and place over medium heat. Add the onion and red pepper and sauté until softened, approximately 5 minutes. Add the raisins, olive oil, lemon juice, honey, garlic and dates and mix until combined. Add to the couscous and mix well. Garnish with the cilantro.

PREPARATION TIME 10 minutes · **COOKING TIME** 10 minutes ·
MAKE AHEAD Cook up to a day in advance and serve at room temperature or reheat gently. · **MAKES** 6 servings.

1 cup (250 mL) low-sodium chicken or vegetable stock

1 cup (250 mL) couscous

2 tsp (10 mL) vegetable oil

¾ cup (185 mL) finely chopped onion

1 cup (250 mL) finely chopped red bell pepper

¼ cup (60 mL) raisins

1 Tbsp (15 mL) olive oil

2 Tbsp (30 mL) freshly squeezed lemon juice

2 tsp (10 mL) honey

1 tsp (5 mL) crushed fresh garlic

¼ cup (60 mL) diced dried dates or apricots

¼ cup (60 mL) chopped cilantro or parsley

 ROSE'S TIP
Do not follow the instructions on the back of the couscous box unless it recommends a one-to-one ratio of stock to couscous. Most brands say to use 2 cups (500 mL) of water, and this makes your couscous too wet and clumpy.

 HEALTH TIP
Dried fruits are the concentrated form of fruits—they have had the water removed—therefore, they are higher in calories. One cup (250 mL) of fresh fruit is equivalent to ¼ cup (60 mL) of dried fruit.

NUTRITION INFORMATION PER SERVING

Calories 162	Protein 4 g	Cholesterol 0 mg
Carbohydrates 31 g	Total fat 2 g	Sodium 159 mg
Fibre 2 g	Saturated fat 0 g	

LIGHT FETTUCCINE ALFREDO WITH SNOW PEAS AND YELLOW BELL PEPPER

Fettuccine alfredo, better known as "heart attack on a plate," is definitely not recommended on a regular basis due to the amount of cheese and butter it contains. The sauce in this version, however, uses stock, evaporated milk and light cream cheese, and it's really delicious.

1. Bring a large pot of water to a boil. Add the fettuccine and cook for 8 to 10 minutes or until just tender. Drain and place it in a large serving bowl. Cover to keep warm.

2. Meanwhile, in a saucepan off the heat, combine the stock, evaporated milk, mustard, pepper and garlic. Slowly whisk in the flour until smooth. Place the saucepan over medium heat and bring to a slight boil. Reduce the heat and simmer, whisking constantly, for 4 to 5 minutes or until slightly thickened. Remove from the heat and whisk in the cream cheese and 4 Tbsp (60 mL) of the Parmesan cheese, whisking just until the cheese is melted. Set aside.

3. Lightly coat a nonstick skillet with cooking spray and set over medium-high heat. Add the peas and bell pepper and sauté for 2 minutes or until warm but still crisp. Add to the cooked fettuccine, pour the sauce over the pasta and toss. Garnish with the remaining Parmesan cheese and basil. Serve immediately.

PREPARATION TIME 10 minutes · **COOKING TIME** 8 to 10 minutes · **MAKE AHEAD** Prepare the sauce early in the day. Gently reheat, adding more stock to thin. Cook pasta right before serving. · **MAKES** 4 servings.

NUTRITION INFORMATION PER SERVING

Calories 345	Protein 18 g	Cholesterol 15 mg
Carbohydrates 55 g	Total fat 6 g	Sodium 244 mg
Fibre 2.9 g	Saturated fat 3.4 g	

½ lb (250 g) fettuccine

1 cup (250 mL) low-sodium cold chicken (or vegetable) stock

¾ cup (185 mL) evaporated 2% milk

½ tsp (2.5 mL) Dijon mustard

½ tsp (2.5 mL) pepper

1 tsp (5 mL) finely chopped garlic

2 Tbsp (30 mL) all-purpose flour

¼ cup (60 mL) diced reduced-fat cream cheese (2 oz/60 g)

⅓ cup (80 mL) grated Parmesan cheese (1¼ oz/40 g)

1 cup (250 mL) sliced snow peas

1 cup (250 mL) sliced yellow bell pepper

2 Tbsp (30 mL) chopped fresh basil

ROSE'S TIP
Adding the light cream cheese to the sauce gives it the richness that heavy cream or butter would with a fraction of the calories and fat.

HEALTH TIP
A traditional fettuccine alfredo is made with loads of butter, cream and cheese, bringing the calories close to 1,000 and the fat close to 45 grams!

FARFALLE WITH SUN-DRIED ROASTED RED BELL PEPPER PESTO, CHICKEN, PINE NUTS AND PARMESAN

Farfalle pasta looks like bowties and has a great texture. You can always substitute a pasta such as rigatoni or larger penne.

1. Grill or sauté the chicken breast just until cooked or temperature reaches 165°F (74°C), about 4 minutes per side. Let cool, then slice thinly.

2. TO MAKE THE PESTO Place the peppers, garlic, half the pine nuts, sun dried tomatoes, basil, mint, half the Parmesan, oil, stock and salt and pepper in a food processor and purée until smooth. (If too thick, add more stock.)

3. Meanwhile cook the pasta just until al dente.

4. Add the chicken and pesto to the pasta and garnish with the remaining pine nuts and Parmesan cheese, basil and bell pepper.

PREPARATION TIME 15 minutes · **COOKING TIME** 28 minutes ·
MAKE AHEAD Make pesto early in the day. Cook pasta and chicken just before serving. · **MAKES** 4 servings.

 ROSE'S TIP
This is a very versatile dish that can use other proteins such as beef, seafood or tofu. Toast the pine nuts by placing in a hot skillet over medium-high heat and cooking for two minutes or until lightly browned. You can make up a batch and freeze for later use.

 HEALTH TIP
Pine nuts have one of the highest amounts of protein of any nuts as well as a notable amount of fibre.

NUTRITION INFORMATION PER SERVING

Calories 409	Protein 22.5 g	Cholesterol 37 mg
Carbohydrates 47 g	Total fat 16.5 g	Sodium 414 mg
Fibre 5.8 g	Saturated fat 3.2 g	

8 oz (250 g) boneless skinless chicken breast

Pesto
1 large red bell pepper, roasted, cut into quarters (½ cup/125 mL)*

1 garlic clove

⅓ cup (80 mL) toasted pine nuts

⅓ cup (80 mL) chopped sun-dried tomatoes

½ cup (125 mL) fresh basil

¼ cup (60 mL) fresh mint

⅓ cup (80 mL) grated Parmesan cheese (1¼ oz/40 g)

¼ cup (60 mL) olive oil

¼ cup (60 mL) low-sodium chicken stock

pinch of salt and pepper

Pasta
8 oz (250 g) farfalle pasta

½ cup (125 mL) chopped basil

½ cup (125 mL) sliced red bell peppers

*ROASTED BELL PEPPERS
In a 425°F (220°C) oven, roast the bell pepper for 20 minutes or just until charred. Cool and remove skin.

SMALL-SHELL PASTA "BEEFARONI"

Better than any packaged version of beef and pasta, which has more preservatives and artificial flavours than you'll ever need. The combination of the meat and light cheese sauce is fantastic.

1. Preheat the oven to 425°F (220°C). Lightly coat a 9- × 13-inch (3.5 L) casserole dish with cooking spray.

2. Bring a large pot of water to a boil. Add the pasta and cook for 8 to 10 minutes or until tender but still firm. Drain and place in the casserole dish.

3. TO MAKE THE MEAT SAUCE Heat the vegetable oil in a large skillet over medium heat. Add the onion and garlic and sauté for 4 minutes or until softened. Add the ground beef and cook, stirring to break up the meat, for 4 minutes or until no longer pink. Stir in the tomato sauce, cover and cook for about 5 minutes. Set aside.

4. TO MAKE THE CHEESE SAUCE Combine the milk, stock and mustard in a saucepan. Slowly whisk in the flour. Place over medium heat and stir until the mixture begins to boil. Reduce the heat to low and simmer, stirring occasionally, for 5 minutes or until the sauce is slightly thickened. Stir in the cheddar cheese and half the Parmesan cheese and stir until melted. Remove from the heat and add to the meat sauce.

5. Pour the sauce over the cooked pasta and stir to combine. Sprinkle with the remaining Parmesan and bake in the preheated oven for 10 to 15 minutes or until completely heated through. Garnish with parsley.

PREPARATION TIME 15 minutes · **COOKING TIME** About 30 minutes ·
MAKE AHEAD Prepare up to a day in advance and bake just before serving. ·
MAKES 6 servings.

8 oz (250 g) small-shell pasta

Meat sauce

1 tsp (5 mL) vegetable oil

⅔ cup (160 mL) finely chopped onion

1½ tsp (7.5 mL) finely chopped garlic

8 oz (250 g) lean ground beef

1 cup (250 mL) homemade or store-bought tomato sauce (see Quick Basic Tomato Sauce on page 369)

Cheese sauce

1¼ cups (310 mL) canned evaporated 2% milk

¾ cup (185 mL) low-sodium beef (or chicken) stock

½ tsp (2.5 mL) Dijon mustard

2 Tbsp (30 mL) all-purpose flour

½ cup (125 mL) shredded aged cheddar cheese (1½ oz/45 g)

¼ cup (60 mL) grated Parmesan cheese (1 oz/30 g)

2 Tbsp (30 mL) chopped parsley

ROSE'S TIP

To bring down the calories, substitute ground chicken, turkey or pork for the beef, or make it vegetarian by using ground soy.

 HEALTH TIP

Evaporated milk is my answer to a substitute for cream. It's thick and rich and works well in sauces. A quarter-cup (60 mL) of 2% evaporated milk has 50 calories and 1 gram of fat versus heavy cream, which has 207 calories and 22 grams of fat!

NUTRITION INFORMATION PER SERVING

Calories 320	Protein 20 g	Cholesterol 34 mg
Carbohydrates 42 g	Total fat 7.8 g	Sodium 290 mg
Fibre 2.1 g	Saturated fat 3.7 g	

GREEK FETA LASAGNA

Everyone has their favourite beef lasagna dish, so I decided to give this a Mediterranean flavour. Ground lamb is delicious, but you can still use beef if desired. Traditional meat lasagnas are high in calories and fat due to the fatty beef, excess cheese and the béchamel (white cream sauce). I drain both the beef and sausage fat. In the cheese layer, I depend on more ricotta and evaporated milk so I don't need a béchamel sauce.

1. Preheat the oven to 350°F (175°C). Lightly coat a 9- × 13-inch (3.5 L) glass casserole dish with cooking spray.

2. Cook the lasagna noodles in boiling water just until tender to the bite, about 12 minutes. Drain and set aside.

3. TO MAKE THE MEAT AND TOMATO SAUCE Lightly coat a large nonstick skillet with cooking spray. Add the ground lamb and sausage and cook until brown, breaking up with a fork, about 3 minutes. Using a slotted spoon, transfer the meat to a plate. Set aside.

4. Respray the pan. Add the oil, onion and garlic to the skillet and sauté until the onion is tender, about 5 minutes. Add the zucchini and sauté for 5 minutes. Return the beef and sausage to the skillet. Add the dried basil, oregano, salt and pepper, bay leaves, sugar and pasta sauce. Bring to a boil. Reduce the heat to medium-low. Cover and simmer until the sauce is thick, about 15 minutes. Place it in the bowl of a food processor and pulse on and off just until still chunky. Do not purée.

5. TO MAKE THE CHEESE FILLING Stir the ricotta, mozzarella, feta, egg, milk, Parmesan and salt and pepper together in a bowl.

9 lasagna noodles

Meat and tomato sauce

8 oz (250 g) ground lamb or beef

6 oz (175 g) spicy sausage (casing removed, chopped)

2 tsp (10 mL) vegetable oil

1½ cups (375 mL) chopped onion

3 cloves of garlic, finely chopped

1½ cups (375 mL) chopped zucchini

2 tsp (10 mL) crumbled dried basil

1½ tsp (7.5 mL) crumbled dried oregano

pinch of salt and pepper

2 bay leaves

1 tsp (5 mL) granulated sugar

4 cups (1 L) homemade or store-bought tomato sauce (see Quick Basic Tomato Sauce on page 369)

Cheese filling

2 cups (500 mL) reduced-fat ricotta cheese (1 lb/500 g)

1 cup (250 mL) grated part-skim mozzarella (3 oz/90 g)

1 cup (250 mL) crumbled reduced-fat feta cheese (4 oz/125 g)

6. Spread 1½ cups (375 mL) of the meat and tomato sauce over the bottom of the prepared casserole dish. Top with 3 noodles. Spread half the cheese filling over the noodles. Add another 1½ cups (375 mL) of the meat and tomato sauce, 3 noodles and the remaining filling. Add another 1½ cups (375 mL) sauce and the remaining 3 noodles. Finish with the remaining meat sauce. Top with the grated mozzarella and feta.

7. Cover the pan tightly with foil. Bake in the centre of the oven for 20 minutes, then another 15 minutes uncovered. Garnish with basil.

PREPARATION TIME 25 minutes · **COOKING TIME** 65 minutes ·

MAKE AHEAD Prepare the entire lasagna up to a day in advance. Bake just before serving. Leftovers are great; just reheat gently. · **MAKES** 10 servings.

1 egg

⅓ cup (80 mL) canned evaporated 2% milk

½ cup (125 mL) grated Parmesan cheese (2 oz/60 g)

pinch of salt and pepper

Topping

¾ cup (185 mL) shredded part-skim mozzarella cheese (2 oz/60 g)

3 Tbsp (45 mL) crumbled reduced-fat feta cheese (¾ oz/23 g)

3 Tbsp (45 mL) chopped fresh basil or parsley

 ROSE'S TIP
This lasagna freezes well. Freeze in individual serving sizes. Defrost, then place in a 300°F (150°C) oven to reheat.

 HEALTH TIP
When cooking ground beef or sausage, the key to reducing the calories and saturated fat is to drain off the excess oil after cooking.

NUTRITION INFORMATION PER SERVING

Calories 259	Protein 24.3 g	Cholesterol 60 mg
Carbohydrates 18.9 g	Total fat 10 g	Sodium 694 mg
Fibre 3.3 g	Saturated fat 5.7 g	

MINIATURE LASAGNAS

My daughter Natalie gave me this idea, and once I created it, I found it hard to go back to regular lasagna! These individual portions maintain calorie and fat control and present beautifully.

1. Preheat the oven to 375°F (190°C). Spray a 12-cup muffin tin with vegetable oil.

2. TO MAKE THE SAUCE In a saucepan, add oil and sauté onions and garlic for 5 minutes. Add the beef, basil, bay leaf and salt and pepper and sauté just until beef is cooked, breaking up with the back of a wooden spoon. Add the tomato sauce, cover and simmer for 15 minutes. Set aside.

3. TO MAKE THE CHEESE MIXTURE Combine the ricotta, mozzarella and Parmesan cheeses, egg, milk and salt and pepper in a bowl.

4. TO ASSEMBLE THE LASAGNAS Place two wonton sheets into the bottom of each muffin cup, overlapping to cover the entire surface. Add half the cheese mixture overtop of the wontons. Then add half the sauce.

5. Place the last 12 wonton sheets overtop, pressing down gently. Add the remaining cheese mixture and sauce and sprinkle with the mozzarella cheese.

6. Bake for 20 to 25 minutes until wontons are crisp. Let cool for 10 minutes, then remove carefully with a knife. Garnish with basil.

PREPARATION TIME 20 minutes • **COOKING TIME** 40 minutes •
MAKE AHEAD Make lasagnas up to a day in advance and bake just before serving. Leftovers are great if reheated gently in a 300°F (150°C) oven. •
MAKES 6 servings.

Sauce

1 tsp (5 mL) vegetable oil

1 cup (250 mL) diced onions

1½ tsp (7.5 mL) crushed garlic

6 oz (175 g) lean ground beef

1 tsp (5 mL) dried basil

1 bay leaf

pinch of salt and pepper

1¾ cups (435 mL) homemade or store-bought tomato sauce (see Quick Basic Tomato Sauce on page 369)

Cheese mixture

1 cup (250 mL) reduced-fat ricotta cheese (8 oz/250 g)

½ cup (125 mL) grated part-skim mozzarella cheese (1½ oz/45 g)

⅓ cup (80 mL) grated Parmesan cheese (1¼ oz/40 g)

1 egg

3 Tbsp (45 mL) 2% milk

pinch of salt and pepper

continued . . .

Miniature Lasagnas (continued)

 ROSE'S TIP

You can also use mini loaf pans for these lasagnas. One is a perfect appetizer or side dish. It's filling if served as a main meal with a side salad or vegetable dish.

 HEALTH TIP

Most lasagnas have double the fat and calories due to an added white sauce called béchamel made with butter and cream as well as additional cheese. With my delicious cheese and tomato sauce, there is no need for this high-fat white sauce.

Lasagnas

36 small wonton sheets

⅓ cup (80 mL) grated part-skim mozzarella cheese (1 oz/30 g)

chopped fresh basil or parsley

NUTRITION INFORMATION PER SERVING (2 MINIATURE LASAGNAS)

Calories 339	Protein 24 g	Cholesterol 62 mg
Carbohydrates 44.4 g	Total fat 6.3 g	Sodium 491 mg
Fibre 3.8 g	Saturated fat 3.5 g	

TURKEY BOLOGNESE OVER LINGUINI

Bolognese is a classic Italian meat sauce originating from where else but Bologna! Instead of beef, I have used ground turkey, which has much less fat and fewer calories than red meat. The sausage adds a kick, but feel free to omit it and just increase the ground turkey.

1. Sauté the sausage until cooked. Pour off the excess fat.

2. Sauté the onions in oil until tender, about 3 minutes. Add the carrots and garlic. Sauté until softened, another 3 minutes. Add the turkey, basil, oregano, bay leaf, chili flakes and salt and pepper and sauté until cooked, breaking with a wooden spoon until no longer pink, about 5 minutes. Add the wine and cook until half is evaporated, about 3 minutes.

3. Add the tomatoes, tomato paste and stock. Simmer, covered, for 20 minutes until thickened, stirring occasionally. Remove the bay leaf and place the sauce in a food processor. Process lightly until still chunky. Add the milk and cheese.

4. Cook the linguini. Pour the sauce over the pasta, adding the basil and Parmesan cheese.

PREPARATION TIME 20 minutes · **COOKING TIME** 35 minutes ·
MAKE AHEAD Make the sauce up to 2 days in advance. Reheat, then pour over the pasta. · **MAKES** 6 servings.

 ROSE'S TIP
This is a rich sauce, perfect over pasta or other grains such as rice, quinoa or other noodles.

 HEALTH TIP
Bolognese sauce is a healthier tomato meat sauce with fewer calories and less fat than pesto or alfredo sauces.

NUTRITION INFORMATION PER SERVING

Calories 359	Protein 25 g	Cholesterol 65 mg
Carbohydrates 40.8 g	Total fat 9.8 g	Sodium 396 mg
7 g fibre	Saturated fat 3 g	

6 oz (175 g) turkey or pork sausage, skin removed and diced

2 tsp (10 mL) vegetable oil

1 cup (250 mL) finely diced onions

½ cup (125 mL) finely diced carrots

2 large garlic cloves, chopped

12 oz (375 g) ground turkey

1 tsp (5 mL) dried basil

1½ tsp (7.5 mL) dried oregano

1 bay leaf

¼ tsp (1 mL) chili flakes

pinch of salt and pepper

½ cup (125 mL) white wine

one 19 oz (540 mL) can diced tomatoes without juice

3 Tbsp (45 mL) tomato paste

¾ cup (185 mL) low-sodium chicken stock

⅓ cup (80 mL) 2% milk

¼ cup (60 mL) grated Parmesan cheese (1 oz/30 g)

8 oz (250 g) whole-grain linguini

¼ cup (60 mL) chopped basil

freshly shaved Parmesan cheese

SPAGHETTI AND CHEESE STUFFED MEATBALLS

Everyone needs a great spaghetti and meatball recipe. But this one is unique with the secret cheese stuffing. Try to use whole wheat spaghetti for the extra nutrients it offers.

1. Preheat the oven to 425°F (220°C). Line a baking sheet with foil lightly coated with cooking spray.

2. TO MAKE THE MEATBALLS Combine the ground beef, breadcrumbs, green onions, barbecue sauce, egg, garlic and basil. Form into 12 round meatballs. Press a cube of cheese in the middle and seal. Place on the baking sheet and bake for about 12 minutes, turning halfway through the cooking time.

3. Meanwhile, place the tomato sauce in a large saucepan and add the cooked meatballs. Bring to a boil over medium-high heat, reduce the heat and simmer, covered, for about 5 minutes, stirring occasionally.

4. Meanwhile, bring a large pot of water to a boil. Add the spaghetti and cook according to the package directions. Drain and serve immediately, with the meatballs and sauce spooned over the spaghetti. Garnish with the Parmesan and basil.

PREPARATION TIME 15 minutes · **COOKING TIME** 12 minutes ·
MAKE AHEAD Complete the meatballs and sauce early in the day. Cook the spaghetti right before serving and gently reheat meatballs. · **MAKES** 4 servings.

Meatballs

1 lb (500 g) lean ground beef

¼ cup (60 mL) seasoned dry breadcrumbs

¼ cup (60 mL) finely chopped green onions

¼ cup (60 mL) barbecue sauce

1 egg

2 tsp (10 mL) finely chopped garlic

1 tsp (5 mL) dried basil

¾ cup (185 mL) part-skim mozzarella cheese cut into 12 small cubes (2 oz/60 g)

Sauce and pasta

3 cups (750 mL) tomato sauce (see Quick Basic Tomato Sauce on page 369)

½ lb (250 g) spaghetti noodles

¼ cup (60 mL) grated Parmesan cheese (1 oz/30 g)

3 Tbsp (45 mL) chopped fresh basil

ROSE'S TIP

If you want to omit the cheese in the meatballs, do so; you can also make the meatballs smaller.

 HEALTH TIP

When buying ground beef, there is a large difference between extra-lean and regular. A 4-ounce (125 g) portion of extra-lean has 193 calories and 7 grams of fat versus the regular ground, which has 300 calories and 20 grams of fat.

NUTRITION INFORMATION PER SERVING

Calories 492	Protein 42 g	Cholesterol 119 mg
Carbohydrates 64 g	Total fat 9.2 g	Sodium 570 mg
Fibre 11 g	Saturated fat 4.3 g	

LOBSTER MACARONI AND CHEESE WITH CHEDDAR AND GRUYÈRE

The latest trend in mac and cheese dishes is the highbrow lobster addition. If lobster is too much for your pocketbook, substitute shrimp or crabmeat. Lobster is most affordable if bought frozen or in a can. Defrost, squeeze out excess moisture and dice. I like to serve this in individual ovenproof dishes, or you can use a 9-inch (23 cm) baking dish.

1. Preheat the oven to 425°F (220°C). Spray 4 individual baking dishes or a 9-inch (23 cm) baking dish with vegetable oil.

2. Boil the macaroni just until firm to the bite, about 5 minutes. Drain and set aside.

3. TO MAKE THE CHEESE SAUCE Combine the milk, stock and flour until smooth. Heat over medium heat and whisk until slightly thickened, approximately 3 minutes. Add the cheeses, cayenne, nutmeg and salt and pepper and mix just until the cheeses are melted.

4. Add the cooked pasta and lobster. Pour into the baking dishes.

5. TO MAKE THE TOPPING Combine the crumbs, oil and both cheeses. Sprinkle overtop of the pasta and bake for 10 minutes just until hot and the topping is browned.

PREPARATION TIME 15 minutes · **COOKING TIME** 15 minutes ·
MAKE AHEAD Make the cheese sauce early in the day. Add more milk to thin it before assembling. Bake just before serving. · **MAKES** 4 servings.

1 cup (250 mL) macaroni

6 oz (175 g) cooked lobster meat, diced

Cheese sauce
1 cup (250 mL) 2% milk

1 cup (250 mL) low-sodium chicken or seafood stock

¼ cup (60 mL) all-purpose flour

¾ cup (185 mL) grated aged white cheddar (3 oz/90 g)

¼ cup (60 mL) grated Parmesan cheese (1 oz/30 g)

⅛ tsp (0.5 mL) cayenne pepper

⅛ tsp (0.5 mL) nutmeg

pinch of salt and pepper

Topping
¼ cup (60 mL) panko crumbs

1 tsp (5 mL) olive oil

1 Tbsp (15 mL) grated Parmesan cheese (¼ oz/8 g)

¼ cup (60 mL) grated aged white cheddar (¾ oz/23 g)

ROSE'S TIP

To save money when buying lobster, go directly to a wholesale fish market instead of your grocery store, which can charge up to double the price. The quality of frozen lobster is excellent.

HEALTH TIP

Lobster is high in protein and low in fat and contains omega-3 fatty acids, which benefit your heart health.

NUTRITION INFORMATION PER SERVING

Calories 282

Carbohydrates 32.5 g

Fibre 2.4 g

Protein 24.9 g

Total fat 6 g

Saturated fat 2.9 g

Cholesterol 68 mg

Sodium 668 mg

ASIAN "SLOPPY JOES" OVER SOBA NOODLES

*A sloppy Joe is an American dish of ground beef, onions, sweet-
ened tomato sauce or ketchup and other seasonings, served on a
hamburger bun. I decided to take an Asian twist to this recipe, which
was incredible. Serving it over soba noodles and topping it with a
quick Asian slaw completes this common fast food.*

1. In a large skillet add the oil, onions, garlic and ginger.
   Sauté for 5 minutes or just until tender. Add the carrots
   and sauté for 3 minutes.

2. Add the beef and sauté for 5 minutes, just until no longer
   rare, stirring constantly to break up the meat. Add the
   hot sauce, hoisin, tomatoes and salt and pepper.

3. Cook on medium heat, uncovered, for 15 minutes, stirring occasionally.

4. Meanwhile, boil the soba noodles just until cooked. Drain
   and place on a serving platter. Add the beef mixture and
   garnish with the green onions and cilantro.

5. To make an Asian slaw, combine the coleslaw mixture,
   cilantro, vinegar, soy sauce and sesame oil.

PREPARATION TIME 20 minutes · **COOKING TIME** 28 minutes ·
MAKE AHEAD Cook the beef mixture up to a day in advance. Make the slaw, if
using, early in the day. Cook the pasta right before serving and reheat the beef
mixture slowly. · **MAKES** 4 servings.

2 tsp (10 mL) vegetable oil

1½ cups (375 mL) diced onions

2 tsp (10 mL) crushed garlic

2 tsp (10 mL) minced ginger

1 cup (250 mL) finely diced carrot

1 lb (500 g) lean ground beef
or chicken

1 tsp (5 mL) hot Asian sauce
(Sriracha)

½ cup (125 mL) hoisin sauce

¾ cup (185 mL) diced tomatoes

pinch of salt and pepper

3 oz (90 g) soba or buckwheat
noodles

⅓ cup (80 mL) chopped green
onions for garnish

¼ cup (60 mL) chopped cilantro
for garnish

1½ cups (375 mL) ready-made
shredded coleslaw mixture

2 Tbsp (30 mL) chopped cilantro

2 tsp (10 mL) rice vinegar

1½ tsp (7.5 mL) low-sodium
soy sauce

2 tsp (10 mL) sesame oil

ROSE'S TIP

Coleslaw mixture can be found in your grocery store prepackaged. If not, thinly slice some green and red cabbage with julienne carrots.

 HEALTH TIP

Sriracha is a hot sauce made from hot red chili peppers, garlic, vinegar and sugar. It is known to protect heart health by boosting the body's ability to dissolve blood clots, which improves blood flow and lowers blood pressure.

NUTRITION INFORMATION PER SERVING

Calories 290	Protein 26.7 g	Cholesterol 71 mg
Carbohydrates 24.7 g	Total fat 8.6 g	Sodium 697 mg
Fibre 3.3 g	Saturated fat 3.1 g	

ORANGE BLACK BEAN SAUCE WITH MUSSELS OVER SOBA NOODLES

The combination of flavours makes this dish sensational. Be sure to buy the freshest mussels you can. If any don't open during cooking, toss them.

1. Combine the orange juice, honey, black bean sauce and cornstarch and mix until smooth.

2. Bring a pot of water to a boil. Add the soba noodles and boil for 5 minutes until tender. Drain and set aside.

3. In a nonstick wok or large saucepan sprayed with vegetable spray, heat the oil over medium-high heat. Add the onions and cook for 3 minutes or until lightly browned. Add the red peppers, green peppers, garlic and ginger and cook for 3 minutes.

4. Add the sauce and mussels to the vegetables. Cover and cook for about 3 minutes just until mussels open. (Discard any that do not open.)

5. On a serving platter, arrange the noodles and pour the mussel mixture overtop. Garnish with cilantro and serve immediately.

PREPARATION TIME 15 minutes · **COOKING TIME** 11 minutes ·
MAKE AHEAD Prepare the sauce and vegetables early in the day. Complete the recipe just before serving. · **MAKES** 4 servings.

1 cup (250 mL) orange juice

3 Tbsp (45 mL) honey

3 Tbsp (45 mL) black bean sauce

1½ Tbsp (22.5 mL) cornstarch

6 oz (175 g) soba noodles

2 tsp (10 mL) vegetable oil

1 cup (250 mL) sliced onions

1½ cups (375 mL) thinly sliced red bell peppers

1 cup (250 mL) thinly sliced green bell peppers

1½ tsp (7.5 mL) minced garlic

1 tsp (5 mL) minced ginger

2 lb (1 kg) fresh mussels, cleaned

½ cup (125 mL) chopped fresh cilantro or parsley

ROSE'S TIP
You can substitute clams, shrimp, scallops or squid for the mussels, or try a combination of seafood.

HEALTH TIP
Mussels contain over 9 times the vitamin B12 of beef and over 8 times the iron of chicken. As well, they have more omega-3 fatty acids than all other shellfish.

NUTRITION INFORMATION PER SERVING

Calories 562	Protein 33.3 g	Cholesterol 87 mg
Carbohydrates 62.5 g	Total fat 6.9 g	Sodium 880 mg
Fibre 3.7 g	Saturated fat 1.7 g	

PAD THAI WITH SHRIMP

Making traditional pad Thai at home is not an easy endeavour, but I've simplified the recipe, and it's so delicious and easy to prepare, you'll love it. Substitute chicken breast or cubed tofu for the shrimp.

1. TO MAKE THE SAUCE Whisk or purée the soy sauce, water, rice vinegar, sesame and vegetable oils, honey, brown sugar, cider vinegar, peanut butter, hot sauce, garlic and ginger until smooth. Set aside.

2. Bring the water to a boil. Add the noodles and boil just until tender, about 5 minutes. Do not overcook. Drain well.

3. In a large skillet sprayed with vegetable spray, add the shrimp and sauté for 5 minutes just until almost cooked. Add the oil, carrots and red pepper and sauté for 3 minutes. Add the cooked noodles and sauce and heat until hot and the sauce thickens slightly.

4. Garnish with cilantro and peanuts.

PREPARATION TIME 15 minutes • **COOKING TIME** 13 minutes •
MAKE AHEAD Prepare the sauce early in the day. Finish off the pad Thai just before serving. • **MAKES** 4 servings.

 ROSE'S TIP
Be sure to use only natural peanut butter, which has peanuts only. The regular varieties contain icing sugar and are only smooth due to hydrogenation, which changes the fat to saturated fat.

 HEALTH TIP
If you want to cut the calories from the noodles, you can use half the noodles and double the protein.

NUTRITION INFORMATION PER SERVING

Calories 406	Protein 16.1 g	Cholesterol 71 mg
Carbohydrates 44 g	Total fat 17.7 g	Sodium 720 mg
Fibre 3.7 g	Saturated fat 2.8 g	

Sauce

3 Tbsp (45 mL) low-sodium soy sauce

2½ Tbsp (22.5 mL) water

3 Tbsp (45 mL) rice vinegar

1 Tbsp (15 mL) sesame oil

1 Tbsp (15 mL) vegetable oil

1 Tbsp (15 mL) honey

1 Tbsp (15 mL) brown sugar

1 Tbsp (15 mL) cider vinegar

¼ cup (60 mL) creamy peanut butter

1 tsp (5 mL) hot sauce (Sriracha)

1½ tsp (7.5 mL) crushed garlic

Pad Thai

1½ tsp (7.5 mL) minced ginger

4 oz (125 g) wide rice noodles

8 oz (250 g) shelled and diced raw shrimp

2 tsp (10 mL) vegetable oil

1 cup (250 mL) julienne carrots

1 cup (250 mL) julienne red peppers

¼ cup (60 mL) chopped cilantro

¼ cup (60 mL) toasted chopped peanuts

MUSHROOM RISOTTO WITH ASPARAGUS AND PARMESAN

I love risottos, but the restaurant versions are loaded with butter, cream or cheese. This risotto is easy to make and has little fat and few calories by comparison. For a more elegant risotto, try adding 2 tsp (10 mL) of truffle oil at the end.

1. Lightly coat a saucepan with cooking spray. Add the oil and set over medium-high heat. Add the onion and garlic and sauté for 5 minutes or until the onions are just tender and lightly browned. Add the mushrooms and sauté for about 8 minutes or until the mushrooms are no longer wet.

2. Add the arborio rice and sauté for 1 minute. Add 1 cup (250 mL) of the stock and simmer until the stock has just been absorbed. Continue adding ½ cup (125 mL) stock at a time, stirring until absorbed; repeat until all the stock has been used (about 20 minutes in total). Add the chopped asparagus with the last ½ cup (125 mL) stock and cook until the asparagus is tender-crisp, about 3 minutes, and the liquid is absorbed.

3. Add all but 2 Tbsp (30 mL) of the grated Parmesan cheese and the salt and pepper and mix well. Garnish with the remaining Parmesan and basil. Serve warm.

PREPARATION TIME 10 minutes · **COOKING TIME** About 35 minutes · **MAKE AHEAD** You can make the dish early in the day right up until you add the first cup (250 mL) of stock. Finish off just before serving. · **MAKES** 4 servings.

2 tsp (10 mL) vegetable oil

1 cup (250 mL) finely chopped onion

2 tsp (10 mL) finely chopped garlic

4 cups (1 L) chopped wild mushrooms (try oyster, shiitake and/or portobello)

1 cup (250 mL) arborio rice

3½ cups (875 mL) low-sodium vegetable (or chicken) stock

1 cup (250 mL) chopped asparagus (cut into 1-inch/2.5 cm pieces)

⅓ cup (80 mL) grated Parmesan cheese (1¼ oz/40 g)

pinch of salt and pepper

¼ cup (60 mL) chopped fresh basil

 ROSE'S TIP
I prefer wild mushrooms in this dish but feel free to use button mushrooms, making sure they are sautéed until all the moisture evaporates.

 HEALTH TIP
Mushrooms are an excellent source of potassium, which helps regulate blood pressure. One medium portobello mushroom has more potassium than a banana or a glass of orange juice!

NUTRITION INFORMATION PER SERVING

Calories 196	Protein 11 g	Cholesterol 5 mg
Carbohydrates 29 g	Total fat 4.9 g	Sodium 450 mg
Fibre 3 g	Saturated fat 1.4 g	

LEMON RISOTTO WITH SHRIMP, SUGAR SNAP PEAS AND PARMESAN CHEESE

Traditional risottos are sensational, but in restaurants they are usually made with excess butter, oil and cheese. My lemon shrimp variety is so delicious with a fraction of the calories and fat.

1. Sauté or grill the shrimp just until no longer pink, about 5 minutes, and set aside. Cut lengthwise to divide into two slices. Set aside.

2. In a large skillet, add the oil and sauté the onions for 5 minutes until soft on medium-low heat. Add the garlic and sauté for 1 minute. Add the rice and sauté for 2 minutes just until lightly browned. Add half the stock and simmer until the liquid has been absorbed (about 5 minutes).

3. Add the remaining stock and simmer just until the liquid is absorbed and rice is just tender (about 5 minutes). Add the peas, 4 Tbsp (60 mL) of the cheese, salt and pepper, lemon juice and zest and half the mint. Place it in a serving bowl with the shrimp overtop and garnish with the remaining mint and Parmesan cheese.

PREPARATION TIME 15 minutes · **COOKING TIME** 23 minutes ·
MAKE AHEAD Sauté the onions early in the day. Best to complete just before eating. · **MAKES** 4 servings.

8 oz (250 g) shelled medium shrimp

2 tsp (10 mL) vegetable oil

1 cup (250 mL) onions, diced

1½ tsp (7.5 mL) crushed garlic

1 cup (250 mL) jasmine rice

3 cups (750 mL) low-sodium chicken stock

1 cup (250 mL) sliced sugar snap peas, cut into thirds

⅓ cup (80 mL) grated Parmesan cheese (1¼ oz/40 g)

pinch of salt and pepper

2 Tbsp (30 mL) lemon juice

2 tsp (10 mL) lemon zest

¼ cup (60 mL) fresh chopped mint

 ROSE'S TIP
Risottos are a wonderful main course meal if they are as healthy as my version. The lemon juice and zest along with the cheese allow the flavours to come through without using butter or excess cheese.

 HEALTH TIP
If you can find Meyer lemons, try them. They are a cross between a lemon and mandarin orange and are high in vitamin C.

NUTRITION INFORMATION PER SERVING

Calories 291	Protein 17.1 g	Cholesterol 77 mg
Carbohydrates 49.9 g	Total fat 2.3 g	Sodium 546 mg
Fibre 2 g	Saturated fat 1.1 g	

QUINOA WITH CHARRED CORN, SPINACH AND FETA

Quinoa is a superfood—low glycemic and with an abundance of nutrients. Containing all eight essential amino acids, it's the only grain that's considered a complete protein, making this recipe a vegetarian's delight. Instead of fresh spinach, you can use half a 10-ounce (300 g) package of frozen spinach, cooked and squeezed dry.

1. Bring the quinoa and stock to a boil. Cover and simmer for 15 minutes, just until the stock is absorbed and the quinoa is tender. Remove from the heat and place in a serving bowl.

2. Spray a small nonstick skillet with cooking oil and place over medium heat. Sauté the corn for approximately 8 minutes, just until browned, stirring constantly. Set aside.

3. Spray a medium nonstick skillet with cooking oil, add the vegetable oil and place over medium heat. Add the diced onion, bell pepper, garlic, cumin and jalapeño pepper and sauté until the onion begins to brown, about 5 minutes.

4. Add the spinach and water. Cook until the spinach wilts, approximately 2 minutes.

5. Remove from the heat. Stir in the green onion, cilantro, feta, olive oil, lemon juice and sautéed corn. Add the mixture to the quinoa and mix well.

PREPARATION TIME 15 minutes · **COOKING TIME** 15 minutes ·
MAKE AHEAD Make early in the day and either serve at room temperature or gently reheat. · **MAKES** 4 servings.

1 cup (250 mL) quinoa

2 cups (500 mL) low-sodium vegetable or chicken stock

1½ cups (375 mL) corn

1 tsp (5 mL) vegetable oil

1 cup (250 mL) diced onion

½ cup (125 mL) diced red bell pepper

2 tsp (10 mL) crushed fresh garlic

½ tsp (2.5 mL) ground cumin

1 tsp (5 mL) seeded minced jalapeño pepper (or 1 tsp/5 mL hot chili sauce or paste)

4 cups (1 L) chopped fresh spinach

1 Tbsp (15 mL) water

⅓ cup (80 mL) chopped green onion

⅓ cup (80 mL) chopped cilantro or parsley

½ cup (125 mL) crumbled reduced-fat feta cheese (2 oz/60 g)

2 Tbsp (30 mL) olive oil

2 Tbsp (30 mL) freshly squeezed lemon juice

ROSE'S TIP

At times there can be a
bitter taste to quinoa due
to the seeds being covered
with a bitter coating called
saponin. Rinse well with
water to eliminate the
bitterness before cooking.

 HEALTH TIP

Quinoa is gluten-free,
so it's a perfect grain for
those with celiac and wheat
allergies.

NUTRITION INFORMATION PER SERVING

Calories 379	Protein 14 g	Cholesterol 5 mg
Carbohydrates 53 g	Total fat 13 g	Sodium 436 mg
Fibre 7.0 g	Saturated fat 2.4 g	

QUINOA MACARONI AND CHEESE WITH CHICKEN AND SUN-DRIED TOMATOES

Quinoa, the supergrain, has crept its way into every meal I can think of. My daughter Natalie gave me this idea, and testing it produced a variation of mac and cheese that we ultimately preferred! You can use tofu or seafood for the chicken.

1. Preheat the oven to 400°F (200°C).

2. In a small pot, add the quinoa and stock. Bring to a boil, cover and simmer for 15 minutes or just until cooked. Set aside.

3. Meanwhile, dust the chicken with flour. In a skillet sprayed with vegetable oil, cook just until done, about 3 minutes. Add to the quinoa along with the sun-dried tomatoes and feta. Place into a 9-inch (23 cm) baking dish.

4. TO MAKE THE SAUCE   In a saucepan, add the milk, stock, flour, mustard and salt and pepper. Whisk until the flour is mixed in and bring to a simmer. Cook for 3 minutes or just until slightly thickened, stirring constantly. Add ¾ cup (185 mL) cheddar and 2 Tbsp (30 mL) Parmesan. Whisk until smooth.

5. Pour over the quinoa and mix.

6. TO MAKE THE TOPPING   Combine the topping ingredients and sprinkle overtop. Bake for 10 minutes just until topping is browned.

PREPARATION TIME 20 minutes • **COOKING TIME** 25 minutes •

MAKE AHEAD This dish can be made up to the point of baking. Bake it just before serving. • **MAKES** 6 servings.

1 cup (250 mL) quinoa

1½ cups (375 mL) water or low-sodium chicken stock

6 oz (175 g) diced chicken breast

2 Tbsp (30 mL) all-purpose flour

½ cup (125 mL) chopped rehydrated sun-dried tomatoes

⅓ cup (80 mL) crumbled reduced-fat feta cheese (1½ oz/45 g)

Sauce

1¼ cups (310 mL) 2% milk

¼ cup (60 mL) low-sodium chicken stock

2 Tbsp (30 mL) all-purpose flour

½ tsp (2.5 mL) Dijon mustard

pinch of salt and pepper

¾ cup (185 mL) grated aged cheddar cheese (2¼ oz/65 g)

2 Tbsp (30 mL) grated Parmesan cheese (½ oz/15 g)

ROSE'S TIP

Substitute diced pork, beef or shrimp for the chicken. To make it vegetarian, use diced firm tofu.

 HEALTH TIP

Panko crumbs are healthier than breadcrumbs because they absorb less oil and have much less sodium. One cup (250 mL) of panko has only 80 mg of sodium whereas one cup (250 mL) of unseasoned dry breadcrumbs has 800 mg!

Topping

⅓ cup (80 mL) panko or unseasoned dry breadcrumbs

2 Tbsp (30 mL) grated aged cheddar cheese (2½ oz/75 g)

2 Tbsp (30 mL) grated Parmesan cheese (½ oz/15 g)

2 tsp (10 mL) olive oil

NUTRITION INFORMATION PER SERVING

Calories 308	Protein 25.6 g	Cholesterol 28 mg
Carbohydrates 32.5 g	Total fat 8.3 g	Sodium 673 mg
Fibre 3.1 g	Saturated fat 3.4 g	

CHICKEN "FRIED RICE" WITH EDAMAME

Fried rice in Asian restaurants is often made with lard or excess oil, adding enormous amounts of calories and fat. In my recipe I use a stock-based sauce that uses only 1 Tbsp (15 mL) of flavoured sesame oil. And instead of the traditional green peas, I have used edamame (Japanese soybeans).

1. Whisk together the chicken stock, soy sauce, sesame oil and chili sauce in a small bowl. Set aside.

2. Add the rice to the stock and bring to a boil. Reduce the heat to low, cover and simmer for 10 minutes. Remove from the heat and let sit for 10 minutes, covered.

3. Lightly coat a large nonstick skillet or wok with cooking spray, add the oil and set over medium–high heat. Add the onion and sauté for 5 minutes or until it is softened. Add the garlic and ginger and sauté for 1 more minute. Add the chicken and sauté for 5 minutes or until no longer pink. Add the edamame, carrots and green onions.

4. Add the cooked rice to the chicken mixture. Add the sauce and stir-fry for 2 minutes or until everything is warmed through and the rice is coated with the sauce. Serve hot.

PREPARATION TIME 15 minutes · **COOKING TIME** 21 minutes ·

MAKE AHEAD Can be prepared early in the day and gently reheated before serving. · **MAKES** 6 servings.

⅓ cup (80 mL) low-sodium chicken stock

3 Tbsp (45 mL) low-sodium soy sauce

1 Tbsp (15 mL) sesame oil

1 tsp (5 mL) hot chili sauce

1½ cups (375 mL) white rice

1½ cups (375 mL) low-sodium chicken stock

2 tsp (10 mL) vegetable oil

1 cup (250 mL) chopped onion

1½ tsp (7.5 mL) each finely chopped garlic and ginger

4 oz (125 g) boneless chicken breast, diced

1 cup (250 mL) frozen shelled edamame

½ cup (125 mL) grated carrots

½ cup (125 mL) chopped green onions

 ROSE'S TIP
Substitute shrimp, beef, pork or tofu for the chicken.

 HEALTH TIP
Fried rice in Chinese restaurants can have over 500 calories and 18 grams of fat in one serving.

NUTRITION INFORMATION PER SERVING

Calories 309	Protein 12 g	Cholesterol 28 mg
Carbohydrates 52 g	Total fat 5.4 g	Sodium 459 mg
Fibre 1.8 g	Saturated fat 0.6 g	

VEGETABLES

ROASTED GREEN BEANS WITH DRIED APRICOTS AND PECANS

Green beans are a staple in most homes because they're so affordable and versatile. But instead of just steaming them, try this unique recipe.

1. Preheat the oven to 400°F (200°C). Line a baking sheet with foil and spray with vegetable oil. Place the green beans on the sheet and bake for 10 minutes or just until tender.

2. Add the olive oil, garlic, ginger, apricots, pecans and orange zest. Toss well and serve.

PREPARATION TIME 5 minutes · **COOKING TIME** 10 minutes · **MAKE AHEAD** Best roasted just before serving. · **MAKES** 4 servings.

ROSE'S TIP
If you're in a hurry, you can steam your beans for about 2 minutes. If not serving immediately, rinse with cold water to stop the cooking process.

HEALTH TIP
Frozen beans have 90% of the nutrients of fresh. Do not use canned beans, where the majority of the nutrients are lost.

1 lb (500 g) green beans, trimmed and cut in half

2 tsp (10 mL) olive oil

½ tsp (2.5 mL) finely chopped garlic

½ tsp (2.5 mL) finely chopped ginger

¼ cup (60 mL) finely chopped dried apricots

3 Tbsp (45 mL) toasted chopped pecans

1 tsp (5 mL) orange zest

NUTRITION INFORMATION PER SERVING

Calories 121	Protein 3 g	Cholesterol 0 mg
Carbohydrates 15 g	Total fat 5 g	Sodium 7 mg
Fibre 4.8 g	Saturated fat 0.6 g	

MEXICAN STUFFED PEPPERS

A classic vegetable side dish or main meal that is always being resur-rected. Make this vegetarian by using ground soy or diced tofu. These are delicious reheated as well.

1. Preheat the oven to 375°F (190°C). Line a baking sheet with foil and lightly coat with cooking spray.

2. In a medium saucepan, bring the stock and rice to a boil. Reduce the heat to low, then cover and simmer for 25 minutes or until the rice is tender. Drain any excess stock.

3. Meanwhile, lightly coat a large saucepan with cooking spray, add the oil and set over medium-high heat. Add the onion and sauté for 3 minutes. Add the corn and sauté another 5 minutes or until the corn starts to brown. Add the ground beef and sauté until no longer pink, about 3 minutes.

4. Add the cooked rice, beans, chili powder, basil, cumin, salt and pepper, and salsa and cook for 1 minute. Remove from the heat and add ½ cup (125 mL) of the cheese, along with the sour cream and cilantro.

5. Carefully remove and discard the top from each of the peppers. Remove the ribs and seeds and discard. Place the peppers on the baking sheet and fill them with the beef stuffing. Bake for 25 minutes.

6. Sprinkle with the remaining cheese. Bake for another 2 minutes or just until the cheese melts.

PREPARATION TIME 15 minutes · **COOKING TIME** 53 minutes ·
MAKE AHEAD Prepare the entire pepper up to a day in advance and bake just before serving. Gently reheat leftovers. · **MAKES** 4 servings.

2 cups (500 mL) low-sodium beef (or chicken) stock

½ cup (125 mL) brown rice

2 tsp (10 mL) vegetable oil

1 cup (250 mL) diced onion

1 cup (250 mL) corn

½ lb (250 g) lean ground beef

1½ cups (375 mL) canned red kidney beans, drained and rinsed

1½ tsp (7.5 mL) chili powder

½ tsp (2.5 mL) dried basil

½ tsp (2.5 mL) ground cumin

pinch of salt and pepper

½ cup (125 mL) medium salsa

¾ cup (185 mL) shredded aged cheddar cheese (2¼ oz/65 g)

⅓ cup (80 mL) reduced-fat sour cream

⅓ cup (80 mL) chopped cilantro or parsley

4 medium bell peppers (any colour)

ROSE'S TIP

Be sure to eat the entire
bell pepper so this becomes
your entire meal. You can
use ground chicken, turkey
or pork instead of the beef.

 HEALTH TIP

Red bell peppers have the
most nutritional benefits
of all peppers. They have
300% of your daily vitamin
C requirement and contain
antioxidants and lycopene,
which gives them their red
colour. Lycopene has been
known to reduce the risk
of cancers of the prostate
and lungs.

NUTRITION INFORMATION PER SERVING

Calories 455	Protein 28 g	Cholesterol 49 mg
Carbohydrates 58 g	Total fat 13 g	Sodium 790 mg
Fibre 9.7 g	Saturated fat 5.1 g	

ROASTED WHITE STRING BEANS WITH TOMATOES AND KALAMATA OLIVES

This is a great Mediterranean vegetable dish. You can substitute green beans, asparagus or broccoli for the white string beans.

1. Preheat the oven to 400°F (200°C). Line 2 baking sheets with foil and lightly coat with cooking spray.

2. Slice the top off the head of the garlic to expose the tops of the cloves. Rub with a little vegetable oil. Wrap in foil and place on the foil-covered baking sheet along with the cherry tomatoes. Place the string beans on the other sheet. Bake for 10 minutes, then remove the tomatoes. Continue baking for another 10 minutes until the beans are slightly browned and the garlic is soft. Squeeze out the garlic cloves.

3. Place the beans on a serving dish along with the cherry tomatoes, olives, olive oil, pepper and garlic cloves. Toss. Garnish with basil.

PREPARATION TIME 5 minutes • **COOKING TIME** 20 minutes •
MAKE AHEAD Cook just before serving. If serving at room temperature, make early in the day. • **MAKES** 6 servings.

1 head of garlic

2 cups (500 mL) halved cherry tomatoes

1½ lb (750 g) white string beans, trimmed

⅓ cup (80 mL) chopped black olives

1 Tbsp (15 mL) olive oil

pinch of pepper

2 Tbsp (30 mL) chopped fresh basil

ROSE'S TIP
If you're in a hurry, you can steam or boil the string beans. If not using immediately, rinse with cold water and serve at room temperature.

HEALTH TIP
Garlic is a superfood. Its antioxidant properties reduce the bad cholesterol (LDL), which in turn reduces the risk of heart disease and may reduce the risk of colon and stomach cancers.

NUTRITION INFORMATION PER SERVING

Calories 87	Protein 3 g	Cholesterol 0 mg
Carbohydrates 13 g	Total fat 3.6 g	Sodium 100 mg
Fibre 4.6 g	Saturated fat 0.5 g	

BABY BOK CHOY AND WILD MUSHROOMS WITH SESAME GINGER SAUCE

The combined flavours of bok choy, mushrooms and this sesame sauce is outstanding. I love to serve this alongside a fish or chicken dish. I use whole oyster mushrooms for their appearance as well as texture. Feel free to substitute other mushrooms, but it is best to slice them in large pieces.

1. **TO MAKE THE SESAME GINGER SAUCE** Combine the soy sauce, sesame oil, oyster sauce, sugar, garlic, ginger and chili sauce in a small bowl and set aside.

2. **TO MAKE THE VEGETABLES** Lightly coat a large nonstick skillet with cooking spray, add the oil and set over medium-high heat. Add the mushrooms and sauté for 5 minutes or until tender. (If using button mushrooms, sauté until the liquid has evaporated.) Add the sauce and cook for 2 minutes, until slightly thickened.

3. Place a shallow layer of water in a large saucepan and bring to a boil. Place the bok choy in the saucepan, cover and cook for 2 minutes or just until it is bright green. Drain well and place on a serving dish. Top with the sautéed mushrooms and sesame sauce, sprinkle with the sesame seeds and serve immediately.

PREPARATION TIME 5 minutes · **COOKING TIME** 9 minutes ·
MAKE AHEAD Make the sauce and prepare the vegetables early in the day. Cook just before serving. If serving at room temperature, make early in the day. · **MAKES** 4 servings.

NUTRITION INFORMATION PER SERVING

Calories 55	Protein 4 g	Cholesterol 0 mg
Carbohydrates 9 g	Total fat 3 g	Sodium 257 mg
Fibre 3.7 g	Saturated fat 0.4 g	

Sesame Ginger Sauce

4 tsp (20 mL) low-sodium soy sauce

1 Tbsp (15 mL) sesame oil

2 tsp (10 mL) oyster sauce

4 tsp (20 mL) brown sugar

1 tsp (5 mL) finely chopped garlic

1 tsp (5 mL) finely chopped ginger

1 tsp (5 mL) hot chili sauce

Vegetables

2 tsp (10 mL) vegetable oil

8 oz (250 g) whole oyster or sliced button mushrooms

8 baby bok choy

1 tsp (5 mL) toasted sesame seeds

 ROSE'S TIP
Buy the baby bok choy rather than the large bok choy. It is milder and has a sweet flavour. It's also known as Shanghai bok choy.

 HEALTH TIP
Bok choy is a member of the cruciferous vegetables, like broccoli and cauliflower. It has antioxidant benefits that may reduce the risk of certain cancers, and one cup (250 mL) has half your daily requirements of vitamin A, C and K.

SCALLOPED YUKON GOLD, SWEET POTATO AND MUSHROOM CASSEROLE

I love scalloped potatoes, but most recipes are filled with fat and calories from the excess butter and cheese used. This dish uses two varieties of potatoes, creating a sweet and savoury flavour. The oyster mushrooms give the dish a wonderful taste and texture, and the evaporated milk gives it a creamy consistency without using heavy cream or butter.

1. Preheat the oven to 400°F (200°C). Line a baking sheet with foil sprayed with vegetable oil and coat a 9- × 13-inch (3.5 L) baking dish with cooking spray.

2. Layer both kinds of potatoes on the baking sheet. Bake for 20 minutes, just until potatoes are tender and lightly browned. Place the overlapping potato slices in the prepared baking dish.

3. Meanwhile, in a large nonstick frying pan sprayed with cooking spray, heat the oil over medium-high heat. Cook the onions and garlic for 3 minutes or until softened. Stir in the mushrooms, thyme and salt and pepper and cook for 8 minutes or until the mushrooms are browned and dry. In a bowl, whisk together the stock, evaporated milk and flour and stir into the mushroom mixture. Cook, stirring, for 4 minutes or until slightly thickened. Pour over the potatoes.

4. In a bowl, stir together the cheddar and Parmesan cheeses and sprinkle over the casserole.

5. TO MAKE THE CRUMB TOPPING In another bowl, stir together the breadcrumbs, oil, water and Parmesan. Sprinkle over the casserole.

6. Bake, uncovered, for 15 minutes.

PREPARATION TIME 20 minutes · **COOKING TIME** 35 minutes ·
MAKE AHEAD Prepare the entire dish early in the day and bake just before serving. · **MAKES** 8 servings.

1 lb (500 g) peeled Yukon Gold potatoes sliced into ¼-inch (6 mm) rounds

1 lb (500 g) peeled sweet potatoes sliced into ¼-inch (6 mm) rounds

2 tsp (10 mL) vegetable oil

1 cup (250 mL) chopped onions

2 tsp (10 mL) minced garlic

3 cups (750 mL) sliced oyster mushrooms

½ tsp (2.5 mL) dried thyme

pinch of salt and ground black pepper

1 cup (250 mL) low-sodium vegetable or chicken stock

1 cup (250 mL) canned evaporated 2% milk

2 Tbsp (30 mL) all-purpose flour

¾ cup (185 mL) shredded cheddar or Swiss cheese (2¼ oz/65 g)

¼ cup (60 mL) grated Parmesan cheese (1 oz/30 g)

continued . . .

Scalloped Yukon Gold, Sweet Potato and Mushroom Casserole (continued)

 ROSE'S TIP

Scalloped potatoes have always been considered a high-calorie and high-fat dish with few nutrients but lots of butter and cream. My version adds sweet potatoes and uses a light cheese sauce, making this an incredibly nutritious dish.

 HEALTH TIP

Most stocks contain large amounts of sodium. One cup (250 mL) of commercial stock contains over 600 mg of sodium. Either purchase low-sodium or no-sodium stock, or prepare your own at home to reduce the sodium by more than half. Add your own sea salt to flavour.

Crumb topping

⅓ cup (80 mL) seasoned dry breadcrumbs

1 tsp (5 mL) vegetable oil

1 tsp (5 mL) water

1 Tbsp (15 mL) grated Parmesan cheese (¼ oz/8 g)

NUTRITION INFORMATION PER SERVING

Calories 220	Protein 9.1 g	Cholesterol 14 mg
Carbohydrates 33.8 g	Total fat 5.6 g	Sodium 218 mg
Fibre 4 g	Saturated fat 2.7 g	

YUKON GOLD POTATO AND CHICKPEA MASH

Instead of traditional mashed potatoes, I added puréed chickpeas and roasted garlic to this potato dish. It's delicious and a nice change from the standard recipes. The evaporated milk takes the place of the butter or cream normally used.

1. Preheat the oven to 450°F (230°C). Slice the top off the head of garlic to expose the tops of the cloves. Rub with a little vegetable oil. Wrap the head in foil and bake for 20 minutes.

2. Place the potatoes in a large pot and add enough cold water to cover. Bring to a boil and cook for 15 minutes or until tender.

3. Meanwhile, lightly coat a nonstick skillet with cooking spray. Add the oil and set over medium-high heat. Add the onion and sauté for 5 minutes or until tender.

4. Drain the cooked potatoes and return to the pot. Squeeze the roasted garlic out of the skins and add to the potatoes. Add the sautéed onion to the potatoes and mash with a potato masher.

5. Combine the chickpeas, evaporated milk, olive oil, salt and pepper in the bowl of a food processor. Purée, then add to the mashed potatoes. If desired, return the potato mixture to the stovetop and heat gently. Garnish with parsley and serve.

PREPARATION TIME 5 minutes · **COOKING TIME** 20 minutes (roast the garlic while making the remainder of the dish) · **MAKE AHEAD** Make this dish up to a day in advance and heat gently before serving. · **MAKES** 4 servings.

NUTRITION INFORMATION PER SERVING

Calories 258	Protein 7.5 g	Cholesterol 2 mg
Carbohydrates 37 g	Total fat 9 g	Sodium 189 mg
Fibre 4.7 g	Saturated fat 1.3 g	

1 head of garlic

1 lb (500 g) Yukon Gold potatoes, peeled and quartered

1 tsp (5 mL) vegetable oil

1 cup (250 mL) chopped red onion

1 cup (250 mL) canned chickpeas, drained and rinsed

5 Tbsp (75 mL) canned evaporated 2% milk

2 Tbsp (30 mL) olive oil

¼ tsp (1 mL) salt

¼ tsp (1 mL) pepper

Garnish
3 Tbsp (45 mL) chopped fresh parsley or basil

ROSE'S TIP
Adding a bean to a regular mashed potato dish increases the flavour and nutrients, especially the fibre and the protein.

HEALTH TIP
One cup (250 mL) of chickpeas has over 10 grams of fibre, which is close to half your daily intake. As well, they are loaded with protein with 12 grams per cup (250 mL).

POTATO "FRIES"

These are the best and healthiest french fries you'll ever eat—forget deep-fried fast-food ones that can contain over 20 grams of fat in a small serving. Experiment and use any seasonings you like. You can cut the potatoes early in the day, as long as you keep them in cold water so they won't turn brown.

1. Preheat the oven to 375°F (190°C). Lightly coat a rimmed baking sheet with cooking spray.

2. Cut each potato lengthwise into 8 wedges. Place on the prepared baking sheet. Combine the oil and garlic in a small bowl. Combine the cheese and chili powder in another small bowl. Brush the potato wedges with half the oil mixture, then sprinkle with half the cheese mixture.

3. Bake for 20 minutes. Turn the wedges, brush with the remaining oil mixture and sprinkle with the remaining cheese mixture. Bake for another 20 minutes or just until the potatoes are tender-crisp. Garnish with parsley.

PREPARATION TIME 5 minutes · **COOKING TIME** 40 minutes ·
MAKE AHEAD Best if baked just before serving. Can be reheated. ·
MAKES 6 servings.

3 large baking potatoes (about 2 lb/500 g), scrubbed

2 Tbsp (30 mL) olive oil

1 tsp (5 mL) finely chopped garlic

2 Tbsp (30 mL) grated Parmesan cheese (½ oz/15 g)

¼ tsp (1 mL) chili powder

3 Tbsp (45 mL) chopped parsley

 ROSE'S TIP
You can add any spice or herb you like to these potatoes. Garlic or onion powder, cumin, cayenne or dried basil add great flavour.

 HEALTH TIP
Do not ban potatoes from your diet even if you are on a low-carbohydrate regime. They are packed with powerful antioxidants, and one potato contains 20% of your daily potassium needs, which lowers blood pressure.

NUTRITION INFORMATION PER SERVING (4 WEDGES)

Calories 156	Protein 3 g	Cholesterol 1.6 mg
Carbohydrates 24 g	Total fat 5.3 g	Sodium 47 mg
Fibre 2.3 g	Saturated fat 1 g	

SWEET POTATO WEDGES WITH MAPLE SYRUP

Sweet potatoes are the newest craze. They are more nutritious than regular potatoes and contain antioxidants that may help in the fight against cancer. Beware of these in restaurants, as they are usually deep-fried

1. Preheat the oven to 425°F (220°C). Lightly coat a rimmed baking sheet with cooking spray.

2. Cut the sweet potatoes in half lengthwise and then cut each half into 6 wedges. Lightly coat with cooking spray. Place on the prepared baking sheet.

3. Combine all the remaining ingredients except the parsley in a small bowl. Brush half the maple syrup mixture over the sweet potatoes.

4. Bake in the centre of the oven for 20 minutes. Turn and brush with the remaining maple syrup mixture. Bake another 15 minutes or until tender. Garnish with parsley.

PREPARATION TIME 10 minutes • **COOKING TIME** 35 minutes •
MAKE AHEAD Prepare the potatoes early in the day. They are best baked just before serving, but can be reheated. • **MAKES** 6 servings.

2 large sweet potatoes (about 1½ lb/750 g), unpeeled and scrubbed

2 Tbsp (30 mL) vegetable oil

4 tsp (20 mL) maple syrup

¾ tsp (4 mL) cinnamon

¼ tsp (1 mL) ground ginger

pinch of nutmeg

3 Tbsp (45 mL) chopped parsley

 ROSE'S TIP
You can cut the potatoes any way you want: either into large wedges, chunks or thin fries. Just watch the baking time, since smaller pieces will require less time.

 HEALTH TIP
Sweet potatoes are a super-food and much healthier than white potatoes. A medium sweet potato contains more than your daily vitamin A require-ment, a third of your vitamin C and 15% of your daily fibre. They are considered a low-glycemic food, which controls blood sugar levels.

NUTRITION INFORMATION PER SERVING (4 WEDGES)

Calories 170	Protein 2.1 g	Cholesterol 0 mg
Carbohydrates 30 g	Total fat 4.5 g	Sodium 12 mg
Fibre 3.9 g	Saturated fat 0.2 g	

ROASTED POTATO, CAULIFLOWER AND EDAMAME MASH

To lighten up a mashed potato dish, roasted cauliflower is a great low-calorie addition.

1. Preheat the oven to 400°F (200°C). Line a baking sheet with foil sprayed with vegetable oil. Cut the top off the garlic head and wrap with foil and place on the baking sheet along with the potato and cauliflower. Spray the vegetables with vegetable oil. Roast for 30 minutes or just until tender, turning occasionally. Squeeze out the cloves of garlic.

2. Meanwhile, add the onions to a skillet along with the vegetable oil and sauté on medium heat for 10 minutes just until tender. Add the brown sugar and sauté for another 5 minutes.

3. Mash the potato wedges with the skin in a large bowl. Place the cauliflower in a food processor along with the olive oil, sesame oil and milk and purée. Add to the mashed potatoes along with the onions, garlic cloves and edamame. Add the salt and pepper.

PREPARATION TIME 15 minutes • **COOKING TIME** 30 minutes •
MAKE AHEAD Make the entire dish early in the day and gently reheat. •
MAKES 8 servings.

NUTRITION INFORMATION PER SERVING

Calories 154	Protein 6.3 g	Cholesterol 0 mg
Carbohydrates 24 g	Total fat 4.1 g	Sodium 73 mg
Fibre 4.3 g	Saturated fat 0.7 g	

1 head roasted garlic

1½ lb (750 g) Yukon Gold potatoes cut into wedges, unpeeled

1 lb (500 g) raw cauliflower, broken into pieces

2 cups (500 mL) diced onions

2 tsp (10 mL) vegetable oil

1 Tbsp (15 mL) brown sugar

1 Tbsp (15 mL) olive oil

1 Tbsp (15 mL) sesame oil

¼ cup (60 mL) 2% milk

¾ cup (185 mL) frozen shelled edamame, blanched

pinch of salt and pepper

ROSE'S TIP

The combination of potato, cauliflower and edamame gives mashed potatoes a new look and taste. I found by roasting the vegetables the flavour was more intense and prevented the cauliflower from adding excess moisture.

HEALTH TIP

Edamame (Japanese soybeans) is a superfood. It contains antioxidants that help fight free radicals to help prevent cancer. As well, it is considered a complete protein, which is perfect for vegetarian diets.

ROASTED CAULIFLOWER, ROASTED GARLIC AND CARAMELIZED ONION MASH

The newest low-carbohydrate craze is to replace old-fashioned mashed potatoes with mashed cauliflower. I found that if I added some caramelized onions, you almost couldn't tell the difference. Try this on your guests next time you're serving roast beef.

1. Preheat the oven or toaster oven to 425°F (220°C). Wrap the garlic in aluminum foil. Place the cauliflower on a baking sheet and spray with vegetable oil. Bake for 25 minutes just until the cauliflower is tender and browned. Cool the garlic, then squeeze out. Set aside.

2. Meanwhile, in a nonstick skillet sprayed with vegetable spray, heat the oil over medium-high heat and cook the onions for 5 minutes. Stir in the brown sugar, vinegar and cinnamon. Reduce the heat to medium-low and cook until the onions are golden, about 10 minutes.

3. Place the cauliflower in a food processor with the stock, olive oil, salt and pepper. Purée until smooth and transfer to a serving bowl. Stir in the onions and garlic until combined. Garnish with parsley.

PREPARATION TIME 10 minutes · **COOKING TIME** 25 minutes ·
MAKE AHEAD Make this dish early in the day and gently reheat. ·
MAKES 6 servings.

1 head garlic, skin on

about 6 cups (1.5 L) chopped cauliflower florets (1½ lb/750 g)

2 tsp (10 mL) vegetable oil

2 cups (500 mL) sliced sweet onions

2 tsp (10 mL) packed brown sugar

1 tsp (5 mL) balsamic vinegar

½ tsp (2.5 mL) cinnamon

¼ cup (60 mL) low-sodium vegetable or chicken stock

1 Tbsp (15 mL) olive oil

⅛ tsp (0.5 mL) salt

⅛ tsp (0.5 mL) ground black pepper

2 Tbsp (30 mL) chopped parsley

ROSE'S TIP
Using non-starchy vegetables to replace starchy ones saves you calories and provides you with more nutrients. I found that roasting the cauliflower prevented the dish from getting watery.

HEALTH TIP
Cauliflower is a cruciferous vegetable that is loaded with health benefits. It contains antioxidants, including vitamin C and manganese, which reduce the risk of heart disease and cancer.

NUTRITION INFORMATION PER SERVING

Calories 100	Protein 3.2 g	Cholesterol 0.2 mg
Carbohydrates 8 g	Total fat 4.2 g	Sodium 42 mg
Fibre 3.8 g	Saturated fat 0.5 g	

ROASTED ASPARAGUS WRAPPED WITH GOAT CHEESE AND PROSCIUTTO

This substantial vegetable dish with its colourful and elegant presentation is a great way to complete the dinner entrée. Prosciutto and goat cheese bring out the subtle flavour of asparagus. You can substitute thinly sliced roast turkey in place of the prosciutto.

1. Preheat the oven to 425°F (220°C). Spray a baking sheet with cooking oil.

2. Place the prosciutto flat on a clean work surface. Divide the goat cheese among the prosciutto slices, spreading it thinly down the centre. Place 3 to 4 asparagus spears crosswise on top of each slice of prosciutto. Wrap the prosciutto tightly around the asparagus and transfer to the prepared baking sheet. Spray the bundles with cooking oil.

3. Bake in the centre of the oven for 10 minutes or just until the asparagus turns bright green and is slightly tender. Garnish with red pepper.

PREPARATION TIME 10 minutes · **COOKING TIME** 10 minutes ·

MAKE AHEAD Make bundles early in the day and bake just before serving. ·

MAKES 6 servings.

6 slices prosciutto (about 4 oz/125 g)

½ cup (125 mL) softened goat cheese (2 oz/60 g)

1 lb (500 g) trimmed asparagus

2 Tbsp (30 mL) finely diced red bell pepper

 ROSE'S TIP

If goat cheese is too strong for your liking, use a light cream cheese.

 HEALTH TIP

Using small amounts of prosciutto is fine in your daily diet. One ounce (30 g), which is two slices, has only 55 calories and 3 grams of fat.

NUTRITION INFORMATION PER SERVING

Calories 130	Protein 5.6 g	Cholesterol 17 mg
Carbohydrates 1.5 g	Total fat 10 g	Sodium 122 mg
Fibre 1.7 g	Saturated fat 4.3 g	

ROASTED ASPARAGUS
WITH PARMESAN DRESSING

Asparagus is always a delicious and elegant vegetable to serve. This caesar-style dressing is sensational overtop. Try thinly slicing some fresh Parmesan, using a cheese slicer or sharp knife, to use as a garnish. This can be served hot or at room temperature.

1. Preheat the oven to 425°F (220°C). Place the asparagus on a baking sheet sprayed with vegetable oil. Roast for about 8 minutes just until bright green and slightly tender. Do not overcook. Place on a serving dish.

2. In a small bowl, mix together 1 Tbsp (15 mL) of the Parmesan, the olive oil, lemon juice, water, anchovies, garlic and mustard. Pour over the asparagus.

3. Sprinkle with the remaining Parmesan and the diced tomato, if using.

PREPARATION TIME 10 minutes • **COOKING TIME** 8 minutes • **MAKE AHEAD** Roast the asparagus early in the day and serve at room temperature. • **MAKES** 4 servings.

1 lb (500 g) asparagus, trimmed

2 Tbsp (30 mL) grated Parmesan cheese (½ oz/15 g)

1 Tbsp (15 mL) olive oil

2 tsp (10 mL) fresh lemon juice

2 tsp (10 mL) water

2 anchovy fillets, minced (optional)

1 tsp (5 mL) crushed garlic

½ tsp (2.5 mL) Dijon mustard

¼ cup (60 mL) diced tomato (optional)

ROSE'S TIP

You can exchange the asparagus for green beans or broccolini, which are equally delicious.

HEALTH TIP

Asparagus is a very good source of vitamins C and A, iron and folate. It's considered one of the best vegetables for providing antioxidants, which help fight free radicals.

NUTRITION INFORMATION PER SERVING

Calories 87	Protein 5.1 g	Sodium 90 mg
Carbohydrates 5.1 g	Total fat 5.1 g	Cholesterol 4.9 mg
Fibre 1.7 g	Saturated fat 1.3 g	

ROASTED BRUSSELS SPROUTS WITH RED PEPPERS, ALMONDS AND PARMESAN CHEESE

Brussels sprouts are the trendy vegetable today. If you're eating them whole and just boiled, I don't blame you for not enjoying them, but cutting them in half and roasting them brings out a wonderful flavour. This dish is also great served at room temperature as a salad.

1. Preheat the oven to 400°F (200°C). Line the baking sheets with foil sprayed with vegetable oil.

2. Place the Brussels sprouts in a bowl and add the Parmesan, olive oil, salt and pepper, and garlic. Mix well and place on the baking sheet along with the red pepper.

3. Roast for 20 minutes, turning occasionally just until tender and slightly browned. Peel the skin off the pepper and cut into large wedges.

4. Garnish with almonds.

PREPARATION TIME 15 minutes: · **COOKING TIME** 20 minutes ·
MAKE AHEAD Prepare the recipe early in the day and bake just before serving.
If serving at room temperature, make early in the day. · **MAKES** 6 servings.

1½ lb (750 g) Brussels sprouts
(stems removed and cut in half)

2 Tbsp (30 mL) grated
Parmesan cheese (½ oz/15 g)

1 Tbsp (15 mL) olive oil

pinch of salt and pepper

1 tsp (5 mL) minced garlic

1 small red pepper, seeded and
cut in half

⅓ cup (80 mL) toasted slivered
almonds

ROSE'S TIP

Roasting Brussels sprouts will turn anyone who doesn't like this vegetable into a convert. The Parmesan cheese and olive oil give them a sweet flavour and crispy texture. Much better than boiled!

HEALTH TIP

Brussels sprouts have 4 grams of fibre for one cup (250 mL), which helps with weight control and regulating your bowels, and helps prevent type 2 diabetes. They are part of the cruciferous family of vegetables, which is what gives them their antioxidant power to reduce the risk of cancer.

NUTRITION INFORMATION PER SERVING

Calories 122	Protein 5.9 g	Cholesterol 1 mg
Carbohydrates 12.6 g	Total fat 6.6 g	Sodium 102 mg
Fibre 5.4 g	Saturated fat 0.9 g	

SHIITAKE MUSHROOMS WITH SESAME SAUCE

Shiitake mushrooms have to be my favourite variety. The key, though, is to cook them until they double in size and then use Asian flavouring overtop. The texture and flavour is like no other mushroom.

1. In a large skillet sprayed with vegetable oil, sauté the mushrooms for 3 minutes. Add the stock, cover and let simmer on medium heat for 5 minutes or just until tender and the stock has evaporated. Add more stock if the mushrooms begin to burn.

2. TO MAKE THE SESAME SAUCE Combine the soy sauce, sesame oil, oyster sauce, garlic, ginger and sesame seeds and pour over the mushrooms. Stir-fry for 3 minutes or until the mushrooms are cooked. Garnish with cilantro.

PREPARATION TIME 10 minutes • **COOKING TIME** 11 minutes •
MAKE AHEAD You can cook this dish early in the day and gently reheat. •
MAKES 4 servings.

1 lb (500 g) shiitake mushrooms, stem removed

¼ cup (60 mL) water or low-sodium stock

Sesame sauce

4 tsp (20 mL) low-sodium soy sauce

2 tsp (10 mL) sesame oil

2 tsp (10 mL) oyster sauce

1 tsp (5 mL) minced garlic

1 tsp (5 mL) minced ginger

1 tsp (5 mL) sesame seeds

2 Tbsp (30 mL) chopped cilantro

ROSE'S TIP

If shiitake mushrooms are unavailable, use any variety you like but be sure to cook them long enough to eliminate excess moisture.

HEALTH TIP

Shiitake mushrooms in particular are known to reduce cholesterol, helping prevent heart disease and stroke. Compounds in these mushrooms also help your immune system to reduce the growth of existing cancer cells, and they are rich in iron.

NUTRITION INFORMATION PER SERVING

Calories 69	Protein 3.1 g	Cholesterol 0 mg
Carbohydrates 9.2 g	Total fat 2.5 g	Sodium 268 mg
Fibre 3.1 g	Saturated fat 0.4 g	

ROASTED VEGETABLE TOWERS WITH BALSAMIC SYRUP

You'll never serve anything more beautiful than these vegetable towers. My catering company does them for our events, and when I saw how easy they were to prepare, I had to include them in this book. The vegetables I've chosen look great and cook for about the same time, but feel free to substitute your favourites. A powerhouse of antioxidants! I often add a bit of goat cheese between the vegetables.

1. Preheat the oven to 425°F (220°C). Spray a baking sheet with vegetable spray. Place the sweet potato, red pepper, zucchini, onion, mushrooms and garlic on the prepared baking sheet, and spray with vegetable spray. Bake the vegetables for 25 minutes, turn over and bake for another 15 minutes. Gently peel the skin from the garlic.

2. TO MAKE THE DRESSING In a small skillet, add the vinegar and maple syrup, bring to a rapid boil and boil for about 5 minutes until bubbles cover the entire surface and the glaze thickens slightly. Do not overcook or the syrup will get too thick.

3. Slice the zucchini, onion slices and mushrooms in half to make 6 pieces. To make the towers, place the sweet potato on the bottom, then add the red pepper, zucchini, onion and mushrooms, and top with garlic cloves. Garnish with basil and drizzle the dressing overtop.

PREPARATION TIME 20 minutes · **COOKING TIME** 45 minutes ·
MAKE AHEAD Cook the vegetables early in the day and assemble. Serve at room temperature or reheat gently. · **MAKES** 6 servings.

NUTRITION INFORMATION PER SERVING

Calories 55	Protein 2 g	Cholesterol 0 mg
Carbohydrates 8 g	Total fat 0.3 g	Sodium 57 mg
Fibre 2.5 g	Saturated fat 0.5 g	

1 small sweet potato, cut into 6 horizontal ½-inch (1 cm) slices (skin on)

1 large red bell pepper, seeded, cored and cut into 6 wedges

1 medium zucchini, cut lengthwise in 3 slices

3 horizontal ½-inch (1 cm) slices of a large onion

3 medium portobello mushrooms (stems removed)

6 large cloves of garlic, skin on, wrapped in foil

Dressing
¾ cup (185 mL) balsamic vinegar

3 Tbsp (45 mL) maple syrup

¼ cup (60 mL) chopped fresh basil or parsley

ROSE'S TIP
This balsamic syrup is so delicious and contains no fat. It is outstanding with these grilled vegetable stacks.

HEALTH TIP
All of these vegetables have bright colours, meaning you're getting an abundance of vitamins, minerals and antioxidants.

CARROT, BROCCOLI AND CHEESE PHYLLO STRUDEL

This strudel is filled with great nutrients and beautiful colours. Sweet potatoes can replace the carrots, but precook them in boiling water for 3 minutes to soften them slightly. You can use parsley or basil instead of the dill, and cheddar or mozzarella instead of the Swiss cheese, though a stronger cheese tastes best.

1. Preheat the oven to 375°F (190°C). Spray a baking sheet with cooking oil.

2. Spray a large nonstick pan with cooking oil and heat the vegetable oil over medium heat.

3. Cook the garlic, onion, broccoli and carrots for 10 minutes or until tender-crisp, stirring occasionally. Remove from the heat and stir in the dill, egg, bread-crumbs, cheese and salt and pepper.

4. Lay one sheet of phyllo on your work surface, with the long side facing you, and spray with cooking oil. Repeat with the remaining phyllo sheets, but do not spray the last sheet. Spread the vegetable mixture over the surface, leaving a 1-inch (2.5 cm) border on all sides.

5. Roll up tightly, jelly roll–fashion, and tuck the ends under. Spray with cooking oil. Place on the prepared baking sheet and bake for 25 minutes or until golden brown.

PREPARATION TIME 10 minutes · **COOKING TIME** 25 minutes · **MAKE AHEAD** The entire strudel can be made early in the day. Keep well covered in the refrigerator and bake just before serving to maintain the phyllo's crispness. · **MAKES** 6 servings.

2 tsp (10 mL) vegetable oil

1½ tsp (7.5 mL) minced fresh garlic

1½ cups (375 mL) chopped onion

3 cups (750 mL) finely chopped broccoli

2 cups (500 mL) finely chopped carrots

⅓ cup (80 mL) chopped fresh dill or parsley

1 egg

¼ cup (60 mL) seasoned dry breadcrumbs

⅔ cup (160 mL) shredded Swiss cheese (2 oz/60 g)

pinch of salt and ground black pepper

6 sheets of phyllo pastry

ROSE'S TIP

When butter is not used to
coat the phyllo sheets, the
crust can become soggy. If
the phyllo becomes soft
because it is baked too
early, just put it back into
a 400°F (200°C) oven
for 10 minutes and it will
become crisp.

 HEALTH TIP

Broccoli, part of the cruciferous group of vegetables,
is considered a superfood.
To retain the nutrients,
be sure not to overcook.
It's known to reduce the
risk of cancer due to its
antioxidants; it reduces
inflammation to help fight
arthritis; the high fibre
content reduces choles-
terol and reduces the risk
of heart disease; and it
contains high levels of vitamins A and K, increasing
bone density.

NUTRITION INFORMATION PER SERVING

Calories 112	Protein 6 g	Cholesterol 40 mg
Carbohydrates 34 mg	Total fat 6 g	Sodium 490 mg
Fibre 2.2 g	Saturated fat 2 g	

SUGAR SNAP PEAS WITH SESAME SAUCE AND TOASTED CASHEWS

This is a simple Asian-style recipe that can be used to accompany any main course. You can substitute snow peas or green beans, but you can't find a sweeter and crisper bean than the sugar snap pea.

1. Combine the honey, vinegar, sesame oil, soy sauce and garlic in a small bowl. Set aside.

2. Heat the vegetable oil in a large nonstick skillet over medium-high heat. Add the snow peas and cook until tender-crisp, about 3 minutes. Pour the sauce over the peas and cook until heated through. Serve immediately, garnished with cashews and sesame seeds.

PREPARATION TIME 10 minutes · **COOKING TIME** 3 minutes ·
MAKE AHEAD Best cooked just before serving. · **MAKES** 6 servings.

 ROSE'S TIP
If you add some cooked tofu cubes to this dish, you have an entire vegetarian meal.

 HEALTH TIP
Always use low-sodium soy sauce due to the high sodium levels of regular soy sauce. One table-spoon (15 mL) of regular soy sauce has 900 mg of sodium, whereas the low-sodium version has only 500 mg.

1 Tbsp (15 mL) honey

1 Tbsp (15 mL) rice vinegar

1 Tbsp (15 mL) sesame oil

1 Tbsp (15 mL) low-sodium soy sauce

½ tsp (2.5 mL) minced fresh garlic

1 tsp (5 mL) vegetable oil

1 lb (500 g) snow peas, trimmed

2 Tbsp (30 mL) chopped toasted cashews

1 Tbsp (15 mL) toasted sesame seeds

NUTRITION INFORMATION PER SERVING

Calories 100	Protein 2.8 g	Cholesterol 0 mg
Carbohydrates 10 g	Total fat 5.3 g	Sodium 93 mg
Fibre 2.2 g	Saturated fat 0.8 g	

VEGETARIAN MAINS

BARLEY AND SUN-DRIED TOMATO PILAF WITH FETA

I often use barley when creating salads. People still tend to think of it only in soup, but it has many uses. This outstanding pilaf can be made into an entire meal just by adding some grilled fish, chicken or tofu overtop.

1. In a saucepan, combine the stock and barley. Bring to a boil. Reduce the heat to a simmer, cover and cook just until tender, about 25 to 30 minutes. Do not overcook. Drain excess liquid. Cool to room temperature.

2. Stir in the sun-dried tomatoes, olives, feta, basil, lemon juice, olive oil, capers, garlic and pepper.

PREPARATION TIME 15 minutes · **COOKING TIME** 25 minutes ·
MAKE AHEAD Prepare up to a day in advance. Serve at room temperature or warm. · **MAKES** 6 servings.

 ROSE'S TIP
Buy sun-dried tomatoes dry in bulk and store them in your freezer. Take out the amount you want, soak in hot water until soft and then chop.

 HEALTH TIP
Barley is a complex carbohydrate and is better for you than white pasta or rice. Try the pot barley, which contains even more nutrients. You have to cook it about 20 minutes longer.

3 cups (750 mL) low-sodium vegetable stock

1 cup (250 mL) pearl barley

½ cup (125 mL) chopped rehydrated sun-dried tomatoes

⅓ cup (80 mL) chopped pitted black olives

⅔ cup (160 mL) crumbled reduced-fat feta cheese (3 oz/90 g)

⅓ cup (80 mL) chopped fresh basil or parsley

3 Tbsp (45 mL) freshly squeezed lemon juice

2 Tbsp (30 mL) olive oil

1 Tbsp (15 mL) chopped drained capers

1½ tsp (7.5 mL) minced garlic

⅛ tsp (0.5 mL) ground black pepper

NUTRITION INFORMATION PER SERVING

Calories 245	Protein 7.9 g	Cholesterol 14.6 g
Carbohydrates 25 g	Total fat 9.6 g	Sodium 287 mg
Fibre 6.3 g	Saturated fat 3.3 g	

SHEPHERD'S PIE WITH TWO BEAN SWEET POTATO TOPPING

Traditional shepherd's pie is made with ground beef and white potato topping. Not the perfect meal for a vegetarian! My veggie version includes beans and a delicious sweet potato topping filled with nutrients.

1. Preheat the oven to 350°F (175°C). Spray an 8-inch (20 cm) square baking dish with vegetable spray.

2. In a large skillet sprayed with vegetable spray, add the oil and garlic and onion and sauté for 3 minutes on medium heat. Add the carrots and sauté another 3 minutes. Add the tomato sauce, both beans, basil and bay leaf and bring to a boil. Cover and simmer on low heat for 12 minutes. Add to the baking dish.

3. Meanwhile place the potatoes in a saucepan and add cold water to cover. Bring to a boil, reduce heat and simmer for 10 minutes or until tender. Drain and mash with the olive oil, milk and salt and pepper. Spoon on top of the sauce in the baking dish. Sprinkle with the cheeses. Bake, uncovered, for 20 minutes or until hot.

PREPARATION TIME 20 minutes · **COOKING TIME** 38 minutes · **MAKE AHEAD** Bake up to a day in advance and reheat gently in a 300°F (150°C) oven. · **MAKES** 8 servings.

2 tsp (10 mL) vegetable oil

2 tsp (10 mL) minced garlic

1 cup (250 mL) chopped onions

½ cup (125 mL) finely chopped carrots

¾ cup (185 mL) homemade or store-bought tomato sauce (see Quick Basic Tomato Sauce on page 369)

½ cup (125 mL) canned red kidney beans, drained and rinsed

½ cup (125 mL) canned chickpeas, drained and rinsed

½ tsp (2.5 mL) dried basil

1 bay leaf

1 lb (500 g) diced sweet potatoes

1 Tbsp (15 mL) olive oil

2 Tbsp (30 mL) 2% milk

pinch of salt and pepper

½ cup (125 mL) shredded cheddar cheese (1½ oz/45 g)

3 Tbsp (45 mL) grated Parmesan cheese (¾ oz/23 g)

 ROSE'S TIP

You can substitute ground soy or diced tofu for half the total beans for a variation.

 HEALTH TIP

This is a great nutritious meal that covers all four food groups: beans as your protein and carbohydrate, sweet potatoes as your vegetable and cheese as your dairy.

NUTRITION INFORMATION PER SERVING

Calories 162	Protein 5.4 g	Cholesterol 3 mg
Carbohydrates 26.9 g	Total fat 4 g	Sodium 219 mg
Fibre 4.9 g	Saturated fat 1 g	

BULGUR WITH CHICKPEAS, TOMATOES AND FETA SALAD

You may think you've never tried bulgur, but just think back to the last time you ate tabbouleh, that wonderful Middle Eastern dish made with tomatoes, cucumbers, parsley and mint. Serve this as a main salad or side dish.

1. In a saucepan, bring the stock to a boil. Stir in the bulgur, remove from the heat, cover and let stand until the liquid is absorbed and the bulgur is tender, about 15 to 20 minutes. Fluff with a fork. Let cool.

2. Stir in the chickpeas, tomatoes, feta, green onions, mint, parsley, lemon zest and juice, olive oil, garlic, oregano and salt and pepper. Serve warm or at room temperature.

PREPARATION TIME 15 minutes · **COOKING TIME** 15 minutes ·
MAKE AHEAD Make early in the day and refrigerate. · **MAKES** 6 servings.

1½ cups (375 mL) low-sodium vegetable stock

1 cup (250 mL) bulgur

1 cup (250 mL) canned chickpeas, drained and rinsed

1 cup (250 mL) diced, seeded plum tomatoes

⅓ cup (80 mL) crumbled reduced-fat feta cheese (2 oz/60 g)

⅓ cup (80 mL) chopped green onions (whole onion)

¼ cup (60 mL) chopped fresh mint

¼ cup (60 mL) chopped fresh Italian parsley

2 tsp (10 mL) grated lemon zest

3 Tbsp (45 mL) freshly squeezed lemon juice

4 tsp (20 mL) olive oil

1½ tsp (7.5 mL) crushed garlic

½ tsp (2.5 mL) dried oregano

pinch of salt and pepper

 ROSE'S TIP

To get the best texture for bulgur, never cook it over direct heat. Only let it soak in hot water until the liquid is absorbed. If cooked over direct heat, the bulgur will be too soft.

 HEALTH TIP

Bulgur is a good source of fibre, protein, iron and vitamin B6. This is a 100% whole grain, which reduces the risk of heart disease. One cup (250 mL) has only 150 calories and 8 grams of fibre, which is a third of your daily requirement.

NUTRITION INFORMATION PER SERVING

Calories 214	Protein 7.9 g	Cholesterol 9.4 mg
Carbohydrates 22 g	Total fat 6.9 g	Sodium 193 mg
Fibre 7.2 g	Saturated fat 2.2 g	

LENTIL FETA SALAD WITH LEMON DRESSING

If you prefer, you can buy canned lentils and forget about the cooking, but I always find that cooking your own produces a better flavour and texture. This is a great vegetarian dish on its own or served as a side dish to any entrée.

2½ cups (625 mL) low-sodium vegetable stock

¾ cup (185 mL) dried green lentils

¾ cup (185 mL) diced red bell pepper

⅓ cup (80 mL) chopped green onions (whole onion)

⅓ cup (80 mL) chopped fresh parsley

¼ cup (60 mL) diced red onion

2 Tbsp (30 mL) olive oil

3 Tbsp (45 mL) freshly squeezed lemon juice

2 tsp (10 mL) balsamic vinegar

1½ tsp (7.5 mL) minced garlic

1 tsp (5 mL) Dijon mustard

⅛ tsp (0.5 mL) salt

⅛ tsp (0.5 mL) ground black pepper

½ cup (125 mL) diced reduced-fat feta cheese (1½ oz/45 g)

1. In a saucepan, combine the stock and lentils. Bring to a boil. Reduce the heat to a simmer, cover and cook just until tender, about 20 to 25 minutes. Do not overcook. Drain any excess liquid. Cool to room temperature.

2. In a large bowl, stir together the cooked lentils, red pepper, green onion, parsley, red onion, olive oil, lemon juice, vinegar, garlic, mustard, salt, pepper and feta. Toss together before serving.

PREPARATION TIME 15 minutes · **COOKING TIME** 20 minutes ·

MAKE AHEAD Make up to a day in advance and serve at room temperature. ·

MAKES 6 servings.

ROSE'S TIP
Serve grilled fish, chicken, pork or tofu overtop to make a complete meal.

HEALTH TIP
Lentils are a wonderful low-glycemic food to enjoy as well as being an excellent source of protein. They're a good source of fibre, which helps prevent hunger. One cup (250 mL) cooked lentils has 230 calories, virtually no fat, 16 grams of fibre and 18 grams of protein. It's a powerhouse of nutrients.

NUTRITION INFORMATION PER SERVING

Calories 160	Protein 8.2 g	Cholesterol 3.2 mg
Carbohydrates 13 g	Total fat 5.9 g	Sodium 165 mg
Fibre 4.5 g	Saturated fat 1.3 g	

TOFU AND VEGETABLE SATAYS WITH BLACK BEAN—HOISIN SAUCE

I love chicken, beef and shrimp satays, but if you're a vegetarian or you just want a healthy alternative, try these tofu satays. Tofu absorbs whatever flavours it's cooked with. Buy firm tofu: medium tofu is too soft and the extra firm too tough. Once opened, cover unused tofu with water in a container and refrigerate for up to 3 days.

1. Thread the peppers, onion and tofu alternately on 4 long or 8 short wooden or metal skewers, dividing the vegetables evenly among them. (If using wooden skewers, soak for at least 20 minutes in water before using them.)

2. TO MAKE THE SAUCE Whisk the hoisin, sugar, bean sauce, soy sauce, sesame oil, garlic and ginger in a bowl until smooth.

3. Spray a barbecue or a nonstick grill pan with cooking oil and heat to medium. Grill the satays, turning occasionally, for 10 minutes or until browned on all sides. Brush half the sauce over the satays and continue cooking, turning occasionally, for another 10 minutes or just until the vegetables are soft. Garnish with cilantro and serve with the remaining sauce on the side.

PREPARATION TIME 15 minutes • **COOKING TIME** 20 minutes •
MAKE AHEAD Prepare the satays up to a day in advance and cook just before serving. • **MAKES** 4 servings.

1 large green bell pepper, cut into 16 squares

1 large red bell pepper, cut into 16 squares

½ sweet onion, cut into 16 pieces

12 oz (375 g) firm tofu, cut into 16 cubes 2 inches (5 cm) square

Sauce

¼ cup (60 mL) hoisin sauce

¼ cup (60 mL) packed brown sugar

5 tsp (25 mL) black bean sauce

5 tsp (25 mL) low-sodium soy sauce

1 Tbsp (15 mL) sesame oil

1½ tsp (7.5 mL) minced fresh garlic

1½ tsp (7.5 mL) minced fresh ginger

¼ cup (60 mL) chopped cilantro or parsley

 ROSE'S TIP

If you don't want to make skewers, you can grill the tofu and vegetables by themselves and serve as a plattered item.

 HEALTH TIP

Black bean sauce and hoisin sauce are high in sodium. Black bean sauce has 650 mg sodium per tablespoon (15 mL) and hoisin sauce has 260 mg sodium. Watch your intake.

NUTRITION INFORMATION PER SERVING

Calories 240	Protein 9.9 g	Cholesterol 0.5 mg
Carbohydrates 38.7 g	Total fat 7 g	Sodium 501 mg
Fibre 5.3 g	Saturated fat 1 g	

BEAN AND BROWN RICE BURGERS WITH TAHINI LEMON DRESSING

The brown rice and white kidney beans make a great combination in a burger. The Tahini Lemon Dressing goes well as a condiment. You could also use hummus.

1. Preheat the oven to 350°F (175°C). Line a baking sheet with foil sprayed with vegetable spray.

2. Bring the rice and stock to boil, cover and simmer for 35 minutes or just until rice is tender. Drain any excess liquid.

3. Meanwhile, sauté the onions in oil for 5 minutes. Add the garlic, cumin and salt and pepper and sauté for 1 minute. Remove from the heat and add to the food processor along with the rice, beans, carrot, breadcrumbs, soy sauce, egg, feta, cilantro and jalapeños. Process off and on until well blended but not puréed. Pat into 8 flat burgers and sauté in a large skillet sprayed with vegetable oil just until browned on both sides. Place on a baking sheet and bake for 10 minutes.

4. Divide the Tahini Lemon Dressing overtop the 8 burgers. Garnish with cilantro and serve.

PREPARATION TIME 20 minutes · **COOKING TIME** 45 minutes ·

MAKE AHEAD Prepare these burgers and sauce up to a day in advance but cook just before serving. · **MAKES** 8 servings.

½ cup (125 mL) brown rice

1½ cups (375 mL) low-sodium chicken or vegetable stock

2 tsp (10 mL) vegetable oil

1 cup (250 mL) chopped onions

2 tsp (10 mL) crushed garlic

½ tsp (2.5 mL) cumin powder

pinch of salt and pepper

8 oz (250 g) canned white kidney beans, drained and rinsed

½ cup (125 mL) grated carrot

½ cup (125 mL) unseasoned dry breadcrumbs

1 Tbsp (15 mL) low-sodium soy sauce

1 egg

⅓ cup (80 mL) crumbled reduced-fat feta cheese (1 oz/30 g)

⅓ cup (80 mL) chopped cilantro

2 tsp (10 mL) minced jalapeño peppers

1 cup (250 mL) Tahini Lemon Dressing (see page 366)

2 Tbsp (30 mL) chopped cilantro

ROSE'S TIP

There are many varieties of brown rice available. For this burger recipe, I like to use short-grain brown rice that has an almost creamy texture when cooked.

 HEALTH TIP

If you're concerned about sodium intake, always use unseasoned breadcrumbs instead of seasoned. A quarter-cup (60 mL) of seasoned has 500 mg of sodium and 3 grams of sugar, and unseasoned has 400 mg and 0 grams of sugar for the amount.

NUTRITION INFORMATION PER SERVING (1 BURGER)

Calories 184	Protein 6.1 g	Cholesterol 20 mg
Carbohydrates 23.1 g	Total fat 7.5 g	Sodium 382 mg
Fibre 3.2 g	Saturated fat 1.5 g	

TOFU STIR-FRY WITH SNOW PEAS IN LIGHT COCONUT BROTH

The tofu absorbs the taste of the coconut sauce to make a rich-tasting dish that's low in fat and calories. You can also serve this over brown rice or just by itself.

1. To make the sauce, whisk the coconut milk, hoisin sauce, honey, soy sauce, sesame oil, vinegar, garlic, ginger and cornstarch in a large bowl. Add the tofu and marinate for 10 to 30 minutes. Drain well, reserving the sauce.

2. Spray a large nonstick wok or skillet with cooking oil and place over medium heat. Add the tofu and stir-fry for 5 minutes, just until browned. Add the snow peas and bell pepper and sauté for 2 minutes. Add the reserved sauce and heat for 2 minutes, just until the mixture is hot and sauce slightly thickens.

3. Cook the noodles in boiling water for 4 minutes, until barely tender. Do not overcook. Drain well and place on a serving dish and top with the tofu mixture.

4. Toss with the cilantro and sesame seeds and serve immediately.

PREPARATION TIME 10 minutes (not including marinating) ·
COOKING TIME 13 minutes · **MAKE AHEAD** Prepare the sauce and marinate the tofu up to a day in advance. Cook just before serving. · **MAKES** 4 servings.

¾ cup (185 mL) light coconut milk

3½ Tbsp (55 mL) hoisin sauce

4 tsp (20 mL) honey

4 tsp (20 mL) low-sodium soy sauce

1½ tsp (7.5 mL) sesame oil

1 tsp (5 mL) rice vinegar

1 tsp (5 mL) crushed fresh garlic

1 tsp (5 mL) crushed fresh ginger

2 tsp (10 mL) cornstarch

12 oz (375 g) firm tofu, cut into 1-inch (2.5 cm) cubes

1 cup (250 mL) sliced snow peas

1 cup (250 mL) sliced red bell pepper

3 oz (90 g) rice noodles (½-inch/ 1 cm wide)

⅓ cup (80 mL) chopped cilantro

2 tsp (10 mL) toasted sesame seeds

ROSE'S TIP
Try to find both black and white sesame seeds. Mix together and freeze. Use these for garnishes and in Asian dishes.

HEALTH TIP
Sesame seeds are loaded with essential minerals. The zinc in them promotes bone health and reduces the risk of osteoporosis.

NUTRITION INFORMATION PER SERVING

Calories 175	Protein 21.5 g	Cholesterol 35 mg
Carbohydrates 16 g	Total fat 2.9 g	Sodium 334 mg
Fibre 1.8 g	Saturated fat 0.5 g	

MUSHROOM QUINOA BURGERS WITH TZATZIKI

Quinoa the supergrain can be used in almost any recipe. It makes for a healthy and delicious veggie burger, especially when combined with mushrooms and served with tzatziki.

1. Bring the quinoa and water to a boil. Cover and simmer for 15 minutes, just until the water is absorbed. Let cool for 15 minutes.

2. Meanwhile, in a large skillet, add the oil and sauté the onion for 5 minutes, just until tender. Add the bell pepper and mushrooms and sauté on medium heat until the mushrooms are no longer wet (about 10 minutes).

3. Add the mixture to the food processor along with the quinoa, parsley, soy sauce, eggs and breadcrumbs and pulse just until combined. Do not purée.

4. Form into 8 burgers.

5. Sauté the burgers in a nonstick skillet sprayed with vegetable oil. Sauté on medium heat just until browned on both sides (about 10 minutes). Respray the pan if necessary.

6. Serve with tzatziki.

PREPARATION TIME 15 minutes • **COOKING TIME** 25 minutes •
MAKE AHEAD Prepare the burgers up to a day in advance and bake just before serving. • **MAKES** 8 servings.

NUTRITION INFORMATION PER SERVING (1 BURGER)

Calories 146	Protein 6.8 g	Cholesterol 35 mg
Carbohydrates 22.6 g	Total fat 3.3 g	Sodium 129 mg
Fibre 3.1 g	Saturated fat 0.7 g	

⅔ cup (160 mL) quinoa

1⅓ cups (330 mL) water

2 tsp (10 mL) vegetable oil

2 cups (500 mL) diced onion

1 cup (250 mL) diced red bell pepper

16 oz (500 g) diced mushrooms

¼ cup (60 mL) chopped parsley

2 tsp (10 mL) low-sodium soy sauce

2 eggs

⅔ cup (160 mL) dry breadcrumbs

½ cup (125 mL) store-bought or homemade tzatziki (see Tzatziki on page 368)

 ROSE'S TIP
Tzatziki is very low in calories and fat.

 HEALTH TIP
Quinoa is ideal for those wanting to cut back on saturated fat proteins, such as beef, pork and poultry. It is a complete protein, and 1 cup (250 mL) has only 220 calories and 8 grams of protein.

MUSHROOM SOY LASAGNA WITH THREE CHEESES

This lasagna is so fabulous that nobody will ever suspect there's no meat in it. Ground soy tastes like ground beef or chicken. If you want a spicier flavour, try the Mexican-flavoured ground soy or add 1 tsp (5 mL) of hot sauce. I have used a smaller casserole dish, since extra lasagna so often goes to waste. You just have to trim the cooked lasagna sheets to fit the pan. If you'd like to increase the yield, use a regular 9- × 13-inch (3.5 L) dish, double the recipe and cook nine lasagna noodles.

1. Preheat the oven to 350°F (175°C). Lightly coat a 9-inch (23 cm) square casserole dish with cooking spray.

2. Bring a large pot of water to a boil. Add the lasagna noodles and cook for 12 to 14 minutes or until tender. Drain and rinse under cold running water and drain again. Set aside. Cut the noodles to fit the casserole dish.

3. TO MAKE THE SAUCE Lightly coat a nonstick saucepan with cooking spray. Add the oil and set over medium-high heat. Add the onion and garlic and sauté, stirring frequently, until browned, about 5 minutes. Add the mushrooms and sauté for 5 minutes or until no longer wet.

4. Stir in the tomato sauce and dried basil. Bring to a boil, then reduce the heat. Cover and simmer for 12 to 15 minutes or until slightly thickened. Stir in the ground soy and simmer for 5 more minutes. Set aside.

5. TO MAKE THE FILLING Combine the ricotta, mozzarella, milk and Parmesan together in a bowl.

6 lasagna noodles

Sauce

1 tsp (5 mL) vegetable oil

¾ cup (185 mL) finely chopped onion

1 tsp (5 mL) finely chopped garlic

3 cups (750 mL) finely chopped mushrooms

2½ cups (625 mL) homemade or store-bought tomato sauce (see Quick Basic Tomato Sauce on page 369)

1 tsp (5 mL) dried basil

8 oz (250 g) soy-based ground-beef substitute

Filling

1¼ cups (310 mL) reduced-fat ricotta cheese (10 oz/300 g)

¾ cup (185 mL) shredded part-skim mozzarella (2 oz/60 g)

3 Tbsp (45 mL) 2% milk

3 Tbsp (45 mL) grated Parmesan cheese (¾ oz/23 g)

6. To assemble, spread one-quarter of the tomato sauce mixture over the bottom of the casserole dish. Top with 2 lasagna noodles, trimming to fit the pan. Spread half the cheese mixture over the noodles. Top with another one-quarter of the tomato sauce. Top with 2 noodles. Spread the remaining cheese mixture over the noodles. Top with another one-quarter of the tomato sauce. Top with the last 2 noodles. Spread the remaining tomato sauce overtop. Sprinkle with the mozzarella cheese.

7. Bake in the centre of the oven for 20 to 25 minutes or until hot. Garnish with basil.

PREPARATION TIME 15 minutes · **COOKING TIME** 50 minutes · **MAKE AHEAD** Prepare the lasagna up to a day in advance and bake just before serving. Leftovers are great; reheat them gently in a 300°F (150°C) oven. · **MAKES** 6 servings.

Topping

⅓ cup (80 mL) shredded part-skim mozzarella cheese (1 oz/30 g)

3 Tbsp (45 mL) chopped fresh basil or parsley

 ROSE'S TIP
You can always use diced tofu or tempeh instead of ground soy.

 HEALTH TIP
To boost the fibre, use whole wheat lasagna sheets. One whole wheat sheet has 4 grams of fibre, whereas one white flour lasagna sheet has 1 gram of fibre. It's a significant difference.

NUTRITION INFORMATION PER SERVING

Calories 240	Protein 20 g	Cholesterol 20 mg
Carbohydrates 26 g	Total fat 6 g	Sodium 334 mg
Fibre 3.9 g	Saturated fat 3 g	

CHICKPEA AND RED KIDNEY BEAN CHILI WITH GROUND SOY

Using two varieties of beans makes this dish full-bodied. I like to eat this on its own or with brown rice or a baked white or sweet potato.

1. Lightly coat a nonstick skillet with cooking spray. Add the oil and set over medium heat. Add the onion and sauté for 3 minutes or until soft. Stir in the corn and garlic and cook for another 5 minutes or until the corn is browned, stirring occasionally. Add the ground soy and sauté for 2 more minutes.

2. Add the kidney beans, chickpeas, tomato sauce, stock, chili powder, dried basil, sugar and cumin. Bring to a boil, cover and reduce the heat. Simmer for 20 minutes or just until the mixture is thickened.

3. Garnish with the cheese, sour cream and fresh basil.

PREPARATION TIME 10 minutes · **COOKING TIME** 30 minutes · **MAKE AHEAD** Make this up to 2 days in advance. Reheat gently, then add the garnishes. · **MAKES** 4 servings.

 ROSE'S TIP
Stocks, whether they are beef, chicken or vegetable, are all high in sodium. If you have the time, try to make your own and freeze. By adding your own spices and salt you'll save yourself from most of the sodium.

 HEALTH TIP
Red kidney beans are a very good source of cholesterol-lowering fibre. They also prevent blood sugar levels from rising, which may prevent type 2 diabetes. They are an excellent fat-free source of protein.

NUTRITION INFORMATION PER SERVING

Calories 439	Protein 28 g	Cholesterol 18 mg
Carbohydrates 60 g	Total fat 9.6 g	Sodium 445 mg
Fibre 16 g	Saturated fat 4 g	

2 tsp (10 mL) vegetable oil

1½ cups (375 mL) chopped onion

1 cup (250 mL) corn

2 tsp (10 mL) crushed garlic

8 oz (250 g) soy-based ground beef substitute

1 cup (250 mL) canned red kidney beans, drained and rinsed

1 cup (250 mL) canned chickpeas, drained and rinsed

2 cups (500 mL) homemade or store-bought tomato sauce (see Quick Basic Tomato Sauce on page 369)

1 cup (250 mL) low-sodium vegetable stock

2 tsp (10 mL) chili powder

1½ tsp (7.5 mL) dried basil

1 tsp (5 mL) granulated sugar

½ tsp (2.5 mL) ground cumin

Garnish
½ cup (125 mL) shredded aged cheddar cheese (1½ oz/45 g)

¼ cup (60 mL) reduced-fat sour cream

3 Tbsp (45 mL) chopped fresh basil

POTATO BAKE (KUGEL) WITH ONION, MUSHROOM AND SPINACH FILLING

This is another classic Eastern European dish. It's usually high in calories and fat due to the excess oil used, but I decided to give it a layered component, which adds flavour and doesn't require the excess oil to taste great.

1. Preheat the oven to 500°F (260°C). Spray a 9-inch (23 cm) aquare baking dish with vegetable oil.

2. Sauté the onions in oil until soft, about 5 minutes. Add the mushrooms and sauté until no longer wet (about 4 minutes). Add the spinach, garlic, oregano and salt and pepper and cook for 2 minutes.

3. Combine the potatoes with the flour, eggs, oil, salt and pepper, garlic and cheese if using.

4. Add half the potato mixture to the prepared dish and place the spinach mixture overtop. Add the remaining potato mixture. Spray the top with vegetable oil. Bake for 20 minutes. Turn the heat down to 400°F (200°C) and bake for another 20 minutes or just until the potatoes are soft and the topping is brown.

PREPARATION TIME 20 minutes · **COOKING TIME** 50 minutes ·

MAKE AHEAD Prepare early in the day and bake just before serving. Leftovers are great; reheat them gently in a 300°F (150°C) oven. · **MAKES** 12 servings.

2 cups (500 mL) diced onions

2 tsp (10 mL) vegetable oil

2 cups (500 mL) diced mushrooms

4 oz (125 g) frozen spinach, chopped, defrosted and squeezed dry, or 4 cups (1 L) chopped fresh baby spinach

2 tsp (10 mL) garlic

1 tsp (5 mL) dried oregano

pinch of salt and pepper

2½ lb (1.25 kg) Yukon Gold potatoes (grated and squeezed dry)

3 Tbsp (45 mL) all-purpose flour

2 eggs

4 Tbsp (60 mL) olive oil

pinch of salt and pepper

2 tsp (10 mL) crushed garlic

3 Tbsp (45 mL) grated Parmesan cheese (¾ oz/23 g) (optional)

 ROSE'S TIP

For a different twist, use half sweet potatoes and half Yukon Gold. This would boost the fibre to 5 grams per serving.

 HEALTH TIP

Frozen spinach goes through a flash-freezing process within hours after it has been picked, which allows it to retain more of its vitamin C than fresh.

NUTRITION INFORMATION PER SERVING (1 SQUARE)

Calories 145	Protein 3.8 g	Cholesterol 23 mg
Carbohydrates 20.1 g	Total fat 5.8 g	Sodium 83 mg
Fibre 2.5 g	Saturated fat 1 g	

THREE ROOT VEGETABLE LATKES (PANCAKES)

Potato latkes are a traditional Jewish or Eastern European dish, especially served on Hanukkah. I wanted to make a healthy version, so I used a blend of root vegetables. Use the grater blade of a food processor to grate the veggies.

1. Preheat the oven to 400°F (200°C). Spray a large oven dish with vegetable oil.

2. In a skillet sprayed with vegetable oil, add the oil, onions and garlic. Sauté on medium heat for 10 minutes until tender. Add the sugar and sauté another 5 minutes. Place in a mixing bowl.

3. Squeeze out the excess moisture from the grated vegetables. Add the vegetables to the onion mixture along with the dill, eggs and salt and pepper.

4. Pat into 12 latkes, flatten and place them in an oven dish. Spray the patties with vegetable oil. Bake for 20 minutes, turning halfway through the baking time, just until the vegetables are tender. Serve with the tzatziki.

PREPARATION TIME 20 minutes · **COOKING TIME** 35 minutes ·
MAKE AHEAD Grate the vegetables early in the day but keep them covered with water and refrigerated. Drain well, then prepare. · **MAKES** 6 servings.

2 tsp (10 mL) vegetable oil

2 cups (500 mL) diced onion

1 tsp (5 mL) crushed garlic

2 tsp (10 mL) brown sugar

2 cups (500 mL) grated peeled sweet potatoes

2 cups (500 mL) grated peeled baking potato

1 cup (250 mL) grated peeled parsnips

3 Tbsp (45 mL) chopped fresh dill or 1 tsp (5 mL) dried

2 eggs

pinch of salt and pepper

½ cup (125 mL) tzatziki (see Tzatziki Sauce on page 368)

ROSE'S TIP

Make large potato *rösti* by using a 12-inch (30 cm) skillet. Spread the root vegetable mixture into a skillet and, on low heat, cook for about 10 minutes per side, until the vegetables are tender.

HEALTH TIP

Parsnips are rich in fibre and promote healthy digestion, regulate blood sugar levels and may reduce cholesterol levels.

NUTRITION INFORMATION PER SERVING (2 LATKES)

Calories 167	Protein 4.2 g	Cholesterol 47 mg
Carbohydrates 32.1 g	Total fat 2.7 g	Sodium 84 mg
Fibre 4.9 g	Saturated fat 0.7 g	

QUINOA FALAFELS

Traditional Middle Eastern falafels are so delicious and oh so high in calories and fat! The deep-frying is the reason. My version is sautéed with just a small amount of oil and when served with diced veggies and tzatziki, is an incredibly tasty and healthy meal.

1. Bring the quinoa and water to a boil. Cover and simmer on the lowest heat for 15 minutes, just until cooked. Drain any excess liquid. Cool for 10 minutes.

2. Place the carrot, onions, peppers, salt and pepper, eggs, Parmesan and feta cheeses, tahini, breadcrumbs, lemon juice, garlic and basil, along with the cooled quinoa, in the bowl of a food processor. Process on and off just until combined. Do not purée. Form into approximately 18 balls.

3. In a large skillet sprayed with vegetable spray, add 2 tsp (10 mL) vegetable oil. Let the pan get very hot so the falafels do not stick. Add the falafels and sauté on medium heat for 3 minutes per side until browned and hot throughout.

4. Cut the pitas in half and put 3 falafels in each half pocket. Add the tzatziki, tomatoes, cucumbers, onions and cilantro.

PREPARATION TIME 25 minutes · **COOKING TIME** 21 minutes ·
MAKE AHEAD Prepare falafels up to a day in advance and sauté just before serving. · **MAKES** 6 servings.

½ cup (125 mL) quinoa

1 cup (250 mL) water or low-sodium stock

⅓ cup (80 mL) shredded carrot

⅓ cup (80 mL) sliced green onions

⅓ cup (80 mL) diced red bell pepper

pinch of salt and pepper

2 eggs

3 Tbsp (45 mL) grated Parmesan cheese (¾ oz/23 g)

⅓ cup (80 mL) crumbled reduced-fat feta cheese (1½ oz/45 g)

2 Tbsp (30 mL) tahini (sesame seed paste)

⅓ cup (80 mL) unseasoned dry breadcrumbs

2 tsp (10 mL) lemon juice

1 tsp (5 mL) crushed garlic

1 tsp (5 mL) dried basil

2 tsp (10 mL) vegetable oil

continued . . .

Quinoa Falafels (continued)

 ROSE'S TIP

You can also bake these falafels for 15 minutes in a 375°F (190°C) oven on a baking sheet sprayed with vegetable oil. They will be delicious, but won't have the browned crisp exterior.

 HEALTH TIP

Whole wheat pitas (large) have 5 grams of fibre versus white pitas, which have only 1.5 grams of fibre.

3 large pitas (whole wheat) sliced in half

½ cup (125 mL) homemade or store-bought tzatziki (see Tzatziki Sauce on page 368)

½ cup (125 mL) tomatoes

½ cup (125 mL) cucumbers

¼ cup (60 mL) onions

¼ cup (60 mL) chopped cilantro or parsley

NUTRITION INFORMATION PER SERVING (½ PITA)

Calories 256	Protein 11 g	Cholesterol 51 mg
Carbohydrates 36.4 g	Total fat 6.9 g	Sodium 430 mg
Fibre 5.3 g	Saturated fat 2 g	

MUSHROOM AND CHEESE STRUDEL

If you love mushrooms, you'll get your fill with this strudel. Use any variety you like, but be sure to sauté them long enough to eliminate any extra moisture.

1. Preheat the oven to 375°F (190°C). Spray a baking sheet with cooking spray.

2. TO MAKE THE FILLING In a large nonstick skillet sprayed with cooking spray, heat the oil over medium-high heat. Cook the onions and garlic for 4 minutes or until softened. Stir in the mushrooms and thyme and cook for 8 to 10 minutes, stirring frequently, or until the mushrooms are tender and most of the liquid is absorbed. Transfer to a bowl. Cool for 5 minutes. Stir in the ricotta, goat cheese, dill, olives, Parmesan and salt and pepper.

3. Keeping the remaining phyllo covered with a cloth to prevent drying out, layer 2 sheets of phyllo, one on top of the other. Spray with the cooking spray. Layer the remaining sheets on top, spraying every other sheet. Spread the filling over the phyllo, leaving a 2-inch (5 cm) border bare around the edges. Starting from the long end, roll several times. Tuck in the short ends and continue to roll. Place on the prepared baking sheet. Spray with cooking spray.

4. Bake in the centre of the oven for 25 to 30 minutes or until golden.

PREPARATION TIME 10 minutes • **COOKING TIME** 40 minutes • **MAKE AHEAD** Prepare the entire phyllo filling up to 2 days in advance. Bake just before serving. • **MAKES** 8 servings.

NUTRITION INFORMATION PER SERVING

Calories 159	Protein 8.6 g	Cholesterol 12 mg
Carbohydrates 15 g	Total fat 7.2 g	Sodium 256 mg
Fibre 2.1 g	Saturated fat 2.8 g	

2 tsp (10 mL) vegetable oil

1 cup (250 mL) chopped onions

2 tsp (10 mL) minced garlic

6 cups (1.5 L) sliced mushrooms (about 1 lb/500 g)

1 tsp (5 mL) dried thyme leaves

¾ cup (185 mL) reduced-fat ricotta cheese (6 oz/175 g)

½ cup (125 mL) goat cheese (2 oz/60 g)

⅓ cup (80 mL) chopped fresh dill

¼ cup (60 mL) sliced black olives

2 Tbsp (30 mL) grated Parmesan cheese (½ oz/15 g)

pinch of salt and pepper

6 sheets phyllo pastry

 ROSE'S TIP
If it's in season, fresh thyme is better. Use 1 Tbsp (15 mL) chopped.

 HEALTH TIP
Phyllo pastry is a great substitute for puff pastry. One ounce (30 g) of phyllo, about 1½ sheets, has only 85 calories and 2 grams of fat; the same amount of puff pastry has 110 calories and 8 grams of fat.

MANICOTTI WITH THREE CHEESE PESTO

Stuffed pasta shells with a creamy cheese mixture are a great and satisfying meal for a vegetarian. You can also use jumbo pasta shells. You will need approximately 18 to 20 shells.

1. Preheat the oven to 350°F (175°C). Lightly coat a 9- × 13-inch (3.5 L) ovenproof casserole dish with vegetable oil.

2. Bring a large pot of water to a boil. Add the manicotti shells and cook for about 8 minutes or until just tender. Drain and rinse with cold water.

3. Combine the ricotta, Parmesan, goat cheese, pesto and egg in the bowl of a food processor and process until well combined.

4. Make a lengthwise split to open up each manicotti. Lay flat and place 3 Tbsp (45 mL) of cheese filling in the middle. Close and repeat with the remaining manicotti.

5. Combine the tomato sauce, milk and dried basil in a bowl. Pour about half into the prepared casserole dish. Place the manicotti overtop, seam side down. Pour the remaining sauce overtop of the manicotti and top with the mozzarella and Parmesan cheeses. Bake uncovered for 20 minutes or until completely heated through and the cheese is melted and bubbling. Garnish with basil and serve.

PREPARATION TIME 10 minutes · **COOKING TIME** 30 minutes ·
MAKE AHEAD Prepare this dish up to a day in advance and bake just before serving. · **MAKES** 4 servings.

8 manicotti shells

1 cup (250 mL) reduced-fat ricotta cheese (8 oz/250 g)

¼ cup (60 mL) grated Parmesan cheese (1 oz/30 g)

¼ cup (60 mL) crumbled goat cheese (1 oz/30 g)

3 Tbsp (45 mL) pesto (see Basil Pesto on page 371)

1 large egg

1½ cups (375 mL) store-bought or homemade tomato sauce (see Quick Basic Tomato Sauce on page 369)

3 Tbsp (45 mL) canned evaporated 2% milk

1 tsp (5 mL) dried basil

½ cup (125 mL) shredded part-skim mozzarella cheese (1½ oz/45 g)

2 Tbsp (30 mL) grated Parmesan cheese (½ oz/15 g)

3 Tbsp (45 mL) chopped fresh basil or parsley

ROSE'S TIP

Shred a few cups of grated cheese and keep them in your freezer stored in an airtight container for up to 4 months. You'll save time.

 HEALTH TIP

By eating manicotti or cannelloni, you're actually saving on carbohydrates by not eating an entire dish of pasta. A normal serving would be 2 manicotti shells, which would have 345 calories and 37 grams of carbohydrates. A normal pasta serving such as fettucine would consist of 3 cups (750 mL) cooked pasta with tomato sauce, which has over 700 calories and 100 grams of carbohydrates!

NUTRITION INFORMATION PER SERVING

Calories 345	Protein 21 g	Cholesterol 86 mg
Carbohydrates 37 g	Total fat 13 g	Sodium 400 mg
Fibre 2.7 g	Saturated fat 6.4 g	

STACKED TORTILLA PIE
WITH BEANS AND CHEESE

This is one of the most beautiful and delicious recipes to serve. Use a variety of coloured tortillas to make it even more spectacular. When this dish is cut open to expose the tomato sauce, vegetables and cheese, it looks amazing.

1. Preheat the oven to 350°F (175°C). Lightly coat a 9-inch (23 cm) springform pan with cooking spray.

2. Lightly coat a nonstick saucepan with vegetable oil and set over medium heat. Add the corn and sauté, stirring often, for about 8 minutes or until slightly charred. Set aside.

3. Add the oil to the saucepan and keep over medium heat. Add the onion and garlic and cook for 4 minutes, stirring occasionally. Stir in the red and green peppers. Cook for 3 minutes, stirring occasionally. Stir in the tomato sauce, charred corn, basil, chili powder and cumin. Cover and cook over medium heat, stirring occasionally, for 10 minutes or until slightly thickened. Remove from the heat.

4. Place the chickpeas in a bowl and mash them roughly with a fork. Add to the vegetable mixture and stir to combine.

5. TO MAKE THE FILLING In a separate bowl, combine the ricotta, mozzarella and cheddar cheeses (but reserve ¼ cup/ 60 mL of the cheddar for garnish). Add the milk and salt and pepper and stir until well combined.

6. Place a tortilla in the prepared springform pan. Spread with one-quarter of the vegetable-chickpea mixture. Sprinkle with one-quarter of the cheese mixture. Repeat the layers 3 times. Top with the final tortilla and sprinkle with the remaining cheddar and Parmesan cheeses. Cover the pan tightly with foil.

1 cup (250 mL) corn

2 tsp (10 mL) vegetable oil

½ cup (125 mL) chopped onion

2 tsp (10 mL) finely chopped garlic

½ cup (125 mL) chopped red bell pepper

½ cup (125 mL) chopped green bell pepper

2 cups (500 mL) homemade or store-bought tomato sauce (see Quick Basic Tomato Sauce on page 369)

1½ tsp (7.5 mL) dried basil

1 tsp (5 mL) chili powder

½ tsp (2.5 mL) ground cumin

2 cups (500 mL) canned chickpeas, drained and rinsed

Filling

1 cup (250 mL) reduced-fat ricotta cheese (8 oz/250 g)

1 cup (250 mL) shredded part-skim mozzarella cheese (3 oz/90 g)

¾ cup (185 mL) shredded cheddar cheese (2¼ oz/65 g)

3 Tbsp (45 mL) 2% milk

pinch of salt and pepper

7. Bake for 20 minutes in the preheated oven, then uncovered for 10 minutes or until it is completely heated through and the cheese has melted. Cut into 8 wedges with a sharp knife.

PREPARATION TIME 20 minutes · **COOKING TIME** 55 minutes · **MAKE AHEAD** Prepare up to a day in advance and bake just before serving. · **MAKES** 8 servings.

Tortillas

5 large flour tortillas

2 Tbsp (30 mL) grated Parmesan cheese (½ oz/15 g)

 ROSE'S TIP
This is a great main meal for a vegetarian. You have vegetables, beans for protein and fibre, and cheese for dairy. Perfect for entertaining.

 HEALTH TIP
Large whole wheat tortillas have 7 grams of fibre each. Large white tortillas have only 3 grams of fibre.

NUTRITION INFORMATION PER SERVING

Calories 280	Protein 14 g	Cholesterol 22 mg
Carbohydrates 39 g	Total fat 8.5 g	Sodium 710 mg
Fibre 5 g	Saturated fat 3.1 g	

MEDITERRANEAN STUFFED PORTOBELLO MUSHROOMS WITH SPINACH AND GOAT CHEESE

Portobello mushrooms are known as "steak" for the vegetarian. They are a delicious, meaty and filling meal. You can always substitute 3 ounces (90 g) of frozen spinach for the fresh spinach.

1. Spray a baking dish with vegetable oil.

2. Combine the egg and milk. Dip the portobellos in the egg wash and then in the breadcrumbs. Spray the mushrooms with vegetable oil.

3. Place in a 400°F (200°C) oven for 15 minutes. Remove from the oven and set the oven to broil.

4. Meanwhile, in a skillet, heat the oil and sauté the onions until softened. Add the garlic and chopped mushroom stems and cook for 5 minutes until tender. Add the bell peppers and spinach and cook just until wilted, about 2 minutes. Add the Parmesan cheese, olive oil and olives. Divide overtop of the mushroom caps and dot with the goat cheese.

5. Broil for 1 minute, just until the goat cheese is browned.

PREPARATION TIME 15 minutes · **COOKING TIME** 16 minutes ·
MAKE AHEAD You can prepare the mushroom mixture early in the day.
Bake the mushrooms just before serving, then continue with the recipe. ·
MAKES 4 servings.

1 egg

2 Tbsp (30 mL) 2% milk

4 medium portobello mushrooms (stems removed)

½ cup (125 mL) seasoned dry breadcrumbs

2 tsp (10 mL) vegetable oil

1 cup (250 mL) finely chopped onions

2 tsp (10 mL) chopped garlic

½ cup (125 mL) finely chopped mushroom stems

½ cup (125 mL) finely diced red bell pepper

3 cups (750 mL) fresh baby spinach

¼ cup (60 mL) grated Parmesan cheese (1 oz/30 g)

2 tsp (10 mL) olive oil

3 Tbsp (45 mL) chopped black olives

⅓ cup (80 mL) crumbled goat cheese (1 oz/30 g)

 ROSE'S TIP

Replace the spinach with arugula or baby kale if you like. Marinating the portobellos for a couple of hours before cooking enhances the flavour.

 HEALTH TIP

Portobello mushrooms are one of the lowest-calorie vegetables. A medium one has only 18 calories and 0 grams of fat. It also contains 350 mg potassium.

NUTRITION INFORMATION PER SERVING

Calories 203	Protein 9.3 g	Cholesterol 45 mg
Carbohydrates 20.5 g	Total fat 9.7 g	Sodium 302 mg
Fibre 3.6 g	Saturated fat 3.4 g	

POLENTA SQUARES WITH ROASTED BELL PEPPERS AND ZUCCHINI

These squares are a complete meal in themselves, or they can be served as a grain or vegetable side dish. Substitute the vegetables and cheese of your choice. Avoid buying pre-rolled polenta, which lacks the flavour and texture of polenta made from scratch.

1. Preheat the oven to 425°F (220°C).

2. Bring the stock to a boil in a large saucepan and set over medium-high heat. Reduce the heat to low and gradually whisk in the cornmeal and Parmesan cheese. Cook, stirring, for about 5 minutes or until the mixture is thick and bubbly.

3. Lightly coat an 8-inch (20 cm) square casserole dish with vegetable oil. Pour the polenta into the dish and smooth the top. Cover and leave to set while roasting the vegetables.

4. Line a large baking sheet with foil and lightly coat it with cooking spray. Cut the top off the head of the garlic so that all the cloves are exposed. Wrap in foil. Place the wrapped garlic on the baking sheet along with the bell peppers, onion rings and zucchini. Lightly coat with vegetable oil and roast in the preheated oven, turning occasionally, for 30 minutes or until tender.

5. Remove from the oven and allow to cool slightly. Squeeze the garlic cloves out of the skin and place in a large bowl. Chop the roasted vegetables and add to the bowl. Drizzle with the olive oil and balsamic vinegar.

6. Cut the set polenta into 4 squares (4 × 4 inch/10 × 10 cm). Lightly coat a large nonstick skillet with vegetable oil and set over medium-high heat. Add the polenta squares and sauté for 3 minutes or until golden. Turn and cook for 1 minute. Place the polenta onto serving plates. Top with the vegetable mixture and sprinkle with the goat cheese.

3 cups (750 mL) low-sodium vegetable stock

1 cup (250 mL) cornmeal

1 Tbsp (15 mL) grated Parmesan cheese (¼ oz/8 g)

1 small head of garlic

½ medium red bell pepper, core and seeds removed

½ medium yellow bell pepper, core and seeds removed

½ medium red onion, cut into ½-inch (1 cm) rings

1 small zucchini, cut in half lengthwise

1 Tbsp (15 mL) olive oil

1 tsp (5 mL) balsamic vinegar

⅓ cup (80 mL) crumbled goat cheese (1½ oz/45 g)

PREPARATION TIME 15 minutes · **COOKING TIME** 40 minutes ·

MAKE AHEAD This dish can be made a day in advance, covered and refrigerated. Reheat gently in a 300°F (150°C) oven. · **MAKES** 4 servings.

 ROSE'S TIP

These are perfect as an appetizer or starter for a meal. They also make an excellent vegetarian meal.

 HEALTH TIP

Cornmeal is rich in anti-oxidants and fibre and is an alternative for those who have gluten allergies or are celiac.

NUTRITION INFORMATION PER SERVING

Calories 250	Protein 8 g	Cholesterol 6 mg
Carbohydrates 39 g	Total fat 7.4 g	Sodium 420 mg
Fibre 4 g	Saturated fat 2.5 g	

SAUCES, DRESSINGS & SPREADS

SMOKED FISH SPREAD

This has to be my number-one appetizer spread. I usually serve it with whole-grain crackers, baked tortilla chips or celery sticks, or I use it as a spread in a sandwich. You can now find prepackaged smoked fish in your local supermarket.

1. Combine the smoked fish, cream cheese, ricotta, sour cream, mayonnaise, lemon juice and pepper in a food processor and purée until smooth. Stir in the chives.

PREPARATION TIME 5 minutes · **MAKE AHEAD** Prepare up to 3 days in advance. · **MAKES** about 1½ cups (375 mL).

4 oz (125 g) boneless skinless smoked fish

¼ cup (60 mL) softened reduced-fat cream cheese (2 oz/60 g)

½ cup (125 mL) reduced-fat ricotta cheese (4 oz/125 g)

¼ cup (60 mL) reduced-fat sour cream

2 Tbsp (30 mL) reduced-fat mayonnaise

1 Tbsp (15 mL) freshly squeezed lemon juice

pinch of ground black pepper

2 Tbsp (30 mL) finely chopped chives or green onions

 ROSE'S TIP
You can buy vacuum-sealed packages of either smoked salmon or trout. Freeze them so you can make this dip at any time.

 HEALTH TIP
Smoked fish, like smoked meats, has excess sodium. A 2-ounce (60 g) serving has 400 mg of sodium. Keep your intake of smoked foods to a minimum.

NUTRITION INFORMATION PER SERVING (1 TBSP/15 ML)

Calories 26	Protein 2.2 g	Cholesterol 7.2 mg
Carbohydrates 0.8 g	Total fat 1.5 g	Sodium 120 mg
Fibre 0 g	Saturated fat 0.6 g	

SPINACH AND RICOTTA DIP

A classic dip that usually contains excess calories and fat due to the mayonnaise and sour cream. My dip is light because it uses reduced-fat yogurt and ricotta cheese. Serve this with crackers or veggies or hollow out a medium-sized bread bowl and fill it with the dip.

1. Boil the spinach for 2 minutes. Drain, rinse with cold water and squeeze dry.

2. In a food processor, combine the spinach, yogurt, ricotta, garlic, parsley, Parmesan and salt and pepper to taste; process just until still chunky. Do not purée.

PREPARATION TIME 10 minutes · **COOKING TIME** 2 minutes ·
MAKE AHEAD Prepare and refrigerate up to a day before. Stir just before serving.
(If filling bread, do so just before serving.) · **MAKES** 1½ cups (375 mL).

half a 10 oz (300 g) package frozen chopped spinach, defrosted and squeezed dry (⅓ cup/80 mL)

½ cup (125 mL) reduced-fat plain yogurt

¾ cup (185 mL) reduced-fat ricotta cheese (6 oz/175 g)

½ tsp (2.5 mL) crushed garlic

2 Tbsp (30 mL) chopped fresh parsley

3 Tbsp (45 mL) grated Parmesan cheese (¾ oz/23 g)

pinch of salt and pepper

ROSE'S TIP
Keep a few packages of chopped frozen spinach in your refrigerator. It's less expensive and easier to use than fresh.

HEALTH TIP
Fresh and frozen spinach have similar nutrients. Often the frozen spinach has more vitamins and minerals because it has been picked at its best and immediately frozen, whereas fresh spinach may be exposed to the elements longer before being eaten.

NUTRITION INFORMATION PER SERVING (1 TBSP/15 ML)

Calories 16	Protein 1.4 g	Cholesterol 2 mg
Carbohydrates 1.1 g	Total fat 0.7 g	Sodium 50 mg
Fibre 0.1 g	Saturated fat 0.4 g	

ARTICHOKE AND ASIAGO SPREAD

Canned artichokes and Asiago cheese are a great combination. You can use this as a dip for crackers or crudités or as a spread for sandwiches.

1. Purée both cheeses, mayonnaise, garlic and artichokes in a food processor until smooth. Garnish with parsley.

PREPARATION TIME 10 minutes • **MAKE AHEAD** Refrigerate for up to 3 days. • **MAKES** about 1 cup (250 mL).

¼ cup (60 mL) grated part-skim mozzarella cheese (¾ oz/23 g)

¼ cup (60 mL) grated Asiago or Parmesan cheese (1 oz/30 g)

3 Tbsp (45 mL) reduced-fat mayonnaise

½ tsp (2.5 mL) minced garlic

4 canned artichoke hearts, drained and diced

1 Tbsp (15 mL) finely chopped parsley for garnish

 ROSE'S TIP
You can also use aged cheddar or Monterey Jack instead of the Asiago if you want a less sharp flavour.

 HEALTH TIP
Only use artichokes packed in water. Two artichoke hearts in water contain only 30 calories and 0 grams of fat. Two artichoke hearts in oil have 60 calories and 5 grams of fat.

NUTRITION INFORMATION PER SERVING (1 TBSP/15 ML)

Calories 32	Protein 2.2 g	Cholesterol 2 mg
Carbohydrates 4.5 g	Total fat 0.5 g	Sodium 104 mg
Fibre 2 g	Saturated fat 0.4 g	

BLUE CHEESE DRESSING

To lighten this dressing, I use reduced-fat sour cream, milk and reduced-fat mayonnaise, which saves you more than half the calories and fat.

2/3 cup (160 mL) crumbled blue cheese (2 oz/60 g)

1/3 cup (80 mL) reduced-fat sour cream

1/3 cup (80 mL) 2% milk

3 Tbsp (45 mL) reduced-fat mayonnaise

1/4 tsp (1 mL) crushed garlic

pinch of salt and pepper

1. In a small food processor, purée the cheese, sour cream, milk, mayonnaise, garlic and salt and pepper until smooth or chunky, depending upon your preference.

PREPARATION TIME 5 minutes · **MAKE AHEAD** Refrigerate for up to 3 days. · **MAKES** 1 cup (250 mL).

 ROSE'S TIP
Use this over salads, as a dip and even over cooked fish, chicken or beef.

 HEALTH TIP
Blue cheese dressing is traditionally made with full-fat mayonnaise, sour cream, oil and excess blue cheese. One tablespoon (15 mL) can have more than 70 calories and 8 grams of fat.

NUTRITION INFORMATION PER SERVING (1 TBSP/15 ML)

Calories 27	Protein 1.1 g	Cholesterol 5 mg
Carbohydrates 1.1 g	Total fat 1.6 g	Sodium 97 mg
Fibre 0 g	Saturated fat 1.1 g	

GOAT CHEESE SAUCE

Goat cheese is one of my favourite cheeses. You could also substitute feta cheese. This is a great sauce over vegetables, burgers, fish or chicken.

1. Combine the goat and cream cheeses, water, olive oil, lemon juice and garlic in the small bowl of a food processor. Purée until smooth. Add the chopped dill.

PREPARATION TIME 10 minutes · **MAKE AHEAD** Refrigerate for up to 3 days. · **MAKES** ⅓ cup (80 mL).

ROSE'S TIP

If you like the sauce thinner, just add a little water. If you will be using it as a dip, remove the water.

HEALTH TIP

Other cheese dressings such as blue cheese can have 70 calories and 8 grams of fat per tablespoon (15 mL).

⅓ cup (80 mL) crumbled goat cheese (1½ oz/45 g)

2 Tbsp (30 mL) softened reduced-fat cream cheese (1 oz/30 g)

1 Tbsp (15 mL) water

2 tsp (10 mL) olive oil

2 tsp (10 mL) lemon juice

½ tsp (2.5 mL) finely chopped garlic

2 tsp (10 mL) finely chopped fresh dill or parsley

NUTRITION INFORMATION PER SERVING (1 TBSP/15 ML)

Calories 32	Protein 1.2 g	Cholesterol 6 mg
Carbohydrates 0.4 g	Total fat 2.9 g	Sodium 42 mg
Fibre 0 g	Saturated fat 1.5 g	

CAESAR DRESSING

A delicious light caesar dressing that can be used over greens or even as a sauce for fish or chicken.

1. Combine the Parmesan, mayonnaise, olive oil, water, lemon juice, garlic and mustard in a small food processor or mix by hand until smooth.

PREPARATION TIME 5 minutes · **MAKE AHEAD** Keep refrigerated for up to 3 days. · **MAKES** ¾ cup (185 mL).

 ROSE'S TIP
You can find light caesar dressings in the super-market if you don't have time to make your own.

 HEALTH TIP
Traditional caesar dress-ings in restaurants contain around 100 calories and 10 grams of fat per serving due to the excess oil and cheese.

2 Tbsp (30 mL) grated Parmesan cheese (½ oz/15 g)

2 Tbsp (30 mL) reduced-fat mayonnaise

3 Tbsp (45 mL) olive oil

1 Tbsp (15 mL) water

2 tsp (10 mL) lemon juice

½ tsp (2.5 mL) finely chopped garlic

½ tsp (2.5 mL) Dijon mustard

NUTRITION INFORMATION PER SERVING (1 TBSP/15 ML)

Calories 51	Protein 0.3 g	Cholesterol 1 mg
Carbohydrates 0.7 g	Total fat 4.7 g	Sodium 49 mg
Fibre 0 g	Saturated fat 0.9 g	

RANCH DRESSING

Ranch dressing is traditionally high in fat and calories due to the excess oil and mayonnaise. My version is light and creamy. If you don't want to buy buttermilk, simply use my tip of creating your own using a mixture of milk and lemon juice.

⅓ cup (80 mL) reduced-fat mayonnaise

½ cup (125 mL) buttermilk (or mix ½ cup/125 mL 2% milk with 2 tsp/10 mL lemon juice and let sit for 5 minutes)

1 tsp (5 mL) Dijon mustard

4 tsp (20 mL) lemon juice

pinch of salt and pepper

½ tsp (2.5 mL) crushed garlic

1½ tsp (7.5 mL) sugar

1. Whisk mayonnaise, buttermilk, mustard, lemon juice, salt and pepper, garlic and sugar until combined.

PREPARATION TIME 5 minutes · **MAKE AHEAD** Refrigerate for up to 3 days. · **MAKES** 1 cup (250 mL).

 ROSE'S TIP

I find it easier to make my own buttermilk unless I use a lot of it, in which case I would purchase it at the store.

 HEALTH TIP

Buttermilk is a low-fat milk and contains no butter. One cup (250 mL) has 98 calories and 2 grams of fat compared to 2% milk, which has 122 calories and 5 grams of fat.

NUTRITION INFORMATION PER SERVING (1 TBSP/15 ML)

Calories 18	Protein 0.4 g	Cholesterol 1 mg
Carbohydrates 1.7 g	Total fat 0.3 g	Sodium 71 mg
Fibre 0 g	Saturated fat 0.3 g	

CREAMY BALSAMIC DRESSING

I love this dressing over spinach leaves. It's creamy and rich tasting without the calories and fat.

1. Whisk the olive oil, sour cream, mayonnaise, vinegar, honey and garlic together in a small bowl.

PREPARATION TIME 5 minutes · **MAKE AHEAD** Keep refrigerated for up to 3 days. · **MAKES** ⅓ cup (80 mL).

ROSE'S TIP

You will get a smoother texture if you use a small food processor to mix the ingredients.

HEALTH TIP

Some varieties of honey have large amounts of friendly bacteria such as lactobacilli, which may explain honey's therapeutic properties.

2 Tbsp (30 mL) olive oil

2 Tbsp (30 mL) reduced-fat sour cream

1 Tbsp (15 mL) reduced-fat mayonnaise

1 Tbsp (15 mL) balsamic vinegar

2 tsp (10 mL) liquid honey

½ tsp (2.5 mL) minced fresh garlic

NUTRITION INFORMATION PER SERVING (1 TBSP/15 ML)

Calories 46	Protein 0.2 g	Cholesterol 1 mg
Carbohydrates 2.4 g	Total fat 3.7 g	Sodium 19 mg
Fibre 0 g	Saturated fat 0.8 g	

RUSSIAN DRESSING

A simple classic dressing made light. Great for vegetables or salads or as a sauce over fish.

1. Combine the mayonnaise, sour cream, chili sauce and water in a small bowl and mix well.

PREPARATION TIME 5 minutes · **MAKE AHEAD** Keep refrigerated for up to 3 days. · **MAKES** ¾ cup (185 mL).

⅓ cup (80 mL) reduced-fat mayonnaise

⅓ cup (80 mL) reduced-fat sour cream

¼ cup (60 mL) sweet tomato chili sauce or ketchup

2 Tbsp (30 mL) water

 ROSE'S TIP
Heinz makes a tomato chili sauce. You can find it in the aisle where ketchup is sold. It consists of ripened tomatoes, garlic, sweet peppers and spices.

 HEALTH TIP
Don't use 0% fat mayonnaise or sour cream; there will be a great loss in flavour.

NUTRITION INFORMATION PER SERVING (1 TBSP/15 ML)

Calories 24	Protein 0.3 g	Cholesterol 3 mg
Carbohydrates 2.2 g	Total fat 0.7 g	Sodium 94 mg
Fibre 0 g	Saturated fat 0.5 g	

CARAMELIZED ONION DIP

I love this dip with crudités or whole-grain crackers. Caramelizing the onions is the key to bringing out their natural sweetness.

1. In a large nonstick skillet sprayed with vegetable spray, heat the oil and add the onion. Sauté for 5 minutes, stirring frequently. On low heat, continue cooking for another 10 minutes or until the onion is soft and browned.

2. Add the sour cream, mayonnaise, cream cheese, salt and pepper and mix until well combined and the cheese is melted. Garnish with parsley and serve with whole wheat crackers, baked tortilla chips or pita wedges.

PREPARATION TIME 10 minutes • **COOKING TIME** 15 minutes •
MAKE AHEAD Keep refrigerated for up to 2 days. • **MAKES** 1 cup (250 mL).

 ROSE'S TIP
Use Vidalia onions if available; they have the sweetest flavour.

 HEALTH TIP
Light cream cheese is reduced in fat by 25%. Never use 0% fat. An ounce (30 g) of real cream cheese has 100 calories and 9 grams of fat compared to light cream cheese, which has 75 calories and 6.8 grams of fat.

2 tsp (10 mL) vegetable oil

3 cups (750 mL) finely diced sweet onion

2 Tbsp (30 mL) reduced-fat sour cream

1 Tbsp (15 mL) reduced-fat mayonnaise

2 Tbsp (30 mL) reduced-fat cream cheese (1 oz/30 g)

⅛ tsp (0.5 mL) salt

⅛ tsp (0.5 mL) ground black pepper

2 Tbsp (30 mL) chopped parsley for garnish

NUTRITION INFORMATION PER SERVING (1 TBSP/15 ML)

Calories 28	Protein 0.6 g	Cholesterol 2 mg
Carbohydrates 3.2 g	Total fat 1.3 g	Sodium 42 mg
Fibre 0.5 g	Saturated fat 0.6 g	

MAPLE APPLE CIDER DRESSING

This is the dressing I created for our salads for Glow Fresh Grill. It goes well with salads that include fruits and nuts.

1. Mix the garlic, mustard, vinegar, maple syrup, olive oil, lemon juice and salt and pepper.

PREPARATION TIME 5 minutes · **MAKE AHEAD** Keep refrigerated for up to 3 days. · **MAKES** ⅔ cup (160 mL).

1½ tsp (7.5 mL) minced garlic

½ tsp (2.5 mL) Dijon mustard

2 Tbsp (30 mL) cider vinegar

3 Tbsp (45 mL) maple syrup

¼ cup (60 mL) olive oil

4 tsp (20 mL) lemon juice

pinch of salt and pepper

ROSE'S TIP
Due to the intense flavour of this dressing, you need only a small amount over your salads.

HEALTH TIP
Maple syrup, a natural sweetener, has over 54 antioxidants that can help prevent diseases caused by free radicals, such as cancer and type 2 diabetes. It also contains high levels of zinc and manganese, keeping the heart healthy and boosting the immune system.

NUTRITION INFORMATION PER SERVING (1 TBSP/15 ML)

Calories 59	Protein 0 g	Cholesterol 0 mg
Carbohydrates 4 g	Total fat 4.8 g	Sodium 29 mg
Fibre 0 g	Saturated fat 0.7 g	

GUACAMOLE

There is nothing more delicious than homemade guacamole. The key is finding a ripe avocado; if it's not ripe, you'll never get the delicate texture and flavour.

1. Combine the avocado, cilantro, mayonnaise, jalapeño, garlic, lemon juice and salt and pepper in a small bowl. Use with crackers or crudités or as a garnish.

PREPARATION TIME 10 minutes • **MAKE AHEAD** Make a couple of hours before serving. Too early and the avocado will brown. • **MAKES** ⅔ cup (160 mL).

½ cup (125 mL) mashed ripe avocado

2 Tbsp (30 mL) chopped cilantro

1 Tbsp (15 mL) reduced-fat mayonnaise

1 tsp (5 mL) finely chopped jalapeño pepper (or ½ tsp/ 2.5 mL hot chili sauce)

½ tsp (2.5 mL) finely chopped garlic

2 tsp (10 mL) lemon or lime juice

pinch of salt and pepper

 ROSE'S TIP

Don't refrigerate an unripe avocado; leave it out at room temperature to ripen.

 HEALTH TIP

Homemade guacamole is a heart-healthy dip, but some commercial brands contain only small amounts of avocado combined with oils and fat, including hydrogenated soybean and coconut oil, corn syrup and modified potato starch. Read the labels.

NUTRITION INFORMATION PER SERVING (1 TBSP/15 ML)

Calories 19	Protein 0.17 g	Cholesterol 0 mg
Carbohydrates 0.9 g	Total fat 1.8 g	Sodium 45 mg
Fibre 0.5 g	Saturated fat 0.3 g	

RED BELL PEPPER HUMMUS

The addition of roasted bell pepper to a hummus dip creates a new flavour and colour. This is great not only as a dip but also as a spread for sandwiches or tortillas.

1. In the bowl of a small food processor, combine the chickpeas, roasted red pepper, tahini, lemon juice, olive oil, water, garlic and chili sauce.

2. Purée until smooth. Garnish with parsley.

PREPARATION TIME 5 minutes · **MAKE AHEAD** Prepare up to a day in advance. · **MAKES** ¾ cup (185 mL).

 ROSE'S TIP
To roast red peppers, cut the pepper in half lengthwise and remove ribs and seeds. Lay on a foil-covered baking sheet and roast at 425°F (220°C) for 25 minutes, or just until browned on all sides. Place bell peppers in a covered bowl and let sit for 10 minutes before peeling off the skin. Store in the fridge for up to 3 days.

 HEALTH TIP
Sesame seeds in tahini have a cholesterol-lowering effect.

½ cup (125 mL) canned chickpeas, drained and rinsed

¼ cup (60 mL) roasted red pepper (about ½ small roasted red pepper) (see Rose's tip, below)

1½ Tbsp (22.5 mL) tahini (sesame seed paste)

1 Tbsp (15 mL) lemon juice

1 Tbsp (15 mL) olive oil

2 tsp (10 mL) water

½ tsp (2.5 mL) finely chopped garlic

½ tsp (2.5 mL) hot chili sauce

2 Tbsp (30 mL) chopped parsley for garnish

NUTRITION INFORMATION PER SERVING (1 TBSP/15 ML)

Calories 33	Protein 0.1 g	Cholesterol 0 mg
Carbohydrates 3.1 g	Total fat 2.1 g	Sodium 32 mg
Fibre 0.7 g	Saturated fat 0.3 g	

TAHINI LEMON DRESSING

This lemony dressing can be spooned over vegetables or used as a dip for sandwiches and wraps. It's also delicious over fish, chicken or beef.

1. Purée the stock, ricotta, tahini, mayonnaise, olive oil, lemon juice, soy sauce and garlic in the bowl of a small food processor until smooth. Add chopped cilantro.

PREPARATION TIME 10 minutes · **MAKE AHEAD** Refrigerate for up to 3 days. · **MAKES** 1 cup (250 mL).

 ROSE'S TIP
This is perfect for a light and healthy falafel dressing.

 HEALTH TIP
Store-bought tahini can have 50 calories and 4 grams of fat per table-spoon (15 mL).

⅓ cup (80 mL) low-sodium chicken or vegetable stock

⅓ cup (80 mL) reduced-fat ricotta cheese (3 oz/90 g)

2 Tbsp (30 mL) tahini (sesame seed paste)

2 Tbsp (30 mL) reduced-fat mayonnaise

2 Tbsp (30 mL) olive oil

1 Tbsp (15 mL) fresh lemon juice

1 Tbsp (15 mL) low-sodium soy sauce

1 tsp (5 mL) minced fresh garlic

¼ cup (60 mL) chopped fresh cilantro or parsley

NUTRITION INFORMATION PER SERVING (1 TBSP/15 ML)

Calories 26	Protein 0.7 g	Cholesterol 1 mg
Carbohydrates 0.9 g	Total fat 2.1 g	Sodium 40 mg
Fibre 0.1 g	Saturated fat 0.5 g	

BLACK OLIVE HUMMUS

A great twist on hummus using black olives. For a change, try green pitted olives. Serve with crackers or veggies or as a spread over sandwiches or wraps.

1. Add the chickpeas, tahini, water, oil, lemon juice, garlic and chili paste to the bowl of a food processor. Purée until smooth. Add the olives and garnish with the basil.

PREPARATION TIME 10 minutes · **MAKE AHEAD** Refrigerate for up to 3 days. · **MAKES** 1½ cups (375 mL).

 ROSE'S TIP
You could use white kidney or navy beans to replace the chickpeas. Omit the water, since these beans have more moisture.

 HEALTH TIP
Hummus dips are healthier and lower in fat and calories than store-bought dips used for crackers or veggies, which can contain over 50 calories and 5 grams of fat per tablespoon.

1 cup (250 mL) canned chickpeas, drained and rinsed

¼ cup (60 mL) tahini (sesame seed paste)

3 Tbsp (45 mL) water

2 Tbsp (30 mL) olive oil

2 Tbsp (30 mL) lemon juice

1 tsp (5 mL) crushed garlic

½ tsp (2.5 mL) chili paste

⅓ cup (80 mL) finely diced black olives

2 Tbsp (30 mL) chopped basil or parsley for garnish

NUTRITION INFORMATION PER SERVING (1 TBSP/15 ML)

Calories 38	Protein 1 g	Cholesterol 0 mg
Carbohydrates 3.2 g	Total fat 2.5 g	Sodium 45 mg
Fibre 0.7 g	Saturated fat 0.4 g	

TZATZIKI

This delicious Middle Eastern sauce is light and healthy, and so easy to make at home. I love using reduced-fat yogurt, which adds to the richness and thickness of the dish. Serve with burgers, sandwiches or wraps. It even works well as a sauce over fish, chicken or beef.

½ cup (125 mL) grated, peeled, seeded cucumber

pinch of salt and pepper

¾ cup (185 mL) reduced-fat plain Greek yogurt

1 tsp (5 mL) fresh chopped dill

1 tsp (5 mL) lemon juice

½ tsp (2.5 mL) minced garlic

1 tsp (5 mL) olive oil

1. Gently squeeze out excess moisture from the cucumber. Then mix with the salt and pepper, yogurt, dill, lemon juice, garlic and olive oil.

PREPARATION TIME 10 minutes · **MAKE AHEAD** Best if served the same day. · **MAKES** 1 cup (250 mL).

ROSE'S TIP
If you don't have time to prepare this sauce, your supermarket will carry some healthy brands. Read the labels to ensure you're not getting mayonnaise. You want yogurt in the product.

HEALTH TIP
A great breakfast item is plain reduced-fat yogurt with fruit and whole-grain cereal. The protein in the yogurt (18 grams per ¾ cup/185 mL) will keep you going all morning.

NUTRITION INFORMATION PER SERVING (1 TBSP/15 ML)

Calories 10	Protein 1.3 g	Cholesterol 0 mg
Carbohydrates 0.8 g	Total fat 0.6 g	Sodium 12 mg
Fibre 0.1 g	Saturated fat 0.1 g	

QUICK BASIC TOMATO SAUCE

This is a great sauce to have in the refrigerator or freezer for pasta or other grains, homemade pizzas or any dish requiring tomato sauce. You can make it more interesting by adding dried herbs, your choice of vegetables, or ground beef, chicken or soy

1. Heat the oil in a large nonstick saucepan over medium heat. Sauté the onion and garlic for 3 minutes, stirring often.

2. Add the tomatoes, basil, oregano, bay leaves, sugar and salt and pepper. Reduce the heat to low and cook for 15 minutes, stirring occasionally, until it has reduced slightly. Add the cheese.

PREPARATION TIME 5 minutes · **COOKING TIME** 18 minutes ·
MAKE AHEAD Refrigerate for up to 2 days or freeze for up to 6 weeks. After defrosting, add 2 Tbsp (30 mL) tomato paste to thicken. ·
MAKES 2½ cups (625 mL).

ROSE'S TIP
To make a thicker sauce, add 2 tablespoons (30 mL) of tomato paste during the cooking.

HEALTH TIP
Cooked tomatoes have more of the antioxidant lycopene than fresh ones. Lycopene is associated with a lower risk of prostate cancer.

2 tsp (10 mL) olive oil

⅔ cup (160 mL) finely chopped onion

2 tsp (10 mL) crushed fresh garlic

one 28 oz (796 mL) can crushed plum tomatoes

2 tsp (10 mL) dried basil

1 tsp (5 mL) dried oregano

2 bay leaves

2 tsp (10 mL) granulated sugar

pinch of salt and pepper

2 Tbsp (30 mL) grated Parmesan cheese (½ oz/15 g) (optional)

NUTRITION INFORMATION PER SERVING (½ CUP/125 ML)

Calories 60	Protein 2 g	Cholesterol 0 mg
Carbohydrates 10 g	Total fat 2 g	Sodium 360 mg
Fibre 1 g	Saturated fat 0 g	

FRESH TOMATO SALSA

There's no comparison between a homemade salsa and a salsa from the grocery store. The key is to use ripe, sweet tomatoes. Serve with tortilla chips, as a side condiment with Mexican dishes, or on top of chicken, fish or meat.

1. Combine the tomatoes, onion, olive oil, lemon juice, cilantro, basil, garlic, salt and pepper and jalapeño.

PREPARATION TIME 10 minutes · **MAKE AHEAD** Prepare up to 4 hours in advance. · **MAKES** 1⅓ cups (335 mL).

ROSE'S TIP
Leave your tomatoes out at room temperature to ripen. If you refrigerate them, they will stop ripening.

HEALTH TIP
Tomatoes are rich in vitamin A. A 1½-cup (375 mL) serving contains 15% of your daily requirement and 40% of your vitamin C requirement. Both these vitamins are antioxidants known to fight free radicals.

1½ cups (375 mL) diced plum tomatoes

¼ cup (60 mL) diced red onion

2 Tbsp (30 mL) olive oil

2 tsp (10 mL) lemon juice

3 Tbsp (45 mL) chopped cilantro

2 Tbsp (30 mL) fresh chopped basil

1 tsp (5 mL) minced garlic

pinch of salt and pepper

1 tsp (5 mL) minced jalapeño pepper

NUTRITION INFORMATION PER SERVING (3 TBSP/45 ML)

Calories 36	Protein 0.3 g	Cholesterol 0 mg
Carbohydrates 0.9 g	Total fat 3.9 g	Sodium 40 mg
Fibre 0.3 g	Saturated fat 0.6 g	

BASIL PESTO

You'll never find a more versatile sauce. I make it in batches when basil is plentiful and freeze it in small containers for use throughout the year. You can substitute other leaves such as parsley, cilantro and spinach for a variety of flavours. Use it over grains or as a topping for fish, meat, chicken or vegetables.

1. Purée the basil, both cheeses, olive oil, stock, pine nuts, garlic and salt and pepper until smooth in a small food processor. If too thick, add a little water.

PREPARATION TIME 10 minutes · **MAKE AHEAD** Refrigerate for up to 3 days or freeze for up to 3 months. · **MAKES** about ⅔ cup (160 mL).

 ROSE'S TIP
For easy use, I put the pesto in ice cube trays and use as needed.

 HEALTH TIP
Never buy "light" olive oil instead of extra virgin olive oil. Light means it has been combined with other oils and diluted.

1 cup (250 mL) packed fresh basil leaves

2 Tbsp (30 mL) grated Parmesan cheese (½ oz/15 g)

2 Tbsp (30 mL) reduced-fat cream cheese (1 oz/30 g)

2 Tbsp (30 mL) olive oil

3 Tbsp (45 mL) water or low-sodium stock

1 Tbsp (15 mL) toasted pine nuts or chopped almonds

1 tsp (5 mL) minced garlic

pinch of salt and pepper

NUTRITION INFORMATION PER SERVING (1 TBSP/15 ML)

Calories 26	Protein 0.5 g	Cholesterol 1 mg
Carbohydrates 0.3 g	Total fat 2.4 g	Sodium 17 mg
Fibre 0.3 g	Saturated fat 0.4 g	

HOISIN SAUCE

I could put hoisin sauce over anything! The sweet Asian flavours go well with grains, vegetables and meat, chicken or fish.

1. Combine the hoisin sauce, soy sauce, rice vinegar, brown sugar, sesame oil, garlic and ginger in a small bowl.

PREPARATION TIME 5 minutes · **MAKE AHEAD** Prepare up to 3 days in advance. · **MAKES** ½ cup (125 mL).

 ROSE'S TIP

I make large batches of this sauce and freeze them in small containers for later use.

 HEALTH TIP

If you want to avoid sodium in rice vinegar, don't use the seasoned variety. One tablespoon (15 mL) has 250 mg of sodium, whereas plain rice vinegar has no sodium.

3 Tbsp (45 mL) hoisin sauce

2 Tbsp (30 mL) low-sodium soy sauce

2 Tbsp (30 mL) rice vinegar

1½ Tbsp (22.5 mL) brown sugar

1 tsp (5 mL) sesame oil

1 tsp (5 mL) finely chopped garlic

½ tsp (2.5 mL) finely chopped ginger

NUTRITION INFORMATION PER SERVING (1 TBSP/15 ML)

Calories 22	Protein 0.4 g	Cholesterol 0 mg
Carbohydrates 3.9 g	Total fat 0.6 g	Sodium 184 mg
Fibre 0.2 g	Saturated fat 0.1 g	

HOISIN TERIYAKI SAUCE

Take the two best flavours from Asian cooking, combine them and you have a winning sauce—so easy to prepare and versatile. You can use this over chicken, fish, meat, rice or noodles.

1. Combine the sugar, soy sauce, rice vinegar, hoisin sauce, water, sesame oil, cornstarch, garlic, ginger and sesame seeds until the cornstarch is dissolved. Place in a skillet and simmer for 2 minutes, just until slightly thickened.

PREPARATION TIME 10 minutes · **COOKING TIME** 2 minutes ·
MAKE AHEAD Refrigerate this sauce for up to 7 days. Add some water when reheating. · **MAKES** ½ cup (125 mL).

ROSE'S TIP
I triple this recipe and spread it over an entire side of salmon and bake it.

HEALTH TIP
Garlic pre-chopped and stored in oil loses its allicin in about one hour. Allicin helps to lower cholesterol and high blood pressure and is an antioxidant. Bottled garlic is inferior to fresh in terms of flavour and nutrients.

3 Tbsp (45 mL) brown sugar

2 Tbsp (30 mL) low-sodium soy sauce

1 Tbsp (15 mL) rice vinegar

1 Tbsp (15 mL) hoisin sauce

1 Tbsp (15 mL) water

2 tsp (10 mL) sesame oil

2 tsp (10 mL) cornstarch

1 tsp (5 mL) chopped garlic

1 tsp (5 mL) chopped ginger

1 tsp (5 mL) sesame seeds

NUTRITION INFORMATION PER SERVING (1 TBSP/15 ML)

Calories 37	Protein 0.3 g	Cholesterol 0 mg
Carbohydrates 6.5 g	Total fat 1.2 g	Sodium 148 mg
Fibre 0.2 g	Saturated fat 0.2 g	

TERIYAKI SAUCE

This has to be the best sauce I've ever made, and it's so versatile. Use it in a stir-fry, over vegetables or over fish, chicken, meat or noodles.

1. Combine the brown sugar, soy sauce, water, rice vinegar, sesame oil, cornstarch, garlic and ginger in a small saucepan. Bring to a boil over medium-high heat, whisking constantly. Reduce the heat to a simmer and cook for 2 minutes or until the sauce has thickened slightly.

PREPARATION TIME 10 minutes • **COOKING TIME** 2 minutes •
MAKE AHEAD Keep refrigerated for up to 7 days. Add more water and reheat to reuse. • Makes ⅔ cup (160 mL).

 ROSE'S TIP
I make this sauce in batches and freeze in small containers.

 HEALTH TIP
If you pre-chop your garlic and store it in oil, be sure to refrigerate immediately and don't keep for over 2 days. Bacteria can grow that could cause botulism.

3 Tbsp (45 mL) packed brown sugar

2 Tbsp (30 mL) low-sodium soy sauce

3 Tbsp (45 mL) water (or low-sodium chicken stock)

2 Tbsp (30 mL) rice vinegar

2 tsp (10 mL) sesame oil

1 tsp (5 mL) cornstarch

1 tsp (5 mL) finely chopped garlic

½ tsp (2.5 mL) finely chopped ginger

NUTRITION INFORMATION PER SERVING (1 TBSP/15 ML)

Calories 24	Protein 0.2 g	Cholesterol 0 mg
Carbohydrates 4.3 g	Total fat 0.8 g	Sodium 98 mg
Fibre 0 g	Saturated fat 0.1 g	

PEANUT SAUCE

Everyone needs a light and delicious peanut sauce. Use it over chicken, fish or meat or over rice noodles. Substitute any other nut butter if there are allergies to peanuts.

1. In the bowl of a small food processor, combine the peanut butter, water, cilantro, honey, rice vinegar, soy sauce, sesame oil, garlic and ginger until smooth.

PREPARATION TIME 10 minutes · **MAKE AHEAD** Refrigerate for up to 3 days. · **MAKES** ½ cup (125 mL).

2 Tbsp (30 mL) natural peanut butter

2 Tbsp (30 mL) water

2 Tbsp (30 mL) chopped fresh cilantro

1 Tbsp (15 mL) honey

1 Tbsp (15 mL) rice vinegar

2 tsp (10 mL) low-sodium soy sauce

1 tsp (5 mL) sesame oil

½ tsp (2.5 mL) minced garlic

½ tsp (2.5 mL) minced fresh ginger

 ROSE'S TIP

Triple this recipe and freeze it in ice cube trays for a quick flavouring for your dishes.

 HEALTH TIP

Natural peanut butter has nothing but peanuts. Commercial peanut butters contain sugar and are often hydrogenated to make them smooth and creamy.

NUTRITION INFORMATION PER SERVING (1 TBSP/15 ML)

Calories 32

Carbohydrates 3.7 g

Fibre 0.2 g

Protein 1 g

Total fat 1.7 g

Saturated fat 0.3 g

Cholesterol 0 mg

Sodium 63 mg

PEANUT COCONUT SAUCE

Peanut butter and light coconut milk are true Asian flavours. This sauce can go over rice, noodles, chicken, beef or fish. It has a multitude of uses.

1. In a bowl, whisk together the coconut milk, peanut butter, soy sauce, sesame oil, rice vinegar, honey, garlic, ginger and chili sauce.

PREPARATION TIME 10 minutes · **MAKE AHEAD** Refrigerate for up to 3 days. · **MAKES** ½ cup (125 mL).

 ROSE'S TIP
Thai Kitchen and Taste of Thai both make a delicious light coconut sauce.

 HEALTH TIP
Restaurant peanut sauces have about 60 calories and 5 grams of fat per tablespoon (15 mL).

¼ cup (60 mL) light coconut milk

2 Tbsp (30 mL) natural peanut butter

2 tsp (10 mL) low-sodium soy sauce

2 tsp (10 mL) sesame oil

2 tsp (10 mL) rice vinegar

1 tsp (5 mL) honey

1 tsp (5 mL) finely chopped garlic

½ tsp (2.5 mL) finely chopped ginger

½ tsp (2.5 mL) hot chili sauce (Sriracha)

NUTRITION INFORMATION PER SERVING (1 TBSP/15 ML)

Calories 37	Protein 1 g	Cholesterol 0 mg
Carbohydrates 2.4 g	Total fat 2.6 g	Sodium 65 mg
Fibre 0.2 g	Saturated fat 0.7 g	

ORANGE SESAME DRESSING

A great dressing over any greens. The orange juice concentrate gives a more intense flavour than just orange juice. Use it straight from the freezer.

1. Whisk the juice concentrate, sugar, vinegar, soy sauce, oil, garlic, ginger, chili sauce and salt in a small bowl.

PREPARATION TIME 5 minutes · **MAKE AHEAD** Make up to 3 days in advance. · **MAKES** ½ cup (125 mL).

 ROSE'S TIP
You can also use apple juice concentrate for salad dressings that will benefit from an apple flavour.

 HEALTH TIP
Sesame oil is a source of vitamin E, which is an antioxidant that can lower bad cholesterol. It also contains copper, which relieves rheumatoid arthritis.

2 Tbsp (30 mL) orange juice concentrate

1½ Tbsp (22.5 mL) packed brown sugar

2 Tbsp (30 mL) rice vinegar

2 Tbsp (30 mL) low-sodium soy sauce

2 tsp (10 mL) sesame oil

1 tsp (5 mL) minced fresh garlic

½ tsp (2.5 mL) minced fresh ginger

½ tsp (2.5 mL) hot Asian chili sauce

pinch of salt

NUTRITION INFORMATION PER SERVING (1 TBSP/15 ML)

Calories 26	Protein 0.4 g	Cholesterol 0 mg
Carbohydrates 3.9 g	Total fat 1.1 g	Sodium 171 mg
Fibre 0.1 g	Saturated fat 0.2 g	

SESAME MAYO SAUCE

Sesame oil and light mayo make a great spread for a sandwich, tortilla or quesadilla.

1. Combine the mayonnaise, sour cream, sesame oil and soy sauce until smooth.

PREPARATION TIME 5 minutes · **MAKE AHEAD** Can be refrigerated for up to 3 days. · **MAKES** ½ cup (125 mL).

 ROSE'S TIP
This sauce is great over a veggie burger or even falafel balls.

 HEALTH TIP
Be sure not to buy imitation mayonnaise like Miracle Whip, which is just a salad dressing not a true mayonnaise. It consists of water, vinegar, soybean oil, modified food starch, high-fructose corn syrup, sugar, eggs and artificial flavour.

2 Tbsp (30 mL) reduced-fat mayonnaise

¼ cup (60 mL) reduced-fat sour cream

2 tsp (10 mL) sesame oil

2 tsp (10 mL) low-sodium soy sauce

NUTRITION INFORMATION PER SERVING (1 TBSP/15 ML)

Calories 33	Protein 0.4 g	Cholesterol 4 mg
Carbohydrates 1.4 g	Total fat 2.2 g	Sodium 93 mg
Fibre 0 g	Saturated fat 0.9 g	

DESSERTS

MINI ESPRESSO
CHOCOLATE MUD PIES

These are the best-selling desserts at Rose Reisman Catering. They are so dense, they will put you into chocolate heaven. You will never believe they are low-fat. Drizzle with melted chocolate for an extra special touch.

1. Preheat the oven to 350°F (175°C). Lightly coat a 12-cup muffin tin with cooking spray.

2. In a small bowl, combine the crumbs, 1 Tbsp (15 mL) water and oil until mixed. Divide and pat into the bottom of the muffin tins.

3. In a small bowl, combine the chocolate chips, 2 Tbsp (30 mL) hot water and instant coffee. Microwave for 40 seconds on High or just until the chocolate begins to melt. Stir until smooth.

4. In the bowl of a food processor, add the sugar, cocoa powder, flour, cream cheese, eggs, sour cream, corn syrup and vanilla. Purée until smooth. Add the chocolate mixture and purée until smooth. Divide among the muffin cups and bake for 12 to 14 minutes or just until the centres are still slightly loose. Cool and chill at least 2 hours before serving. Carefully remove from the tin with a knife. Decorate with icing sugar.

PREPARATION TIME 15 minutes · **BAKING TIME** 12 minutes ·
MAKE AHEAD Make these a day in advance and keep refrigerated. ·
MAKES 12 servings.

1 cup (250 mL) chocolate wafer crumbs

1 Tbsp (15 mL) water

2 tsp (10 mL) vegetable oil

2 Tbsp (30 mL) semisweet chocolate chips

2 Tbsp (30 mL) hot water

1 tsp (5 mL) instant coffee

1 cup (250 mL) packed brown sugar

½ cup (125 mL) cocoa powder

2 Tbsp (30 mL) all-purpose flour

¼ cup + 1 Tbsp (75 mL) reduced-fat cream cheese (2½ oz/75 g)

2 large eggs

¼ cup (60 mL) reduced-fat sour cream

3 Tbsp (45 mL) corn syrup

1 tsp (5 mL) vanilla extract

icing sugar for decoration

 ROSE'S TIP
To make a 9-inch (23 cm) pie from this recipe, bake for about 25 minutes or just until the centre is slightly loose.

 HEALTH TIP
Cocoa powder is great in low-fat cooking because it has the base flavour of chocolate without the butterfat.

NUTRITION INFORMATION PER SERVING (1 PIE)

Calories 220	Protein 3.6 g	Cholesterol 23 mg
Carbohydrates 30 g	Total fat 5.8 g	
Fibre 1.5 g	Saturated fat 2.1 g	

CHOCOLATE BROWNIE BANANA CAKE WITH CREAM CHEESE FROSTING

I love banana cake and I love brownies. Well, take the elements of both and make a new dessert! These flavours have always gone well together. Use the ripest bananas you have. I always freeze my leftover ripe bananas in their skin and use them for baking.

1. Preheat the oven to 350°F (175°C). Lightly coat a 9-inch (23 cm) square baking pan with cooking spray.

2. TO MAKE THE BROWNIE CAKE Combine the sugar, oil, egg and vanilla in a bowl until well mixed. Add the cocoa and mix well. Add the flour, baking powder, yogurt and chocolate chips, mixing just until combined and smooth. Don't overmix. Pour the batter into the pan.

3. TO MAKE THE BANANA CAKE Combine the sugar, oil, egg, vanilla and banana in a bowl until well mixed. Add the yogurt, flour, baking powder and baking soda. Mix until just combined. Pour over the brownie cake.

4. Bake for 25 minutes or just until a tester comes out dry.

5. TO MAKE THE FROSTING Blend all the icing ingredients in a blender or food processor until smooth. If too thick, add a few drops of water. Spread on the cake once cool, and serve.

PREPARATION TIME 20 minutes • **BAKING TIME** 25 minutes •
MAKE AHEAD Make a day in advance and keep refrigerated. •
MAKES 16 servings.

Brownie cake

⅔ cup (160 mL) granulated sugar

¼ cup (60 mL) vegetable oil

1 egg

1 tsp (5 mL) vanilla extract

⅓ cup (80 mL) unsweetened cocoa powder

⅓ cup (80 mL) all-purpose flour

1 tsp (5 mL) baking powder

¼ cup (60 mL) reduced-fat plain yogurt (or reduced-fat sour cream)

¼ cup (60 mL) semisweet chocolate chips

Banana cake

½ cup (125 mL) granulated sugar

3 Tbsp (45 mL) vegetable oil

1 egg

1 tsp (5 mL) vanilla extract

1 large ripe banana, mashed (about ½ cup/125 mL)

3 Tbsp (45 mL) reduced-fat plain yogurt (or reduced-fat sour cream)

ROSE'S TIP

If you ever need a larger cake, you can double this recipe and use a 9- × 13-inch (3.5 L) rectangular baking pan. You will need to bake about 15 minutes longer or until a tester comes out dry.

HEALTH TIP

Chocolate chips are fine in moderation and to highlight a dessert like this. A quarter-cup (60 mL) contains 280 calories and 16 grams of fat.

¾ cup (185 mL) all-purpose flour

1 tsp (5 mL) baking powder

½ tsp (2.5 mL) baking soda

Frosting

¼ cup (60 mL) softened reduced-fat cream cheese (2 oz/60 g)

⅔ cup (160 mL) icing sugar

1½ tsp (7.5 mL) cocoa powder

NUTRITION INFORMATION PER SERVING

Calories 213	Protein 3.6 g	Cholesterol 29 mg
Carbohydrates 32 g	Total fat 8.5 g	
Fibre 1.5 g	Saturated fat 1.8 g	

PEANUT BUTTER BROWNIE CHEESECAKE

Peanut butter, cheesecake and chocolate flavours combine to make this an outstanding, decadent dessert. I keep the fat and calories down by using a combination of ricotta and light cream cheese and more cocoa powder than chocolate.

1. Preheat the oven to 350°F (175°C). Lightly coat a 9-inch (2.5 L) springform pan with cooking spray.

2. **TO MAKE THE BROWNIE LAYER** Beat together the sugar, oil, egg and vanilla in a bowl. In another bowl, stir together the flour, cocoa and baking powder. Stir the wet mixture into the dry mixture just until combined. Stir in the sour cream and chocolate chips. Pour the mixture into the pan.

3. **TO MAKE THE CHEESECAKE LAYER** Combine the ricotta, sugar, cream cheese, sour cream, peanut butter, egg, flour and vanilla in a food processor. Process until smooth. Pour the mixture on top of the brownie layer.

4. Bake the cheesecake in the centre of the oven for 35 minutes. The brownie layer may rise slightly around the edges. Chill before serving. Decorate with the icing sugar.

PREPARATION TIME 15 minutes • **BAKING TIME** 35 minutes •
MAKE AHEAD Make cheesecake up to a day early. Keep refrigerated. •
MAKES 12 servings.

Brownie layer

⅔ cup (160 mL) granulated sugar

¼ cup (60 mL) vegetable oil

1 large egg

1 tsp (5 mL) vanilla extract

⅓ cup (80 mL) all-purpose flour

⅓ cup (80 mL) unsweetened cocoa powder

1 tsp (5 mL) baking powder

¼ cup (60 mL) reduced-fat sour cream

¼ cup (60 mL) semisweet chocolate chips

Cheesecake layer

1½ cups (375 mL) reduced-fat ricotta cheese (12 oz/375 g)

1 cup (250 mL) granulated sugar

½ cup (125 mL) softened reduced-fat cream cheese (4 oz/125 g)

⅓ cup (80 mL) reduced-fat sour cream

ROSE'S TIP
Always buy peanut butter
with peanuts only. The
processed varieties contain
icing sugar.

 HEALTH TIP
Light (5%) ricotta cheese is
a smooth and tasty product
and has only 80 calories
and 4 grams of fat per
⅓ cup (80 mL). Whole
milk ricotta has 140 calories and 10 grams of fat per
⅓ cup (80 mL).

⅓ cup (80 mL) smooth
natural peanut butter

1 large egg

2 Tbsp (30 mL) all-purpose
flour

1½ tsp (7.5 mL) vanilla extract

icing sugar for decoration

NUTRITION INFORMATION PER SERVING

Calories 304	Protein 8.1 g	Cholesterol 53 mg
Carbohydrates 36 g	Total fat 14 g	
Fibre 1.6 g	Saturated fat 4.4 g	

S'MORES CHOCOLATE LAYER CAKE

This has to be the most delicious and fun-to-make cake I have ever created. Think of your summertime memories of making s'mores around the bonfire. Now take that idea and turn it into a cake! All the people who tested this with me had permanent smiles on their faces!

1. TO MAKE THE CAKE Preheat the oven to 350°F (175°C). Lightly coat two 8-inch (20 cm) round baking pans with cooking spray.

2. Combine the chocolate chips and hot water in a small bowl. Microwave on High for 30 seconds. Mix until smooth.

3. In a large mixing bowl, combine the sugar, oil, eggs and vanilla with a whisk until smooth. Add the cocoa powder, sour cream, mayonnaise and melted chocolate. Mix until combined. Add the flour, baking powder and baking soda. Mix just until combined.

4. Pour into the pans and bake for 18 minutes or until a tester comes out dry. Let cool.

5. TO MAKE THE TOPPING Melt the 1 cup (250 mL) of chocolate and the milk in the microwave for 20 seconds just enough to mix the chocolate and milk until smooth. Let cool for 5 minutes to thicken.

6. Heat the marshmallow fluff for 10 seconds in the microwave to soften.

7. Place one cake layer on a plate, spread half the chocolate sauce over the top and sides of the cake, then half the marshmallow, and sprinkle with 1 Tbsp (15 mL) of the chocolate chips and ½ the broken graham cookie crumbs.

continued ...

Cake

⅓ cup (80 mL) semisweet chocolate chips

¼ cup (60 mL) hot water

1 cup (250 mL) granulated sugar

¼ cup (60 mL) vegetable oil

2 large eggs

1 tsp (5 mL) vanilla extract

½ cup (125 mL) cocoa powder

¾ cup (185 mL) reduced-fat sour cream

⅓ cup (80 mL) reduced-fat mayonnaise

1 cup (250 mL) all-purpose flour

1½ tsp (7.5 mL) baking powder

½ tsp (2.5 mL) baking soda

Topping

1 cup (250 mL) semisweet chocolate chips

⅓ cup (80 mL) canned evaporated 2% milk

1 cup (250 mL) marshmallow fluff

2 Tbsp (30 mL) semisweet chocolate chips

7 graham cookie wafers, broken into small pieces

S'mores Chocolate Layer Cake (continued)

8. Place the other cake layer overtop, pour the remaining chocolate sauce on top and spread around the sides, then add the remaining marshmallow, chocolate chips and cookie crumbs.

PREPARATION TIME 20 minutes · **BAKING TIME** 18 minutes ·
MAKE AHEAD Assemble the cake up to a day in advance and keep covered and refrigerated. · **MAKES** 16 servings.

 ROSE'S TIP
You will find marshmallow fluff, made by Kraft and Jiffy, in the baking aisle of your supermarket. It's best to slightly heat the fluff in a microwave oven for 10 seconds to make it more spreadable.

 HEALTH TIP
The saying "to have your cake and eat it too" goes well for this dessert. A regular piece of chocolate cake would have at least double the calories and fat.

NUTRITION INFORMATION PER SERVING

Calories 280	Protein 3.3 g	Cholesterol 23 mg
Carbohydrates 36.3 g	Total fat 13.4 g	
Fibre 1.9 g	Saturated fat 4 g	

PEANUT BUTTER BROWNIES

If you love peanut butter and chocolate, these brownies will become a favourite treat. Using cocoa and reduced-fat yogurt prevents using excess sugar and oil or butter. Peanut butter chips are in the baking section of your grocery store

1. Preheat the oven to 350°F (175°C). Spray an 8-inch (20 cm) square pan with cooking oil.

2. FOR THE BROWNIES Combine the sugar, oil, egg and vanilla in a bowl and mix well. Add the cocoa, mixing it in well. Add the flour, baking powder, yogurt and peanut butter chips, mixing just until combined and smooth. Don't overmix.

3. Pour the batter into the prepared pan. Bake in the centre of the oven for 15 to 20 minutes just until set. Do not overbake. Cool on a rack for 15 minutes before icing.

4. TO MAKE THE ICING Place cream cheese, icing sugar, peanut butter and water in a blender or food processor and process until smooth. Spread overtop of the brownies. Dust with icing sugar.

PREPARATION TIME 10 minutes · **BAKING TIME** 20 minutes ·
MAKE AHEAD Bake up to a day in advance. These can be frozen for up to a month. · **MAKES** 12 squares.

NUTRITION INFORMATION PER SERVING (1 SQUARE)

Calories 164	Protein 2 g	Cholesterol 20 mg
Carbohydrates 24.9 g	Total fat 6.8 g	
Fibre 1 g	Saturated fat 2.1 g	

Brownies

⅔ cup (160 mL) granulated sugar

¼ cup (60 mL) vegetable oil

1 large egg

1 tsp (5 mL) pure vanilla extract

⅓ cup (80 mL) unsweetened cocoa powder

⅓ cup (80 mL) all-purpose flour

1 tsp (5 mL) baking powder

¼ cup (60 mL) reduced-fat plain yogurt or reduced-fat sour cream

¼ cup (60 mL) peanut butter chips

Icing

¼ cup (60 mL) reduced-fat cream cheese (2 oz/60 g)

½ cup (125 mL) icing sugar

1 Tbsp (15 mL) smooth peanut butter

2 Tbsp (30 mL) water

ROSE'S TIP

If there is a peanut allergy, just use chocolate chips and another nut butter such as almond or cashew butter in the icing.

HEALTH TIP

Peanut butter chips have more fat (7 g) per ounce than semisweet chocolate chips (9 g).

TRIPLE CHOCOLATE BROWNIES WITH CREAM CHEESE FROSTING

You will never taste a better brownie that's lighter in calories and fat. I've featured them in my catering company and they rank as the number-one dessert. The cocoa, oil and yogurt that replace the traditional butter and chocolate are the way to keep the calorie and fat count low.

1. Preheat the oven to 350°F (175°C). Spray an 8-inch (20 cm) square pan with cooking oil.

2. TO MAKE THE BROWNIES Combine the sugar, oil, egg and vanilla in a bowl and mix well. Add the cocoa, mixing it in well. Add the flour, baking powder, yogurt and chocolate chips, mixing just until combined and smooth. Don't overmix.

3. Pour the batter into the prepared pan. Bake in the centre of the oven for 15 to 20 minutes, just until set. Do not overbake. Cool on a rack for 15 minutes before icing.

4. TO MAKE THE ICING Place all the icing ingredients in a blender or food processor and process until smooth. Add a few drops of water if too thick. Spread over the top of the brownies.

5. Cut into squares and garnish with a dusting of icing sugar.

PREPARATION TIME 10 minutes · **BAKING TIME** 15 to 20 minutes ·
MAKE AHEAD Make these brownies a day in advance. Keep refrigerated.
They also freeze well for up to 2 months. · **MAKES** 12 servings.

Brownies

⅔ cup (160 mL) granulated sugar

¼ cup (60 mL) vegetable oil

1 large egg

1 tsp (5 mL) pure vanilla extract

⅓ cup (80 mL) unsweetened cocoa powder

⅓ cup (80 mL) all-purpose flour

1 tsp (5 mL) baking powder

¼ cup (60 mL) reduced-fat yogurt or reduced-fat sour cream

¼ cup (60 mL) semisweet chocolate chips

Icing

¼ cup (60 mL) reduced-fat cream cheese (2 oz/60 g)

⅔ cup (160 mL) icing sugar

1½ tsp (7.5 mL) cocoa powder

dusting of icing sugar for decoration

ROSE'S TIP

These brownies go so fast
I tend to triple the recipe
and bake in a 9- × 13-inch
(3.5 L) pan. Bake for about
25 minutes or until the
centre is just set.

 HEALTH TIP

I like to use only mono-
unsaturated oils such as
organic canola, peanut and
grapeseed oil. They have
the lowest amount of saturated fat. Corn, safflower
and sunflower oil are
polyunsaturated fats and
contain more saturated fat.

NUTRITION INFORMATION PER SERVING

Calories 140	Protein 2.3 g	Cholesterol 19 mg
Carbohydrates 20 g	Total fat 7 g	
Fibre 1.2 g	Saturated fat 1.5 g	

CHOCOLATE FUDGE CHEESECAKE WITH SOUR CREAM TOPPING

You'll never eat a cheesecake that's so dense and rich tasting, yet so low in fat and calories. The combination of semisweet chocolate and cocoa powder gives this cheesecake its velvety chocolate flavour. Garnish with fresh berries if desired.

1. Preheat the oven to 350°F (175°C). Spray a 9-inch (2.5 L) springform pan with cooking oil.

2. FOR THE CRUST Combine the wafer crumbs, water and oil in a small bowl and mix well. Pat onto the bottom and slightly up the sides of the springform pan.

3. FOR THE FILLING Combine the chocolate chips and water in a small microwaveable bowl and heat in a microwave oven for 40 seconds. Stir until smooth.

4. Combine the chocolate mixture with the ricotta and cream cheeses, sugar, cocoa, egg, sour cream and flour in the bowl of a food processor and purée until smooth. Pour over the crust. Bake for 30 minutes. The centre should still be slightly loose.

5. FOR THE TOPPING Mix the sour cream and sugar. Carefully spoon over the cake. Bake for another 10 minutes. Cool on a rack, then chill completely before removing the sides of the pan and serving.

PREPARATION TIME 10 minutes • **BAKING TIME** 40 minutes •
MAKE AHEAD Make the cake up to a day in advance. Keep refrigerated. •
MAKES 12 servings.

Crust

2 cups (500 mL) chocolate wafer crumbs

2 Tbsp (30 mL) water

1 Tbsp (15 mL) vegetable oil

Filling

⅓ cup (80 mL) semisweet chocolate chips

2 Tbsp (30 mL) water

1½ cups (375 mL) reduced-fat ricotta cheese (12 oz/375 g)

½ cup (125 mL) reduced-fat cream cheese (4 oz/125 g)

1 cup (250 mL) granulated sugar

¼ cup (60 mL) unsweetened cocoa powder

1 large egg

½ cup (125 mL) reduced-fat sour cream

2 Tbsp (30 mL) all-purpose flour

Topping

1¼ cups (310 mL) reduced-fat sour cream

2 Tbsp (30 mL) sugar

ROSE'S TIP

Chocolate wafer crumbs
are made by Nabisco, but
if you want to save money,
purchase the chocolate
wafers and process them in
a food processor.

 HEALTH TIP

A half-cup (125 mL)
portion of ricotta cheese
contains 260 mg of
calcium, which is 26% of
your daily requirement.
Calcium helps to build
strong bones and prevent
osteoporosis.

NUTRITION INFORMATION PER SERVING

Calories 259	Protein 6.2 g	Cholesterol 34 mg
Carbohydrates 36 g	Total fat 10 g	
Fibre 1.2 g	Saturated fat 5.0 g	

CARAMELIZED BANANA STREUSEL CAKE

This blows traditional banana cake away. Sautéing the bananas in brown sugar and vegetable oil gives the cake a totally different taste and texture!

1. Preheat the oven to 350°F (175°C). Spray a 9-inch (2.5 L) springform pan with oil.

2. Slice the bananas thinly and add to a large skillet with the sugar, oil and cinnamon. Sauté for 4 minutes. Let cool for 10 minutes and mash.

3. TO MAKE THE CAKE In a large bowl, combine the oil, sugar, eggs, vanilla and sour cream until smooth. Add the mashed banana. Add the flour, baking powder and soda and combine just until the flour is incorporated.

4. TO MAKE THE STREUSEL Combine the brown sugar, cocoa, cinnamon and chips if using.

5. Pour half the cake batter into the pan, sprinkle with half the streusel, add the remaining batter and top with the rest of the streusel. Bake for 40 to 45 minutes or until a tester comes out clean.

PREPARATION TIME 15 minutes · **BAKING TIME** 45 minutes ·
MAKE AHEAD Make the cake up to a day in advance. It freezes well for up to a month. · **MAKES** 14 servings.

ROSE'S TIP
The riper your bananas the more banana flavour you'll have. Bananas can never get too ripe— just freeze them.

HEALTH TIP
Brown sugar is not healthier than white sugar; it just has molasses added. It's a matter of taste.

NUTRITION INFORMATION PER SERVING

Calories 292	Protein 2.5 g	Cholesterol 21 mg
Carbohydrates 48 g	Total fat 8.5 g	
Fibre 1.2 g	Saturated fat 1.6 g	

3 large ripe bananas (about 3 cups/750 mL)

¾ cup (185 mL) brown sugar

2 Tbsp (30 mL) vegetable oil

¼ tsp (1 mL) cinnamon

Cake

⅓ cup (80 mL) vegetable oil

1 cup (250 mL) granulated sugar

2 eggs

1½ tsp (7.5 mL) vanilla extract

⅓ cup (80 mL) reduced-fat sour cream

1¾ cups (185 mL) all-purpose flour

1½ tsp (7.5 mL) baking powder

1 tsp (5 mL) baking soda

Streusel

¾ cup (185 mL) brown sugar

4 tsp (20 mL) cocoa

½ tsp (2.5 mL) cinnamon

¼ cup (60 mL) semisweet chocolate chips (optional)

MINI CHOCOLATE CHEESECAKES WITH MARSHMALLOWS AND PECANS

Individual cheesecakes are so elegant, especially these, which are almost mousse-like in texture. Light cream cheese is 25 percent reduced in fat, and when combined with ricotta cheese, it gives a smooth, delicious flavour and texture.

1. Preheat the oven to 350°F (175°C). Line a 12-cup muffin tin with paper liners.

2. Combine the ricotta, cream cheese, sour cream, egg, sugar, cocoa and flour in a food processor. Purée until smooth. Divide the mixture among the prepared muffin cups.

3. Set the muffin tin in a larger pan. Pour enough hot water into the pan to come halfway up the sides of the muffin cups.

4. Bake in the centre of the oven for 20 minutes. Remove and sprinkle the marshmallows, chocolate chips and nuts evenly over the cheesecakes. Return to the oven and bake for 5 minutes longer or until the marshmallows and chocolate chips begin to melt.

5. Remove the muffin tin from the water bath and cool on a rack. Chill well before removing the paper liners and serving.

PREPARATION TIME 10 minutes · **BAKING TIME** 25 minutes ·
MAKE AHEAD Make these up to a day in advance. Keep refrigerated. ·
MAKES 12 servings.

NUTRITION INFORMATION PER SERVING (1 MINI CHEESECAKE)

Calories 185	Protein 6.5 g	Cholesterol 36 mg
Carbohydrates 20.5 g	Total fat 8.8 g	
Fibre 0.9 g	Saturated fat 4 g	

1½ cups (375 mL) reduced-fat ricotta cheese (12 oz/375 g)

½ cup (125 mL) softened reduced-fat cream cheese (4 oz/125 g)

½ cup (125 mL) reduced-fat sour cream

1 large egg

¾ cup (185 mL) granulated sugar

3 Tbsp (45 mL) unsweetened cocoa powder

1½ Tbsp (22.5 mL) all-purpose flour

⅓ cup (80 mL) miniature marshmallows

3 Tbsp (45 mL) semisweet chocolate chips

3 Tbsp (45 mL) finely chopped toasted pecans

 ROSE'S TIP

If you don't have mini marshmallows, use scissors to cut the large ones into small pieces.

 HEALTH TIP

If you ever need a sweet treat without all the calories and fat, try ½ cup (125 mL) of mini marshmallows, which has only 100 calories and 0 grams of fat.

CHOCOLATE CHIP COOKIE AND BROWNIE SQUARES

If you love chocolate chip cookies and brownies, wait until you try this combination. OMG!! That's all I can say. The crunchy cookie on the bottom and the creamy brownie on top are too good to be true!

1. Preheat the oven to 350°F. Line a 9-inch (23 cm) square baking dish with parchment paper.

2. TO MAKE THE COOKIE BASE In a small bowl, combine both sugars, oil, egg and vanilla. Mix until smooth. Add the flour, baking powder and chocolate chips. Mix until well combined. Spread over the bottom of a baking dish with a wet knife. Bake for 25 minutes or just until browned and slightly crisp.

3. TO MAKE THE BROWNIE TOPPING In a small bowl, combine the sugar, oil, egg and vanilla until mixed. Add the cocoa, flour, baking powder and sour cream until combined. Pour over the cookie base and bake for 15 minutes or just until set. Cool and garnish with icing sugar.

PREPARATION TIME 15 minutes • **BAKING TIME** 40 minutes •
MAKE AHEAD Make up to a day in advance and refrigerate. •
MAKES 24 squares.

 ROSE'S TIP
You can double this recipe and use a 9- × 13-inch (3.5 L) pan. Bake the cookie base for 30 to 35 minutes and the brownie topping for about 20 minutes or just until set.

 HEALTH TIP
This cookie brownie is decadent and still has less than half the calories and fat of a regular dessert due to the smaller amounts of fat, eggs and chocolate.

Cookie base

⅓ cup (80 mL) granulated sugar

½ cup (125 mL) packed brown sugar

¼ cup (60 mL) vegetable oil

1 large egg

2 tsp (10 mL) vanilla extract

¾ cup (185 mL) all-purpose flour

½ tsp (2.5 mL) baking powder

⅓ cup (80 mL) miniature semi-sweet chocolate chips

Brownie topping

⅔ cup (160 mL) granulated sugar

¼ cup (60 mL) vegetable oil

1 large egg

1 tsp (5 mL) vanilla

⅓ cup (80 mL) unsweetened cocoa powder

⅓ cup (80 mL) all-purpose flour

1 tsp (5 mL) baking powder

⅓ cup (80 mL) reduced-fat sour cream

icing sugar for garnish

NUTRITION INFORMATION PER SERVING (1 SQUARE)

Calories 140	Protein 1.6 g	Cholesterol 16 mg
Carbohydrates 20.4 g	Total fat 6.1 g	
Fibre 0.7 g	Saturated fat 1.6 g	

OLD–FASHIONED DATE SQUARES

Date squares, often known as matrimonial squares, have been a classic for decades. The oatmeal crust traditionally contains a cup (250 mL) or more of butter or vegetable shortening. My version uses only ⅓ cup (80 mL) oil mixed with water, and the squares are still incredibly delicious and rich tasting.

1. In a saucepan, combine dates, sugar and 1 cup (250 mL) of the water. Bring to a boil, reduce the heat to medium and cook for 15 minutes or until the dates are soft and the liquid is absorbed. Mash the mixture and let it cool.

2. Preheat the oven to 350°F (175°C). Spray an 8-inch (20 cm) square baking dish with cooking spray.

3. In a bowl, stir together the oats, flour, brown sugar, oil, pecans, cinnamon and the remaining ¼ cup (60 mL) of water, until combined. Press half onto the bottom of the prepared dish. Spread the cooled date mixture on top. Sprinkle the remaining oat mixture on top of the dates.

4. Bake in the centre of the oven for 25 minutes or until the top is golden. Cool in the pan on a wire rack.

PREPARATION TIME 20 minutes · **BAKING TIME** 25 minutes ·
MAKE AHEAD Make up to 2 days in advance. · **MAKES** 16 servings.

1½ cups (375 mL) chopped pitted dates (8 oz/250 g)

¼ cup (60 mL) granulated sugar

1¼ cups (310 mL) water

1⅓ cups (335 mL) quick-cooking oats

1 cup (250 mL) all-purpose flour

¾ cup (185 mL) packed brown sugar

⅓ cup (80 mL) vegetable oil

¼ cup (60 mL) chopped toasted pecans

½ tsp (2.5 mL) cinnamon

ROSE'S TIP
I buy pitted dates at a bulk food warehouse and keep them in my freezer. They defrost quickly or you can put them in your microwave oven for 20 seconds.

HEALTH TIP
When eating dates, remember that dried fruit is always higher in calories. A 3½-ounce (105 g) serving of dried dates contains 280 calories, whereas fresh dates have 142 calories.

NUTRITION INFORMATION PER SERVING

Calories 211	Protein 2.4 g	Cholesterol 0 mg
Carbohydrates 36 g	Total fat 6.4 g	
Fibre 2.1 g	Saturated fat 0.5 g	

TWO-LAYER LEMON COCONUT TART

The taste, texture and appearance of this dessert are wonderful. It's a smaller cake but rich tasting.

1. Preheat the oven to 350°F (175°C). Spray an 8-inch (2 L) springform pan with oil.

2. TO MAKE THE CRUST In a small bowl, combine graham crumbs, oil, water and ¼ cup (60 mL) toasted coconut. Pat onto the bottom of the pan.

3. TO MAKE THE TART In another bowl, add ⅓ cup (80 mL) lemon juice, eggs, ¾ cup (185 mL) of the condensed milk and the vanilla until smooth and pour into the pan. Bake for 15 to 20 minutes or just until firm.

4. In a small food processor, add both cheeses, ¼ cup (60 mL) lemon juice and the lemon zest and purée until smooth. Pour over the tart and chill until firm, about 2 to 3 hours. Garnish with the 1 Tbsp (15 mL) coconut.

PREPARATION TIME 15 minutes • BAKING TIME 15 minutes •

MAKE AHEAD Can be made a day in advance. Keep refrigerated. •

MAKES 8 servings.

 ROSE'S TIP
Always use freshly squeezed lemon juice when a recipe depends on it for flavour. The bottled versions don't compare and will give your dessert an aftertaste.

 HEALTH TIP
A half-cup (125 mL) of regular condensed milk has 500 calories and 13 grams of fat. The low-fat version has 340 calories and 4 grams of fat for the same amount.

Crust
1 cup (250 mL) graham crumbs

1 Tbsp (15 mL) vegetable oil

2 Tbsp (30 mL) water

¼ cup (60 mL) toasted coconut

Tart
⅓ cup (80 mL) lemon juice

2 large eggs

1 can (300 mL) low-fat condensed milk

1 tsp (5 mL) vanilla extract

½ cup (125 mL) reduced-fat cream cheese (4 oz/125 g)

½ cup (125 mL) reduced-fat ricotta cheese (4 oz/125 g)

¼ cup (60 mL) lemon juice

2 tsp (10 mL) lemon zest

1 Tbsp (15 mL) toasted coconut for garnish

NUTRITION INFORMATION PER SERVING

Calories 255	Protein 6.3 g	Cholesterol 62 mg
Carbohydrates 22.1 g	Total fat 15.6 g	
Fibre 1.8 g	Saturated fat 10.2 g	

CINNAMON DATE CAKE WITH COCONUT TOPPING

This has to be the moistest cake I've ever tasted. Dates are a good way to lower the fat in desserts—they have a buttery taste when puréed and provide the moisture that fat would supply. To chop dates easily, use kitchen shears—or cook whole pitted dates and use a food processor to mash them after they're cooked. Dates are a good source of protein and iron.

1. Preheat the oven to 350°F (175°C). Spray a 9-inch (23 cm) square cake pan with cooking oil.

2. TO MAKE THE CAKE Place the dates and water in a saucepan and bring them to a boil. Reduce the heat to low, cover and cook, stirring often, until the dates are soft and most of the liquid has been absorbed, about 10 minutes. Set the pan aside to cool for 10 minutes.

3. Mix the oil and granulated sugar in a large bowl or food processor. Beat in the eggs. Add the cooled date mixture and mix well.

4. Combine the flour, baking powder and baking soda in a bowl, mixing well. Stir the flour mixture into the date mixture until everything is just blended. Pour into the prepared pan.

5. Bake in the centre of the oven for 35 to 40 minutes or until a tester inserted in the centre comes out dry. Cool in the pan on a rack until no longer hot.

6. TO MAKE THE TOPPING Combine the coconut, brown sugar, milk and oil in a small saucepan. Cook over medium heat, stirring, for 2 minutes or until the sugar dissolves. Pour the topping over the cooled cake and cut into squares.

PREPARATION TIME 10 minutes · COOKING TIME 45 minutes ·
MAKE AHEAD Make the cake up to a day in advance. Keep refrigerated. ·
MAKES 16 servings.

Cake

12 oz (375 g) pitted dried dates, chopped (2½ cups/625 mL)

1¾ cups (435 mL) water

¼ cup (60 mL) vegetable oil

1 cup (250 mL) granulated sugar

2 large eggs

1½ cups (375 mL) all-purpose flour

1½ tsp (7.5 mL) baking powder

1 tsp (5 mL) baking soda

Topping

⅓ cup (80 mL) unsweetened coconut

¼ cup (60 mL) packed brown sugar

¼ cup (60 mL) canned evaporated 2% milk

2 Tbsp (30 mL) vegetable oil

ROSE'S TIP

You can now purchase
diced dried dates, which
are easier to use in this
recipe than whole dates,
at a bulk food warehouse.
Store them in the freezer.

 HEALTH TIP

Be sure you buy unsweet-
ened coconut instead of
sweetened. A half-cup
(125 mL) of unsweetened
coconut has 100 calories,
and sweetened coconut has
145 calories for the same
amount.

NUTRITION INFORMATION PER SERVING

Calories 217	Protein 3 g	Cholesterol 27 mg
Carbohydrates 41 g	Total fat 5 g	
Fibre 2 g	Saturated fat 2 g	

LEMON POPPY SEED LOAF WITH LEMON GLAZE

This loaf was featured in my first light cookbook, Rose Reisman Brings Home Light Cooking, *and to this day people tell me it's still their go-to dessert. This is a delicious and versatile loaf that can be served at breakfast or brunch or for dessert at dinner. You can even make it into muffins. Just spray a 12-cup muffin pan with vegetable oil, pour in the batter and bake in a 375°F (190°C) oven for 15 to 20 minutes. If you like a strong lemon taste, add an extra teaspoon (5 mL) of grated lemon rind.*

1. Preheat the oven to 350°F (175°C). Spray a 9- × 5-inch (2 L) loaf pan with cooking oil.

2. TO MAKE THE CAKE Combine the granulated sugar, oil, egg and lemon zest and juice in a large bowl or a food processor and mix well. Add the milk, mixing it in thoroughly.

3. Combine the flour, poppy seeds, baking powder and baking soda. Add to the wet mixture alternately with the yogurt, mixing just until incorporated. Do not overmix.

4. Pour into the prepared pan and bake for 35 to 40 minutes or until a tester inserted in the centre of the cake comes out dry. Set the pan on a rack to cool for 10 minutes. The centre of the cake may sink slightly when it cools.

5. TO MAKE THE GLAZE Combine the icing sugar and lemon juice. Prick holes in the top of the loaf with a fork or wooden skewer and pour the glaze over the loaf.

PREPARATION TIME 10 minutes · **BAKING TIME** 35 to 40 minutes ·
MAKE AHEAD Make the cake up to a day in advance and keep refrigerated.
Can be frozen for up to a month. · **MAKES** 16 servings.

Cake

¾ cup (185 mL) granulated sugar

⅓ cup (80 mL) vegetable oil

1 large egg

2 tsp (10 mL) grated lemon zest

3 Tbsp (45 mL) lemon juice

⅓ cup (80 mL) 2% milk

1¼ cups (310 mL) all-purpose flour

1 Tbsp (15 mL) poppy seeds

1 tsp (5 mL) baking powder

½ tsp (2.5 mL) baking soda

⅓ cup (80 mL) reduced-fat plain yogurt (or reduced-fat sour cream)

Glaze

¼ cup (60 mL) icing sugar

2 Tbsp (30 mL) lemon juice

ROSE'S TIP

This outstanding cake
doesn't rise like some loaf
cakes. Be sure to poke lots
of holes in the cake so the
icing penetrates.

 HEALTH TIP

Lemons are rich in vitamin
C and just ¼ cup (60 mL)
gives you 23 mg, which is
about 33% of your daily
recommended amount.
They also contain vitamins
A and C, which are anti-
oxidants that can lessen
the risk of heart disease
and various cancers.

NUTRITION INFORMATION PER SERVING (½ SLICE)

Calories 126	Protein 1.2 g	Cholesterol 13 mg
Carbohydrates 18 g	Total fat 3.7 g	
Fibre 0.6 g	Saturated fat 0.2 g	

CARROT CAKE WITH DRIED CRANBERRIES AND CREAM CHEESE FROSTING

People often think carrot cake is healthier than other desserts, but beware of recipes that sound healthy! Most carrot cakes are full of oil, butter, eggs and regular sour cream. This version greatly reduces the fat by using pineapple, extra carrots, reduced-fat yogurt and ripe banana to create the moist texture typical of carrot cake.

1. Preheat the oven to 350°F (175°C). Spray a 9-inch (23 cm) Bundt pan with cooking oil.

2. TO MAKE THE CAKE   Beat the oil and sugar in a large bowl until smooth. Add the eggs and vanilla, beating the mixture well (it may look curdled). Add the banana, carrots, cranberries, pineapple and yogurt. Stir until everything is well combined.

3. Combine the flour, baking powder, baking soda, cinnamon and nutmeg in a separate bowl, mixing well. Add to the carrot mixture and stir just until everything is combined.

4. Pour the mixture into the prepared pan.

5. Place the pan in the centre of the oven and bake for 40 to 45 minutes or until a tester inserted in the centre comes out clean. Cool in the pan on a rack. When it's no longer hot, invert the cake onto a serving plate.

6. TO MAKE THE ICING   Beat the cream cheese, icing sugar and milk in a bowl or food processor until smooth. Drizzle over the cake.

PREPARATION TIME 15 minutes · **BAKING TIME** 40 minutes ·

MAKE AHEAD Make this cake a day in advance and keep refrigerated. It freezes well for about a month. · **MAKES** 16 servings.

Cake

⅓ cup (80 mL) vegetable oil

1 cup (250 mL) granulated sugar

2 large eggs

1 tsp (5 mL) pure vanilla extract

1 large ripe banana, mashed

2 cups (500 mL) grated carrots (about 6 oz/175 g)

⅔ cup (160 mL) dried cranberries

½ cup (125 mL) canned crushed pineapple, drained

½ cup (125 mL) reduced-fat plain yogurt

2 cups (500 mL) all-purpose flour

1½ tsp (7.5 mL) baking powder

1½ tsp (7.5 mL) baking soda

1½ tsp (7.5 mL) ground cinnamon

¼ tsp (1 mL) ground nutmeg

Icing

⅓ cup (80 mL) softened reduced-fat cream cheese (3 oz/90 g)

⅔ cup (160 mL) icing sugar

1 Tbsp (15 mL) 2% milk or water

ROSE'S TIP

You can replace the dried cranberries with dried raisins, chopped dates or apricots.

HEALTH TIP

A traditional piece of classic carrot cake has over 800 calories and 45 grams of fat! There's usually 1 cup (250 mL) of butter or oil, at least 4 eggs and a cup (250 mL) of full-fat sour cream. My version uses only ⅓ cup (80 mL) of vegetable oil due to the banana, crushed pineapple and reduced-fat sour cream.

NUTRITION INFORMATION PER SERVING

Calories 223	Protein 4 g	Cholesterol 30 mg
Carbohydrates 41 g	Total fat 5 g	
Fibre 1 g	Saturated fat 1 g	

CHOCOLATE CHIP CRUMB CAKE

If I had to choose my number-one dessert of all time, it would be this crumb cake. I created it for Enlightened Home Cooking *in 1996 and I still whip it up all the time. My children can bake it blindfolded! I adapted it from a recipe from the original Silver Palate bakery in New York City, using cocoa, oil, ricotta cheese and yogurt to reduce the amount of fat and calories. Here's proof you don't have to eliminate chocolate when you eat light.*

1. Preheat the oven to 350°F (175°C). Spray a 9-inch (23 cm) Bundt pan with cooking oil.

2. Beat the ricotta, oil and granulated sugar in a large bowl or food processor. Add the eggs and vanilla, mixing well.

3. Combine the flour, baking powder and baking soda in a separate bowl. Add the flour mixture to the cheese mixture in batches, alternating with the yogurt. Mix just until everything is incorporated. Stir in the chocolate chips. Pour half the batter into the prepared pan.

4. Combine the brown sugar, cocoa and cinnamon in a small bowl. Sprinkle half the sugar mixture over the batter in the pan. Add the remaining batter and top with the remaining sugar mixture.

5. Bake in the centre of the oven for 35 to 40 minutes or until a tester inserted in the centre comes out dry.

6. Cool the cake in the pan on a rack. When it's completely cool, invert it carefully onto a serving plate.

PREPARATION TIME 15 minutes · **BAKING TIME** 35 minutes ·

MAKE AHEAD Make the cake a day in advance. Keep refrigerated. Freezes well for up to a month. · **MAKES** 16 servings.

1 cup (250 mL) reduced-fat ricotta cheese (8 oz/250 g)

⅓ cup (80 mL) vegetable oil

1¼ cups (310 mL) granulated sugar

2 large eggs

2 tsp (10 mL) pure vanilla extract

1½ cups (375 mL) all-purpose flour

2 tsp (10 mL) baking powder

½ tsp (2.5 mL) baking soda

¾ cup (185 mL) reduced-fat plain yogurt

½ cup (125 mL) semisweet chocolate chips

½ cup (125 mL) packed brown sugar

4 tsp (20 mL) unsweetened cocoa powder

½ tsp (2.5 mL) ground cinnamon

ROSE'S TIP

You can use a 9-inch
(2.5 L) springform pan
instead of a Bundt pan—
just check the cake at 30 to
40 minutes to see if it
needs to cook a few minutes
longer. Sprinkle lightly
with icing sugar or drizzle
with melted chocolate.

 HEALTH TIP

If you want to add some
protein to your dessert,
substitute 0% fat Greek
yogurt for the reduced-
fat plain yogurt: ¾ cup
(185 mL) has 18 grams
of protein.

NUTRITION INFORMATION PER SERVING

Calories 226	Protein 5 g	Cholesterol 42 mg
Carbohydrates 36 g	Total fat 7 g	
Fibre 2 g	Saturated fat 4 g	

COCONUT LAYER CAKE WITH ITALIAN MERINGUE ICING

A mouth-watering dessert that tastes so decadent due to the moistness of the cake and Italian meringue. No high-fat icing here! Just beaten egg whites and sugar without butter and cream. To toast the coconut, brown it in a skillet over high heat for approximately 2 to 3 minutes.

1. Preheat the oven to 350°F (175°C). Spray two 9-inch (23 cm) round cake pans with cooking oil.

2. TO MAKE THE CAKE Beat 1 cup (250 mL) of the sugar, the coconut milk, oil, eggs and vanilla in a large bowl, using a whisk or an electric mixer.

3. Combine the flour, baking powder, salt and coconut in another bowl, mixing well. Stir the dry ingredients into the coconut milk mixture by hand, mixing just until combined.

4. Beat the egg whites with the cream of tartar in a clean bowl until foamy. Gradually add the remaining ¼ cup (60 mL) sugar, beating until stiff peaks form. Stir one-quarter of the egg whites into the cake batter. Gently fold in the remaining egg whites. Divide the mixture between the prepared pans.

5. Bake in the centre of the oven for approximately 15 minutes or until a tester inserted into the centre comes out clean. Cool in the pans on a rack.

6. TO MAKE THE ICING Combine the egg whites, sugar, water and cream of tartar in the top of a double boiler over simmering water (or use a glass or metal bowl over a saucepan). Beat the mixture with an electric mixer for 6 to 8 minutes or until it thickens and soft peaks form. Remove it from the heat. Beat for 1 minute or until stiff peaks form. Stir in 2 Tbsp (30 mL) of the toasted coconut.

Cake

1¼ cups (310 mL) granulated sugar

¾ cup (185 mL) light coconut milk

⅓ cup (80 mL) vegetable oil

2 large eggs

1½ tsp (7.5 mL) pure vanilla extract

1¼ cups (310 mL) all-purpose flour

1½ tsp (7.5 mL) baking powder

¼ tsp (1 mL) salt

2 Tbsp (30 mL) toasted coconut

2 large egg whites

¼ tsp (1 mL) cream of tartar

Icing

3 large egg whites

¾ cup (185 mL) granulated sugar

¼ cup (60 mL) water

¼ tsp (1 mL) cream of tartar

3 Tbsp (45 mL) toasted coconut

7. When the cakes are completely cooled, place one cake layer on a platter. Spread approximately one-quarter of the icing overtop. Place the second layer on top of the first and ice the top and sides with the remainder. Sprinkle with the remaining 1 Tbsp (15 mL) toasted coconut.

PREPARATION TIME 20 minutes · **BAKING TIME** 15 minutes ·

MAKE AHEAD Make the cake a day in advance and keep refrigerated. ·

MAKES 14 servings.

 ROSE'S TIP
Italian meringue will not "weep" the way regular meringues do, meaning they exude excess liquid from the egg whites. This icing holds well for a couple of days.

 HEALTH TIP
Light coconut milk, now available, has 25% of the fat and a fraction of the calories of regular coconut milk.

NUTRITION INFORMATION PER SERVING

Calories 270	Protein 3.7 g	Cholesterol 30 mg
Carbohydrates 63 g	Total fat 7.5 g	
Fibre 2.2 g	Saturated fat 2.2 g	

TURTLE CHEESECAKE

Who doesn't love Turtle chocolate pecan clusters? Well, think about eating this in cheesecake form. To die for! And since I lighten it up, you won't die from it!

1. Preheat the oven to 350°F (175°C). Spray a 9-inch (2.5 L) springform pan with vegetable oil.

2. TO MAKE THE CRUST Place the crumbs, water and oil in a small bowl and mix well. Pat into the bottom of the pan.

3. TO MAKE THE CHEESECAKE Place both cheeses, both sugars, the egg, vanilla, sour cream and flour in a large food processor. Purée until smooth. Remove one cup (250 mL) of the batter and place in a small bowl.

4. Melt ⅓ cup (80 mL) of the chocolate chips in a bowl and microwave on Defrost for 2 minutes or until almost melted. Mix until smooth. Add to the reserved 1 cup (250 mL) cheesecake batter and pour over the cookie crust.

5. Drizzle the caramel sauce overtop. Pour the remaining batter overtop and bake for 45 minutes or until almost set. Cool.

6. TO MAKE THE TOPPING Melt the chocolate and milk on High in a microwave oven for 25 seconds. Mix until smooth. Cool, then spread on top of the cheesecake. Sprinkle with chopped pecans.

PREPARATION TIME 20 minutes · **BAKING TIME** 45 minutes · **MAKE AHEAD** Make the cheesecake up to a day in advance. Keep refrigerated. · **MAKES** 14 servings.

continued ...

Crust

1½ cups (375 mL) chocolate wafer crumbs

2 Tbsp (30 mL) water

1 Tbsp (15 mL) vegetable oil

Cheesecake

2 cups (500 mL) reduced-fat ricotta cheese (1 lb/500 g)

¾ cup (185 mL) cubed reduced-fat cream cheese (6 oz/175 g)

⅔ cup (160 mL) white sugar

⅔ cup (160 mL) brown sugar

1 large egg

1½ tsp (7.5 mL) vanilla extract

¾ cup (185 mL) reduced-fat sour cream

2 Tbsp (30 mL) all-purpose flour

⅓ cup (80 mL) semisweet chocolate chips

¼ cup (60 mL) caramel sauce (ice cream topping)

Topping

⅓ cup (80 mL) semisweet chocolate chips

2 Tbsp (30 mL) canned evaporated 2% milk

¼ cup (60 mL) chopped pecans

Turtle Cheesecake (continued)

 ROSE'S TIP
This cake makes 14 slices
since it is very dense and
rich while still being lower
in calories and fat.

 HEALTH TIP
At the Cheesecake Factory
in the United States, the
average cheesecake slice has
around 1,000 calories and
80 grams of fat!

NUTRITION INFORMATION PER SERVING

Calories 295	Protein 7.7 g	Cholesterol 31 mg
Carbohydrates 38 g	Total fat 12 g	
Fibre 1 g	Saturated fat 6 g	

PISTACHIO AND DRIED CRANBERRY BISCOTTI

I couldn't complete my book without one of my biscotti recipes. I have launched a line of biscotti that is being widely distributed. Here is one of our customers' favourites.

1. Preheat the oven to 350°F (175°C). Line a baking sheet with foil and spray with vegetable oil.

2. Mix the eggs, oil, sugar and vanilla in a large bowl.

3. Add the flour, oats, baking powder and soda, salt, zest, cranberries and pistachios and mix until all is combined. Form into two long rolls (approximately 12 × 2 inches/ 30 × 5 cm).

4. Bake for 30 minutes. Turn the oven to 300°F (150°C). Slice the biscotti into 15 pieces per roll, lay them on their side and bake for 40 more minutes.

PREPARATION TIME 15 minutes · **BAKING TIME** 70 minutes ·
MAKE AHEAD These can be baked and kept at room temperature in an airtight container for up to 2 weeks. · **MAKES** 30 servings.

2 large eggs

⅓ cup (80 mL) vegetable oil

1 cup (250 mL) granulated sugar

1½ tsp (7.5 mL) vanilla extract

2 cups (500 mL) all-purpose flour

½ cup (125 mL) rolled oats

1 tsp (5 mL) baking powder

½ tsp (2.5 mL) baking soda

⅛ tsp (0.5 mL) salt

1 Tbsp (15 mL) chopped orange zest

1 cup (250 mL) dried cranberries

⅔ cup (160 mL) whole pistachios

 ROSE'S TIP
You can have fun with this recipe and substitute any variety of nuts and dried fruits. Dried apricots, mango and cherries are delicious, as are pecans, walnuts and almonds.

 HEALTH TIP
Biscotti are a much healthier treat than most desserts. With only 114 calories and 4 grams of fat, these are fine for a snack or alongside your coffee.

NUTRITION INFORMATION PER SERVING (1 BISCOTTI)

Calories 114	Protein 1.4 g	Cholesterol 10 mg
Carbohydrates 17 g	Total fat 3.9 g	
Fibre 0.9 g	Saturated fat 0.5 g	

INDEX